The Black Book
of Canadian Foreign Policy

By
Yves Engler

Fernwood Publishing, RED Publishing
in association with The Dominion (www.dominionpaper.ca)

Cover design Working Design

Printed and bound in Canada by Transcontinental Printing
A co-publication of
RED Publishing
2736 Cambridge Street
Vancouver, B.C. V5K 1L7 and
Fernwood Publishing
32 Oceanvista Lane
Black Point, Nova Scotia B0J 1B0
and 8 - 222 Osborne Street, Winnipeg, Manitoba R3L 1Z3.
www.fernwoodpublishing.ca

Fernwood Publishing Company Limited gratefully acknowledges the financial support of the Department of Canadian Heritage, the Nova Scotia Department of Tourism and Culture and the Canada Council for the Arts for our publishing program.

Library and Archives Canada Cataloguing in Publication
Engler, Yves, 1979-
    The black book of Canadian foreign policy / Yves Engler.
Includes bibliographical references.
ISBN 978-1-55266-314-1
    1. Canada--Foreign relations. I. Title.
FC242.E53 2009   327.71   C2009-901313-4

few people who own Canadian corporations active abroad? Do those of us with pensions or RRSPs invested in Canadian corporations operating abroad also share responsibility when people are poisoned by a mine, or rivers are destroyed by oil exploration?

Events in Haiti made me question Canada's peacekeeper self-image. Canada helped overthrow the democratically elected Haitian government of Jean-Bertrand Aristide in February 2004 and then supported an interim "illegal" government that killed thousands. When I first learned about the situation in Haiti I assumed Canadian diplomats had simply followed Washington, not fully understanding the consequences of their actions. But as I learned about the extent to which Canada participated in this crime against the Haitian people I began to question my assumptions of Canada's role in the world. While acting in concert with the USA, it was clear that Canada was also an independent player with its own self-interests, including those of Canadian companies. Seeing Canada simply as a junior partner with the USA did not adequately explain our role in overthrowing the elected Haitian government or our ongoing relationship with that country. Was Haiti an anomaly? Or has Canada used its wealth and power to act like an imperial bully elsewhere?

I decided to devote my time to reading everything I could find about Canadian foreign policy. If you know where to look, there's a vast amount of material about Canada's role around the world.

I am not a foreign policy expert or veteran diplomat; I have never worked as foreign correspondent for a major media outlet. Instead, I am a moderately well educated, politically active, independent journalist and author. I believe Earth is our home and we are its stewards. While citizens of Canada, we are also neighbours to everyone who shares this planet. We must be good neighbours. That should be the underlying premise of Canada's foreign policy. This book is aimed at people who share this basic political viewpoint and who also believe that democracy requires citizens to keep themselves informed about what their government is doing. Canadians have a right and a responsibility to know, debate and ultimately shape what is being done in our name around the world.

Informing citizens about what their governments, corporations and other institutions are doing is a central task of journalists. In order for our government to be held to even minimal standards of democracy Canadians must know what our institutions are doing. If a mining company based in Vancouver destroys a watershed in Ecuador, we are not being good neighbours. If a Canadian-funded NGO works with the U.S. National

Endowment for Democracy to destabilize a government that favours its citizens' interests over those of giant corporations, we are not being good neighbours. If the Canadian government takes part in a military campaign designed to subordinate the interests of a country or region to ours and the USA, we are being terrible neighbours.

The chapters that follow discuss examples of Canada's role in various regions of the world as well as in international organizations. When reading, please think about the following questions: Is this what a "good neighbour" would do? Are we really "a force for good" in the world? Have our government policies been as they should be or must citizens demand change?

Unfortunately, most of us pay more attention to the words than to the deeds of our governments and corporations. Much of the media has abdicated its responsibility in favour of some combination of entertainment and cheerleading for the rich and powerful. Nowhere is this more true than in the realm of foreign policy. The foreign affairs establishment, the military and corporate interests dominate discussion of Canada's role in the world.

This book is an attempt to understand what "the government does in our name" and is also a warning to ordinary Canadians that ignorance is no excuse. We are all complicit in the actions of our elected government. Every year tens of billions of our tax dollars are spent on the military, foreign aid and other forms of diplomacy. While elections are inevitably fought over healthcare, the economy, social services and dealing with crime, we ignore foreign affairs at our peril.

This book is offered in the spirit of democratic accountability. Only when the majority of Canadians pay attention to the reality of foreign affairs and demand altruistic aid, real international cooperation, benevolent peacekeeping instead of militarism, and the rule of law instead of an empire's might, will these things happen. That is because there are powerful actors in business and government who make sure their interests are satisfied before all others. The first step is to understand what our government, corporations and other institutions do abroad. That is the least that can be expected of responsible citizens in a democracy.

The goal of this book is to reveal a side of international relations that our governments and corporations have kept hidden from the vast majority of us. This black book, unlike a secret list of girlfriends kept by a lothario, has a progressive purpose: To inspire Canadians to demand change.

The Caribbean

The best place to start this look at Canada's role in the world is in our foreign affairs backyard, which, for geographical, linguistic, economic and historical reasons, is the Caribbean. Our relationship with this part of the planet is longstanding and allows us to explore most of the themes that will emerge throughout the book. Canada's role there has been both junior partner to the world's major imperial power (Great Britain or the USA, depending on the era) and an independent actor with its own distinct self-interest.

The English-speaking Caribbean

Canada has long been influential in the English-speaking Caribbean and, given our colonial past, it should not be surprising that this country's role was usually one of supporting Great Britain. "For Canadian foreign policy the 19th century opened with participation in British campaigns against the slave rebellions in the Caribbean, for which Upper and Lower Canada, as well as the Maritimes, provided resources, troops and commanding officers."[3]

So colonial were this country's attitudes that some prominent Canadians once wanted to add Britain's Caribbean colonies to Canada's expanding territory. In the late 1870s the Canada First Movement sought "a closer political connection" with the British West Indies. By the early 1900s official Canadian policy supported annexing the British Empire's Caribbean possessions (the various islands as well as British Honduras [Belize] and Guyana).[4]

The West Indies Union movement reached its apex in the early 1900s, but the idea continued to find support after World War One. At the end of the conflict the other British Dominions (South Africa, Australia and New Zealand) that fought alongside London were compensated with German properties. With no German colonies nearby Ottawa asked the Imperial War Cabinet if it could take possession of the British West Indies as compensation for Canada's defence of the Empire.[5] London balked.[6]

Ottawa was unsuccessful in securing the British "properties" partly because the request did not find unanimous domestic support. Prime Minister Robert Borden was of two minds on the issue. From London he dispatched a cable noting "the responsibilities of governing subject races would probably exercise a broadening influence upon our people as the dominion thus constituted would closely resemble in its problems and its duties the empire as a whole."[7] But, on the other hand, Borden feared that the Caribbean's black population might want to vote. He remarked upon "the difficulty of dealing with the coloured population, who would probably be more restless under Canadian law than under British control and would desire and perhaps insist upon representation in Parliament."[8]

Canadian-owned business

Support for taking on the colonies was driven by commercial relations.[9] "For many years, the chief lobbyist for closer Canada-West Indies relations was T. B. Macaulay, the president of Sun Life."[10] Sun Life Assurance Company of Montréal established an office in Barbados in 1879 and began the Planter's Bank of Canada in that country in 1882.[11]

In later years the insurance industry's lobbying was surpassed by that of the banks. In his critical account of the Canadian banking industry Walter Stewart notes: "The business was so profitable that in 1919 Canada seriously considered taking the Commonwealth Caribbean off mother England's hands and running it ourselves."[12] The Canadian banking presence in the Caribbean began when the Halifax Banking Company signed an agreement in 1837 with the Colonial Bank, a London headquartered operation that had a preeminent place in the British Caribbean.[13] Prior to opening a branch in Montréal, in 1882, the Merchants Bank of Halifax (later the Royal Bank) established itself in Bermuda.[14] Two other Maritimes-based banks quickly followed suit. The Bank of Nova Scotia became active in Trinidad in 1889 and the Union Bank of Halifax discovered that country at the turn of the century. Montréal- and Toronto-based banks were a little slower to join the rush. The Royal Securities Corporation of Montréal entered Bermuda in 1903 and the Canadian Bank of Commerce (now CIBC) moved into the region after World War One.[15]

In 1912 the Royal Bank bought the Bank of British Honduras, the colony's main financial institution, from London interests and for nearly three decades after 1916 the Royal Bank was the only bank in the Bahamas. By 1926 Canadian banks operated 140 branches across the Caribbean.[16] In the mid-1970s Canadian banks controlled 60-90 percent of banking in the Commonwealth Caribbean.[17] One commentator wrote: "The status of single banks on some of the Island states rises to the level of quasi sovereign."[18]

After a decline in their influence in the 1980s and 1990s Canadian banks have regained their prominence. As of April 2008 Canadian banks controlled "the English-speaking Caribbean's three largest banks, with $42 billion in assets, four times those commanded by its forty-odd remaining locally owned banks."[19]

Caribbean nationalists have long opposed foreign banking domination. In the early 1970s Canadian banks, particularly in Trinidad, were targeted in demonstrations and even fire bombings.[20] As far back as the 1925 Canada-West Indies Conference one attendee remarked: "When a country like Canada or the United States wants to build a big hotel, companies are formed and the money is supplied by either the banks or the insurance companies... In Jamaica, we can neither get the banks nor the insurance companies to loan us any money to put up hotels."[21]

Canadian banks have traditionally been conservative in releasing capital to local manufacturers, retailers and farmers. This has stunted the region's development and heightened these countries dependency on foreign imports.[22] Further stunting Caribbean development, the banks' profits are mostly repatriated to Canada.

Canadian banking practices in the Caribbean would simply not be accepted here. Even after a quarter-century of deregulating the economy, the federal government maintains strict laws concerning foreign ownership of Canadian banks. The banking sector is considered too vital to the economy to be left in the hands of foreign corporations.

When Canadian banks entered the Caribbean the region's people were under British rule, with the majority of the population working on plantations. A history of colonialism (and slavery) gave most of the population little say over who owned their countries' banks. In fact, Canadian citizens may have had a greater say over the region's banking. "[The Canadian] federal government has the power to control banking behaviour in the Commonwealth Caribbean," one author noted in the mid 1970s. "Indeed, it may well be that the Canadian government has greater capacity to bring about certain banking behaviour than the governments of the Commonwealth Caribbean themselves."[23]

At times Ottawa has taken a proactive approach to Caribbean banking regulation. Beginning in 1955, a former governor of the Bank of Canada and director of the Royal Bank, Graham Towers, along with a representative from the Ministry of Finance, helped write the Bank of Jamaica law of 1960 and that country's Banking Law of 1960. These laws, which became the model for the rest of the newly independent English Caribbean, pleased Canadian banks.[24] "The overall and firm impression with which one is left after reading the [Bank] Act is that its drafters did not intend to control the foreign operations of Canadian banks, or that if they intended to, they failed to do so."[25] More to the point, "West Indian banking laws, when they were written, were written with our help and advice and for our benefit. ... [The Jamaican Bank Act] left discretion in most areas of banking entirely up to the Minister of Finance, who had a convenient habit of acting in a way that benefited the banks."[26]

Banking and insurance were not the only sectors of the Caribbean economy that Canadian capital staked out. In 1900 a syndicate led by Canadian capitalist William Van Horne acquired electric railway and lighting franchises in three English Caribbean cities.[27] The next year Oil Explorations Syndicate of Canada became the first company to search for oil in Trinidad.[28] In the 1940s the Aluminum Company of Canada (Alcan) began extracting bauxite in Jamaica and by the mid-1970s the company owned 48,000 acres of land. For a time Alcan was the largest investor on the island.[29]

"Driving into Nassau [in the 1960s] from Windsor Field Airport you can see Canadian money sprinkled along the route like icing on a cake."[30] At that time the Financial Post reported that (well known Toronto financier) EP Taylor was likely the most powerful voice in the Bahamas economy. In addition to significant property interests, Taylor chaired the Trust Corps of the Bahamas, which handled the affairs of 1,000 registered companies. Taylor was also chairman of RoyWest Ltd, the island's leading source of venture capital, and unpaid chairman of the country's economic council.[31]

Canadian business continues to be a major force in the Caribbean economy. In Belize, for instance, Newfoundland's Fortis has a monopoly over electricity. In March 2008 the Economist reported "Canadian firms make chemicals in Trinidad and drill for natural gas offshore, mine nickel in Cuba and gold in Surinam, seek oil off Guyana and run cable television in the Bahamas and Jamaica. A tax treaty with Canada underpins offshore finance in Barbados."[32]

Canadian capital played a major part in building the region's leading industry, tourism. Commonwealth Holiday Inns of Canada and CN Realty were largely responsible for the introduction of Holiday Inns to Antigua, St. Kitts, St Lucia, Grenada, Barbados and Trinidad. Air Canada has long flown to the islands and the company purchased 40 percent of Air Jamaica in 1968.[33] That same year it was reported "Toronto mine promoter, Lou Chesler, lavishly cultivated politicians to extract a gambling concession from the Bahamas government with the idea of turning the area into a new Monte Carlo ... At least $1 million in 'consultant fees' went to finance minister Sir Stafford Sands, who also held down a chair on the board of the country's largest bank, the Royal Bank of Canada. The resulting casino [Lucayan Beach Hotel] with its 'whites only' policy soon fell out of Canadian control and into the hands of American gangland syndicates."[34]

A boon to Canadian-owned hotels and airlines, development aid was used to expand Caribbean tourism. In the 1970s the Canadian International Development Agency (CIDA) gave ten million dollars on soft terms to upgrade Trinidad's Piarco International airport and another ten million to expand Barbados' Seawell airport.[35] "At least seven [Caribbean] nations have received CIDA support for building or expanding airports specifically designed to increase tourism."[36]

From the tarmac to room service, Canadian aid has benefited the Caribbean traveler. Canadian advisors helped establish a school to train hotel workers in Jamaica and Barbados in the 1970s and the CIDA-spawned Canadian Executive Services Overseas has long trained the region's hotel and restaurant management. In 2008 the Trade Facilitation Office, another CIDA-spawned organization, arranged a trade mission to the Caribbean that was designed to expand medical tourism on the islands.[37]

CIDA not only provides practical assistance to the tourism sector, it provides political support as well. The aid agency has financed a number of tourism-related studies, largely designed to justify expanding the region's tourism industry.[38] Studies financed by CIDA and market economists argue tourism is the Caribbean's "competitive advantage." But does a tourism-based economy benefit the people of the region? Not very much, according to the Canadian Senate's Standing Committee on Foreign Affairs. Its 1970 report on aid to the region noted: "The Committee is concerned about too great a reliance [in the Caribbean] on the development of tourism."[39]

While the situation is better today, many managerial and executive positions in the hospitality industry are still filled by foreigners and along with tourists, profits usually leave the islands. Even most of the food consumed by tourists is imported, often from North America.

Despite the drawbacks of a tourism-based economy, Canadian aid, both bilateral and multilateral, continues to be channeled to the sector. Through the Caribbean Development Bank (CDB), Canadian financial consultants have worked to improve the region's transport systems. CDB loans have also been used for port improvements designed to stimulate the cruise industry.[40] The CDB and CDC (Commonwealth Development Corporation), notes the author of Commonwealth Caribbean, "have financed infrastructure, including transport and public utilities, directly beneficial to tourism."[41]

The CDB is a multilateral bank that provides Ottawa with influence over the region's economy. The idea for a Caribbean development bank first came up at the 1966 Canada-Commonwealth Caribbean conference in Ottawa. It was initially staffed by Canada and the U.K., the only two non-regional members, which each controlled 20 percent of the bank's voting shares. The two countries now hold 10.44 percent each and have been joined by three other non-regional members.[42] Canada was the CDB's largest donor by the early 1990s, providing more than a $100 million to a bank few Canadians had heard of.[43]

Canadian aid

Canadian "aid" to the region dates back to the region's independence. Amidst fears the British Empire's former territories would fall under the influence of the communist bloc, the South Asian Colombo Aid Plan was extended to the Commonwealth Caribbean (and Africa) in the late 1950s. The 1959 Cuban Revolution heightened Ottawa's fears of a communist menace, spurring the aid flow.[44] Aid officials "singled out Cuban revolutionary activity as the main threat to political and thus economic stability in the region and implied that developmental aid staved off Cuban interference."[45]

From anti-communist geopolitics to free market economics, Canadian aid has been used to extend Ottawa's influence in the Caribbean. In a 1981 speech to the Canada-CARICOM (Caribbean Community) Joint Trade and Economic Committee, Mark MacGuigan, Canada's secretary of state for external affairs, promised to make emergency balance of payments assistance available to CARICOM states that concluded structural adjustment programs with the International Monetary Fund (IMF).[46] A decade later CIDA began providing a million dollars a year for Canadian advisors to assist CARICOM in industrial development planning and implementation.[47] And, in 2009, a CIDA/CARICOM project provided "financial donations to the CARICOM Secretariat for business development within the region as we move toward a single market economy."[48]

Canadian aid to CARICOM has targeted the investor-friendly aspects of the trade group. Since independence Ottawa has supported West Indian trade groupings designed to attract foreign capital.[49] In February 1966 Prime Minister Lester B. Pearson announced that Trinidad, Jamaica and Canada hoped to organize a conference to promote regional economic cooperation. The prime minister of British Guyana, Forbes Burnham, replied that he did not want to participate in a conference led by Canadians since it was "time

Caribbean countries stopped running to conferences called by outsiders."[50] As this book goes to press Ottawa is negotiating a trade agreement with CARICOM. Of course Ottawa already has an investor centric economic accord with the English Caribbean. Introduced in 1986, CARIBCAN "is heavily geared to reinforcing the prevailing patterns inherent in the global economy. ... Canadian businesses are certain to gain a large part of the region's growing demand for imports and the guaranteed duty free access to the Canadian market will make Canada's direct investments in the commonwealth Caribbean more profitable."[51] In addition, CARIBCAN, like the 1983 U.S. Caribbean Basin Initiative, sought to isolate Cuba from the region.[52] This may come as a surprise to some since it's widely perceived that Ottawa has somewhat cordial relations with Havana. Still, Canada has generally sided with U.S. fear mongering about the "Cuban menace" — propaganda largely designed to justify keeping the region subservient to western capitalist domination.

For example, in October 1983, 7,000 U.S. troops invaded Grenada, to reassert U.S. hegemony in a country supposedly overrun by Cuban doctors. In the lead up to the U.S. intervention, Grenada's prime minister, Maurice Bishop, accused the Royal Bank of "promoting destabilization" in the economy. For its part, Ottawa abstained on a U.N. resolution calling for the withdrawal of all foreign troops (predominantly American) from Grenada.[53] During a House of Commons debate Liberal Secretary of State for International Trade, Harold Reagan explained that "the position of this government was that we were concerned about the political orientation of Grenada under the late PM Bishop since the coup of 1979 which overthrew the unpopular government of Sir Eric Gairy."[54]

Mild support for U.S. aggression is the best way to describe Canada's role in Grenada. Trudeau's Liberals took a similar position in the late 1970s when the U.S. worked to undermine Jamaica's democratic socialist government of Michael Manley (who served with the Royal Canadian Air Force during World War Two). "Capital being withheld by the United States, Canada and the international lending agencies" created the crisis that led to Manley's defeat.[55] In public Trudeau was sympathetic to Manley, but upon Manley's 1980 loss to pro-business candidate, Edward Seaga, Canadian assistance to Jamaica increased from $9 million a year to $34 million.[56]

Canadian military

While Canadian diplomacy and aid have been employed to keep the region in order, so has the Canadian military. Canadian soldiers garrisoned

Bermuda from 1914-1916 and St. Lucia from 1915-1919.[57] They also replaced British forces in Jamaica from 1940-1946, as well as in Bermuda and the Bahamas during segments of this period.[58] Perceptions of race underlay the use of Canadian troops during World War Two. According to Defence Minister Norman Rogers, the governor of Jamaica "had intimated that it will be risky to remove all white troops."[59] The situation in the Bahamas was even more sensitive. In June 1942 rioting broke out over the low wages received by black labourers. Canadian troops arrived in the Bahamas just after the riots and their main task was to protect a paranoid governor, the Duke of Windsor.[60]

Ottawa was not particularly concerned that Canadian troops supported a racist colonial system. Rather, "the complications affecting Canadian troops in the West Indies, as it turned out, did not arise from the internal situation of Jamaica, but instead came from United States opposition to the British occupation of Curacao."[61]

Canadian military planners seemed to have enjoyed Canada's presence in the Caribbean. Just after World War Two came to a close Canada's chief military planner put forward a scheme for Canada to take over British military responsibilities in the Caribbean/Atlantic region. "For Canada to assume these responsibilities might be a happy solution to an otherwise confusing situation of overlapping defence interests," he wrote.[62]

In late 2006 Ottawa announced financing for a Jamaican military school to train the country's pilots as well as soldiers from across the region.[63] Since not long after independence Ottawa has trained Jamaica's security forces. Canada "cooperated closely with Jamaica in setting up the latter's national security organizations. Cadet training schemes were followed by reciprocal high-level military visits and consultations. Aircraft were sold to Jamaica and pilot training was undertaken. Technical assistance was initiated and expanded to include joint training exercises."[64]

For nearly four decades Canada has been training Caribbean military personnel at the Jamaica-based Caribbean Junior Command and Staff College, "the only source of in theatre staff college training for the Caribbean states."[65] Since 1970 the Military Training Assistance Program has educated Jamaican and Trinidadian police and military forces in methods to maintain "internal security and stability."[66]

Canadian military training in Jamaica has been particularly controversial. When "a battalion of 850 Canadian troops landed in the mountainous Jamaican interior to conduct a tropical training exercise" in the early 70s, Abeng, a leftist Jamaican paper, cried foul.[67] The paper's editors claimed Ottawa was preparing to intervene to protect Montréal-based Alcan's bauxite facilities in the event of civil unrest and/or in case a socialist government took office.

While numerous books dealing with Canadian-Caribbean relations scoff at Abeng's accusations, the archives confirm the paper's suspicions. "Subsequent [to 1979] planning for intervention seems to bear out the Abeng accusations," notes military historian Sean Maloney.[68] Code-named, NIMROD CAPPER, "the objective of the operation revolved around securing and protecting the Alcan facilities from mob unrest and outright seizure or sabotage."[69]

Later, Canadian military planning resumed from where NIMROD CAPPER began with an exercise titled "Southern Renewal" beginning in 1988. "In this case a company from two RCR [Royal Canadian Reserves] was covertly inserted to 'rescue' Canadian industrial personnel with knowledge of bauxite deposits seized by Jamaican rebels and held hostage."[70] In addition to defending commercial interests, Maloney says Canada's navy and military regularly exercise in Jamaica as part of an economic competition with the U.S.[71]

The Canadian navy has a long history of intervention in the Caribbean. A May 2008 Frontline magazine article described a trip to the region aboard HMCS Iroquois designed "to reaffirm the fact that Canada takes the Caribbean seriously as an area of strategic interest."[72] According to Maloney, "Since 1960, Canada has used its military forces at least 26 times in the Caribbean to support Canadian foreign policy. In addition, Canada planned three additional operations, including two unilateral interventions into Caribbean states. Sixteen out of these 29 operations have involved the use or planned use of Canadian maritime forces."[73]

One example cited is Barbados in 1966. (See Haiti appendix.) Two Canadian gunboats were deployed to that country's independence celebration in a bizarre diplomatic maneuver designed to demonstrate Canada's military prowess. "We can only speculate at who the 'signal' was directed towards, but given the fact that tensions were running high in the Caribbean over the Dominican Republic Affair [1965 U.S. invasion], it is likely that the targets were any outside force, probably Cuban, which might be tempted to interfere with Barbadian independence."[74] Of course, Canadian naval vessels (which regularly dock in Barbados on maneuvers) were considered no threat to Barbadian independence.[75] Intervening in another country to defend it from possible outside intervention may be the pinnacle of the imperial mindset.

The sentiment that Canada has imperial tendencies in the Caribbean is widely held there. "Canada is in fact, already sometimes classed with the United States and Britain as an imperialist exploiter in Jamaica and elsewhere," noted a book published in 1988.[76] In the midst of protests in the early 1970s against Canadian banks in Trinidad, Maclean's magazine quoted an External Affairs official who noted that "we're not colonialists by intent, but by circumstances. We've taken on a neocolonial aura there."[77] When RCMP officers were hired to run Antigua's police force in early 2008 the National Post quoted a Canadian expat explaining how "some see a climate of neocolonialism."[78]

The non-English-speaking Caribbean

Even outside the English-speaking islands of the Caribbean, Canada has a long record of acting like an imperial power, usually in concert with the U.S.

Dominican Republic

Beginning on April 24, 1965, 23,000 U.S. troops invaded the Dominican Republic. In response to the U.S. invasion, Prime Minister Lester Pearson told Parliament "the United States government has intervened in the Dominican Republic for the protection of its own citizens and those of other countries."[79] Defence Minister Paul Hellyer added that a Canadian warship was sent to Santo Domingo "to stand by in case it is required."[80]

Pearson told the Commons he was concerned about Canadian investments in the Dominican. "We have ... been in touch by telephone with the Falconbridge Nickel plant ... and we are told that all is well in that quarter." Later he said "the embassy is also investigating reports that the main branch of the Royal Bank of Canada has been looted."[81]

Concern for Canadian corporate assets was driven by the size of the investments. By 1965 Canadian banking interests held nearly 70 percent of the Dominican's foreign-owned banking assets.[82] The Royal Bank of Canada had been in the Dominican since 1912 and the Bank of Nova Scotia entered during the U.S. occupation of 1916-1924.[83]

Falconbridge's interests in the Dominican were not insignificant either and the U.S. intervention was good for business. The year after the invasion Falconbridge quadrupled the size of its experimental pilot plant in the country. Prior to commencing nickel production, the company got the post-invasion U.S.-backed Joaquin Balaguer government to send soldiers to break a strike. "When Falconbridge workers went on strike on

May 11, 1970 and then formed a union affiliated with the Confederation of Christian Trade Unions, the company refused to recognize the union and fired 60 workers. Falconbridge called in the military and police to remove the strikers, some of whom were beaten. ... The police and military broke up a union meeting of 150 workers, threatening them with death, beating some, and arresting 92 of them."[84]

Falconbridge President Marsh Cooper was pleased with the Balaguer government's actions. He gave thanks for "the whole-hearted cooperation offered by President Balaguer, his ministers and officials of the Dominican government."[85] By 1972 Falconbridge controlled the single largest foreign investment in the country and the company continued its antiunion activities.[86] In October 1974 Falconbridge fired 25 union leaders, shut down their office and prohibited future worker meetings.[87] Some alleged that Falconbridge also associated with the right wing Cuban exile terrorist group, Coordination of the United Revolutionary Organizations.[88]

Balaguer was the U.S.-backed candidate in the "demonstration election" organized after the invasion. Edward Herman notes: "After invading, decimating the democratic forces and recreating a climate of fear, the United States was able to follow president Lyndon Johnson's order to 'get this guy [Balaguer] in office down there!' — and simultaneously prove its devotion to self-determination and the democratic process!"[89] (Ballot box stuffing and coercion meant the election was fraudulent, even in the simple technical sense.[90])

Ottawa supported Belaguer with its first bilateral grant to a Latin American country. Canada gave $298,000 in food aid to the Dominican Republic in 1966 as part of the "mop-up in the wake of the 1965 military invasion of that country."[91] Canadian troops also participated in the OAS mission designed to relieve U.S. troops after the invasion.[92]

To this day Canadian companies continue to benefit from the climate created by the 1965 U.S. invasion. In 2007 Canada's two biggest gold mining companies, Barrick and Goldcorp, began a controversial $3 billion investment at the Pueblo Viejo mine, which the Dominican government was convinced to privatize partly by Louis Guay, a Canadian diplomat who then worked for Placer Dome (acquired by Barrick).[93] In February 2009 "a delegation of Barrick Gold headed by its CEO Aaron W. Regent visited [Dominican] president Leonel Fernandez in the National Palace, to provide information and details of its projects in the gold mines at Pueblo Viejo, Sanchez Ramirez province (northeast). Also present at the meeting were the Venezuelan mogul Gustavo Cisneros, the Dominican Manuel Alejandro

Grullón, president of the bank group Popular, Felix Garcia, president of the group Caribe, former United States ambassador Hans H. Hertell and the lawyer Luis Rafael Pellerano, of the law firm Pellerano & Herrera."[94]

Cuba

If Canada has acted like a traditional colonial power in the rest of the Caribbean, at least Canadian policy towards Cuba proves that we can stand up to the USA and follow a more independent policy, right? Rather than participate in hundreds of CIA assassination attempts on the life of Fidel Castro, Canadian Prime Minister Pierre Trudeau declared "Viva Castro" during an official trip to Cuba in 1976. But it's not so simple as Canadian relations with Cuba have been good, while those of the U.S. with Cuba have been bad.

Business is business seems to be Canada's slogan for relations with Cuba from the U.S. occupation in 1898 through the dictator Batista to Castro's revolution in 1959.[95] In 1900 the Canadian Journal of Commerce noted: "Canadian capital and clearer northern brains" were turning Cuba into a "modern hive of industry."[96] A few months after the U.S. began its 1898-1902 occupation the Royal Bank opened its first branch in Havana.[97] According to one bank history: "[Royal Bank] General Manager, Mr. E.L. Pease, took a quick trip to Cuba at the end of the Spanish-American War and got in on the ground floor of banking there; his American friends, who put capital into the bank, helped him to expand there. (The bank was appointed agent for the payment of claims of the Army of Liberation.)"[98] Before his trip to Havana Pease asked Henry White of New York's Chase National to "smooth the way through the American authorities."[99] And once in that beautiful city Pease befriended U.S. Consul Joseph Springer, who indicated that the U.S. planned to reform Cuba's financial sector.[100] (It was relatively easy for the Royal to get priority of place because, until 1914, national U.S. banks were forbidden from establishing foreign branches.[101])

The Canadian bankers saw themselves as American and after the U.S. occupation formally ended they felt covered by the protective umbrella of the Platt amendment. (Inserted into the Cuban constitution by Washington, the Platt amendment gave the U.S. the right to intervene on the island whenever necessary). "The United States authorities have the affairs of the Island well in hand at the present time," Pease told the Financial Post in 1907.[102] Royal Bank branches sprouted up across the island, usually along the newly built railroad through central Cuba. "The bank consciously established its branches wherever it could facilitate the spread of foreign investment entering Cuba."[103] The Royal Bank's best customer was Canadian businessman William Van Horne's Cuba Company and its offspring, the Cuba Railroad. Famous for his role in constructing the Canadian Pacific Railway, Van Horne "took advantage of Spain's defeat and his influence in U.S. financial circles to start building a trans-island railway before any government had the power to stop him."[104] Van Horne had two U.S. generals sit on the company's board and "land for the railroad was not purchased, but seized by the [U.S. military]."[105] Van Horne also benefited from Cuba's postwar railway law. He and a colleague wrote it.[106] The Cuban railway was completed in 1902 and Van Horne proceeded to purchase tramways and sugar mills on the island.[107]

With a wave of foreign investment into Cuba, business was good for the Royal Bank. By the mid-1920s, the Royal had 65 branches in the country.[108] Popularly known as "Banco de Canada" during this period, "the Canadian bank acted as Cuba's de facto central banker."[109] A quarter century later, Canadian banks still controlled 28 percent of total deposits in commercial Cuban banks. U.S. interests controlled 36 percent and Cuban interests 35 percent.[110] Beyond banking, Canadian insurance companies sold two-thirds of the country's total annual premiums in the mid 1950s, while the Cuban-Canadian sugar company owned 66,000 acres and 2,720 head of cattle.[111] Another Canadian-owned ranch covered 75,000 acres and the Canada-Cuba Land and Fruit Company ran 100 tobacco plantations.[112]

"Since Canada's ties with Cuba are primarily commercial," External Affairs advised the Canadian ambassador to Cuba in March 1949 that his two "main duties" were to defend Canadian commercial interests and increase trade opportunities on the island.[113] Ottawa's focus on Canadian commercial interests helps explain the embassy's attitude to the pro-capitalist dictator, General Fulgencio Batista. Twenty months before the brutal despot was overthrown, the Canadian ambassador said Batista was "still the best hope for the future" because he "has offered the stability demanded by foreign investors."[114] A year earlier the Canadian ambassador said "the benevolence of President Batista is not to be questioned. He may be lining his pockets at Cuba's expense but it is traditional for Cuban Presidents to do so and it is in part made necessary by the uncertainty of political life here. But as a dictator he is a failure, if the standard is Hitler or Mussolini. Public protests against the regime are possible; an opposition is in existence and is weak only because of fundamental weaknesses in the personalities of the opposition."[115]

After Batista's downfall in January 1959 the new government tried to gain greater control over the economy. Among other steps, U.S. banks were nationalized without compensation. Canadian banks were also nationalized, but more amicably — with compensation. In response to these moves by the new Cuban government, U.S. hostility rose and Uncle Sam eventually cut off trade and diplomatic relations with the country. The U.S. also supported an invasion of Cuba, which Ottawa endorsed. Just days after the CIA-backed Bay of Pigs invasion, Prime Minister John Diefenbaker claimed Castro was a threat to the security of the hemisphere.[116] On April 19, 1961, he told the House of Commons that events in Cuba were "manifestations of a dictatorship which is abhorrent to free men everywhere."[117]

Despite tacit support for U.S. actions against Cuba Ottawa never broke off diplomatic relations, even though most other countries in the hemisphere did. Three Nights in Havana explains why Ottawa maintained diplomatic and economic relations with Cuba: "Recently declassified State Department documents have revealed that, far from encouraging Canada to support the embargo, the United States secretly urged Diefenbaker to maintain normal relations because it was thought that Canada would be well positioned to gather intelligence on the island."[118] Washington was okay with Canada's continued relations with the island. It simply wanted assurances, which were promptly given, that Canada wouldn't take over the trade the U.S. lost.[119]

Ottawa has not let Washington down in regards to intelligence gathering. For nearly half a century Canada has spied on Cuba. Since the start of the 1960s the Communications Security Establishment (CSE), an intelligence department of the federal government, has listened to Cuban leaders secret conversations from an interception post in the Canadian embassy in Havana.[120] A senior Canadian official, close to Washington, "admitted that the U.S. made 'far greater use' of our intelligence during the [October 1962] Cuban Missile Crisis than has been revealed."[121] Pentagon and State Department sources cite the U.K. and Canada as the only countries that "supply any real military information on Cuba" with Canada providing "the best" military intelligence.[122] Canada has even spied on Cuba from outside that country. The CSE wanted to establish a communications post in Kingston, Jamaica, to intercept "communications from Fidel Castro's Cuba, which would please [the US government's] NSA to no end."[123]

Alongside ongoing intelligence gathering efforts, today there are growing indications that Ottawa is in the midst of a low-level "democracy promotion" campaign in Cuba. Embassy magazine reported in 2008 that "Gerald Hyman, former director of USAID's office of democracy and governance, noted that Canada can be active in many places the U.S. cannot

— for example, Cuba."[124] Well-known columnist Gwynne Dwyer described funding he received from Foreign Affairs: "I was contacted early last year [2007] by the Canadian Embassy in Cuba, which was bringing in various Canadian experts to explain how things are done in free countries to groups that they hoped would be influential after Fidel finally dies. Cubans have been living in a cave for the past 50 years, and a bunch of Western embassies in Havana thought that it might help to bring some key groups in Havana into contact with people from the real world."[125]

Canadian officials, including former Canadian ambassador to Haiti Claude Boucher and the head of Rights and Democracy, Jean-Louis Roy, have cited Ottawa's role in Haiti as preparation for post-Castro transition.[126] "Cuba has been cited by certain Canadian and Latin America VIPs as the next place that lessons learned in Haiti might be applied," noted Stephen Baranyi from the North-South Institute at a Canadian Foundation for the Americas (FOCAL) conference.[127] The Globe & Mail echoed this idea, reporting that "The U.N. presence [in Haiti] is widely regarded as a test case for what might happen in Cuba after the Castro regime falls."[128]

Haiti

Canada's role in the most impoverished country of the Americas, Haiti, reveals the extent to which this country is prepared to act as an imperialist power.

On February 29, 2004 Canadian special forces commandos called JTF2 "secured" the airport from which Haiti's elected president Jean-Bertand Aristide was bundled ("kidnapped" in his words) onto a plane by U.S. Marines and deposited in the Central African Republic.[129] Almost immediately after Aristide was gone, 500 Canadian troops patrolled the streets of Port-Au-Prince. Aristide's overthrow was the culmination of a U.S.-led and Canadian supported destabilization campaign that included "civil society building," military and paramilitary interventions, an aid embargo that would cripple the country's economy, a full-scale disinformation campaign waged by Haitian elite-owned and international corporate media, and concerted diplomatic efforts directed at guaranteeing regime change would be both acceptable to the international community and believable to a confused public. (See Damming the Flood, Canada in Haiti and An Unbroken Agony for more detail)

Ottawa played an important role in consolidating the international forces that planned and carried out the coup. On January 31 and February 1, 2003, Jean Chrétien's Liberal government organized the "Ottawa Initiative" on Haiti to discuss that country's future. No Haitian officials were invited to this meeting at Meech Lake where high level U.S., Canadian and French government officials decided that Haiti's elected president "must go", the army should be recreated and that the country would be put under U.N. trusteeship.[130]

Liberal officials justified cutting off assistance to Haiti's elected government and then intervening militarily in the country by citing the Canadian-sponsored "responsibility to protect" doctrine.[131] Secretary of State for Latin America and Minister for La Francophonie Dennis Paradis explained that "there was one thematic that went under the whole meeting [Ottawa Initiative]... the responsibility to protect."[132] In a highly censored February 11, 2004 cable from the embassy in Port-au-Prince to Foreign Affairs, Canadian ambassador Kenneth Cook explained that "President Aristide is clearly a serious aggravating factor in the current crisis" and that there is a need to "consider the options including whether a case can be made for the duty [responsibility] to protect."[133]

The responsibility to protect doctrine was a showpiece of the Liberal party's foreign-policy. In September 2000 Canada launched the International Commission on Intervention and State Sovereignty. The commission's final report, The Responsibility to Protect, was presented to the U.N. in December 2001. At the organization's 2005 World Summit, Canada advocated that world leaders endorse the new doctrine. It asserts that where gross human rights abuses are occurring, it is the duty of the international community to intervene, over and above considerations of state sovereignty. The doctrine asserts that "the principle of non-intervention yields to the international responsibility to protect."

To some this Canadian-promoted "responsibility to protect" doctrine sounds like a good idea. But who gets to decide when a country becomes a "failed state" or when "gross human rights abuses" are occurring? What if a government is "failing" because powerful countries have destablized it? What if the destablization is a result of government policies that challenge corporate and elite interests in those powerful countries? Rather than be a force for good the "responsibility to protect" could just as easily be a cover for imperialism. Certainly the record of the most recent foreign intervention in Haiti, justified by Canada under the responsibility to protect, does not bode well for the doctrine, if humanitarianism is a criteria by which we judge it.

A study published in the prestigious Lancet medical journal released at the end of August 2006 revealed there were 8,000 murders, 35,000 rapes and thousands of incidents of armed threats in the 22 months after the overthrow of the elected government in Haiti.[134] Confirming numerous prior human rights investigations, the study estimated that 8,000 people in Port-au-Prince were killed in the 22 months after the toppling of Aristide's government. (Investigations by the Institute for Justice and Democracy in Haiti, University of Miami, Harvard University, National Lawyers Guild etc. all found significant evidence of persecution directed at Aristide sympathizers in the months after the coup.) The published research gives an idea of the scale of the persecution of those close to Aristide's Lavalas movement. Of the estimated 8,000 people murdered — 12 people a day — in the greater Port-au-Prince area, nearly half (47.7 percent) were killed by governmental or anti-Aristide forces. 21.7 percent of the killings were attributed to members of the Haitian National Police (HNP), 13.0 percent to demobilized soldiers (many of whom participated in the coup) and 13.0 percent to anti-Aristide gangs (none were attributed to Aristide supporters and the rest were attributed to common criminals).[135]

Throughout the March 2004 to May 2006 coup period the Haitian police killed peaceful demonstrators and carried out massacres in poor neighbourhoods, often with help from anti-Aristide gangs. Canadian troops and later police trainers often supported the Haitian police operations, usually by providing backup to the police killers. Canada commanded (and still commands at press time) the 1,600-member U.N. police contingent mandated to train, assist and oversee the Haitian National Police.

The study also found a "shocking" level of sexual violence committed after the coup, with an estimated 35,000 women raped in Port-au- Prince, with more than half of the victims under eighteen. Much of the rape had a political character. In a harrowing account the co-author of the study, Athena Kolbe, discussed interviewing a mother who had been raped with a metal bar, which destroyed her cervix. Gravely ill, the woman was transported by Kolbe's crew to a hospital, where they offered to pay for medical costs. On discovering that a uniformed police officer was implicated, the hospital refused medical treatment. The victim eventually received medical attention at another facility, but ultimately succumbed to her injuries. Kolbe then paid for relocation of the traumatized family (this necessitated not including the rape in the survey data published in the Lancet).

Throughout the period investigated by the researchers Canada was heavily involved in Haitian affairs. Ottawa provided tens of millions of dollars in foreign aid to the installed government, publicly supported coup officials and employed numerous officials within coup government ministries. Haiti's deputy justice minister for the first 15 months of the foreign installed government, Philippe Vixamar, was on CIDA's payroll.[136] He was then replaced by long-time CIDA employee Dilia Lemaire.[137] During this period hundreds of political prisoners, including the former prime minister and interior minister, languished in prolonged and arbitrary detention.

There is some evidence that Canadian forces in Haiti participated directly in the political repression. The Lancet researcher noted above recounted an interview with one family in the Delmas district of Port-au-Prince: "Canadian troops came to their house, and they said they were looking for Lavalas [Aristide's party] chimeres, and threatened to kill the head of household, who was the father, if he didn't name names of people in their neighbourhood who were Lavalas chimeres or Lavalas supporters."[138] A January 2005 human rights report from the University of Miami quoted a Canadian police officer saying that "he engaged in daily guerrilla warfare."[139] Afghanistan and Haiti were cited by the Canadian Forces 2007 draft counterinsurgency manual as the only foreign countries where Canadian troops were participating in counterinsurgency warfare. According to the manual, Canadian Forces have been "conducting COIN [counter-insurgency] operations against the criminally-based insurgency in Haiti since early 2004."[140]

While our security forces fought a counterinsurgency campaign Canadian diplomats pressured others to contribute to the fight. In early 2005 the head of the U.N. force (MINUSTAH), General Augusto Heleno Ribeiro, told a congressional commission in Brazil that "we are under extreme pressure from the international community [specifically citing Canada, France and the U.S.] to use violence."[141] Not long after Ribeiro complained about pressure to get tough, U.N. forces committed their worst massacre in Haiti. Marketed by its architects as an action against a "gang" leader, at dawn on July 6, 2005, 400 U.N. troops, backed by helicopters, entered the capital's densely populated slum neighbourhood of Cité Soleil. Eyewitnesses and victims of the attack claim MINUSTAH helicopters fired on residents throughout the operation. The cardboard and corrugated tin wall houses were no match for the troops' heavy weaponry, which fired "over 22,000 rounds of ammunition."[142] The raid left at least 23 civilians dead, including numerous women and children.[143] The U.N. claimed they only killed "gang" leader Dread Wilme. For their part community members responded to Wilme's death by painting a large mural of him next to one of Aristide and Che Guevara.

In the months just prior to the February 2006 election there was a spike in U.N. military operations. After nominally democratic, but largely powerless, President René Preval took office repression subsided. But Haiti's business elite and the international powers began to demand further U.N. repression of "gangs." In a January 15, 2007 interview with Haiti's Radio Solidarité Canada's ambassador, Claude Boucher, praised the U.N. troops, urging them to "increase their operations as they did last December."[144]

Boucher's public support for operations "last December" was an unmistakable reference to the December 22, 2006, U.N. assault on Cité Soleil. Dubbed the "Christmas Massacre" by neighbourhood residents, Agence France Presse indicated that at least 12 people were killed and "several dozen" wounded. A Haitian human rights organization, AUMOHD, reported 20 killed. The Agence Haitienne de Presse (AHP) reported "very serious property damage" following the U.N. attack, and concerns that "a critical water shortage may now develop because water cisterns and pipes were punctured by the gunfire." Red Cross coordinator Pierre Alexis complained to AHP that U.N. soldiers "blocked Red Cross vehicles from entering Cité Soleil" to help the wounded.

After his interview, Boucher got what he wanted. A U.N. raid on Cité Soleil on Jan. 25 left five dead and a dozen wounded, according to Agence France Presse. On February 3 the U.N. killed several people in Cité Soleil including two little girls, Alexandra and Stephanie Lubin.[145] And a week later, MINUSTAH operations in Cité Soleil left "four dead and 10 injured all of which were innocent civilians" according to AHP. (Kevin Pina's film Haiti: We Must Kill the Bandits documents the chilling brutality of U.N. forces.)

Since the February 2004 coup tens of millions in Canadian "aid" dollars have been spent to reestablish foreign and elite control over Haiti's armed forces. In August 2007 Montréal's Le Devoir newspaper quoted an unnamed CIDA official who said the organization was spending $25 million on a police academy to train Haitian officers and then in early 2009 Ottawa announced it was seeking a private company to fulfil a $15 million contract to train Haiti's police.[146] "We are going to help double the number of Haitian police trained," explained Foreign Affairs Minister Maxime Bernier in 2008. "This needs to increase from 600 to 1,200 a year to reach a force of 12,000 by 2011."

Beyond increasing the size of the force, Canadian trainers have overseen the militarization of Haiti's police force. In the months following the coup, nearly all new police were former military and, according to Reuters in

March 2005, "only one of the top 12 police commanders in the Port-au-Prince area does not have a military background, and most regional police chiefs are also ex-soldiers." The head of the police, Mario Andresol (who was appointed by the coup government), is a former military man who still wears his combat garb.

The new Haitian National Police (HNP) is responsible for all aspects of policing in the country, from beat cops and border patrol to the SWAT team and palace security. This concentration of the security force command structure places those in charge of the police in a better position to overthrow a government or exert political influence.

Canada's role in building the HNP has an important historical parallel dating back to 1918 when U.S. forces established a Haitian army three years after invading. This "Haitian" military helped maintain the 19-year U.S. occupation and once their troops left the country the army became a primary tool for the U.S. to retain power. Until its dissolution by the Aristide government in 1995 this army never fought a foreign power. Its sole function was to repress the domestic population. Immediately after that army was disbanded, the U.S. tried to militarize the newly created police force (the army had been responsible for policing activities), until the Haitian government finally expelled U.S. police trainers and Washington responded by withholding aid.

Historically the Haitian elite and their foreign backers have had near absolute control over the country's armed forces. This control was severely weakened by 2004. That was what made it necessary for U.S. marines and Canadian forces to invade the country to overthrow Aristide, a process more laborious than past coups when the army simply killed or expelled the head of state (with U.S. support of course).

The re-establishment of elite control over the police force was accomplished almost entirely under the radar of the media. If this new force overthrows the next government attempting to narrow Haiti's class divide, Canadian officials will be able to claim they had no role in the affair.

Haiti's February 2006 election provides another striking example of Canada's support for the country's elite. The election was marred by two years of political violence directed at supporters of Aristide; peaceful demonstrations were regularly shot at by the police; hundreds of Lavalas officials and activists were locked away for their political affiliation and hundreds more were in exile. In addition to systematic violence directed at Lavalas, the party's presidential candidate, Gérard Jean Juste, was blocked from participating because he was in jail (a "prisoner of conscience," according to Amnesty International). Canadian-backed electoral officials refused to accept his nomination via a third-party even though there is a provision to do so in Haiti's electoral regulations.

On simple procedural grounds the election was a farce. During the election in 2000 there were more than 10,000 registration centres and some 12,000 polling stations across the country. In 2006 the coup government reduced that number to 500 registration centres and a little more than 800 polling stations, even though they had some $50 million to run the election (most of the money came from the U.S., France and Canada, with Ottawa providing the largest slice).[147] In the poorest neighbourhoods, where opposition to the coup was strongest, registration centres were few and far between.

On Ottawa's initiative the International Mission for Monitoring Haitian Elections (IMMHE) was organized in June of 2005. The IMMHE was chaired by the then chief electoral officer of Elections Canada, Jean-Pierre Kingsley. After widespread fraud in the counting, including thousands of ballots found burned in a dump, the country was gripped by social upheaval. In response, Kingsley released a statement claiming "the election was carried out with no violence or intimidation, and no accusations of fraud."[148] Kingsley's statement went on to laud Jacques Bernard, the head of the electoral council despite the fact that Bernard had already been widely derided as corrupt and biased even by other members of the coup government's electoral council.

Kingsley's connections in Ottawa put his impartiality into serious doubt. In addition, his close ties to the International Foundation of Electoral Systems (IFES), which receives about 80 percent of its funding from the U.S. government, helps explain his partisan statements. At the time of Haiti's election, Kingsley sat on the board of IFES and a year after the election Kingsley stepped down from Elections Canada to become president of IFES. A University of Miami Human Rights Investigation that appeared more than a year before the election summarised the "multi-million dollar" IFES project in Haiti: "IFES workers ... completely take credit for ousting Aristide. ... IFES ... formulated groups that never existed, united pre-existing groups, gave them sensitization seminars, paid for people to attend, paid for entertainment and catering, and basically built group after group. ... They reached out to student groups, business ... [and] human rights groups which they actually paid off to report human rights atrocities to make Aristide look bad. ... They bought journalists, and the IFES associations grew into the Group of 184 that became a solidified opposition against Aristide....

Gérard Latortue, the [coup] prime minister, was an IFES member for a couple of years before the ouster of Aristide. ... Bernard Gousse, the [coup] justice minister ... in charge of prisons and police, was in [IFES] for many years."[149]

But it's not just U.S.-based "non-governmental organizations" that were paid to influence events in Haiti. Canadian aid has been a bonanza for mostly Québec-based NGOs that received tens of millions of dollars for work in Haiti. Montréal-based Alternatives, considered to be one of Québec's most left-leaning non-governmental organizations, is but one example. With no operations in Haiti when the Canadian military invaded, the post-coup influx of Canadian dollars was too good an opportunity to pass up. The Haiti file was given to an Alternatives employee who was having difficulty raising money for his Africa dossier. Canadian imperialism at that moment showed a definite preference for media work in Haiti over Ghana and Alternatives was rewarded when it obliged. (Alternatives, which is heavily involved in the World Social Forum, also followed Canadian "aid" to Afghanistan and Iraq.)

Since the coup Alternatives has received millions of dollars for Haiti work. Coincidentally, Alternatives parroted the neoconservative narrative about Haiti. Sixteen months after the coup an Alternatives article accused, without a shred of evidence, prominent Bel-Air activist Samba Boukman and human rights worker Ronald St. Jean of being "notorious criminals."[150] This was exceedingly dangerous in an environment where the victims of police operations were routinely labelled "bandits" and "criminals" after they were killed. Alternatives' "progressive" credibility was put to work countering opposition to Brazil's leadership of the U.N. occupation of Haiti. "With the support of the Canadian government" in March 2005 Alternatives established a "trialogue" in Brazil between "the governments and organizations of civil society of Brazil, Haiti and Canada" on how to support the "transition" government. "Several ministers of the interim [coup] government of Haiti" assisted Alternatives in this task.[151]

At the August 2007 Québec Social Forum political activist Chavanne Jean-Baptiste was Alternatives' guest speaker on Haiti. Jean-Baptiste was the coup government's liaison to the peasantry and a prominent supporter of the failed presidential campaign of right-wing business candidate, Charles Henry-Baker. (It was alleged that Jean-Baptiste's organization, the MPP, provided support to the ex-military who led the armed assault against the elected government in February 2004.) Alternatives' other main Haitian invitee to the Québec Social Forum was René Colbert, editor of AlterPresse, who told this author in a private conversation that there was no coup in February 2004 since Aristide was never elected.

At the start of 2008 Alternatives co-published a report that clearly articulated this group's colonial attitude vis-a-vis Haiti. The most disturbing statement in the report titled "Haiti: Voices of the Actors" reads: "In a country like Haiti, in which democratic culture has never taken hold, the concept of the common good and the meaning of elections and representation are limited to the educated elites, and in particular to those who have received citizen education within the social movements."[152]

According to Alternatives, Haitians are too stupid to know what's good for them, unless, that is, they've been educated by a foreign NGO. The report, which was financed by Ottawa, is full of other attacks against Haitians and the country's popular movement.

Many of the other Canadian NGOs that benefited from the coup called for Aristide's overthrow. The Concertation Pour Haiti (CPH), an informal group of half a dozen NGOs including Development and Peace, AQOCI (Québec's NGO umbrella group) and Entraide Missionaire branded Aristide a "tyrant," his government a "dictatorship," and a "regime of terror" and in mid-February 2004 called for Aristide's removal.[153] This demand was made at the same time CIA-trained thugs swept across the country to oust Aristide. Throughout the coup period from March 2004 to May 2006 the CPH organized numerous events in Ottawa and Montréal that effectively justified Canada's intervention into Haiti.

A regular co-sponsor of CPH events and press statements, Rights & Democracy is a Montréal-based political group created by an act of Parliament and funded almost entirely by Ottawa. In a January 27, 2006 letter — also signed by the CPH — to Allan Rock, Canada's ambassador to the U.N., the two groups echoed the extreme right's demand for increased repression in the country's largest poor neighbourhood, Cité Soleil. A couple of weeks after a business-sector "strike" demanding that U.N. troops aggressively attack "gangsters" in Cité Soleil, Rights & Democracy questioned the "true motives of the U.N. mission." The letter questioned whether U.N. forces were "protecting armed bandits more than restoring order and ending violence."[154] Criticizing the U.N. for softness in Cité Soleil flew in the face of evidence suggesting the opposite. In fact, just prior to the Rights & Democracy/CPH letter, Canadian solidarity activists documented a murderous U.N. attack on a hospital in the slum neighbourhood. Statements published on the Rights & Democracy website have followed a pattern that belies the organization's professions of support for either human rights or democracy. A couple of days before Aristide took office in 2001 after winning an election with over 90 percent of the vote (it was boycotted by parties of the elite, but a poll by the U.S. State Department confirmed Aristide's overwhelming popularity), Rights & Democracy noted: "Mr. Aristide's election came amidst widespread doubts about his own and the [first] Préval government's commitment to democracy." Yet when the Canadian-backed, unelected government of Gérard Latortue took power in March 2004 after a coup, Rights & Democracy published no such statement. Nor did the group criticize the unconstitutional interim government's terrible human rights record. Yet in an April 2002 statement Rights & Democracy claimed, "the elected officials of the Lavalas Family [Aristide's party] and representatives of 'popular organizations' close to that party are often implicated in the most flagrant violation of Haitian laws."[155]

A few months prior to the February 29, 2004 coup that overthrew Aristide for the second time, Rights & Democracy released a report that described Haiti's pro-coup Group of 184 as "grassroots" and a "promising civil society movement."[156] The truth is that the Group of 184 was spawned and funded by the International Republican Institute (funded by the U.S. government) and headed by Haiti's leading sweatshop owner, Andy Apaid.[157] Apaid had been active in right-wing Haitian politics for many years and, like former Group of 184 spokesperson Charles Henry Baker, is white.

In addition to Rights & Democracy's public campaign to undermine governments elected by Haiti's poor majority, the group used "civil society" to undermine real democracy. In October 2005 Rights & Democracy began a $415,000 CIDA-financed project to "foster greater civil society participation in Haiti's national political process."

The Haitian coordinator of the project, who later became director of Rights & Democracy's Haiti office, was Danielle Magloire, a member of the "Council of the Wise" that appointed Gérard Latortue as interim prime minister after the coup ousted the elected president. Magloire's status as a "wise" person, moreover, arose largely out of her positions at EnfoFanm (Women's info) and the National Coordination for Advocacy on Women's Rights (CONAP). Both were CIDA-funded feminist organizations that would not have grown to prominence without international funding. They were virulently anti-Lavalas groups that shunned the language of class struggle in a country where a tiny percentage of the population owns nearly everything. Interestingly, EnfoFanm and CONAP expressed little concern about the dramatic rise in rapes targeting Lavalas sympathizers after the coup. In mid-July 2005 Magloire issued a statement on behalf of the seven-member "Council of the Wise" saying that any media that gives voice to "bandits" (code for Aristide supporters) should be shut down. She also asserted that the Lavalas Family should be banned from upcoming elections.[158] One must ask whose rights and what sort of democracy Rights & Democracy supports, when it effectively aligns itself with fascistic elements in Haiti?

Regarding Haiti, Rights & Democracy revealed itself to be similar to the U.S. National Endowment for Democracy, the International Republican Institute and many more government-funded institutions around the world that work to undermine real democracy. These groups do the destabilization work that the CIA or the British Foreign Service or agents of the French government once performed.

Why did Canada help overthrow Haiti's elected government in 2004? That's a question I heard over and over when speaking about Canada in Haiti: Waging War on the Poor Majority, a book I co-authored with Anthony Fenton. Most people had difficulty understanding why their country — and the U.S. to some extent — would intervene in a country so poor, so seemingly marginal to world affairs. Why would they bother?

I would answer that Canada participated in the coup as a way to make good with Washington, especially after (officially) declining the Bush administration's invitation (order) to join the "coalition of the willing" in Iraq. Former Foreign Affairs Minister Bill Graham explained: "Foreign Affairs view was there is a limit to how much we can constantly say no to the political masters in Washington. All we had was Afghanistan to wave. On every other file we were offside. Eventually we came on side on Haiti, so we got another arrow in our quiver."[159]

It is also worth noting that at the start of 2003 the Haitian minimum wage was 36 gourdes ($1) a day, which was nearly doubled to 70 gourdes by the Aristide government. Of course, this was opposed by domestic and international capital, which used Haiti's lowest wages in the hemisphere as a way to beat back workers' demands in other countries. Canadian capital was especially hostile to raising the minimum wage. The largest blank T-shirt maker in the world, Montréal-based Gildan Activewear was the country's largest employer after the state, employing up to 8,000 Haitians (directly and indirectly) in Port-au-Prince's assembly sector by 2007.[160] Most of Gildan's work was subcontracted to Andy Apaid, who led the Group 184 domestic "civil society" that opposed Aristide's government. Coincidentally, two days after the coup, Foreign Affairs stated "some Canadian companies are looking to shift garment production to Haiti."[161]

It is also clear that some Canadian mining companies saw better opportunities with a post-Aristide government. In 2007, "Another Canadian-backed company recently resumed prospecting in Haiti after abandoning its claims a decade ago. Steve Lachapelle — a Québec lawyer who is now chair of the board of the company, called St. Genevieve Haiti — says employees were threatened at gunpoint by partisans of ex-president Jean-Bertrand Aristide."[162]

Another reason for the intervention came out of the contempt, heightened during the country's 200-year anniversary of independence, directed at Haiti ever since the country's 1791-1804 revolution dealt a crushing blow to slavery, colonialism and white supremacy. The threat of a good example — particularly worrisome for the powers that be, since Haiti is so poor — contributed to the motivation for the coup. Aristide was perceived as a barrier to a thorough implementation of the free market agenda, particularly because of his opposition to the privatization of the country's five remaining state-owned companies. The attitude seems to have been, "if we can't force our way in Haiti, where can we?"

But I was never entirely satisfied with my answers. That was one motivation for spending hundreds of hours researching this history of Canadian foreign policy. So, why did Canada help overthrow the elected Haitian government?

Historically, countries' foreign affairs were mostly about "projecting force" in a hostile world. This meant the use of power (military or economic) for protection or to gain advantage. In the modern era, the "advantage" to be gained and then protected is capitalist entitlement, the ability to make a profit. In other words, foreign affairs have mostly been about asserting and protecting the "rights" of a country's wealth owners.

The Canadian government, from its beginning, was part of the command and control apparatus of the world economic system. At first Canada served as an arm of the British Empire, but, given the country's location as well as racial and economic makeup, it quickly became intertwined with the USA. Canada's role over the past five decades, as assigned by the dominant power, has typically been some sort of "policing" operation, usually called peacekeeping. Since Canada has primarily been a "policing" rather than "military" power one must look to the language of policing to discover the motivations for our Haitian policy.

Over the past decade there has been much discussion of something called "pulling our weight" in external affairs. In laymen's terms this means spending more of the country's resources on defending and expanding the ability to make a profit around the world, for Canadian capitalists in particular, but also for the system in general. While the less sophisticated neoconservatives simply call for more military spending and a pro-U.S. foreign policy, the more liberal Canadian supporters of capitalism have been busy creating an ideological mask, called the "responsibility to protect" that will accomplish the same end.

The "responsibility to protect" is essentially a justification for imperialism using the dialect of policing instead of the old language of empire and militarism. It says there are "failed states" that must be overthrown because they do not provide adequately for their own citizens and because they threaten world order. This is the international equivalent of the "zero tolerance" (also called the "broken window") strategy of the New York City police department. The policy is to aggressively police petty crimes in order to create an environment that discourages more serious law breaking. In the same fashion, the international community should go after "failed states" not because they threaten other countries with invasion but since they create an environment where "crime" may thrive. (Noam Chomsky has used the Mafia analogy to explain the less sophisticated, older imperialist version of this policy. Any and all challenges, even minor ones, must be met with violence until "order" is established. The "responsibility to protect" differs in form but not in substance.)

The coup in Haiti was a Canadian-managed experiment in the use of the "responsibility to protect" doctrine. Aristide was overthrown precisely because Haiti is so unimportant to the world economic system and because cracking down on it is the international economic equivalent of the New York City police cracking down on graffiti writers. Once again Haiti was an example to the rest of the world, a message from the world's rich and powerful.

Discussion

Canadian policy towards the Caribbean reveals a legacy of seeing the region through the eyes of a colonial master instead of as a fellow country sharing a common goal of independence. This is partly explained by historical notions such as the "white man's burden" or other racist attitudes towards Afro-Caribbean people. But to understand Canadian policy also requires an economic analysis. Canadian companies and the members of the economic elite who owned/own them had, and have, interests in the region. They make profits from investments and want those investments to do well. Canadian business, as well as their local elite partners, desire

Caribbean governments that help them increase their profit and dislike governments that threaten their investments. To the extent that Canadian companies have power to influence Ottawa's policy they do so in their corporate self-interest.

Canadian-owned companies large enough to own foreign subsidiaries often wield significant political power inside Canada. Yet even when they are not particularly influential inside Canada they often still play a part in determining Ottawa's actions in a particular country. An explicit goal of foreign policy is to defend and enhance Canadian interests. And how are these 'interests' determined? At least partly by listening to Canadian companies operating in a particular country. And, if there are no countervailing voices speaking up for poorly paid miners or peasants whose land is being destroyed, or a hundred other scenarios, Canadian foreign policy can be anti-democratic, colonial and environmentally destructive.

Of course, "Canadian interests" are rarely defined entirely by a particular company or industry. Sometimes Canadian interests, as determined by a particular government, are shaped by ideology or by seeing this country as a junior partner to a more powerful country.

Chapter Notes

1   La Presse March 7 2007
2   June 2005 Pew Research Center Global Attitudes Project
3   http://auto_sol.tao.ca/node/3047
4   Canadian-Caribbean relations, 286; Northern shadows, 19
5   Canada and the Commonwealth Caribbean, 222
6   Canada and the Commonwealth Caribbean, 233
7   Northern shadows, 20
8   Towers of Gold, 188; Canada and the Commonwealth Caribbean, 230
9   Canada and the Commonwealth Caribbean, 192
10   Canada and the Commonwealth Caribbean, 17
11   Canadian-West Indian Union, 16
12   Towers of Gold, 187
13   Canada in the European Age, 482
14   Canada and the Commonwealth Caribbean, 17
15   Northern Shadows, 21; Canadian-West Indian Union, 30; Canada and the Commonwealth Caribbean, 17
16   Land of Lost Content, 26; Canada and the Commonwealth Caribbean, 17
17   Imperialism and the National Question in Canada, 80
18   The Banks of Canada in the Commonwealth Caribbean, 50
19   The Economist March 29, 2008
20   Ties that Bind, 113
21   Ties that Bind, 112
22   Canadian Caribbean relations, 271
23   The Banks of Canada in the Commonwealth Caribbean, 29
24   The Banks of Canada in the Commonwealth Caribbean, 32
25   The Banks of Canada in the Commonwealth Caribbean, 30
26   Towers of Gold, 189; Anatomy of Big Business 117
27   Anatomy of Big Business, 138
28   Transnational Corporations and Caribbean Inequalities, 21
29   But not in Canada, 260
30   Last Post Vol 1 #4
31   Last Post Vol 1 #4
32   The Economist Mar 29th 2008
33   Land of Lost Content, 27
34   Last Post Vol 1 #4
35   Canada and the Commonwealth Caribbean, 329; Half a Loaf, 194
36   Perpetuating Poverty, 83
37   Toronto Star April 5 2008
38   The Commonwealth Caribbean, 157; Canada and the Third World, 228; Contact January 1968
39   The Banks of Canada in the Commonwealth Caribbean, 99
40   Canadian Caribbean relations, 284; The Commonwealth Caribbean, 172
41   The Commonwealth Caribbean, 157
42   The Banks of Canada in the Commonwealth Caribbean, 107; The Caribbean Development Bank, 12
43   Perpetuating Poverty, 52; Canadian Caribbean Relations, 283
44   Canada and the Third World, 211
45   Canadian Gunboat Diplomacy, 155
46   Canadian Foreign Policy Spring 1993, 64
47   Canadian Foreign Policy Spring 1993, 65
48   http://www.sknvibes.com/News/NewsDetails.cfm/8405
49   Canadian-West Indian Union, 45; Canada and the Third World, 211; Canadian Gunboat Diplomacy, 157
50   Canadian-West Indian Union, 42
51   Canadian Caribbean relations, 289
52   Canadian Caribbean relations, 245
53   Conflicts of Interest, 301
54   Conflicts of Interest, 300
55   Democracy by Default, 111
56   Ties that Bind, 59
57   Canada and the Commonwealth Caribbean, 280
58   The Caribbean Basin, 71
59   Canada Commonwealth Caribbean, 285
60   Canada Commonwealth Caribbean, 291
61   Canada Commonwealth Caribbean, 286
62   Canada Commonwealth Caribbean, 296
63   La Presse Dec 7 2006
64   Canadian Caribbean Relations in Transition, 62
65   Canadian Military Journal Autumn 2001, 64
66   Perpetuating Poverty, 53
67   Last Post Vol 1 #4
68   Canadian Gunboat Diplomacy, 162
69   Canadian Gunboat Diplomacy, 163
70   Canadian Gunboat Diplomacy, 163
71   http://www.irpp.org/events/archive/

nov00/maloney.pdf
72   http://cmss.ucalgary.ca/news/
spotlight/2008-04-28
73   Canadian Gunboat Diplomacy, 147
74   Canadian Gunboat Diplomacy, 153
75   Land of Lost Content, 35
76   Canada and the Commonwealth
Caribbean, 313
77   Imperialism and the National Question
in Canada, 80
78   National Post Apr 9 2008
79   Latin America Working Group Letter Vol
11 #8
80   Latin America Working Group Letter Vol
11 #8
81   Latin America Working Group Letter Vol
11 #8
82   Latin America Working Group Letter Vol
11 #8
83   The Caribbean Basin, 124
84   Transnational Corporations and
Caribbean Inequalities, 65
85   Latin America Working Group Letter Vol
11 #8
86   Latin America Working Group Letter Vol
11 #8
87   Transnational Corporations and
Caribbean Inequalities, 65
88   Transnational Corporations and
Caribbean Inequalities, 67
89   Demonstration Elections, 51
90   Demonstration Elections, 42
91   Perpetuating Poverty, 64; Latin America
Working Group Letter Vol 3 #4
92   Canadian Foreign Policy Vol 12 #2, 20
93   Alternatives Journal February 2009
94   Dominican Today Feb 10 2009
95   Canada-Cuba Relations, 9
96   Profits and Politics, 54
97   Canada-Cuba Relations, 14
98   The Banks of Canada in the
Commonwealth Caribbean, 19
99   Quick to the Frontier, 176
100 Quick to the Frontier, 170
101 Canada in the European Age, 482
102 Quick to the Frontier, 177
103 Quick to the Frontier, 179
104 Last Post Vol 1 #4
105 Our Generation, Vol 10 #4, 34
106 Canada in the European Age, 484
107 Canada-Cuba Relations, 13
108 Canada-Cuba Relations, 14
109 Quick to the Frontier, 173-174
110 Canada-Cuba Relations, 16
111 Canada-Cuba Relations, 16; Anatomy of
Big Business, 128
112 Latin America Working Group Letter,
Vol 4 #3/4, 5
113 Canada-Cuba Relations, 8
114 Canada-Cuba Relations, 28
115 Canada-Cuba Relations, 27
116 Canadian Policy Toward Nikita
Khrushchev's Soviet Union, 297
117 Canadian Policy Toward Nikita
Khrushchev's Soviet Union, 297
118 Three Nights in Havana, 65
119 Three Nights in Havana, 65
120 Enquetes sur les services secret, 116
121 Inside Canadian Intelligence, 144-5
122 American British Canadian Intelligence
Relations, 146-147
123 Spy World, 118
124 Embassy magazine 2008
125 National Post August 12 2008
126 http://www.youtube.com/
watch?v=Za4u87ezBC8
127 www.nsiins.ca/english/pdf/speech_SB_
march08.pdf
128 Globe & Mail ROB Magazine May 30
2008
129 Canadian Military Journal Winter 2005
130 http://www.haiti-progres.com/2003/
sm030305/eng03-05.html
131 http://upsidedownworld.org/main/
content/view/1638/51/
132 http://www.dominionpaper.ca/
weblog/2004/09/interview_with_denis_
paradis_on_haiti_regime_change.html
133 http://www.dominionpaper.ca/foreign_
policy/2006/04/07/declassify.html
134 The Lancet Vol 368 Issue 9538, 864
135 The Lancet Vol 368 Issue 9538, 864
136 http://www.law.miami.edu/cshr/CSHR_
Report_02082005_v2.pdf
137 ZNet April 19 2006
138 Canwest News Service Sept 2 2006
139 http://www.law.miami.edu/cshr/CSHR_
Report_02082005_v2.pdf
140 IPS Mar 22 2007
141 http://74.125.47.132/search?q=cache:
gTPbdHoefbUJ:www.blackcommentator.
com/117/117_cover_haiti.html+ percent22w
e+are+under+extreme+pressure+from+the+
international+community+to+use+violence
percent22&hl=en&ct=clnk&cd=4&gl=ca
142 http://www.cod.edu/people/faculty/

yearman/cite_soleil.htm

143 http://www.independent.co.uk/news/
world/americas/peacekeepers-accused-after-
killings-in-haiti-500570.html

144 Agence Haitienne de Presse Jan 15 2007

145 haitiaction.net Feb 3 2007

146 http://canadahaitiaction.ca/?p=384

147 Radical Philosophy July/August 2006

148 Media release IMMHE Feb 17 2006

149 http://www.law.miami.edu/cshr/CSHR_
Report_02082005_v2.pdf

150 ww.alternatives.ca/article1913.html

151 Alternatives en Haiti

152 http://www.narconews.com/Issue50/
article3013.html

153 http://www.medialternatif.org/
alterpresse/spip.php?article1166

154 http://74.125.47.132/search?q=cache:
AtWpr27uYtAJ:www.dd-rd.ca/site/

what_we_do/index.php percent3Fid
percent3D1619 percent26lang percent3Dfr
percent26subsection percent3Dwhere_
we_work percent26subsubsection
percent3Dcountry_documents+Concertation
+Pour+Haiti+rock+allan&hl=fr&ct=clnk&cd=
2&gl=ca

155 http://www.dd-rd.ca/site/media/index.
php?id=493&subsection=news

156 http://www.dd-rd.ca/site/_PDF/
publications/americas/haiti_en.pdf

157 http://www.globalpolicy.org/empire/
history/2004/0716otherchange.htm

158 www.alterpresse.org

159 Unexpected War, 126-27

160 FOCALPoint July/August 2007 Vol 6 #6

161 zmag.org Mar 5 2004

162 Toronto Star July 21 2007

The Middle East

For the past 150 years the Caribbean has been of relatively limited geostrategic importance. The same cannot be said for the Middle East. In this oil-rich part of the world, foreign powers have vied for influence since well before the destruction of the Ottoman empire in World War One. This strategic region illustrates another major theme of Canadian foreign policy, namely the usefulness of its "good guy" image both domestically and internationally. Or as Jean Chrétien recounts telling Bill Clinton: "Keeping some distance will be good for both of us. If we look as though we're the fifty-first state of the United States, there's nothing we can do for you internationally, just as the governor of a state can't do anything for you internationally. But if we look independent enough, we can do things for you that even the CIA cannot do."[1]

Canada's status as an "honest broker" and "peacekeeper" is called into question by our military and diplomatic activities across the Middle East. Despite the image, Ottawa has acted, often in a low profile manner, as a strategic ally of the primary imperialist power of the day.

Egypt

Former Canadian Prime Minister Lester Pearson won a Nobel Peace Prize for his part in establishing the peacekeeping force in Egypt that helped resolve what is known as the Suez crisis. From Suez on, peacekeeping became a major part of Canadian identity. Memorialized on a postage stamp and the ten-dollar bill, Parliament passed a motion in 2007 for a peacekeeping day. Even a Molson beer ad claimed, "I believe in peacekeeping, not policing. I am Joe and I am Canadian." Since it began in Egypt, this is the place to begin unravelling Canada's peacekeeper myth.

Maintaining the seven-year-old NATO alliance was a priority of Canadian policymakers when they decided to intervene in Egypt in 1956. After Britain, France and Israel invaded Egypt, Canada helped establish a U.N. peacekeeping force to smooth over hostilities inside NATO. Ottawa was primarily concerned with disagreement between the U.S. and the U.K. over the intervention, not Egyptian sovereignty or the plight of that country's people.[2] External affairs minister Lester B. Pearson explained that Canada's "interest is prejudiced when there is division within the Commonwealth or between London, Washington or Paris."[3] Washington opposed the western invasion because it feared this would add to Soviet prestige in a geo-strategically important region. The U.S. even threatened to cut off Britain's much needed IMF funding as a result of the invasion.

After coordinating with U.S. secretary of state John Foster Dulles, Pearson proposed the U.N. mission to Egypt. Although he sided with the Americans, Pearson also sought to help Britain and France save face. On October 31, 1956, Pearson told Dulles that "we are interested in helping Britain and France. I would like to make it possible for them to withdraw with as little loss of face as possible and bring them back into realignment with the U.S."[4] Pearson made numerous declarations sympathetic to the aggressors. According to Pearson, U.K. and French actions in Egypt took place, "against the background of those repeated violations and provocations."[5] Pearson added that he would try to postpone or amend any resolution critical of Britain or France regarding Suez.[6] On November 29, 1956, Pearson declared: "I do not for one minute criticize the motives of the governments of the United Kingdom and France ... I may have thought their intervention was not wise, but I do not criticize their purposes."[7]

The invasion's primary aim was to re-establish European control over the Suez Canal and weaken Arab nationalism. For France the goal was largely to end Egyptian support for Algeria's independence movement. Ottawa sympathized with these objectives. Prime Minister Louis St. Laurent claimed that Egypt's nationalization of the Suez canal, which included full financial compensation, would somehow destabilize the region. He said: "The Egyptian action introduced a threat to the trade on which the economic life of many countries depends."[8]

In the years leading to the Suez crisis Canada's interest in Egypt grew. In 1954 Ottawa opened an embassy in Cairo. "The need for Canadian representation in the region has been recognized for some time, particularly because of the frequency with which Middle Eastern Affairs are discussed in the United Nations and because of the importance to the free world of maintaining peace in this strategic area," noted a government report.[9] A year before the invasion Pearson visited Egypt "to warn Nasser against the historic Russian designs in the Mediterranean and the Middle East."[10]

Some have concluded that during the Suez affair Pearson wanted "a compromise that would, in part, 'legitimize' the Franco-British action."[11] This thesis is supported by the fact that British forces initially provided the U.N. force with motor transport and Canada took over protecting British interests in the country.[12] In addition, in a speech to the British House of Commons, Prime Minister Anthony Eden called for "police action [in Egypt]

... to separate the belligerents and to prevent the resumption of hostilities between them. If the U.N. were then willing to take over the physical task of maintaining peace, no one would be better pleased than we."[13]

Canadian pronouncements regarding the U.K./France/Israel intervention initially led Egypt to reject Canadian troops. Canada's membership in NATO also made Egypt suspicious of Ottawa's motivations.[14] Egypt was correct to worry about Canadian involvement. This is how one Canadian peacekeeper explained his posting to Egypt: "I thought we [were] here to clear the Egyptians out of the Canal Zone. Instead damned if they aren't treating us as prisoners of war."[15]

Eight months into the U.N. mission, in May 1957, Lester Pearson explained: "We feel that Egypt had the right to be consulted and to agree to the entry of an international force, but having given that consent as she did, she has no right to control the force, to order it about, to tell the force when it shall leave. If Egypt is dissatisfied with the operation of the force, or if anybody else is dissatisfied, or if Egypt wants the force to withdraw, feels its work is completed, Egypt should make its views known to the Secretary-General who would take it up with the Committee of Seven [of which Pearson was a member] and then it would go to the full assembly, and until the assembly had decided the force would carry on."[16]

Contrary to the views of the Arab countries, India and many other former colonies, Pearson saw the U.N. troops largely as an occupation force. At a time when Egypt was militarily weak, he used the U.N. force's presence to demand policy changes from Nasser. In the spring of 1957 Pearson warned Nasser that the U.N. force would leave if he continued to pursue nationalistic reforms.[17]

A decade later, on May 28, 1967, U.N. troops were ultimately expelled from the country. Canada's 800-man contingent was ordered to leave within 48 hours.[18] In the lead-up to Israel's invasion of Egypt, Prime Minister Pearson's Liberals, along with Denmark, sponsored an emergency Security Council meeting to call attention to Egypt's blockade of Israeli shipping. This helped create the sense of crisis used by Israel to justify invading Egypt.[19] Ottawa also supported a British and American proposal to establish a maritime force to protect Israeli shipping through the strait of Tiran on the Gulf of Aqaba.[20] On May 26, 1967, Pearson told the House that he and Lyndon B. Johnson were "in complete agreement" on the "importance of maintaining the right of access to an innocent passage through the Gulf of Aqaba." In fact, Ottawa "ordered some Canadian warships into the Mediterranean during the 1967 Arab-Israeli crisis in case the peacekeeping troops in Suez needed assistance and as a gesture of Canadian concern."[21] Made during a politically turbulent time that led to Israel's invasion, these moves were considered a threat by the Egyptians, which prompted Nasser to expel U.N. troops.

Secretary General U Thant acceded to Nasser's demand to withdraw U.N. forces from Egypt. But Ottawa objected, joining the U.S./British push for a meeting of the General Assembly to override U Thant's decision.[22] Secretary of State for External Affairs Paul Martin argued that "in giving its consent to the establishment of the force the Egyptian government accepted a limitation of its sovereignty and that it is now the prerogative of the United Nations rather than the UAR [Egyptian] government to determine when the United Nations force has completed its task."[23]

In response to Canada's action, public protests took place at the Canadian Chancellery building in Egypt.[24] Al Ahram newspaper wrote that Canada was "a stooge of the Western powers who seek to colonize the Arab world with Israel's help."[25] Nasser complained about the Canadian government's "biased stand in favour of Israel."[26] He explained: "On May 16th we requested the withdrawal of the United Nations Emergency Force ... a big world wide campaign led by the United States, Britain, and Canada began opposing the withdrawal of UNEF from Egypt. Thus we felt that there were attempts to turn UNEF into a force serving neo-imperialism. It is obvious that UNEF entered Egypt with our approval and therefore cannot continue to stay in Egypt except with our approval. A campaign is also being mounted against the United Nations Secretary General because he made a faithful and honest decision and would not surrender to the pressure brought to bear upon him by the United States, Britain and Canada to make UNEF an instrument for implementing imperialism's plans."[27]

During the 1967 U.N. crisis the Department of National Defence drew up a top secret plan for a Canadian military invasion of Egypt. Code named Exercise Lazarus, former Canadian ambassador to Egypt, John Starnes, unearthed parts of the plan. According to archives of the Lazarus plan, "it is envisaged that the host nation would not be friendly but that the landing and build-up would not be actively opposed. ... this implies the ability to engage in offensive action of a sporadic nature against indigenous hostile elements of up to battalion size."[28] Starnes suggested that the KGB intercepted the Lazarus plan and passed it on to the Egyptians. This is why, according to Starnes, Nasser became exceedingly hostile to Canada. It would also help explain why Egyptian officials became nervous when Canadian vessels entered the region to remove Canadian peacekeepers.[29]

Ottawa did help keep the peace in Egypt, but it was between two sides of a dispute within NATO. Canada's policies and actions helped declining superpowers Great Britain and France save face over a disastrous invasion and those actions were supported by the new superpower, the United States. This reality has been spun into the myth of this country's vital peacekeeping role, which is a testament to the lack of a critical Canadian foreign policy historiography.

Iraq

Another more recent myth about Canadian foreign policy in the Middle East is that this country did not participate in the 2002 invasion of Iraq, which most neutral observers say was a war crime under international law. Yes, Canada was not cited in U.S. Secretary of State Colin Powell's "coalition of the willing" speech. But, after listing the countries which were taking a direct part in the coalition Powell said that "there are 15 other nations, who, for one reason or another do not wish to be publicly named but will be supporting the coalition."[30] Was Canada one of the 15? Some of the evidence:

• Carrying thousands of troops, U.S. warplanes enroute to Iraq flew through Canadian air space and stopped to refuel in Newfoundland. Some countries gained entry into the "coalition of the willing" simply for allowing U.S. flyovers.[31]

• In the months just before and after the invasion, between January 2002 and December 2003, at least ten Canadian naval vessels conducted maritime interdictions, force-support and force-projection operations in the Arabian Sea.[32] These Canadian frigates usually accompanied U.S. warships used as platforms for bombing raids in Iraq. A month before the commencement of the U.S. invasion, Canada sent a command and control destroyer to the Persian Gulf to take charge of Taskforce 151 — the joint allied naval command.[33] Opinion sought by the Liberal government concluded that taking command of Taskforce 151 could make Canada legally at war with Iraq.[34]

• As the lawyers debated whether this country was legally at war, Canadian soldiers fired their rounds. There were at least 30 Canadian soldiers incorporated into U.S. and British units that invaded Iraq.[35] "At least one of the Canadians … is with the British 7th Armoured Brigade, a unit now taking part in heavy fighting near Basra," reported the Ottawa Citizen a week after the invasion.[36] For his efforts Maj. Ghislain Sauve received the Most Excellent Order of the British Empire pinned to his uniform by the

Queen at Buckingham Palace. Other countries that chose not to participate in the invasion withdrew their exchange officers assigned to British and American units. No Canadian soldier was pulled from an exchange because of Iraq.[37]

• Ottawa provided three CC-130 aircraft to support the U.S.-led war and Canadian pilots flew AWAC surveillance planes that helped guide fighter jets over Iraq.[38] In April 2008 the Ottawa Citizen reported that "Canadian Forces Personnel learned to operate Canada's newest military plane, the giant Boeing C-17, by training on American jets, including flying those planes into Iraq in support of the U.S. war."[39]

• Much of modern air war takes place from the ground and through NORAD Canadian forces provided logistical support to U.S. air strikes.[40] More generally, Canadian war planners helped mastermind the invasion from U.S. Central Command (CENTCOM) in Tampa. When the planning centre was moved on February 11, 2003, Ottawa transferred 25 "military planners" from Tampa to the U.S. military's forward command post in the Persian Gulf state of Qatar. "Canada has helped to determine the whole strategy for fighting this war," noted Richard Sanders from the Coalition to Oppose the Arms Trade.[41]

• Now the head of the Canadian military, General Walt Natynczk helped plan the invasion from American headquarters in Kuwait and then served as deputy commander of U.S. forces in Baghdad.[42] Natynczyk was in charge of 35,000 troops in Iraq and Governor General Michael Jean presented him with the Meritorious Service Cross for his service in the U.S.-led mission.[43]

• In January 2008 the Ottawa Citizen reported that Canadian forces Brig.-Gen. Nicholas Matern took over as deputy commanding general of the 18th Airborne in Iraq.[44] Matern served as deputy to U.S. Lt. Gen. Lloyd Austin III, commander of the 170,000-strong Multi National Corps-Iraq.[45] Matern was Canada's third general to serve in the command group of Operation Iraqi Freedom. His predecessor, Major General Peter Devlin, told the Washington Post that the multinational element brings "greater legitimacy to the effort here in Iraq."[46]

• After the invasion JTF2 commandos were reported to be working alongside their British and U.S. special forces counterparts in Iraq. While Ottawa refused to confirm or deny JTF2 operations, in March 2006 the Pentagon and the British Foreign Office "both commented on the instrumental role JTF2 played in rescuing the British and Canadian Christian Peace Activists that were being held hostage in Iraq."[47] Numerous JTF2 soldiers also quit to work for private companies operating in Iraq.[48]

Reportedly, they could earn up to $350,000 for a 10-month stint protecting payroll trucks for U.S. contractors such as Halliburton.[49]

Despite the Canadian government and media spin, it is clear that Canada was a close and willing ally in the invasion and occupation of Iraq. "What the Canadian government has done with regard to Iraq is to involve itself militarily, in largely covert fashion, but to publicly try to take the moral high ground in opposition to the war."[50] Former U.S. ambassador to Ottawa Paul Cellucci provided a good summary of Canada's role in Iraq. "Ironically, the Canadians indirectly provide more support for us in Iraq than most of those 46 countries that are fully supporting us. It's kind of an odd situation."[51] To gain favour in Washington, Canadian officials echoed the ambassador's comments. "Senior Canadian officials, military officers, and politicians were … privately telling anyone in the State Department or the Pentagon who would listen that, by some measures, Canada's indirect contribution to the American war effort in Iraq — three ships and 100 exchange officers — exceeded that of all but three other countries that were actually part of the coalition."[52]

A skeptic might respond that Ottawa felt the need to tout Canada's contribution to U.S. power brokers because they didn't provide what the Bush administration wanted above all else: diplomatic support for the invasion. True. But not entirely. Three weeks before the war Chrétien suggested the U.N. mandate for military action against Iraq already existed. "If the Americans or the Brits have great evidence that Saddam Hussein — who is no friend of mine — is not following the instructions of the U.N. … if the proof is made of that of course Canada will support an activity there … we have a resolution … that calls for action if Saddam Hussein is not following these instructions of the United Nations. It is mentioned in that resolution that action can be taken against them if they don't accept and conform with that resolution."[53]

After the start of the air war, Chrétien told the House of Commons: "It was the Americans' privilege and right to make the decision that they made. We respect that… Of course, I hope that the Americans will do as well as possible." He continued: "At this point, I think there is no use debating the reasons why some people think war is necessary and some people think it is not. We should not say anything that would comfort Saddam Hussein."[54]

Chrétien's comments were a sign that once the invasion was complete Canada would do its part. In 2003 the Liberals pledged $300 million, the second largest ever post-conflict package, in aid for Iraqi reconstruction.[55] "DFAIT [Foreign Affairs] augmented the Canadian Embassy in Kuwait with a senior officer to act as a point of contact and to work alongside international participants, including the CENTCOM Office of Reconstruction and Humanitarian Assistance in Baghdad. [Five weeks after the beginning of the invasion,] on 29 April 2003 Canada sent a diplomatic note to the U.S. offering police, detention facility experts, legal officers, combat engineers, and transport planes to help in reconstructing post-war Iraq."[56] At a November 2004 conference in Egypt Foreign Affairs Minister Pierre Pettigrew called on regional governments to play a greater role in the reconstruction of Iraq and until 2007 Ottawa chaired the International Reconstruction Fund Facility for Iraq.[57] In a March 2007 international donors meeting Canada was cited as "one of the key powers seeking to involve as many countries as possible in the reconstruction of the violence-ridden country."[58]

Canadian aid and reconstruction efforts included training Iraq's military. High-level Canadian military personnel joined the NATO Training Mission in Iraq to "train the trainers" of Iraq's military. A Canadian colonel, under NATO command, was chief of staff at the Baghdad-based training mission and Ottawa's initial $810,000 was the largest donation to this training centre.[59]

On a much larger scale, one year after the invasion the RCMP began training Iraqi police at the U.S.-built Jordan International Police Training Center. The RCMP helped "train 32,000 new Iraqi police officers who are being deployed to replace war-weary U.S. soldiers."[60]

A Maclean's article in 2006 described a Canadian police officer who helped the Iraqi police develop bomb disposal capabilities. "During his year there [Insp. Ron] van Straalen was highly involved in the fight against the insurgency."[61] To help build Iraq's security forces high-level Canadian police worked in the Iraqi Interior Ministry.[62] "Canada provides advisors and financial support to this ministry which has been caught running torture centres. Thousands of its officers have been withdrawn for corruption, and it has been accused of working with death squads that executed a thousand people per month in Baghdad alone in the summer of 2006."[63]

A number of private Canadian security companies also supported the U.S. occupation of Iraq. Canadian-based Globe Risk, Global Impact, Gladius and Executive Security Services International, as well as Canadian-owned High Energy Access Tools, operated in Iraq.[64] Iraq represented $150 million of $683 million in 2006 revenue for Montréal based GardaWorld.[65] When four Garda employees were kidnapped in May 2007, the company's operations garnered significant media attention.[66] In a front page Ottawa Citizen article headlined "How a nice Québec firm found itself in a war zone", the head of the company deflected criticism of its 1,800 private soldiers in Iraq by claiming "we're perceived differently because we're Canadian."[67] Of course he didn't mention if the Iraqi mothers whose children have been shot by mercenaries (unaccountable to any law) feel that way on discovering the bullets were shot by an employee of a Canadian company.

All too often these bullets were manufactured in Canada. Montréal-based SNC Technologies Inc. joined a multinational consortium of ammunition producers providing occupation forces with 300 to 500 million bullets per year for five years beginning in 2004. To kill the terrorists, insurgents and freedom fighters — as well as Iraqi civilians — you need a lot of bullets. Eric Hugel, a defence industry analyst, told the Financial Times that "we're using so much ammunition in Iraq there isn't enough [U.S. manufacturing] capacity around. ... They have to go internationally."[68]

Beyond the regular flow of Canadian-manufactured weapons to the U.S. army, a Burlington, Ontario firm, L-3 Wescam, a division of Titan group, supplied "interrogation" teams allegedly implicated in torture at Abu Ghraib.[69] The company also produced guidance systems for missiles and unmanned drones, as well as components for the Cobra Attack Helicopter. Bell Helicopters Director of Business Development Michel Legault justified the use of the company's aircraft in Iraq by saying: "Have you heard of Honda Civic? It's used in car bombings in Iraq."[70]

In addition to security and arms companies, Canadian oil interests were buzzing like flies over the wreckage in Iraq. Mother Jones magazine reported that the Kurdistan Regional Government (KRG) "has signed more than 20 oil deals with foreign firms; eight Canadian companies have stakes in at least six of those deals."[71] In May 2008 Vast Exploration, along with two other Canadian companies, signed a contract for "one of the largest [oil] blocks in Kurdistan" a concession with as much as 600 million barrels of oil. The company CEO explained that former U.S. Iraqi administrator Jay Garner "was influential in introducing me to Kurdistan and the opportunity here."[72] Garner was named to the company's board of directors, joining a list of prominent Washington lobbyists. These concessions in Kurdish areas are not recognized by Iraq's central government, which claims the regional government has no right to enter into production-sharing agreements.[73] "This is flagrant violation of the Iraqi law," said Minister of Oil Osama Al-Nejefi.[74]

The U.S. agreed with Iraq's central government but Ottawa held no such policy. In 2005 the U.S. State Department complained about "Canadian investment in Kurdistan (especially a deal between the KRG and a Canadian company called Heritage Oil), saying, 'You need to inform your companies [about] the problems this is causing,' according to the State Department official."[75]

Iran

Iran is another country where Canada has a long history of being a junior partner to whatever the U.S. is up to. If Iraq illustrates the "big lie" — Canada did not support the U.S. invasion/occupation — Ottawa's policy towards Iran reveals the "big hypocrisy". While we are told that this country stands for certain principles — democracy, women's rights, peaceful settlement of disputes etc. — the overriding imperative in Iran has been and remains support for the U.S.

Throughout 2007 and 2008 Canadian naval vessels regularly patrolled Iran's coast. "About 800 Canadian sailors are patrolling the politically turbulent waters near Iran and Pakistan," the National Post reported.[76] In February of 2008, another paper reported that HMCS Charlottetown was patrolling 1,500 metres from Iranian territorial waters as part of a 50-ship armada under the USS Harry Truman carrier strike group.[77] A reporter on board a Canadian naval vessel explained: "The usual tense games were played this weekend as this Canadian warship responsible for refueling and replenishing a coalition task force in the Indian Ocean passed in a heavy haze through one of the world's most dangerous flashpoints. Iranian radio operators trying to hail the [Canadian vessel] Protecteur were interrupted by Omanis who firmly told their neighbours not speak to the Canadians who were making an 'innocent passage' through Omani territorial waters."[78]

The military assistance this country offers is only a small part of Canada's contribution to the war on Iran. We also gather intelligence and Ottawa has been accused of spying for the U.S. In late 2006 members of the Iranian parliament claimed the Canadian embassy in Tehran was a "den of spies."[79] Unexpected War claims that some Foreign Affairs officials wanted Canada's headquarters in Afghanistan located in the west of the country "so that Canada could get a better window on Iran."[80]

From the military sphere to the economic realm Ottawa is trying to squeeze Iran. Foreign Affairs trade website makes it "clear doing business with Iran is thinly-tolerated and much-controlled."[81] At the U.N., Canada voted for the ongoing trade embargo in strategic materials against Iran and worked diligently to discredit Iran's human rights record. In November 2007 the Ottawa Citizen reported: "In what one western diplomat described as a 'division of labour', among western governments to keep up the pressure on Iran, the big European powers and the United States lead western efforts to convince Iran to roll back its nuclear program while Canada has spearheaded resolutions denouncing the way Iran treats huge numbers of its people."[82] Ottawa has sponsored an annual U.N. resolution condemning Iran's "ongoing systematic violations of human rights." In an embarrassing outcome for Canadian officials, the motions have barely passed (77-75 in 2007). Iran's U.N. representative responded to the resolution by saying, "Canada and other sponsors of this resolution [against Iran] are themselves implicated in serious rights violations for which they must be held accountable."[83] He specifically cited Canada's treatment of aboriginal people.

"Pushing through the censure [of Iran] has become one of Canada's most important diplomatic tasks at the U.N."[84] In 2008 both Foreign Affairs Minister Lawrence Cannon and Minister of State Peter Kent lobbied other U.N. member states for the Canadian-sponsored resolution.[85] The Canwest news service reporter at the U.N. has alluded to Ottawa using its aid to influence countries to vote for the resolution and did a detailed breakdown of how major Canadian aid recipients voted.[86] Not coincidentally, the federal government-funded "arms length" human rights group, Rights & Democracy, also focused considerable energy attacking Iran. It gave its 2007 John Humphrey Freedom Award to Akbar Ganji, a leading Iranian dissident.

There is a concerted campaign to portray Iran as a threat. Members of the Bush administration accused Iran of arming anti-occupation forces in Iraq. So did the Canadian government. In May 2007 Peter MacKay released a statement claiming that "maintaining a relationship with Iran tests the bounds of diplomacy … peace is Canada's goal and we support the United States' effort to engage all regional partners in supporting the Iraqi government's attempts to bring safety and security to the area."[87] In Kandahar on Christmas Day 2007, MacKay accused Iran of arming that country's long-time enemy, the Taliban. McKay's allegation was even dismissed by Canadian Brigadier General, Marquis Hainse, NATO's second in command in southern Afghanistan.[88]

While perhaps less ignorant than her minister, Eugenie Cormier-Lassonde, spokeswoman with Foreign Affairs, was nonetheless spectacularly hypocritical when she told the Calgary Herald: "Rather than seeking to intimidate its neighbours with its nuclear and missile programs, Canada calls upon Iran to abide by the U.N. Security Council resolutions, co-operate fully with the International Atomic Energy Agency, halt its nuclear program and enter into negotiations to resolve its nuclear dispute with the international community."[89] When Lassonde made her statement Canada had a couple thousand troops occupying a nation bordering Iran and Canadian warships were running provocative maneuvers off the coast of Iran. But this was only part of the hypocrisy; Canadian policy toward Iran's nuclear program is also two-faced.

While Canadians should oppose Iran's human rights violations, its interference in Iraq or Afghanistan and its desire to develop nuclear weapons, it is hypocritical for the Canadian government to use Iran's human rights violations and nuclear program as a justification for supporting a U.S. destabilization campaign.

Throughout the 1970s, the Canadian government's Defence Programs Bureau had a representative in Tehran and Canada sold about $60 million worth of arms to Iran during the decade.[90] This was during a time when Amnesty International reported "no country in the world has a worse record in human rights than Iran."[91] The Shah's brutal SAVAK intelligence forces killed tens of thousands, which prompted little condemnation from Ottawa. In fact, in the early 1970s, $250,000 worth of Canadian aid went to the University of Montréal's International Center for Comparative Criminology (ICCC) whose advisors in Iran (as well as the Ivory Coast and Brazil), according to ICCC director Dennis Szabo, "trained police forces in the use of the most modern methods to suppress protest demonstrations and the causes of criminality."[92]

Canada even played a small part in the Shah's rise to power. Ottawa supported the British-led embargo on Iranian oil following Prime Minister Mohammed Mossadeh's nationalization of his country's oil industry in May 1951.[93] This move was designed to destabilize his government. Canada did not protest when in 1953 the U.S. and Britain finally overthrew Mossadegh, Iran's first elected prime minister. Instead, it followed the lead of the U.K. and U.S. in doing business with a dictator. Canadian diplomatic relations with Iran began in 1955 with an embassy opening six years later.[94] Throughout the Shah's reign Canadian politicians visited regularly. Ontario Premier William Davis, for instance, went to meet the Shah in September 1978.[95]

Canada did significant business with the Shah's Iran. In 1978 Canadian exports to Iran reached nearly $600 million.[96] An October 1978 Globe and Mail article headlined "Canadians in Iran" described a massive Export Development Canada (EDC)-financed forestry project along with numerous other Canadian ventures in that country. "Acres International Ltd. of Toronto has been hired for $100-million worth of engineering on an irrigation-power project. Ircan of Montréal has won a $37-million contract to supply mobile training centres and 800 hours of videotaped vocational teaching. Two Canadian drilling companies help Iran explore for oil. A four-firm consortium is bidding for a $1.2-billion thermal power plant. Keith Sjogren, the Bank of Commerce's man in Tehran, actually lends money to the Shah's government companies. A Canadian firm is trying to revolutionize the bread industry by automatic baking of barbari, the traditional Iranian loaves that are shaped like a canoe paddle. Tridon windshield-wipers, made in Burlington, Ont., are advertised on Iranian TV."[97]

By the time the Shah was overthrown in late 1979, there were 850 Canadians in Iran (along with thousands of Americans), most working for foreign owned oilrigs, power projects etc. At the time of the revolution EDC had more than $100 million in outstanding export insurance and Canadian banks held billions of dollars worth of loans to Iran's Shah, which were put into doubt (the loans were eventually honoured).[98] Not happy with the Shah's departure, Canada closed its embassy in 1980. Ottawa also supported Washington's sanctions against Iran.[99]

Canadian hypocrisy has been on full display regarding Iran's drive to develop nuclear energy or atomic weapons. In January 2007 Foreign Affairs Minister Peter McKay said: "Canada is deeply concerned with the direction that Iran is headed. The regime in Tehran cannot be allowed to acquire nuclear weapons."[100] McKay's comment was made in Israel, a regional rival of Iran that possesses nuclear weapons. Referring to "genocidal" Iran a few months later, Jason Kenny (a federal cabinet minister) told a pro-Israel conference that Canada "will pursue every possible avenue in concert with our allies to ensure that [Iran] does not come into possession of nuclear weapons, which could unleash unimaginable violence." Kenny concluded: "He [Iranian President Mahmoud Ahmadinejad] must be stopped by the civilized world."[101]

But, when the Shah was in power, Canada was prepared to sell Iran nuclear reactors. In October 2008 Iranian Prime Minister Mahmoud Ahmadinejad complained that Canada, France, the U.K. and U.S. worked with the Shah on nuclear technology. "When there were no elections in Iran, they wanted us to be a nuclear power," said Ahmadinejad. "As soon as there were elections, they didn't want us to be a nuclear power."[102]

More broadly, after selling 29 nuclear reactors to foreign countries, any reasonable person would say Canada has lost the right to criticize any country's desire for nuclear power.[103] As one book points out, "Canadian nuclear reactors have primarily been sold to dictatorships with very poor human rights records: Pakistan and Taiwan in the 1960s; Argentina, South Korea and Romania in the 1970s; and China in the 1990s."[104] In 1974 Atomic Energy Canada Ltd. (AECL) even tried to sell a Candu reactor to Saddam Hussein's Iraq (one selling point was that the reactor could produce plutonium, the basis of atom bombs).[105]

Canada has not only been willing to sell nuclear reactors, we have spent millions of aid dollars on the cause. Most Canadian nuclear exports have been financed in some way with aid dollars. In the 1950s, for instance, AECL received money from the Colombo Aid Plan to help India set up a nuclear reactor.[106] Ditto in Pakistan where Canada provided $48,000,000 in loans and grants for the construction of its KANUPP nuclear reactor.[107] CIDA has spent millions of dollars promoting "the benefits of nuclear energy." Canadian assistance to Thailand in the mid 1990s was used to produce videos, leaflets and booklets praising nuclear energy. CIDA's goal, according to critics, was "to revive the moribund Canadian nuclear industry."[108]

Some say Iran's push to get the bomb dates back to 1974 when India exploded a nuclear bomb. Canada provided the reactor (called Cyrus) that India, Iran's regional competitor, used to develop the bomb. Canada proceeded with its nuclear commitment to India despite signals from New Delhi that it was going to detonate a nuclear device.[109] At the time Ottawa prioritized nuclear sales over safeguards.[110] "The Indians chose to use Cyrus for their supply of plutonium and not one of their other reactors, because Cyrus was not governed by any nuclear safeguards."[111] In support of the Bush administration's move to support India as a counterweight to China, Ottawa decided it no longer objected to India's atomic weapons program. "Canada has changed its policy on nuclear nonproliferation to accommodate India's entry into the club of countries that can trade openly in nuclear fuel and technology, despite its nuclear weapons programs."[112] In November 2008 Ottawa signed an agreement to export nuclear reactors and energy to India, even though India refused to sign the International Nuclear non-Proliferation Treaty. International Trade Minister Stockwell Day "accompanied by top executives from Atomic Energy of Canada Ltd., the crown corporation that designs nuclear reactors; nuclear engineering firm SNC-Lavalin Nuclear; and Cameco Corp., the Saskatoon-based uranium supplier" visited India in January 2009. Day noted: "India recognizes that Canada was one of the significant voices in terms of seeing some of the past restrictions which have been placed on India lifted when it comes to civilian nuclear production. And we think we're going to be in a good position to make [the] pitch on the benefits of going with Canadian technology and Canadian supply."[113]

Canada also aided another of Iran's regional rivals, Pakistan, in its successful program to build nuclear weapons. In 2008 Canada signed a nuclear energy deal with the monarchy in Jordan and an agreement with Turkey, Iran's neighbour, was on the table.[114]

Canada's opposition to nuclear warfare has never included curtailing the atomic bomb's building blocks. Uranium from Great Bear Lake was used in the only two nuclear bombs ever dropped on a human population. After Hiroshima and Nagasaki Prime Minister Mackenzie King declared: "It gives me pleasure to announce that Canadian scientists played an important role, having been intimately connected, in an efficient manner, to this great scientific development."[115] By 1959 Canada had sold $1.5 billion worth of uranium to the U.S. bomb program (uranium was then Canada's fourth biggest export).[116] In 1982 Canada regained its position as the world's largest producer of uranium, an industry that receives significant sums in taxpayer support.[117] By 2004 Canada was producing about 30 percent of the world's uranium.[118]

Most Canadians have no idea about the extent of Canada's nuclear history, which includes allowing the U.S. to station nuclear weapons on its soil only a few years after the first one was built. The first "nuclear weapons came to Canada as early as September 1950, when the USAF temporarily stationed eleven 'Fat Man'- style atomic bombs at Goose Bay Newfoundland."[119] The Canadian military has also carried nukes on its foreign stationed aircraft. At the height of Canadian nuclear deployments the government had between 250 and 450 atomic bombs at its disposal in Europe.[120] Based in Germany, the CF-104 Starfighter, for instance, operated without a gun and carried nothing but a thermal nuclear weapon.[121]

On the diplomatic front, Ottawa supported its allies' nuclear weapons. "The record clearly shows that Canada refuses to support any resolution that specifies immediate action on a comprehensive approach to ridding the world of nuclear weapons."[122] In the late 1940s Ottawa voted against a U.N. call to ban nuclear weapons.[123] Since that time "numerous U.N. resolutions on nuclear weapons convention [have] pass [ed] with large majorities with Canada never voting in favour."[124] At a meeting of the International Atomic Energy Agency (IAEA) on Sept. 20 2007, Canada abstained in a vote that asked Israel to place its nuclear weapons program under IAEA controls (the same controls demanded of Iran). The resolution passed with 53 countries in favour and two against (the U.S. and Israel) and 47 abstentions. In October of that year Ottawa also abstained on an important U.N. resolution calling for nuclear armed countries to remove their weapons from high alert status. Marius Grinius, Canada's ambassador to the U.N. Disarmament Conference, explained that the resolution was incompatible with NATO policy, which argues that nuclear weapons are "a fundamental component" of the alliance's defence strategy.

If Canada is to have any credibility regarding nuclear non-proliferation perhaps it should begin by getting its own house in order. Then, it would make sense to criticize its allies when they build weapons of mass destruction or break international laws and treaties. Only after doing all that would Ottawa have the authority to condemn Iran's nuclear program.

Israel/Palestine

While Ottawa considers Iran's nuclear energy program a major threat, Israel's atomic bombs have not provoked similar condemnation from Canada. In fact, Ottawa has taken Israel's side on almost every issue of importance, despite Canada's supposed "honest broker" status.

The creation of Israel sparked a massive injustice for the majority population in that region. Long under Ottoman rule, then British control after World War One, the Palestinians were an oppressed and relatively powerless people. Arab Palestinians also had the misfortune of living on land claimed by a predominantly European political movement that called itself Zionism.

When Britain prepared to hand its mandate over Palestine to the U.N. in 1947, the international body formed the First Committee on Palestine. The committee was charged with developing the terms of reference for a special committee that would develop proposals for a political settlement. Lester Pearson, a staunch Zionist, chaired the committee, which established the United Nations Special Committee on Palestine (UNSCOP) in May 1947. Sensing an unjust move, Arab countries boycotted UNSCOP, which was to find a solution for the mandate. Under U.S. pressure, Canada agreed to participate on UNSCOP as one of eleven "neutral" states. The State Department had two different lists of countries it wanted to participate — Canada was at the top of both of these non-alphabetical lists.[125]

Canada's representative to UNSCOP was Supreme Court Justice Ivan C. Rand who is famous for his role in establishing the legal basis for union dues collection (the Rand formula). Rand was sympathetic to Zionism. Rand, according to Israeli historian Ilan Pappe, "claimed that weighty moral issues were involved in the question of Palestine, though he was more inclined to see it as a struggle between the forces of progress and democracy on the one hand (the Jews) and backward societies on the other (the Palestinians)."[126]

Rand challenged members of the UNSCOP committee who failed to recognize the legitimacy of the Balfour Declaration, which was the British Empire's 1917 statement of support for a Jewish homeland on land occupied by Palestinians. He also opposed proposals for a Jewish-Arab unitary state.[127] With Britain viewed as an obstacle to Zionist aspirations, Rand's views carried added weight since Canada was seen as a loyal dominion to Britain.[128] Ultimately, Rand drafted the majority report calling for partition into a Jewish and Arab state. "Justice Rand was by far the main contributor to the partition scheme with economic union," Rand's assistant Leon Mayrand cabled External Affairs with satisfaction.[129]

After UNSCOP put forward majority and minority reports, a special U.N. ad-hoc committee was established to find a solution to the Palestine problem. Having recently concluded a term as Canadian ambassador in Washington, Lester Pearson (then under-secretary of state for External Affairs) headed the ad-hoc committee and is widely considered to have played a central role in the final partition vote. Both the New York Times and Manchester Guardian ran articles about Pearson's role in the partition committee with some Zionist groups calling him "Lord Balfour" of Canada and "rabbi Pearson".[130] Pearson wrote: "I have never waivered in my view that a solution to the problem was impossible without the recognition of a Jewish state in Palestine. To me this was always the core of the matter."[131] After stepping down as prime minister in 1968, Pearson received the Theodore Hertzel award from the Zionist Organization of America for his "commitment to Jewish freedom and Israel."[132]

In State in the Making, David Horowitz (the first governor of the Bank of Israel and first director general of Israel's ministry of finance) writes: "The dynamic force and pathfinder was Lester Pearson. His adherence to the pro-partition fold was an important turning point. His influence, as one of the foremost figures at the U.N. was tremendous. It may be said that Canada more than any other country played a decisive part in all stages of the UNO discussions of Palestine. The activities at Lake Success of Lester Pearson and his fellow delegates were a fitting climax to Justice Rand's beneficent work on UNSCOP."[133]

On October 17, 1947, Ottawa joined 14 U.N. members in approving the partition plan in principle. Thirteen countries opposed partition.[134] In supporting partition Canadian officials opposed Arab moral and political claims.[135] Ottawa supported a plan that gave the new Jewish state the majority of Palestine despite the Jewish population owning only 6 percent of the land and representing less than a third of the population.[136] Even "within the borders of their U.N.-proposed state," Pappe explains, "they owned only eleven percent of the land, and were the minority in every district. In the Negev ... they constituted one percent of the total population."[137]

Rand's assistant on UNSCOP, Leon Mayrand, provides a window into the dominant mindset at External Affairs. "The Arabs were bound to be vocal opponents of partition but they should not be taken too seriously. The great majority were not yet committed nationalists and the Arab chiefs could be appeased through financial concessions, especially if these accompanied a clearly declared will to impose a settlement whatever the means necessary."[138] A dissident within External Affairs, the department's only Middle East expert, Elizabeth MacCallum, claimed Ottawa supported partition, "because we didn't give two hoots for democracy."[139]

Far from an "honest broker," Prime Minister St. Laurent admitted that Canada gained a reputation for "having taken up the Jewish cause."[140] The Canadian Jewish Congress echoed this statement claiming it was "heartwarming to Canadians to have history record that Canada played a most important part in the international deliberations which preceded this decision [on partition]."[141] Conversely, a representative from the Canadian Arab Friendship League explained "Our Canadian government at one time also favoured the creation of a federated State of Palestine which had at least some resemblance to a democratic solution. Unfortunately, as you all know, Canadian delegates, Mr. Lester B. Pearson and Mr. Justice C Rand, changed that official position of our government. Instead of the democratic solution, these gentlemen did their utmost to impose upon the Arabs the infamous partition scheme. The Arab world, I am sure, will remember them."[142]

Why did Canada push for partition? Some believe Ottawa supported the creation of a Jewish state under pressure from a Jewish Zionist lobby. Many Jewish Canadians, including prominent businessman Samuel Bronfman, did call for the creation of Israel. The notion, however, that a Jewish Zionist lobby forced Ottawa to support partition is exaggerated. The book None is Too Many documents the organized Jewish community's inability to reverse Canada's anti-Semitic immigration policy in the years preceding, during and following the Second World War. Despite millions exterminated in Nazi concentration camps, Canada accepted fewer than 5,000 Jewish refugees from 1933 to 1945. Immediately after the Second World War, the Jewish community did not suddenly gain the necessary political clout to drive Canadian policy on Palestine.

In fact, the anti-Semitism underlying Canada's "none is too many" policy towards Jewish refugees helps explain support for Israel. In February

1947 Liberty Magazine reported, "no spokesman will link Canada with Palestine but what everyone is going to know soon is that the displaced persons of Europe either come to Canada or go to Palestine. Politically it's a big question."[143] Ottawa, along with Washington and other capitals, supported partition partly to redirect displaced Jews to Israel, lessening the pressure to accept them. "The Canadian delegation at the United Nations went into the Palestine debate briefed from Ottawa on what a negative majority vote on partition would mean to future discussions of European displaced persons. And Canada voted for partition."[144]

More important than either the Jewish Zionist lobby or Jewish immigration, support for partition was driven by geopolitics. Ottawa was concerned with Anglo-American disunity over Palestine, more than the Palestinian crisis itself.[145] Despite having supported Zionism for decades, at the time of partition Britain was under significant Arab pressure to oppose the creation of Israel. But as Canada moved closer to the U.S. sphere of influence (epitomized by Lester Pearson), Washington's perspective drove Canadian policy. An internal report circulated at External Affairs explained: "The plan of partition gives to the western powers the opportunity to establish an independent, progressive Jewish state in the Eastern Mediterranean with close economic and cultural ties with the West generally and in particular with the United States."[146]

The Ottawa mandarins supported Israel as a possible western outpost in the heart of the Middle East. The idea was decades old. Before there was a Jewish Zionist movement, in 1882, Canada's preeminent Christian Zionist, Henry Wentworth Monk, called for the British Empire to establish a "Dominion of Israel", similar to the Dominion of Canada.[147] Zionism's leading ideological architect, Theodore Hertzel, also tried to sell his ideology to Europe in the 1890s by highlighting its usefulness to western imperialism.

The Canadian-backed U.N. partition contributed to the forced displacement of 700,000-900,000 Palestinians. The U.N. plan put the fate of more than a million Palestinians into the hands of a Zionist movement that openly discussed transferring the Arab population.[148] Palestinian scholar, Walid Khalidi, complained that U.N. partition Resolution 181 was "a hasty act of granting half of Palestine to an ideological movement that declared openly already in the 1930s its wish to de-Arabise Palestine."[149]

Canadian Zionists, with at least some direct support in Ottawa, played a role in this de-Arabising of Palestine. Representatives from Haganah, the primary Zionist military force, recruited more than 300 Canadians to serve in Israel's ranks during the war unleashed by partition and Zionist ethnic cleansing.[150] Ben Dunkelman, Haganah Canada's main recruiter, claimed "about one thousand" Canadians "fought to establish Israel."[151] Almost all of these volunteers were veterans of the Canadian Armed Forces.[152]

Tired of recruiting others, Dunkelman, whose family owned Tip Top Tailors, left for Palestine to put his Canadian acquired military skills — he was particularly adept with mortars — at the service of the Zionist project. "By the summer of 1948, he [Dunkelman] was in command of a Brigade actively depopulating Palestinian villages by force — a unit so heavily comprised of recruits from Canada, the United States and South Africa that it came to be known as the 'Anglo-Saxon Brigade.'"[153]

The Dunkelman-led troops were particularly brutal. "In many of the Palestinian oral histories that have now come to the fore," Ilan Pappe notes, "few brigade names appear. However, [Dunkelman's] Brigade Seven is mentioned again and again, together with such adjectives as 'terrorists' and 'barbarous.'"[154]

During the 1948 war, Israel's air force was almost entirely foreign with at least 53 Canadians, including 15 non-Jews, enlisted.[155] It was not a secret that Canadians fought for Israel. Drawing wide media attention, Canada's top World War Two fighter ace went to fight for Israel (he died enroute). According to an always-boastful Dunkelman, "Canadian pilots accounted for one-third of all Arab planes shot down in that war."[156]

Ottawa did little to stop this recruitment even though the federal government outlawed recruiting for a foreign army during the Spanish civil war.[157] Far from stopping it, Canadian diplomacy helped gain the release of Canadians detained in Lebanon enroute to fight in Palestine.[158] In 1948-9 Canadians, mostly Jewish Zionists, sent more than $9 million to Israel (a total of $18.2 million from 1940-1950).[159] The Purchasing Commission of the United Zionist Council, the umbrella organization of Canadian Zionism, bought weapons and other materials for the war effort.[160] Even though Ottawa caught wind of the arms exports, nobody was ever charged with the illegal export of arms.[161] In fact, Alex Skelton, a functionary at Trade and Commerce and son of well known External Affairs official O. D. Skelton, arranged export permits to Palestine for numerous militarily useful items.[162] Skelton came up with the idea of sending jets to a non-existent "Tel Aviv Spring Fair" — created to justify exporting a number of single-engine Harvard trainer monoplanes from Ontario that were easily convertible to military uses.[163] "Canadian Jews may have contributed only a handful of planes and guns to the Jewish war effort, but Canadian radio sets and other radio equipment became the backbone of Israel's military communications network."[164]

For more than a century Canadian Zionists have financed Jewish colonialism in Israel/Palestine. After the 1967 war, Canada Park was built in the West Bank, on land once occupied by Palestinians.[165] Canadians provided $15 million to construct the park, which contributed to the displacement of many people.[166] By 2007, "Walking around the park the only visible signs of previous inhabitants are a crumbling cemetery with stones engraved in Arabic and a series of old village walls. Some of these near the park entrance bear rows of plaques to Canadian donors — the city of Ottawa, the Metropolitan Toronto Police Department, former Ontario premier Bill Davis and Toronto city councillor Joe Pantalone."[167] Also in 2007, a Palestinian human rights organizations, Al-Haq released a report blaming the Israeli government, the Jewish National Fund Canada (JNF) and the Canadian government for the violation of international law and human rights caused by Canada Park. Al-Haq argued that Ottawa holds some responsibility for the Palestinian dispossession caused by the park since the federal government provided tax rebates for donations to the JNF, which is fundraising for "renewal and development" of the park. (In 1998 the U.N. found that the JNF systematically discriminated against Arab Israelis. Israel's Supreme Court came to similar conclusions in 2005.)

Canada Park is but one example of direct Canadian ties to Israel's post-1967 occupation of Palestinian land. In July 2008 a West Bank village filed suit in Montréal Superior Court against two Québec-based companies, Green Park International and Green Mount International, for building an Israeli settlement in the West Bank. The village claimed the Canadian companies built part of Israel's largest settlement, Modiin Illit, on land seized after Israel captured the West Bank in 1967. "The defendants... as de facto agents of the State of Israel are, and have been, illegally constructing residential and other buildings," the suit reads. "In so doing, the defendants are aiding, abetting, assisting and conspiring with the state of Israel in carrying out an illegal purpose."[168]

Companies involved in the Trans-Israel highway were also directly tied to the infrastructure of occupation. With Canadian financing, the Canadian Highways Infrastructure Corporation headed a private sector consortium building a $3 billion (Jewish) settler-only highway.[169] One writer explains: "Israel's network of bypass roads is designed very deliberately to reach from the core areas of Israel itself into settlements in the West Bank without allowing traffic or communication between West Bank towns. These bypass roads are an integral component of … the 'matrix of control', by which Palestinians are isolated, surrounded, and disconnected from each other, made wholly dependent on the whims of the Israeli regime. It is an appalling program of imprisoning an entire population. It is also good business for the Canadian Highways Infrastructure Corporation."[170]

Ottawa has directly endorsed Israel's occupation in a number of ways. Israel was only the fourth country with which Ottawa signed a free trade agreement.[171] Begun January 1997, the Canada-Israel Free Trade Agreement included the West Bank and Gaza Strip as part of where Israel's custom laws were applied. In short, Canada's trade agreement was based on the areas that Israel maintained territorial control over, not on internationally recognized borders. The European Union's trade agreement with Israel, on the other hand, explicitly precluded the territories that Israel captured in the 1967 war and occupied against international law.

Beginning in 2007, Stephen Harper's Conservatives actively supported U.S. moves to create a Palestinian police force to oversee Israel's occupation and to act as a counterweight to the Hamas government.[172] In a meeting with U.S. Lt. Gen Keith Dayton, the man in charge of organizing the Palestinian force, Foreign Affairs Minister Peter MacKay offered $1.2 million for the U.S. general's mission. "About a fifth of Dayton's staff are Canadian and Condoleeza Rice told reporters in a briefing alongside MacKay in Jerusalem, that Dayton, 'has a Canadian counterpart with whom he works very closely'."[173] A June 2008 Conservative press release noted "Canada is a strong supporter of Palestinian security system reform, particularly through our contribution to the mission of Lt. General Keith Dayton, the U.S. security coordinator, and to the European Union Police Coordinating Office for Palestinian Police Support."[174]

The federal government also signed a security agreement with Israel in early 2008. Columinst Linda McQuaig wrote: "The Harper government last month signed a wide-ranging agreement with Israel establishing cooperation in 'border management and security' — even though we don't share a border with Israel. Does this mean Israel will become involved with intelligence gathering about Canadian Muslims or other Canadians supporting Palestinian rights? Does it mean Canada will help Israel in its military operations in the West Bank or Gaza?"[175]

Despite Israel's four decade-long occupation of Palestine, Canadian diplomatic support for Israel has been unflinching. A 1987 survey of U.N. members ranked Canada second only to the U.S. in perceived support for

Israel.[176] Canadian diplomats echoed this pro-Israeli perception. A study of former ambassadors and diplomats in the late 1980s found that the vast majority felt Canada's relations were "unbalanced" with respect to Israel in Middle East peace negotiations. None of the ambassadors felt Canada was unbalanced in the Palestinians favour.[177]

In 1974 Ottawa was one of only a handful of countries that voted against a U.N. General Assembly resolution affirming the right of the PLO "to participate on equal footing in all U.N. deliberations in the Middle East."[178] On December 11, 1982, the Globe and Mail reported that "The United Nations General Assembly called yesterday for the creation of an independent Palestinian state and for Israel's unconditional withdrawal from territories it occupied in 1967. Israel, Canada, the United States and Costa Rica cast the only negative votes as the assembly passed the appeal by 113 votes to 4, with 23 abstentions."[179]

Prior to 1986, Canada was isolated with Israel and the U.S. in its opposition to an international Middle East peace conference put forward by the U.N. General Assembly.[180] At the September 1987 Francophonie summit in Québec City, Canada was the only country (41 participated) that failed to support a resolution calling for Palestinian self-determination. External Affairs Minister Joe Clark explained that "self-determination is a phrase we've had a lot of difficulty with. We think it could be a synonym for the establishment of an independent Palestinian state. The use of that language could prejudice the results of a conference on the Palestinians."[181] Eighteen months later Joe Clark reminded everyone: "I want to take this occasion to reiterate that Canada does not recognize the Palestinian state proclaimed last November."[182]

Echoing Prime Minister Harper's comment on Lebanon two decades later, when the first Intifada (uprising) broke out in 1987, then PM Brian Mulroney told the CBC that Israel's brutal suppression of rock throwing Palestinian youth was handling the situation with "restraint".[183] When questioned by a CBC reporter about the similarity between the plight of Palestinians and Blacks in South Africa, Mulroney replied that any comparison between Israel and South Africa was "false and odious and should never be mentioned in the same breath."[184]

Fast forward to the second Intifada and again Canada supported Israel. Against world opinion, in December 2000, Jean Chrétien's Liberals opposed a U.N. resolution calling for observers to the occupied territories to protect the security of Palestinian civilians. Canada's reason for rejecting the resolution was that Israel, the occupying power, had not accepted the idea of observers.[185] At a 2002 United Nations Commission on Human Rights (UNCHR) meeting, Canada and Guatemala were the only countries to oppose a resolution to send the organization's representative, Mary Robinson, on a brief fact finding tour of the occupied territories.[186]

While Paul Martin's short-lived government was more pro-Israel than Jean Chrétien's, the Harper government was still more pro-Israel. When Hamas won Canadian monitored and facilitated legislative elections in 2006, Canada was the first country (after Israel) to cut its assistance to the Palestinian Authority.[187] "The response of Canada, under Harper, to this democratic result was to cut aid to the starving and besieged Palestinians. Harper was following senior advisor to [Israeli Prime Minister] Ariel Sharon, Dov Wiseglass, who announced a plan to 'put Palestinians on a diet.'"[188] The aid cutoff was devastating. A Globe and Mail headline said "Open warfare among Gazan families a byproduct of aid freeze."[189] Ostensibly the aid cut-off was due to Hamas' refusal to recognize Israel, yet Canada has not severed relations with Likud governments, a party that does not recognize Palestinians' right to a state.[190]

By fall 2008 the Conservatives were publicly proclaiming that Canada was the most pro-Israel country in the world.[191] In January 2008 the Globe and Mail reported "by refusing to condemn the building [of illegal settlements near Jerusalem] at Harhoma, [Foreign Affairs Minister] Mr. Bernier appeared to have made Canadian foreign policy the most pro-Israeli in the world. Last week, even the United States, usually Israel's staunchest ally, slammed the new construction here."[192]

Canada was the first country to withdraw from the second U.N. Conference on Racism ("Durban II"), much to the delight of the Israeli government, which was the second country to pull out. "When Canada left Durban II it said it would not be 'party to an anti-Semitic, anti-western hate fast dressed up as an antiracism conference.'"[193] Israeli Foreign Affairs Minister Tzipi Livni congratulated Ottawa. "The Canadian decision, at this early stage, undoubtedly will shake the entire foundation of those wishing to repeat the 2001 Durban Conference" where it is alleged that criticism of Zionism was "anti-Semitic".[194]

Just after withdrawing from Durban II, Canada was the only country at the U.N. Human Rights Council to vote against a resolution that called for "urgent international action to put an immediate end to Israel's siege of Gaza." The resolution was adopted by 30 votes, with 15 abstentions. A few months later, 33 members of the 47-seat Human Rights Council endorsed a resolution accusing Israel of war crimes for its March 2008 incursion into the Gaza strip that claimed more than 120 lives. Thirteen countries abstained and only Canada opposed that resolution.[195]

During Israel's December 2008-January 2009 assault on Gaza the Harper government publicly supported Israel and voted alone at the U.N. Human Rights Committee in defence of Israel's actions. After Venezuela broke off diplomatic relations with Israel Canada took over Israeli diplomacy. The Jerusalem Post reported that "Israel's interests in Caracas will now be represented by the Canadian Embassy."[196] Canada officially became Israel, at least in Venezuela.

Lebanon

The Conservative government and Canadian corporations supported Israel's summer 2006 military invasion (Israel's fifth) of Lebanon. "Canadian companies and taxpayers played an important role in the production of much of the military equipment that is currently being used to bomb villages, neighbourhoods and key infrastructure in Lebanon."[197] Canadian companies produced many of the electronic components in the weapons the U.S. passed onto Israel. A dozen Canadian firms made parts for infrared guidance systems, radar equipment and training simulators for the F-15s Israel used in Lebanon (and Palestine).[198] And 10 Israeli F16s were among 200 warplanes that took part in NATO's annual Maple Flag war games at Cold Lake Alberta in May 2005.[199]

When Stephen Harper told reporters that Israel's assault on Lebanon was a "measured response" to Hezbollah incursions, he probably regretted it. Two days later, Israel wiped out an entire Lebanese-Canadian family, including four children aged 1 to 8. Harper's comment brought the kind of publicity even a staunchly pro-Israel Prime Minister should have shied away from. But with 1,200 (1,100 civilians) Lebanese dead and much of the country's infrastructure destroyed, the Conservatives continued to endorse Israel's aggression. Three months after the conclusion of hostilities, Harper vetoed a 55 member Francophonie statement that "'deplored' the effect of the month-long conflict on the Lebanese civilians it endangered."[200] For Harper the statement was too one-sided, even if the 33-day war caused more than ten times the deaths on the Lebanese side in a country with a little more than half of Israel's population.

During its bombing of Lebanon Israel destroyed a U.N. compound, killing Canadian Major Paeta Hess-Von Kruedener. At the time of the bombing Harper publicly questioned the U.N. for keeping its forces in the war zone and demanded answers. When a U.N. inquiry concluded that on the day of the fatal bombing, Hezbollah fighters were nowhere near the U.N. post the "pro-military" Conservative government ignored the report.[201] Israel's ambassador to Canada, Alan Baker, said "there was no high-level push for accountability from Canada."[202]

Lebanon's fractured political/religious landscape is ripe for outside intervention, from Iran and Syria's support for Hezbollah to Saudi Arabian and U.S. support for the Sunni-led government. After the 2006 war Ottawa strengthened its relations with the Lebanese groups least resistant to Israel's aggression. Canada followed Washington's lead in arming the Lebanese army as a counterweight to Hezbollah's military force.[203] With much of Beirut blockaded and the majority of Lebanese calling for a change in government, Parliamentary Secretary Jason Kenny and Liberal MP Irwin Cotler traveled to Beirut in late 2006 to deliver a message of "full moral support" to Lebanese Prime Minister Fouad Siniora.[204] During the same period, Foreign Affairs Minister Peter McKay called Hezbolah, which headed the opposition, the "Taliban on steroids."[205] Eighteen months later AFP reported that "Canada blasts Hezbollah for Lebanon unrest." Foreign Affairs Minister Maxime Bernier told Parliament: "We are supporting the Lebanese government and we hope that peace and security will come back to Lebanon."[206]

Ottawa has long supported Lebanon's westernized elite. In January 2005 the National Post reported that CIDA gave $925,000 to the University of the Hariri Foundation to help implement a Canadian business school curriculum (Rafic Hariri was Lebanon's Prime Minister).[207] For the National Post, the scandal was not that Canada supported Lebanon's western elite. Rather "just weeks after the Canadian government announced" the grant "the government of Lebanon awarded a consortium led by Québec engineering giant SNC-Lavalin Inc. and Canada Post a 12-year contract to modernize its derelict postal system."[208] For a time the project was thought to be worth as much as $1.2 billion.[209]

Ottawa also gave $281,000 in foreign aid to help retrain Lebanese postal workers, which was paid directly to an SNC-Lavalin affiliate. The Canada Post/SNC-Lavalin deal was among "contracts awarded on a basis other than merit" according to the U.S. Embassy in Lebanon. Canadian officials responded by claiming that bidding for the post office contract was "standard business" and part of diplomatic efforts to develop "good social and civil society relationships."[210]

Unlike Harper in 2006, Pierre Trudeau at least publicly criticized Israel's 1982 invasion of Lebanon. But Canadian opposition was at best symbolic.

"As a result of strong pro-Israel bias in the cabinet, the government was unable to take any unequivocal public position on the invasion of Lebanon or the massacre of Palestinian refugees in the Sabra and Chatila refugee camps in September 1982."[211] After Israeli-backed right-wing Christian militias slaughtered between 800 and 2,000 defenceless Palestinian civilians on the 15th and 16th of September 1982, the House of Commons failed to unanimously support a resolution pronouncing "its disgust for those forces that were responsible for the slaughter and urge upon them a policy of restraint."[212]

Ottawa failed to unequivocally condemn Israel's invasion, let alone impose sanctions on Israel like it did with the Soviet Union for invading Afghanistan three years earlier. Instead of breaking off diplomatic relations with Israel for its 18-year occupation of Lebanon, Ottawa signed a trade agreement with Israel and continued business as usual.

Canada also supported Lebanon's westernized elite in the late 1950s. Seventy-seven of 591 members of a U.N. force sent to Lebanon in 1958 were Canadian.[213] One goal of that U.N. mission was to "monitor the borders and confirm that Lebanon was free of [Egypt's Pan-Arabist President Abdul] Nasserite infiltration."[214] Canadian ambassador to the UN Charles Ritchie explained how "the UAR [Egypt's] aim was... to bring into power in Lebanon a government which would be more in sympathy with UAR policies and in fact subservient to Nasser. Moreover the real and more sinister intent behind this move was to weaken the union of Iraq and Jordan and ultimately to isolate Iraq.[215]"

While the initial disbursement of U.N. observers was in the country, American troops invaded Lebanon on July 15, 1958, the day after Iraq's monarchy was overthrown. Fearing the rise of Arab nationalism, Canada supported this U.S. intervention, as well as British forces deployed to Jordan two days later. The Canadian government "informed the [American] embassy that Canadian support for the Lebanese case can be taken for granted."[216] Ottawa worked to increase the U.N. involvement in Lebanon to relieve U.S. forces and reduce tensions in the region.[217] "The U.N. presence in the country gave the United States political cover for a speedy and reasonably graceful exit by allowing it to hand over its stabilizing mission to UNOGIL [United Nations Observation Group in Lebanon]."[218] "It was clear that Canada's involvement in UNOGIL was intended to and did positively contribute to NATO interests in protecting the southern flank and access to Middle East oil."[219]

Discussion

For the past half-century Canadian policy towards the Middle East has been largely designed to enable U.S. imperial designs on a strategic part of the planet. The region's geopolitical importance to Washington — combined with limited Canadian business activity in the region — means that Canadian policymakers are largely focused on the interests of our southern neighbour. Noam Chomsky has commented that U.S. policy in the region — from its invasion of Iraq to its unflinching support of Israel — is largely motivated by a desire to control the region's "stupendous energy reserves." To continue the logic it would be fair to say that Canadian policy towards the Middle East is designed, above all else, to guarantee U.S. control over the region's energy resources.

Chapter Notes

1   My Years as Prime Minister, 87
2   Canada and U.N. Peacekeeping, 63
3   Seize the Day, 157
4   Canada and the Third World, 249
5   Canadian Foreign Policy: 1945-2000, 39
6   Seize the Day, 147
7   Canadian-Arab Relations, 17
8   Canada in Egypt, 3
9   Canada in Egypt, 1
10   Canada in Egypt, 2
11   Peacekeeping, 45
12   Canada and U.N. Peacekeeping, 69;
Closely Guarded, 119
13   More Than a Peacemaker, 80
14   Peacekeeping, 129
15   Canada in Egypt, 197
16   The Commonwealth and Suez, 342
17   The Commonwealth and Suez, 343
18   Alliance and Illusion, 266; Canadian-
Arab World Relations, 22
19   Alliance and Illusion, 266
20   Canada and the World Order, 99
21   Journal of Conference of Defense
Association Institute fall 1991, 13
22   Canada as a Principle Power, 382
23   Canadian-Arab Relations, 10;
Peacekeeping, 139
24   Closely Guarded, 121
25   Canadian-Arab Relations, 65
26   Canada and the Third World, 254
27   Canadian-Arab Relations, 22
28   Closely Guarded, 198
29   Canada in Egypt, 7
30   http://www.sourcewatch.org/index.
php?title=Coalition_of_the_willing
31   Ottawa Citizen March 22 2003
32   Canada Among Nations 2004, 81
33   Dreamland, 67
34   Unexpected War, 82
35   Unexpected War, 64
36   Ottawa Citizen Mar 27 2003
37   Unexpected War, 89
38   www.urbanoperations.com/oifcentaf.pdf
39   Ottawa Citizen Apr 22 2008
40   The Canadian Forces and
Interoperability, 99
41   Coalition to Oppose the Arms Trade Feb
1 2006
42   Unexpected War, 88
43   Ottawa Citizen Jan 19 2008
44   Ottawa Citizen Jan 19 2008

45   IPS Jan 23 08
46   IPS Jan 23 08; Ottawa Citizen Jan 19 2008
47   http://shadowspear.Com/jtf2.htm
48   Toronto Star Nov 21 2006
49   Ottawa Citizen June 4 2007
50   Dreamland, 68
51   http://www.knowledgedrivenrevolution.
com/Articles/200602/20060201_CAN_Iraq_
War_Support.htm
52   Unexpected War, 90
53   Unexpected War, 53
54   Coalition to Oppose the Arms Trade Feb
1 2006
55   IPS Jan 23 08
56   In Harms Way, 171
57   http://embassymag.ca/page/view/.2004.
november.24.tp; Canada and the Middle East,
56
58   Canada and the Middle East, 56
59   http://www.globalresearch.ca/index.
php?context=va&aid=8110
60   Coalition to Oppose the Arms Trade
Canada's secret war in Iraq
61   Maclean's May 29 2006
62   IPS Jan 23 08
63   Press for Conversion, http://coat.ncf.
ca/articles/links/Canada_in_Iraq.htm
64   Foreign Policy Vol 11 #2, 3
65   La Presse June 13 2007
66   National Post June 28 2008
67   Ottawa Citizen June 04 2007
68   Financial Times May 26 2004
69   Toronto Star Nov 11 2006
70   http://www.montrealmirror.
com/2006/033006/front.html
71   Mother Jones Nov 24 2008
72   Mother Jones Nov 24 2008
73   Globe and Mail Oct 18 2007
74   Globe and Mail Oct 18 2007
75   Mother Jones Nov 24 2008
76   National Post July 28 2008
77   Ottawa Citizen Feb 8 2008
78   National Post July 7 2008
79   Globe and Mail Nov 30 2006
80   Unexpected War, 133
81   http://calsun.canoe.ca/News/Columnists/
Kaufmann_Bill/2008/07/18/6194071-sun.php
82   Ottawa Citizen Nov 9 2007
83   Canwest News Nov 22 2006
84   Montréal Gazette Nov 20 2008
85   Montréal Gazette Nov 20 2008

86 Ottawa Citizen Dec 1 2008

87 Canwest May 15 2007

88 Ottawa Citizen Jan 9 2007

89 Canwest July 10 2008

90 Arms Canada, xi

91 Arms Canada, xii

92 Latin American Working Group Letter Vol 3 #4

93 In/Security, 345

94 Toronto Star Nov 30 2006

95 Globe and Mail Sept 25 1978

96 Globe and Mail Nov 24 1979

97 Globe and Mail Oct 23 1978

98 Globe and Mail Nov 24 1979; Towers of Gold, 199

99 Canada and the International Political/ Economic Environment, 104

100 Globe and Mail Jan 23 2007

101 Canadian Jewish News Mar 8 2007

102 http://www.thenation.com/blogs/ dreyfuss/364292/ahmadinejad_meets_us_ peace_movement

103 National Post Oct 25 2008

104 The Politics of Candu Export, 62

105 Canada's International Policies, 248

106 Nucleus, 357

107 Pakistan-Canada Relations

108 Canadian Dimension May 2001

109 Canadian Foreign Policy: Contemporary Issues and Themes, 205

110 Exporting Danger, 81

111 The Politics of Candu Export, 62

112 Globe and Mail Aug 2 2008

113 Globe and Mail Jan 17 2009

114 http://news.xinhuanet.com/english/2008-12/15/content_10509717.htm

115 Relations Mar 2007

116 Exporting Danger, 77; Relations Mar 2007

117 Exporting Danger, 107/124

118 http://www.dominionpaper.ca/ articles/2147

119 Canadian Nuclear Weapons, 18

120 Canadian Nuclear Weapons, 23

121 Canadian Nuclear Weapons, 93

122 Just Dummies, 206

123 Cold War Canada, 373

124 Canada and the New American Empire, 24

125 Canada and the Birth of Israel, 60; Personal Policy Making, 5

126 The Making of the Arab-Israeli Conflict, 29

127 Canadian-Arab Relations, 10

128 Canada and the Birth of Israel, 105

129 Personal Policy Making, 26

130 The Domestic Battleground, 136; Le Canada et le conflit Isrealo-Arab, 33

131 The Domestic Battleground, 129

132 Canada and the Middle East, 10

133 Canadian-Arab Relations, 62

134 The Domestic Battleground, 130

135 Canada and the Birth of Israel, 117

136 Ethnic Cleansing of Palestine, 18

137 Ethnic Cleansing of Palestine, 34

138 The Domestic Battleground, 129

139 Personal Policy Making, 94

140 Canada and the Birth of Israel, 129

141 Canada and the Birth of Israel, 135

142 Canada and Palestine, 123

143 None is Too Many, 278

144 None is Too Many, 278

145 Canada and the Birth of Israel, 237

146 The Domestic Battleground, 31/137

147 Canada and Palestine, 10

148 Ethnic Cleansing of Palestine, 8

149 Ethnic Cleansing of Palestine, 29-38

150 The Domestic Battleground, 45; The Secret Army, 60

151 Dual Allegiance, 159

152 Canada's Jews, 364

153 http://www.zmag.org/znet/ viewArticle/17553

154 http://mostlywater.org/canada_origins_ israelpalestine_conflict_part_2_3

155 Canada's Jews, 364; The Secret Army, 188

156 Dual Allegiance, 159

157 The Secret Army, 64

158 The Secret Army, 118

159 The Domestic Battleground, 45

160 The Secret Army, 45

161 The Secret Army, 44

162 The Secret Army, 47

163 The Secret Army, 47-48

164 The Secret Army, 48

165 Canadian Dimension Feb 1981

166 Canada and the Middle East, 10

167 http://www.nowtoronto.com/news/story. cfm?content=161037

168 Toronto Star July 11 2008

169 Canadian Jewish News Oct 22 1998

170 http://www.zmag.org/znet/ viewArticle/826

171 In/Security, 402

172 Canadian Dimension Jan 2008

173 http://jonelmer.ca/files/elmer_cd_

jan2008.pdf

174 http://www.international.gc.ca/missions/westbank-gaza/bilateral-relations-bilaterales/menu-eng.asp

175 Toronto Star Apr 8 2008

176 The Domestic Battleground, 198

177 The Domestic Battleground, 191

178 Canada and the Middle East, 45

179 Globe and Mail Dec 11 1982

180 The Domestic Battleground, 198

181 The Domestic Battleground, 191

182 Canadian Foreign Policy, 36

183 The Domestic Battleground, 199

184 The Domestic Battleground, 208

185 In/Security, 402

186 Human Rights and Democracy, 20

187 Canada and the Middle East, 91

188 Dominion Foreign Policy issue, 27

189 Globe and Mail Oct 14 2006

190 Globe and Mail Oct 25 2006

191 http://www.israelnationalnews.com/News/News.aspx/127730

192 Globe and Mail Jan 14 2008

193 The economist Nov 29 2008

194 Globe and Mail Feb 25 2008

195 Toronto Star Mar 17 2008

196 Jerusalem Post Jan 29

197 http://www.dominionpaper.ca/foreign_policy/2006/08/07/making_war.html

198 À bâbord Oct 2006

199 This Magazine Sept 2005

200 Canada and the Middle East, 55

201 Toronto Star Feb 21 2008

202 Embassy Magazine Feb 6 2008

203 New York Times Oct 26, 2008

204 Globe and Mail Nov 24 2006

205 Montréal Gazette Nov 2 2006

206 AFP May 12 2008

207 National Post Jan 18 2005

208 National Post Jan 18 2005

209 National Post Jan 18 2005

210 National Post Jan 18 2005

211 Canadian-Arab Relations, 33

212 Canadian-Arab Relations, 34

213 In the Eye of the Storm, 148

214 The Canadian Way of War, 303

215 Canada and U.N. Peacekeeping, 93

216 Canada and U.N. Peacekeeping, 93

217 Canada and U.N. Peacekeeping, 96

218 The Evolution of U.N. Peacekeeping, 177

219 Canada and U.N. Peacekeeping, 97

Mexico, Central and South America

In the second decade of the 1900s Prime Minister Robert Borden wanted Canada to build an empire in southern Mexico and Central America. "In the early part of the last century," notes the author of Northern Shadows, "Canadian Prime Minister Robert Borden wanted Canada to build its own parallel empire to compete with the U.S. He encouraged a group of Canadian businessmen to buy out the Isthmus of Tehuantepec railway, which traversed southern Mexico from the Atlantic to the Pacific."[1]

Borden's plan never came to fruition. Still, Canada, especially its companies, were important actors in the region and the goal of an empire never completely died. As the 20th century rolled into the 21st, our relationship with Mexico, Central and South America became a sort of "branch plant" neo-colonialism, integrated with the U.S. in some respects and yet sometimes quite independent.

Most Canadians would be surprised to discover just how important this country has been, especially in certain economic sectors, in the United States' backyard. While most Canadian are aware of the "ugly American" few of us are familiar with its northern counterpart.

Mexico

Business has been at the forefront of determining Canada's relations with Mexico, at least since the 1910 revolution, which was a reaction to foreign economic domination and a brutal dictator. At the time Canadian corporate interests in Mexico were substantial. About 75 percent of the country's tramways were in the hands of Canadian investors.[2] In the capital, the Bank of Montréal controlled half of all foreign exchange dealings and the Montréal-based Mexican Light and Power Co. supplied Mexico City with electricity through a concession acquired from the dictator Porfirio Diaz.[3] R.T. Naylor explained: "The secret behind the Canadian willingness to venture into Mexico could be summed up in one word: Diaz. In 1908, the general manager of the Bank of Montréal returned from a reconnaissance mission to Mexico and announced that he was 'particularly struck with the stability of the present Mexican government and the powerful character of the ministry.'"[4] The Canadian banker argued that investing in Mexico was safer than Canada where there were growing calls for publicly owned utilities.[5]

Like British and American investors, Canadian businessmen were concerned with the social upheaval caused by the Mexican Revolution. Naylor writes about "the invasion of Mexico City late in 1910 by the Canadian directors of a number of these firms. Among them was Sir Edmund Walker, who proceeded to give advice to the military on how to deal with [famous peasant revolutionary Emiliano] Zapata whose activities were taking their toll of Canadian profits."[6]

Canadian investors began calling for British troops to intervene to defend their property.[7] When that failed the Canadians turned to the Americans. At the height of the Mexican Revolution, the Canadian-owned Monterey Tramways, Light and Power Company, the Bank of Montréal and the Bank of Commerce jointly asked Washington to help preserve Canadian interests in Mexico.[8] According to military historian Sean Maloney, the first recorded instance of Canadian gunboat diplomacy was during the Mexican Revolution. In 1915 HMCS Rainbow was dispatched to protect British interests and the expatriate community in the Pacific port city of Mazalatan. Later that year, Ottawa sent the Athabascan destroyer a little further south to Manzanillo.[9]

Fast forward to 2006. Mexico's presidential election was hotly contested. The former social democratic mayor of Mexico City, Andrés Manuel López Obrador (AMLO), claimed victory and his supporters refused to accept defeat. In the lead-up to the inauguration of right wing president Felipe Calderon, AMLO's partisans blockaded much of the capital. Inside the parliamentary building, legislators from AMLO's PRD party camped out to disrupt the inauguration. In response, legislators from Calderon's PAN camped out to disrupt the planned disruption.

Unwashed members of congress met Stephen Harper, the only head of state to attend Calderon's inauguration. A Globe and Mail headline explained that "Harper's visit to Mexico seen as boost to Calderon."[10] The Conservatives supported Calderon — electoral discrepancies or not — because his party strongly favoured foreign investment and NAFTA, to which Ottawa was committed, preferably in its most extreme form. "Canada considera inoportuno revisar el capitulo agropecuario del TLCAN," read a January 2008 headline in the Mexican Daily La Jornada.[11] In the face of hundreds of thousands of campesinos demonstrating against the elimination of tariffs on corn imports, Jeffrey Jones, Canada's secretary of agricultural negotiations, categorically opposed reopening NAFTA's agricultural policies.[12]

Jones' comments were similar to those of Michael Hart, a senior federal trade official, during the initial NAFTA negotiations 15 years earlier. Hart explained: "Any efforts by Mexico to seek permanent differential treatment for more than a few specific instances should be treated as a non-starter."[13] (To get a leg up, Ottawa spied on Mexico during NAFTA negotiations.[14]) Ottawa wanted NAFTA, and an indigenous Zapatista revolt in the southern state of Chiapas was not going to deter Canada's enthusiasm for the accord. Foreign Affairs spokesman Eduardo del Buey was reported in the January 6, 1994, Vancouver Sun to have said: "There is no link between the free trade agreement and what is going on in Chiapas."[15] In Mexico City, eight days later, Liberal Trade Minister Roy McClaren insisted that "there is no connection between NAFTA and Chiapas. Trade and human rights have nothing to do with each other."[16] The Zapatistas, who timed their uprising to coincide with NAFTA's implementation, called the agreement a "death sentence for indigenous peoples."[17]

NAFTA spurred Mexico's neoliberal transformation, which began with a debt default and peso devaluation in 1982. Canada played a small part in creating the conditions for the default. In the early 1980s Mexico owed Canadian banks $4 billion.[18] Numerous commentators have pointed out that the U.S. promoted megaprojects as part of a plan to swamp Third World countries in debt. (see *Confessions of an Economic Hitman*) "Canadian banks were generally willing to follow the U.S. lead and lend to Latin American countries."[19] After the country's default in 1982, a Canadian Senate Standing Committee on Foreign Affairs investigation into outstanding Canadian loans to Mexico found: "Several Canadian banking authorities told the committee that they were personally aware that U.S. State Department and treasury officials had urged the international banking community to 'accept the responsibility of being the first channel for moving the new petrol dollars' in the 1970s."[20] For his part, Mexico's minister of finance told the Canadian Standing Committee: "I had many bankers chasing me trying to lend me more money."[21]

Pro-market reforms adopted after Mexico's debt default were deepened in the lead-up to NAFTA. Mexico modified its 1917 constitution, which was largely a reaction to an earlier liberal economic period that sparked the seven year revolution. This progressive constitution dictated that land, subsoil and its riches were property of the Mexican state and recognized the collective right of communities to land through the "ejido" system. Constitutional changes in 1992 allowed for sale of lands to third parties, including multinational corporations.[22] Combined with a new Law on Foreign Investment, the Mining Law of 1992 allowed for 100 percent foreign control in exploration and production of mines.

With 375 projects in Mexico, Canadian mining companies were the biggest winners from these reforms.[23] As of March 2008, Canadian investors controlled 84 percent of Mexico's mining concessions.[24] Few Mexicans, however, benefited from Canadian mining operations in their country. Concluding a three-part series on the role of Canadian mining companies in Mexico, daily newspaper La Jornada asked: "Is this the contribution of that great country that is Canada to the development of our people? A new type of barbaric and predatorial colonialism that under the name of globalization imposes its companies in countries with weak and corrupt governments."[25]

Canadian mining interests did not shy away from areas of Mexico facing political unrest. In Chiapas Canadian-based Linear Gold Corp and Fronteer Development Group controlled concessions covering more than 300,000 hectares of land. These concessions were granted by Mexico's federal government without consultation from local communities.

Bordering Chiapas, the state of Oaxaca was another impoverished and politically volatile state where Canadian companies dominated mining. Vancouver-based Continuum Resources had ten projects, covering more than 70,000 hectares of land. Protesting the company's Natividad mine near Capulalpam, demonstrators blocked a highway for five hours in October 2007. Community members demanded an end to the mining concession, which they said destroyed many of the area's streams and springs as well as the frogs that are a big part of the region's diet.[26]

The most controversial Canadian mining venture in Mexico was Vancouver-based Metallica Resources' extraction of gold and silver from Cerro de San Pedro, a small town in the central state of San Louis de Potosi. Opponents of the project protested from Montréal to Mexico City where a hundred protestors, including several members of congress, blockaded the Canadian embassy for six hours in February 2007.[27] More than 200 legislative deputies and 57 Mexican senators signed a bill to close the Cerro de San Pedro mine and to require Metallica pay for environmental damages. Opponents claimed that cyanide from the 1.5 km long and 300m deep mine contaminated a water supply used by 1.5 million people. The mine, which was in a nationally protected area, was demolishing a mountain that was an important part of the town's heritage and a symbol on the state's coat of arms. A mine opponent, who fled to Montréal after receiving death threats, compared it to destroying Mount Royal, Montréal's namesake.[28] Concern for environmental and historical degradation led Mexican courts to revoke the mine's permit on a number of occasions between 2002 and

2006. In September 2008 the mine's environmental permits were once again revoked.[29] But court orders were not enforced, leading many to believe that Metallica had close relations with the highest levels of Mexican government.[30]

Guyana

In the early 1900s Ottawa tried to annex British Guyana, which sits between Venezuela and Surinam on the northeastern tip of South America. Despite failing to directly take over the country, Canada has had significant influence there ever since. The Royal Bank and Bank of Montréal both began operating in the country a century ago. In the early 1900s a syndicate led by Canadian railway tycoon William Van Horne built Georgetown's electric lighting and trolley system with $600,000 from the Bank of Montréal.[31] For its part, the Royal Bank helped U.S.-based Alcoa develop its Guyanese bauxite operations in 1909.[32]

Beyond the economic sphere Canada has long trained Guyana's military. From 1942 to 1945, Canada garrisoned a company of soldiers and a naval ship in the country.[33] Pressure from Montréal-based Alcan, which inherited Alcoa's operations, played a central part in Ottawa's decision to send troops to Guyana even though the official request came from London.[34] In January 1942 Alcan's Fraser Bruce wrote to External Affairs that "responsible company officials at McKenzie will not feel satisfied with respect to the guarding of the works until imperial or Canadian troops are stationed there." In a follow-up letter he bluntly referred to "our recent request for white soldiers."[35] The official request from London made clear the racial nature of Canada's mission. "Local coloured guards are already provided on the ships, but United Kingdom authorities recognize that there would be an advantage if these guards could be strengthened by a small number of whites and NCOs [non-commissioned officers]."[36]

Alcan was closely enmeshed with colonial policy until Britain lost control over Guyana in 1966. The company "thought that because of its contribution to the colonial economy, one of its officials ought to have a seat on the legislative council."[37] In the early 1950s "Alcan repeatedly informed Governor [Sir Alfred] Savage of its disappointment that he was not appointing any of its people, and Alcan officers thought that governor Savage himself was far too leftist, far too sympathetic to unions and socialists, to be kept in his job by a [British] Conservative government."[38]

On occasion Alcan personnel directly enabled Britain's occupation. When anti-colonial upheaval swept the country in 1953 (Guyana was a pseudo colony at the time) the British governor made prominent foreigners special constables, including Charles K Ward, then public relations officer for Alcan's Guyanese subsidiary and a former Royal Canadian Navy officer. As one of the few naval officers in the colony, Ward was summoned to serve as liaison with the Royal Navy. "Other Alcan personnel" notes a company history "were required to patrol the dark city streets by night to guard against troubles."[39]

As Guyana's leading trade partner for many years Canada benefited from the unequal international division of labour created by colonialism. Guyana's bauxite industry provides a stark example of this inequity.[40] In 1970 the price per ton of bauxite ore was G$18, G$160 for alumina and G$1000 for aluminum ingot. "The smelting and semi-fabrication stages being in Canada the result was that Guyana would obtain royalties and taxes on G$72, being the value of four tons of bauxite, while Canada would derive benefit from G$1000, being the value of the equivalent of one ton of aluminum ingot."[41]

While Guyana lost the value-added components of the aluminum process to Canada its workforce fell victim to the worst aspects of aluminum production. The home of Alcan's mine, McKenzie, was the worst sort of company town. Well into the 1960s "the workers live[d] in a depressed slum area to the north called, 'the village.' Staff members live[d] in the plush area of Waatooka, with exclusive clubs and social amenities such as a golf club."[42] Those not living in the town needed to present passes to enter Mackenzie.

Alcan's operations didn't escape the notice of social justice activists. The Student Society of the University of Guyana organized a May 1966 demonstration in front of Alcan's office and the Canadian High Commission (as well as a Royal Bank office).[43] ASCRIA, the country's foremost black nationalist movement, explained: "They [the workers] have, until recently, been bound to live in the most stratified community in Guyana, with its South African and USA idea of neighbourhood living and of white supremacy. The physical arrangements were such also that the whole imperialist machinery could be clearly seen: the extraction of the ore, the processing and added value, the shipping away of wealth, the importation of raw chemicals, the small group of expatriate decision-makers, the tokenism, the social gaps, the misery of the poorer districts, the hilltop luxury of the white population, the buying out of leaders, the divide and rule tactics, the process of exploitation which they could feel in their skin."[44]

In the late 1960s pressure built in Guyana to nationalize Alcan's operations. In response Alcan turned to the American government to help negotiate the nationalization dispute. "When an Alcan executive told a Canadian cabinet minister of his company's intent to request aid from the U.S. State Department, the minister thought it was an excellent idea, adding that if he were a corporate lawyer, he would advise likewise."[45] Alcan's resistance to Guyana's desire to gain greater control over its bauxite industry was partly explained by a desire to dissuade Jamaica and other bauxite producers from following suit.[46] Despite corporate resistance the mine was nationalized in 1971.

While the nationalization of Alcan was a step back for Canadian influence in Guyana, it was not a fatal blow. From the early 1980s Canada pushed neoliberal economics in Guyana. CIDA was involved in Guyana's first (1980-1982) structural adjustment loan from the World Bank designed "to turn over significant sectors of the economy to the private sector, both local and foreign."[47] A December 1982 Globe and Mail article continued "the government denies that the program exists but copies of the agreement are widely circulated in Georgetown. ... They [Canadian officials] are reluctant to discuss the effort to impose conditions, however, since it is apparently CIDA's first foray into this sensitive area of internal economics."[48]

After refusing to expand this initial structural adjustment program, Guyana was blacklisted by the international financial institutions in the mid-1980s. At the same time Canadian bilateral assistance declined from $3.15 million in 1983-84 to $700,000 in 1985-86.[49]

By the late 1980s pressure from Ottawa and the international financial institutions was growing on Guyana to adopt a series of more drastic economic reforms. Ottawa chaired the Guyana Support Group and gave $60 million to a highly controversial IMF structural adjustment program.[50] The Canadian money was tied to Guyana's adherence to IMF macro-economic prescriptions. Frank Jackman, the Canadian high commissioner to Guyana, said "there is great admiration within the government of Canada for the steps that are being taken here, and for the budgetary moves, albeit unpopular, that have been introduced."[51] Jackman claimed Guyana was setting a "precedent" for other indebted Third World countries and told the Guyanese to "take heart" since the austerity package would encourage Canadian investments. The people failed to "take heart" and instead demonstrators threw stones at the Canadian high commission office.[52]

After the structural adjustment programs in the 1980s some Canadian investment did flow into Guyana. Part of this foreign investment led to a terrible tragedy six years later. In August 1995 the tailings dam at Québec-based Cambior's Omai mine in Guyana failed. More than 1.2 billion litres of cyanide-laced sludge spilled into the Essequibo River, the country's main waterway. Huge numbers of fish were killed and thousands of riverbank inhabitants temporarily lost their livelihood. The area was declared a disaster zone.[53] To sidestep possible legal claims stemming from the spill, in September 1995 the company paid off local fisherman. "The fishermen, who were mostly illiterate, were required to sign forms absolving Omai of any future claims in exchange for $1.50 each. About two weeks later, it was reported that [Canadian High Commissioner] Louis Gignac had pressured Guyanese Prime Minister Samuel Hinds to reduce the scope and duration of the government-sponsored commission of inquiry investigating the spill. In a closed-door meeting on September 8 in Georgetown, and later in a follow-up letter leaked to the [Montréal] Gazette, he urged the Prime Minister to limit expert testimony and wrap up the inquiry in thirty days."[54]

Ecuador

According to many scientists, Ecuador's Intag region is the global centre of biodiversity.[55] The area is full of exotic wildlife, pristine rivers and primary cloud forests. Local opposition to mining in this ecologically sensitive area dissuaded companies from entering the region until May 2004, when Toronto-based Ascendant Copper decided to try to make some money, environment be damned. Community resistance was strong. All of the area's local governments (including the provincial, county and seven parish-township governments) and the majority of communities and organizations in the area publicly opposed the project.[56] On July 12, 2005, hundreds of Intag residents marched in Ecuador's capital, Quito, against Ascendant's plans. Mine opponents also brought their objections to Canadian officials. In June 2006 the Intag Solidarity Network provided the Canadian embassy with a 12-page report on the company's harmful activities.[57] Prior to that, the local mayor asked the TSX to block the listing of Ascendant shares because the company "caused serious internal conflicts and confrontations ... and had developed a divisive strategy provoking confrontations within the community, which could lead to the loss of human lives."[58] These pleas to Canadian institutions were to no effect.

Ascendant's response to community opposition was to co-opt groups, demonize mine opponents and repress dissidents. A company press release described opponents of its project as "eco-terrorists", "extremists" and "radicals." Ascendant spearheaded at least 10 criminal lawsuits against more than 70 individuals opposing the project.[59] The company also hired dozens of retired military officials who sprayed teargas and bullets at mining opponents. This prompted Amnesty International to conclude that opponents of Canadian mining operations in Ecuador were "facing death threats and attacks."[60]

A new, more progressive Ecuadorian government finally heeded community calls. In the summer of 2007 the Ministry of Energy and Mines asked the company to stop its community relations work saying it was "intended to divide the community."[61] Ascendant's spokesperson responded by claiming "the ministry doesn't have the right to control our corporate responsibility policies."[62] Ultimately, in late 2007, Ascendant's concessions were revoked "after it was found that the company contracted security firms to rough up local opposition leaders."[63]

While Ascendant was battling community opposition to its plans another Canadian-owned mine in Ecuador was embroiled in a violent struggle. In early 2007 the Ottawa Citizen reported that "an Ecuadorian congressman says he was beaten and nearly suffocated to death in the compound of a Canadian mining company in southern Ecuador by armed forces defending the venture ... A woman was bound, sexually assaulted and threatened with rape."[64]

Along with numerous other demonstrators Congressman Salvador Quishpe was abducted by Ecuadorian soldiers working alongside private security agents hired by Vancouver-based Corriente Resources. The Human Rights Observatory of Ecuador described what happened: "A still undetermined number of campesinos and indigenous people, including women, were victims of repression with tear gas, firearms, physical aggression and illegal detentions."[65]

In an attempt to defeat mining opposition, Corriente backed an indigenous delegation to Ottawa to denounce watchdog group Mining Watch.[66] During the delegation's October 2007 visit to Ottawa, a mining industry public relations firm, Kokopell, organized a presentation titled "The Business of Poverty" that blamed anti-mining groups for profiting from Ecuador's poverty.[67]

A few months after the delegation's visit, Corriente released a press release entitled "Responsible Mining Activities Supported by Major Ecuadorian Indigenous Association." The release explained: "CONFENIAE, an association representing approximately 220,000 people from all 16 indigenous nationalities of the Ecuadorian Amazon, held a Special Assembly on Thursday, November 29th in Puyo, Ecuador. During the Special Assembly, the CONFENIAE leadership overwhelmingly voted in favour of a resolution supporting the responsible mining activities of

EcuaCorriente S.A. (Corriente) in the Zamora Chinchipe and Morona Santiago Provinces of Ecuador, as part of their goal to eradicate indigenous poverty in the region."[68]

But, it turns out, the indigenous representatives Corriente brought to Ottawa were paid by the company.[69] Already expelled from the organizations they claimed to represent, one of them had been publicly denounced as early as 1998.[70] A communiqué by the legitimate CONFENIAE explained: "The mining and oil companies and others that have invaded our territories in Amazonia have organized a campaign by a false CONFENIAE, lead by José Aviles, who is sending out communiqués in the international arena, to confuse public institutions, governments, and international cooperation organizations about what is happening in the Ecuadorian Amazonia. The indigenous Mafia lies in the most shameless and condemnable way, usurping the name of the CONFENIAE and of the Federation Shuar de Zamora Chinchipe FEPNASH-ZCH, presided over by our colleague Ángel Awak. They are not ashamed to send communiqués prepared in the public relations offices of the mining companies, affirming such ridiculous things as that mineral exploitation provides education, hospitals, and culture to our communities. If we have received so many benefits, how is it possible that we live in the situation of misery and abandonment that they themselves recognize in their writings?"[71]

In the midst of this controversy between Corriente and a sector of Ecuador's indigenous community Canada's vice consul to Ecuador represented Ottawa at the June 2007 launch of a pro-mining indigenous group along with the vice president of Project Development for EcuaCorriente and the individuals expelled from the above mentioned native groups. "It remains to be explained," noted MiningWatch, "why officials from the Canadian Embassy would publicly support [expelled indigenous representatives] Naichap and Aviles, who have been denounced through official channels by the legitimate leaders of Indigenous organizations in Ecuador."[72]

These two Canadian companies, Corriente and Ascendant, were at the centre of a debate about resource extraction in Ecuador. In 2007, a constitutional assembly was set up to rewrite the country's constitution and mining law was a hot topic. Canadian companies, which controlled 90 percent of the country's concessions, launched a full-court press. Carlos Zorrilla, the executive director of Defensa y Conservación Ecológica de Intag, noted: "The companies and their public relations firms are using scare tactics, suggesting the [mining] mandate and new mining law will cause thousands [of] lost jobs, the country will go bankrupt, and investors will flee. Furthermore they've issued threats of international lawsuits unless their demands are met.... a lot of money is being spent on trying to convince Ecuadorians that mining will really lift them out of poverty and will solve all of the country's problems — and that it won't contaminate!"[73]

Ottawa took a keen interest in the mining debate. Ian Harris, senior VP of EcuaCorriente wrote that "The Canadian Embassy in Ecuador has worked tirelessly to affect change in the mining policy — including facilitating high-level meetings between Canadian mining companies and President Rafael Correa."[74] Along with a number of Canadian mining representatives, Canada's ambassador to Ecuador, Christian LaPointe, discussed mining regulations with Ecuador's president in early 2008. According to the CBC, LaPointe "attended the meeting with the mining companies and presented the Canadian government's concerns over the mining rules."[75]

Corporate and government officials reminded Ecuadorian representatives that Canada has a Foreign Investment Promotion and Protection Agreement (FIPA) with that country. The agreement says that Canadian investments cannot be expropriated "without prompt and adequate compensation" and, according to Foreign Affairs official Michael O'Shaughnessy, Canadian companies have "access to binding international arbitration for disputes arising from a breach of the treaty."[76]

Social movements responded to this diplomatic pressure. In December 2008 "about 200 activists from around the country including executive members of the influential Confederation of Indigenous Nationalities of Ecuador (CONAIE) participated in a festive march to the Canadian Embassy in Quito.... A letter delivered to Embassy representatives states that Canadian miners are 'unwelcome.'"[77]

Unfortunately, Ecuador is not the only country where Canadian diplomatic might has been used to promote the interests of predatorial mining corporations over the objections of local communities.

Peru

For some, Peru is a Canadian success story. Before 1990, no Canadian mining company operated in Peru. By 2008, Canadian corporations dominated the country's mining sector with a hundred mines under their control. As an illustration of the size of Canadian mining investment in Peru, in late 2006 ScotiaBank announced plans to expand its operations in the country to do more business with mining clients.[78] By 2008 the Toronto-based bank was the third-largest in Peru and only a small part of the "around $5 billion" Canadians had invested in the country.[79]

Where some see Canadian success, others see problems, at least for Peruvians. "In Peru," noted McGill University professor Daviken Stuenicki Gizbert, "40 percent of conflicts involving local communities are over mining. The majority of the mining sector in Peru is Canadian."[80]

In early 2008 Canadian resource companies in Peru were responsible for a number of socially damaging events; an oil and gas company entered an area inhabited by a nomadic tribe that refused contact with the outside world; a mine destroyed pre-Columbian carvings; the government declared a state of emergency over fears that arsenic, lead and cadmium from a mine near Lima could pollute the capital's main water supply.[81] And then, in October 2008, Zuniga, the president of the Achuar indigenous group FENAP, told a local radio: "We, as indigenous people, reject the Canadian company Talisman. We do not want them working in our territory. We want the Peruvian state to respect us and the armed forces to stop helping the company."[82]

The indigenous communities said oil development caused ecological harm and social conflict. "We do not want our forests, rivers and earth polluted, because this is our natural market ... We have proof that pollution already exists, damage to nature and to indigenous people in the communities where petroleum activities are developed. For 37 years in the Achuar brother communities of the Corrientes River, petroleum has not brought any development to them; on the contrary they are sick and poverty stricken."[83]

In the first decade of the 21st century Toronto-based Barrick Gold was embroiled in a number of conflicts in Peru. "Violent conflict at Barrick Gold's Tierina in North Central Peru," blared a 2005 Canadian newspaper headline, as the story reported two protesters killed.[84] A year earlier Reuters reported "thousands of protesters angry at a court decision to waive a $141 million tax payment levied on Canadian miner Barrick Gold Inc. clashed with riot police in Peru's central Andes on Monday, the latest in a run of anti-mining protests in the mineral-rich nation."[85]

The most high profile mining conflict in Peru took place earlier in the decade at Vancouver-based Manhattan Minerals $240 million US project in Tambogrande, a small town in the north of the country. This open pit gold mine would have forced half of the town's 16,000 residents to relocate while creating only a few hundred jobs. Godofredo Garcia Baca, a leader of the anti-mining opposition movement, was shot and killed under suspicious circumstances.[86] Ojeda Irofrio, the president of the Front in Defence of Tambogrande and mayor of the municipal government of Tambogrande, explained: "The company continues trying to buy us or scare us. They follow us, they record us, they infiltrate our meetings. They have a man there who worked for ten years with [disgraced former president Alberto] Fujimori, and before that was a leftist, burning cars and confronting the army, making a big mess. Now, in Tambogrande, he hires local people to confront us."[87]

A community referendum was held with the question: "Do you agree with the development of mining activities in the urban area; urban expansion area; agricultural zone and agricultural expansion zones in the district of Tambogrande?" More than 93 percent of 27,015 residents participated in the referendum and over 73 percent of the population responded "no" to the question.[88] The overwhelming success of the nonbinding referendum forced the company to put the project on hold. (Tambogrande's community referendum became a model for resistance to Canadian mining elsewhere in Latin America.)

Manhattan Minerals obtained its concession in Tambogrande six months after participating in a Department of Natural Resources trade mission to Peru. The federal government has supported many individual mining projects in the country and has worked to provide the industry with a profitable investment climate. In 2002 CIDA began a six-year $9.6 million Mineral Resources Reform Project to provide technical assistance and technological support to the country's Ministry of Energy and Mines. At the end of 2008 CIDA added $4 million to the project and the agreement was extended until 2012.[89] The official goal of the Mineral Resources Reform Project is "development of activities oriented to the consolidation of the institutional capacity of the sector, which means the services provided by the Ministry of Mines and Energy, and to contribute to the generation of greater confidence in the Ministry and its regional offices."[90]

CIDA's push to improve the prospects for Canadian miners through the Mineral Resources Reform Project warranted a visit in early 2008 by the minister of international cooperation. "Ms. [Bev Oda] ... arrived in Peru meeting with the Latin American nation's energy and mines minister, as well as Canadian and Peruvian mining companies and NGOs to discuss mining sector reform."[91]

Five months after Oda's visit the federal government signed a trade agreement with Peru largely designed to improve the prospects for Canadian investors. According to Foreign Affairs, "an investment chapter in the Canada-Peru FTA [free-trade agreement] locks in market access for Canadian investors in Peru and provides greater stability, transparency and protection for their investments."

In truth the FTA — with environmental and labour safeguards that are "even weaker than NAFTA's" — might be better characterized as subverting meaningful democracy. "The FTA with Peru," notes journalist Dawn Paley, "eliminates the possibility that Peru would enact such a thing as the recent 'Mining Mandate' passed in Ecuador by the Constituent Assembly, which suspends all large scale mining activity (exploration) in Ecuador for 180 days while a new Mining Law is written."[92] Above all else Ottawa wanted to remove any future Peruvian government's ability to raise taxes, change mining regulations or expropriate properties of Canadian companies.

Canada has also been involved militarily in Peru. In late 1996 the Túpac Amaru guerrilla group took dozens of foreign diplomats (including Canadians) hostage at the Japanese embassy in Lima. Canada's JTF-2 special forces participated in the U.S.-led rescue effort that left all 14 guerrillas dead, many of them reportedly executed.[93] This was not the first time Canadian forces helped Peru's security apparatus fight the country's guerrillas. Ottawa supplied intelligence-gathering equipment and the RCMP trained Peru's security forces in the late 1980s when Peru's government was engaged in a civil war with leftist guerillas. At the time, many commentators complained that the U.S. was militarizing the region.[94]

Bolivia

On December 26, 1996, 10 community members of Amayapampa Bolivia were killed by more than 800 members of the country's police and military forces.[95] The dead, along with 40 injured, were protesting a mining project owned by Vancouver-based Da Capo Resources, which later merged with a U.S. company to create Vista Gold Corporation.

In a November 19, 1996, letter to now disgraced Bolivian President Gonzalo Sanchez de Lozada, Vista asked the government to intervene in the conflict. They even called for a particular military force. "Currently there is a force lead by colonel Eduardo Rivas of 150 armed men at Catavi awaiting instructions," read the letter.[96] One author explained that "the Vista Gold Corporation and regional government officials actively promoted the idea that the local opposition amounted to a terrorist group against the state. The company demanded that both the regional and national governments ensure compliance with the mining code, which stated that nobody had the right to oppose mining concessions granted by the state."[97]

Resource companies such as Vista operated in Bolivia under conditions Canada helped develop. Ottawa supported opening Bolivia's resource sector to multinational interests. Beginning in 1989, CIDA, Petro-Canada and the Bolivian government began working together to "modernize [the country's] public oil and gas industry through the Bolivia Oil and Gas Project," according to a 1996 report by the Auditor General of Canada. The report claimed the project benefited numerous Canadian corporations. "Twenty-two Canadian firms received spin-off benefits from the Bolivian Oil and Gas Project; [and] approximately $20 million in related commercial spin-offs in South America for Canadian firms since April 1995."[98]

Impasse in Bolivia explained that "an increasingly important component of development assistance includes 'institutional capacity building' — creating the environment needed for markets to operate."[99] One example cited is CIDA's $8.25 million Hydrocarbon Regulatory Assistance Project, initially granted to PriceWaterHouseCoopers (then reassigned to IBM). Impasse in Bolivia claimed that "rather than working for the interests of Bolivia, [Canadian] 'assistance' was designed by the international agency (in this case bilateral) to serve the interests of either international corporations or those based in their own countries." The book quotes a 2004 CIDA report that concludes "the project was successful in linking Canadian petroleum companies to Bolivia's oil and gas sector ... more than $70 million [worth of] commercial spin-offs for Canada have been achieved as a result."[100]

Interestingly, both Bolivia and Ecuador elected governments in the last half of the decade that were less accommodating to the interests of foreign investors. It seems reasonable to speculate that the actions of Canadian corporations contributed to the popularity, amongst ordinary citizens, of these new, more left-wing, administrations.

Guatemala

Canadian mining companies are also active in Central America. In 2008, Canadian companies owned 80 percent of Guatemala's mining concessions.[101] Taking advantage of Guatemala's 1997 World Bank-backed mining liberalization, a number of Canadian companies trampled on Guatemala's impoverished indigenous communities. "There are over a dozen Canadian companies ... involved in mining operations that have been denounced in Guatemala and internationally as contributing to environmental and community development harms and human rights violations (including some killings), while reaping (in the case of Goldcorp) huge profits for company directors, shareholders and investors."[102]

Protests against Canadian-based Glamis Gold's (purchased by Vancouver's Goldcorp in 2006) Marlin mine project in the western highlands of Guatemala left 20 injured and two dead in early 2005.[103] Protestor Raúl

Castro Bocel was killed on January 11, 2005, when the Guatemalan army and police attacked a blockade set up to stop the flow of equipment to the mine. Two months later a leading anti-mine organizer, according to eyewitnesses, "left the church and headed towards his home, [where] two employees of the private security company hired by Glamis, the Golan Group, shot five or six bullets, killing Álvaro Benigno."[104]

In the midst of the conflict between members of the Mayan community and Glamis, Canada's ambassador to Guatemala, James Lambert, said protestors were "breaking the law" and that "we had people complaining to us that they could not get their products to port." The ambassador also claimed that environmental groups were manipulating indigenous communities.[105] In an op-ed published in Guatemala's leading daily, Prensa Libre, Lambert argued that mining would be good for indigenous Guatemalans because it benefited aboriginal communities in Canada. To prove the point the embassy sponsored a visit by chief Jerry Asp, from the Telegraph Creek Band in B.C., to tout the benefits of mining. Coincidentally, when Asp was in Guatemala his office was occupied by the Tahltan Elders Council who claimed he didn't represent their interests. The elders also demanded a mining moratorium on their lands.[106]

In a nonbinding 2006 referendum, communities near the Guatemalan mine overwhelmingly rejected the project. The town of Sipakapa, where much of the mine's gold processing took place, voted 98 percent against the project.[107] Concerns surrounding the ecological impact of open pit mining spurred the opposition. The Marlin mine required removing huge amounts of earth for each ounce of gold and "the mine operations will require massive amounts of water — as much as 450,000 litres per hour according to company estimates — diverting its use from vital irrigation of local farm lands."[108] When water quality studies near the mine found high levels of heavy metals, the company responded to these detailed accusations by lodging a formal complaint against the Guatemalan ecological collective and Italian biologist who produced the research. Opposition to the mine was also driven by the limited number of jobs created (much of the investment was for imported machinery). And, for many years, the mine paid no income taxes.

About the same time that the communities near the Marlin mine asserted their rights through a community referendum, in late 2006 more than 400 families, who claimed ancestral rights to the land, moved onto property purchased by Toronto-based Skye Resources in the northeastern part of the country. Four months after the land reclamation, Guatemala's military violently evicted the "squatters" by burning dozens of houses. Much to the dismay of Canada's new ambassador, Kenneth Cook, the evictions were videotaped by Canadian researchers and journalists. Cook told a visiting Canadian human rights delegation that the video was old and that the photographs were not taken at the evictions. He also claimed that an impoverished Mayan Q'eqchi' woman filmed railing against the forced evictions was an actress paid to "perform." Cook's allegations were categorically denied by the Canadian researchers.[109] Opposition to the Skye Resources mine was motivated by more than the question of property rights. The surrounding community expected to be contaminated by the byproducts of nickel mining, and due to Guatemala's liberal mining code, Skye would pay nothing for its water. The townspeople, on the other hand, collectively paid $20,000 a year, even though the company would use 13 times more water than the entire town.[110]

Skye's property was once owned by the Sudbury, Ontario-based International Nickel Company (Inco). At one point the largest investment in Central America, by 1980 Inco had invested a quarter billion dollars in its "Exmibal" project yet it never created more than 500 jobs for Guatemalans. And not the best of jobs, as Inco made prospective workers sign a form asking if they had previously been a member of any trade union.[111] The mine also left a gouged earth and polluted lake.[112]

Poor labour standards and environmental destruction appear practically inconsequential compared to the violence engendered by the Exmibal property. Inco worked closely with a brutal dictatorship that helped pacify the region surrounding its mine. In the mid to late 1960s, the Guatemalan army is thought to have killed an incredible three to six thousand (mostly indigenous) people in the region around the mine.[113] On May 29, 1978, 53 people were killed after protesting the expropriation of their land, homes and crops to make way for Inco's mine. The New York Times, BBC and Le Monde reported on the slaughter, but no Canadian newspaper picked up the story.[114]

Both the "Nunca Mas" (Never Again) report by the Human Rights Office of the Archbishop of Guatemala and the United Nations Commission for Historical Clarification in Guatemala, found Inco complicit in human rights violations against mine opponents. Inco was linked to the gunning down of two law professors from the National University of San Carlos and a congressman who formed a commission to study the terms of Guatemala's agreement with Inco.[115]

Inco's investment in Guatemala was not simply a case of corporate Canada jumping into bed with a brutal regime. Ottawa was directly complicit. EDC provided Inco with more than $55 million in loans for the Eximbal project.[116] Ottawa's support for the mine was at a high point, symbolically, when the Canadian ambassador, a group of Inco executives and Guatemalan General Kjell Laugerud Garcia launched the project. The general cut the mine' s opening ribbon, the Canadian flag was raised and a Guatemalan military band played O Canada.[117]

Pierre Trudeau's Liberals supported Inco and the Guatemalan generals, even after President Jimmy Carter temporarily halted U.S. arms sales to that country in the late 1970s.[118] Ottawa only discovered the repression in Guatemala after Inco announced it was pulling out of the Eximbal project in 1980.[119]

Canadian concern for human rights in Guatemala was short lived once the new U.S. Republican administration proved keen to support the Guatemalan regime. In the early 1980s Canada gave more than $100 million in Inter-American Development Bank (IDB) and IMF disbursements to Guatemala despite the regime's horrible human rights record.[120] During this same period, Canadian banks provided $180 million for "military and commercial interests who are pushing for control of the nation's forestry, agricultural and mineral resources, with the result of further marginalizing Guatemala's peasant population."[121]

Throughout the 1980s, Canadian-manufactured munitions and weapon components sold to our southern neighbours found their way into the hands of Guatemala's regime. On a couple of occasions, Ottawa even approved the direct sale of technology with military applications to Guatemala.[122]

From weapon sales to election support Canada helped the Guatemalan government fight a brutal civil war. In December 1985, Ottawa sent an official delegation to observe (some would say legitimate) Guatemala's election. They did so despite massive human rights violations taking place in the midst of a civil war.[123]

Unfortunately, siding with anti-democratic forces in Guatemala was nothing new for Canada's foreign policy establishment. In 1954, the U.S. overthrew the country's social democratic President Jacob Arbenz. Despite CCF questioning, the Liberal government of Louis St. Laurent refused to acknowledge U.S. involvement in the invasion of Guatemala. Canada also helped isolate Arbenz. In 1953, External Affairs refused the Guatemalan foreign minister's request for the two nations to open embassies in each other's countries. A similar request was denied again the next year.[124] Prior to Arbenz's 1950 election, a study by Canada's trade commissioner in Guatemala claimed that "businessmen and landowners do not have any cause to view the prospect of Arbenz as future president with any optimism.... He is unscrupulous, daring and ruthless, and not one to be allayed in his aims by bloodshed or killing. He is a drug addict and is especially egotistical and sadistic when under the influence of drugs or alcohol."[125]

After Arbenz's election the trade commissioner continued his attacks. "Unionism has been encouraged and no effort made to discourage labour leaders from bedeviling the United Fruit Company, foreign coffee interests and the foreign-owned railway which crosses the country."[126] Echoing the U.S. rationale for overthrowing Arbenz, in 1953 the Canadian ambassador to Mexico observed that "there are indications that the Soviet embassy here is the contact through which Communists in Guatemala are directed."[127]

Within a few years of the coup against Arbenz, Inco controlled the Lake Izabal nickel property. The company benefited from having John Foster Dulles, the U.S. secretary of state and mastermind of Washington's role in overthrowing Arbenz, on its board of directors.[128]

Canadian capital had other historic ties to Arbenz's overthrow. In the early 1900s Canadian capitalist Sir William Van Horne helped the United Fruit Company, which played an important role in getting rid of Arbenz, build the railway required to export bananas from the country. "Van Horne played a significant role in consolidating the financial control of Guatemala's resource economy in the hands of outside interests."[129] The foreign railway interests convinced a weak Guatemalan government to grant them a monopoly. Describing the negotiations, Van Horne explained, "we asked for everything we could think of, and we got all we asked for."[130] Still, the railway owners broke their promise to the government by charging Guatemalan industry among the highest freight rates in the world.[131] When Arbenz was overthrown the railway line Van Horne built was still controlled by the United Fruit Company and was Guatemala's only outlet to the Atlantic coast. Arbenz's government tried to complete a highway to the Atlantic to break United Fruit's transportation monopoly.[132]

El Salvador

Another country where Canada has had a long history of supporting anti-democratic forces is El Salvador. A January 1932 front page Vancouver Sun headline read: "El Salvador alive with Red Revolt." The subheadline noted: "Canadian destroyers from British Columbia to the rescue."[133] London informed Ottawa that a "communist" uprising was underway in El Salvador and there was "a possibility of danger to British Banks, railways and other British lives and property."[134] Ottawa was also concerned that the

Canadian-owned utility company, International Power, would be targeted by the rebels.[135] When the insurrection began, two Canadian naval vessels in the region were immediately directed to El Salvador's Atlantic Coast. Once there, Canadian troops landed.[136] (Prime Minister R.B. Bennett followed the operation closely, receiving as many as three reports a day from Canadian and British sources in the region.[137]) Canadian vessels arrived to discover a cautious El Salvadoran military regime led by Hernandez Martinez. But the junta was bolstered by the Royal Canadian Navy's presence. Canadian commander Victor Brodeur explained: "There is no doubt that the presence of the ships on the coast strengthened the President's hand considerably as he immediately started sending troops out of town. ...The landing of that platoon had a wonderful moral effect on his troops."[138] It wasn't only Canada's naval presence that helped get the soldiers out of their barracks. International Power lent Martinez money to pay his troops back pay.[139]

The military regime's response to the social upheaval was ferocious. Canada's "two-ship convoy would standby and observe one of the worst massacres of civilians in the history of the Americas."[140] Famous revolutionary leader Farabundo Marti (the namesake of El Salvador's social democratic party, the FMLN, which won the March 2009 presidential election) would ultimately be killed in the violence.

Even though there were many voices within this country calling on Ottawa to do otherwise, throughout the 1980s Canada once again supported state terrorism in El Salvador. Canada supported Inter-American Development Bank and IMF disbursements to El Salvador in 1981 despite the military junta's horrible human rights record. Most western European countries opposed the loans and even IMF staff refused to support them.[141] On the diplomatic front "Ottawa repeatedly sought to moderate the direct denunciations of El Salvador drafted by countries like France and Mexico."[142] In June 1984 Canada sent a delegation of election observers to supervise El Salvador's elections even though the left opposition parties were not able to participate. Ottawa's official observers pronounced the dubious election "fair", "well administered" and "conclusive".[143]

A few months after the electoral farce, Canada renewed bilateral aid to El Salvador.[144] "In support of President Duarte's desire to further improve the human rights record and to alleviate economic hardship," an External Affairs statement noted, "Canada has decided to resume aid to El Salvador ... it will provide encouragement to continued efforts to improve the situation in El Salvador."[145] A CIDA memo provided a more convincing explanation for the restoration of aid. "It should also be recognized that the

United States, which has accorded a very high priority to El Salvador, would welcome (and has encouraged) the restoration of Canadian assistance to that country."[146] Not surprisingly, the aid largely went to those who needed it the least. Salvadorian labour leaders complained "that Canadian aid was being controlled by the Salvadoran military and corrupt government officials."[147]

Two decades on and Salvadorian social movements continued to express frustration with Canadian diplomacy. In May 2007 it was reported that "busloads of people surrounded the Salvador del Mundo monument in front of the Canadian Embassy in San Salvador today to protest the Canadian Government's role [in] Central American mining, and specifically in the 29 mining projects currently active in El Salvador. The event was the culmination of the Central American Alliance against Metallic Mining conference held last weekend in Cabañas, El Salvador, where the Canadian Pacific Rim company is currently operating."[148]

Communities near Pacific Rim's planned mine were worried their land and health would be affected by a project that scientists claimed would contaminate local water supplies. With protests mounting and an election on the horizon, the Salvadoran government refused to issue Vancouver-based Pacific Rim the necessary permits to begin extraction. The company responded in late 2008 by suing (through a Nevada-based subsidiary) "the El Salvadorian government for millions of dollars under CAFTA-DR (Central America-Dominican Republic-United States Free Trade Agreement) for not granting the company a mining license."[149]

"Under their laws and through CAFTA, they are obligated to give us a permit, and if they don't they could face a very sizable CAFTA settlement," said the head of the company, Catherine McLeod-Seltzer.[150] Canadian bankers added to the pressure on the El Salvadoran government. John Hayes, an analyst at BMO Capital Markets, warned that "the thing we'll look for is what kind of response this gets from the government and whether they realize that you can't expect people to invest if they don't have some certainty of an outcome."[151]

Nicaragua

Support for military dictatorships in El Salvador and Guatemala was in stark contrast with Canadian diplomacy towards a neighbouring country. Unlike El Salvador and Guatemala, in the 1980s Nicaragua was governed by a political party working to redress the country's inequality and poverty. Unlike El Salvador and Guatemala, parties of all political persuasions were free to participate in elections. Yet unlike in El Salvador and Guatemala, Ottawa refused to send an official delegation to observe Nicaragua's 1984 election.[152] The reason? Despite their democratic credentials Canada did not support the Sandinista government.

Prior to the Sandinistas rise to power, Ottawa supported U.S. moves to thwart them. On the eve of the downfall of the four decade-long Somoza family dictatorship Canada supported a $66 million IDB loan to Nicaragua despite Sandinista opposition to the grant. Predictably, Anastasio Somoza took the money when he fled and the Sandinistas were forced to repay the loan.[153] A couple of weeks before the Sandinistas' victory in July 1979 Prime Minister Joe Clark endorsed a U.S. proposal to the OAS for a "peacekeeping force, made up mostly of U.S. troops, to be dispatched to Nicaragua to prevent the Sandinistas from taking power."[154] The proposal failed when no OAS members supported it.[155]

Once the Sandinistas were in office Ottawa held them to higher standards than previous Nicaraguan governments. In 1980 Canada's ambassador to Nicaragua, R. Douglas Sirrs, complained to a Costa Rican paper that the Sandinistas' literacy campaign had a Marxist flavor and they were moving "too far" to the left.[156] A few years later a new Canadian ambassador explained "it is just pathetic to see what five years of this regime [Sandinistas] has done for the country. Instead of helping the people to develop, it has resulted in sub-development."[157] Even though they were under assault from the U.S.-backed Contra rebels, who by any reasonable definition engaged in terrorism, including blowing up schools, illiteracy was reduced from 50 percent to 12 percent, polio was eliminated and measles as well as infant mortality rates were significantly decreased.[158]

When not criticizing the Sandinistas' domestic policies, Canadian diplomats found time to denounce their international ties. In the summer of 1984, Canadian ambassador to Panama, Francis Filleul, complained that "Nicaragua has been penetrated so badly by Cuba and other [eastern bloc] countries that it is destabilizing. It was not that the people of Nicaragua … chose to welcome the Russians and the Cubans. It was that the FSLN [Sandinistas] had gained control of the revolutionary movement and that was their policy."[159] A few months earlier, Secretary of State for External Affairs Allan MacEachen told a University of Ottawa audience that "we are dismayed by the increasing tendency toward authoritarianism [in Nicaragua]. Departures from professed non-alignment and support for insurgencies in neighbouring countries only adds to the risk of violence and impedes progress towards peaceful change." Referring to Nicaragua, not the U.S., he continued, "for Canada, no ideology justifies the export of violence."[160]

During most of the 1980s EDC provided unconditional financial support for transactions relating to Guatemala and Honduras, but not for Nicaragua.[161] Any Canadian assistance to Nicaragua was conditional upon adherence to "principles of political pluralism and non-intervention in the affairs of other countries." There was no similar condition placed on aid to El Salvador, Guatemala or Honduras.[162] Throughout the 1980s Honduras maintained its "priority" status for Canadian aid, even though the country openly harboured the U.S.-backed Contras, who were attacking Nicaragua. At one point, Ottawa financed a forestry road that turned out to be infrastructure for a major military base at Fort Mocoron. The road improved the Honduran army's mobility and is suspected to have been used by the Contras.[163]

While the RCMP and CSIS spied on Nicaragua solidarity groups "there seems to have been minimal CSIS interest in fundraising inside Canada for the Contra rebels in Nicaragua."[164] Canadian arms trader Manny Weigensberg sold the Contras more than $2 million worth of weapons (SAM missiles, RPG-7 rocket launchers and rifle bullets) through his company TransWorld Inc.[165] A Québec company, Propair Inc., sold the Contras two Caribou airplanes. The company's staff also maintained the planes at a known Contra base in El Salvador, taught mechanics how to maintain the Caribous and trained pilots to fly them. In both cases the RCMP investigated, but no charges were ever laid against Transworld and Propair because of loopholes in Canadian law regarding weapons purchased and shipped via third countries.[166]

Washington and the Contras, with some Canadian support, finally claimed victory against the Sandinistas in 1990. With the U.S. providing tens of millions of dollars to the political opposition and threatening to continue to back the Contra war, the Sandinistas were defeated in the 1990 election. In response, Canada significantly increased its aid to Nicaragua.[167]

Ottawa's hostility towards the Sandinistas (who were supported by a significant Canadian solidarity movement) has usually been explained as deference to Washington, but there's more to it than that. The Sandinistas toppled a Somoza regime that Ottawa and its corporate friends supported.[168] Just prior to Somoza's downfall in 1979, the Royal Bank held 15 percent ($42.8 million) of Nicaragua's private bank debt. On CBC's the Fifth Estate, Somoza explained "that the attitude of the Canadian bank has been very profitable for Nicaragua."[169] Canadian mining interests also supported

Somoza. In the final years of the dictatorship Toronto-based Noranda made millions annually from its El Setentrion gold mine in Nicaragua.[170] Upon seizing power the Sandinistas immediately nationalized the mine. Canadian mining companies worked with the Somoza familly for decades. In the mid-1940s Canadian mines paid hundreds of thousands of dollars a year into Somoza's secret bank accounts and supplied the strongman with weapons to fight an insurrection.[171] In 1947 the U.S. charge d'affaires in Managua wrote to the Canadian ambassador in Washington that "the rebels have a legitimate grievance against Canadian- and American-owned goldmines as they are, in a manner of speaking, the backbone of the Somoza regime."[172]

In the summer of 1947 Falconbridge's lawyer in Nicaragua, along with the company's headquarters in Toronto, worked out a deal with the U.S. State Department to save the first Anastasio Somoza and create a government of national unity.[173] As part of the agreement Somoza installed Mariano Vargas, Falconbridge's Nicaraguan lawyer, as vice president. This solidified relations between the company and dictator. For his part, Somoza was good to Falconbridge. The "National Guard was used to guarantee the union-free operation of their mines."[174]

In the late 1940s "despite External Affair's own reports, which had painted Somoza as a ruthless profiteer, the department continued to show a curious lack of concern for the fact that Canadian nationals working for two giant Canadian companies were intervening directly in the Nicaraguan civil war, on the dictator's side. Even six months later, when the FBI informed External Affairs that another Canadian, H.D. Adkins, was running guns to Somoza, the department kept its collective head in the sand."[175]

Panama

The conflicts in Nicaragua, El Salvador and Honduras throughout the 1980s provide part of the explanation for why the U.S. invaded Panama in December 1989. George Bush Sr. was not happy when Panamanian President Manuel Noriega, formerly close to the CIA, decided to support Central American-led peace negotiations. It seems Washington was of the opinion that the Central American peace process was something it should define. The U.S. quest to oust Noriega, which left 4,000 Panamanians dead, was endorsed by Ottawa.[176] Prime Minister Brian Mulroney said "we regret the use of force... but the United States was justified" in invading that country, which was effectively created by the U.S..[177] Parroting the U.S. justification, Mulroney called Noriega "a drug-running thug and assassin who looted his own country."[178] True, but many said some rotten things about Mulroney and that wouldn't make it okay for the U.S. to invade Canada. In addition, when Noriega was committing the worst of his abuses he was Washington's man. It is only when he failed to fall into line, particularly regarding the U.S.-backed war in Central America, that Washington and, by extension, Ottawa began to care about Noriega's human rights violations and drug-running.

To Ottawa's dismay the OAS (Canada was not officially a member until 1990) voted 20 to 1, with eight abstentions "to deeply regret the military intervention in Panama."[179] Despite opposition from Canadian unions, church and solidarity groups, Canada was the only country in the Americas, besides El Salvador, to support the U.S. invasion.[180] "The United States found itself virtually isolated at the United Nations ... as country after country criticized the U.S. invasion of Panama. Canada, Britain and El Salvador were the only countries to speak in favour of Washington's military action against strongman Manuel Noriega."[181]

Costa Rica
In 1917 the Royal Bank loaned $200,000 to an unpopular Costa Rican dictator, Federico Tinoco. The money was handed over just as he was about to flee the country. A prosaic Costa Rican diplomatic note explained: "When that business was transacted, the soil of the fatherland had already been sprinkled with the blood of the defenders of its liberties. When that transaction was made, the government was already so discredited that it could not obtain a single resolution of support from its very employees ... When that transaction was made, the teachers and pupils of the public schools and colleges had already run over the streets in clamorous protest. When that transaction was made, people in rebellious mood had already reduced to ashes the principle bulwark of that Government ...When that transaction was made, there was nearly no home in Costa that was not a revolutionary Centre ...When that transaction was made, it was already known by everybody that the men with whom the Royal Bank had entered into negotiations were getting their baggage ready to sail away."[182]

The new government refused to honour the debt. Despite having signed a treaty that said it would abide by the country's commercial laws and not resort to diplomatic action the Royal Bank tried to intimidate the Costa Rican government with threats of imperial retribution.[183] "In 1921," *Canadian Gunboat Diplomacy* notes, "in Costa Rica, [Canadian vessels] Aurora, Patriot and Patrician helped the Royal Bank of Canada satisfactorily settle an outstanding claim with the government of that country."[184]

In 1948 Canadian businessmen, who had invested in the country's mines and banks, played a leading role in setting up and running an intelligence operation that helped topple Costa Rica's left-leaning government.[185] "Alexander Murray, a Canadian World War Two secret agent, was heavily involved in Costa Rica's late 1940s toppling of leftist governments. Murray was in contact with the Canadian government throughout the 1946 to 1948 period with Ottawa considering Murray important enough to merit a visit from Trade and Commerce Minister James MacKinnon during his stay in Costa Rica in 1946. Murray corresponded with MacKinnon's aide for two years after the visit."[186]

Brazil

During the first half of the 20th century, Brazilian Traction (otherwise known as Brascan or the Light) was Canada's largest foreign investment. At its high point in the 1940s, the company employed almost 50,000 Brazilians.[187] Trolleys and electricity production were the company's backbone, but the company also owned a sardine cannery, fishing boats, a tin mine, a brewery, banks as well as real estate.[188] Possibly the biggest firm in Latin America by the end of the 1950s, Brascan was commonly known as the "the Canadian octopus" since its tentacles reached into so many areas of Brazil's economy.[189] Between 1918 and 1952 more than $200 million was taken out of this underdeveloped country and sent to Canada.[190]

As Brascan sucked cash from Brazil, the company also squeezed local competitors. "The Monopoly created by the Light Company inhibited Brazilian initiatives. ... [It] slowly absorbed the local competition."[191] Putting the squeeze on local businesses went hand and hand with poor labour practices. In a confidential September 1923 letter between Brascan's Rio and Toronto offices, company officials admitted they paid their workers poorly even by Brazilian standards. The letter further noted that "our secret agents have just informed us that [some] of our men are taking part in meetings at which an early strike is advocated and we are all becoming somewhat concerned over the situation."[192]

The company was well connected in Ottawa. The initial group of investors included Frederic Nicholls, the vice vonsul for Argentina and Senator George Albertus.[193] Henry Borden, the nephew of former Prime Minister Robert Borden, became Brazilian Traction president in 1946 ("he was like a son to Robert").[194] A decade later, Mitchell Sharp went from deputy minister in the Department of Trade and Commerce to vice-president of Brazilian Traction.[195] He then returned to Ottawa, became an MP and was appointed minister of trade and commerce, minister of finance and then secretary of state for external affairs in various Liberal governments.[196] A colleague, Minister of Trade and Commerce Robert Winters, left politics in 1968 to become president of Brazilian Traction.[197]

The Brazilians were aware of the company's political clout in Ottawa. In June 1940 Brazil's foreign affairs minister bypassed the British ambassador (who had been Canada's representative in Brazil) and went directly to a senior official of Brascan to request that Canada and Brazil establish diplomatic relations.[198] Brascan's political clout helped the company get public support. Brascan was the first company to receive World Bank financing in Latin America. In 1949 the company was given $75 million and received a total of $120 million from the World Bank through 1959.[199] In the late 1960s CIDA's financing for improvements in Brazil's electrical system went more or less directly to Brascan.[200] "[CIDA] is pumping millions into Brazil for development, coincidentally, of hydroelectric power … The foreign aid money goes formally to the Brazilian government, which is responsible for the generation of electric power, but the transmission and distribution of electric energy in the industrial regions of Brazil is the responsibility of Light, which is therefore the ultimate benefactor of that government 'aid.'"[201] In 1974 EDC lent Brazil $40 million, "$26.5 million of which went to the Sao Paulo Tramway, a Brascan subsidiary."[202]

The company put its extensive Brazilian political connections to good use. "To extend the time limit on its original telephone concession in Sao Paulo from 1950 to 1990, the company engaged a former president of Brazil, who fought the legal battle for it through several judicial levels up to the Supreme Court, where in 1923, the judges — appointees of that ex-president — extended the concession, contrary to the stipulations of the original contract."[203] Two decades later Brascan blocked a competitor from entering Rio's electricity market. "In Rio de Janeiro the company was able to prevent the construction of a competing electrical facility through political influence and straight bribery."[204]

Brascan had influence with pro-business politicians and the company actively supported Brazil's right wing. Antonio Gallotti, who was a top executive of Brascan's Brazilian operations for a couple decades, was secretary for international affairs in the Brazilian fascist party, Acao Integralista. Gallotti quit the party in 1938, but began working as a lawyer for Brascan in 1932.[205]

Like its earlier spying on union activists the company appears to have spied on politicians as well. In 1957 the Canadian ambassador to Brazil stated: "During a recent conversation, a senior executive of the Light told me that his office had been keeping track of the number of Brazilian politicians who've been officially invited to visit the USSR and that during the last 18 months the list of visitors had grown to some 300."[206]

Spying was part of Brascan's role in beating back rising economic nationalism in the late 1950s and early 60s. A study of the company noted that "Gallotti had to struggle hard against the nationalization policies of Kubischek (Brazilian president 1955-60) and especially Joao Goulart. Gallotti doesn't hide his participation in the moves and operations that led to the coup d'etat against Goulart in 1964."[207] Just prior to the coup against Goulart, Brazilian Traction president Grant Glassco remarked that "more and more, the various agencies of the government were infiltrated by extremists, many of whom were Communist inspired and directed."[208] After the elected government was overthrown Glassco stated: "The new government of Brazil is...made up of men of proven competence and integrity. The President, Humberto Castello Branco, commands the respect of the entire nation."[209]

Putting a stop to the Goulart government, which made it more difficult for companies to remit profits from Brazil, was good business.[210] After the 1964 coup, the Financial Post noted "the price of Brazilian Traction common shares almost doubled overnight with the change of government from an April 1 low of $1.95 to an April 3 high of $3.06."[211] Between 1965 and 1974, Brascan drained Brazil of another $342 million (out of total Brazilian profits of $648 million).[212] When Robert Winters, Brazilian Traction's Canadian president, was asked why the company's profits grew so rapidly in the late 1960s his response was simple: "The Revolution."[213]

The post-coup military regime succumbed to popular demands by nationalizing parts of Brascan's operations. But they did so amicably. They bought shares of Brascan for $5.90, more than three times the stock price before the coup. When Brascan sold its final stake in the country to the military government it asked for a lump sum payment. The company wanted to "get all the money out of Brazil quickly and cleanly before the nationalistic backlash, certain to surface after the sale was announced."[214]

Following Brascan (and Washington's) lead, Prime Minister Pearson failed to publicly condemn the overthrow of President João Goulart.[215] "The Canadian reaction to the military coup of 1964 was careful, polite and allied with American rhetoric."[216] As Canadian political opposition to the military regime's human rights violations grew, Ottawa downplayed the gravity of the human rights situation. In a June 1972 memo to the embassy in Rio, the Director of the Latin American Division at Foreign Affairs stated: "We have, however, done our best to avoid drawing attention to this problem [human rights violations] because we are anxious to build a vigorous and healthy relationship with Brazil. We hope that in the future these unfortunate events and publicity, which damages the Brazilian image in Canada, can be avoided."[217] A year later, an External Affairs memo called for strengthened relations with Brazil's right-wing military regime. Canada should "take fullest advantage of opportunities offered by significant pace of Brazilian development and initiatives."[218]

Chile

Thousands of refugees from the Pinochet (1973-90) dictatorship found asylum in Canada, leaving many people with the impression that Canada was somehow sympathetic to Chile's Left. This view of Canada's relationship to Chile is as far from the truth as Baffin Island is from Tierra del Fuego.

In 1964 Eduardo Frei defeated openly Marxist candidate Salvador Allende in Chile's presidential elections. Worried about growing support for socialism, Ottawa gave $8.6 million to Frei's Chile, its first aid to a South American country.[219] When Allende won the next election Canadian assistance disappeared. EDC also refused to finance Canadian exports to Chile, which contributed to a reduction in trade between the two countries.[220] This suspension of EDC credits led Chile's Minister of Finance to criticize Canada's "banker's attitude".[221] But suspending bilateral assistance and export insurance was not enough. In 1972 Ottawa joined Washington in voting to cut off all money from the IMF to the Chilean government.[222] (When Allende was first elected all western banks, including Canada's, withdrew from Chile.[223]) From economic asphyxiation to diplomatic isolation Ottawa's policy towards Allende's Chile was clear. After he won office in 1970 Allende invited Pierre Trudeau to visit Santiago. Ottawa refused "for fear of alienating rightist elements in Chile and elsewhere."[224]

Days after the September 11, 1973, coup against Allende, Andrew Ross, Canada's ambassador to Chile cabled External Affairs: "Reprisals and searches have created panic atmosphere affecting particularly expatriates including the riffraff of the Latin American Left to whom Allende gave asylum ... the country has been on a prolonged political binge under the elected Allende government and the junta has assumed the probably thankless task of sobering Chile up."[225] Within three weeks of the coup, Canada recognized Augusto Pinochet's military junta. Ross stated: "I can see no useful purpose to withholding recognition unduly. Indeed, such action might even tend to delay Chile's eventual return to the democratic process."[226] Pinochet stepped down 17 years later.

Diplomatic support for Pinochet led to economic assistance. Just after the coup Canada voted for a $22 million Inter American Development Bank loan "rushed through the bank with embarrassing haste."[227] Ottawa immediately endorsed sending $95 million from the IMF to Chile and supported renegotiating the country's debt held by the Paris Club.[228] After refusing to provide credits to the elected government, on October 2nd, 1973, EDC announced it was granting $5 million in credit to Chile's central bank to purchase six Twin Otter aircraft from De Havilland.[229] Around the same time, the Canadian Defence Quarterly lauded the Twin Otter's capabilities in carrying troops to and from short makeshift strips.[230] Right after the coup the World Bank chose Noranda Inc. to assess Chile's mining laws. Noranda was chosen because it was a Canadian rather than American corporation.[231] Noranda was also the first foreign company to announce plans to invest in Pinochet's Chile.[232] El Mercurio newspaper noted that "the agreement reached with Noranda mines, in the present national and international conjunction, reiterates the confidence that foreign investors are demonstrating towards our country."[233]

By early 1978, Canadian support for the coup d'etat was significant. It included:

• Support for $810 million in multilateral loans with Canada's share amounting to about $40 million.

• Five EDC facilities worth between $15 and $30 million.

• Two Canadian debt re-schedulings for Chile, equivalent to additional loans of approximately $5 million.

• Twenty loans by Canadian chartered banks worth more than $100 million, including a 1977 loan by Toronto Dominion to DINA (Pinochet's secret police) to purchase equipment.

• Direct investments by Canadian companies valued at nearly $1 billion.[234]

In the late 1970s a magazine noted that "Canadian economic relations, in the form of bank loans, investments and government supported financial assistance have helped consolidate the Chilean dictatorship and, by granting it a mantle of respectability and financial endorsation, have encouraged its continued violation of human rights."[235]

Ottawa continued to support Pinochet into the 1980s. Canada voted yes on a major World Bank plan for Chile in June 1985 even though the project was opposed by Scandinavian representatives on human rights grounds and by Italy and Belgium (both representing a number of other countries) for technical reasons.[236] Ottawa supported Pinochet because Washington helped put him in place but also because Canadian capitalists supported the dictator. At its annual general meeting in Toronto on May 9, 1996, Peter Munk, chairman of Barrick Gold, praised Pinochet for "transforming Chile from a wealth-destroying socialist state to a capital-friendly model that is being copied around the world."[237] Concerning Pinochet's human rights record Munk explained that "they can put people in jail, I have no comment on that, I think that may be true ... I think [the end justifies the means] because it brought wealth to an enormous number of people. If you ask somebody who is in jail, he'll say no. But that's the wonderful thing about our world; we can have the freedom to disagree."[238] It's no surprise that Munk was fond of Pinochet. In the last days of his dictatorship, gold, silver and copper mines were effectively exempted from most taxes and royalties.[239] Not one Canadian mining company paid any income tax in Chile during the 1990s due to the favourable tax code and "measures taken by mining companies to defraud the Chilean state."[240]

Barrick Gold's Pascua Lama mine in Chile was among the world's most controversial mining projects. To access nearly 17 million ounces of gold and huge amounts of silver, Barrick planned to remove several glaciers from a 5,500 metres (18,000 feet) high mountain along the Argentinian border. Fierce opposition put a stop to plans to move the glaciers. Nevertheless, Barrick's exploration activities significantly depleted the glaciers near the mine site, contradicting assurances in their environmental assessment.[241] By 2008 dozens of miners had already died on the Pascua Lama project and Barrick had released little information about the circumstances of these fatal accidents.[242] As with many gold mines, the Pascua Lama project planned to use cyanide to break the gold from the rock. For each ounce of gold, 30 tonnes of rock must be extracted and bathed in cyanide, which is highly toxic. If leaked from a mine site or spilled during transportation, cyanide can quickly cause toxicity problems for an entire ecosystem. Inhabitants of the Huasco Valley worried that their water source would be poisoned by the mining operations. Mining activity had already released large dust plumes. In a letter to the Chilean president, a community group from the Huasco Valley explained: "The air we breathe, the water we drink and the land we cultivate have more value than the gold coveted by multinationals."[243]

A delegation to Chile from Manitoba's Black River First Nation described the attitude of indigenous people in the area: "The Diaguita People are very much opposed to the Pascua Lama mining project as they are concerned about the effects this project will have on the environment, the impact on their cultural way of life, as well as the social fabric of their communities... As one leader informed our delegation, he said this project as it stands today, 'it is nothing more than cultural genocide of the Diaguita People and if Barrick Gold is allowed to continue the project in its present form, the Diaguita will become extinct."[244]

Barrick responded to people opposing the mine — as many as ten thousand Chileans marched against their project in June 2006 — with a major TV ad campaign championing "responsible mining." The company also put $10 million US into local educational and cultural endeavours.[245] Barrick gained important support for its Pascua Lama operations during a July 2007 trip to Chile by Prime Minister Stephen Harper. He visited the company's Chilean office and said: "Barrick follows Canadian standards of corporate social responsibility."[246] Harper was greeted with signs from mine opponents stating "Harper go home" and "Canada: What's HARPERing here?"

Other Canadian companies, with Ottawa's support, participated in a number of environmentally and socially destructive projects in Chile. With $17 million in EDC financing, Alstom Power Canada had a major stake in the Ralco dam.[247] Along Chile's Biobio River, the planned dam would flood 3,400 hectares of land, displace 600 (400 of them Pehuenche indigenous people) and threaten the existence of dozens of animals and aquatic species. Three cases against the dam were brought to Chilean courts.[248]

Further south, Toronto-based Brookfield Asset Management Inc. (Brascan's successor) led a consortium, including a $364 million US investment from the Canadian Pension Plan and $356 million from the pension plan for British Columbia public sector workers, pushing to industrialize Chile's Patagonia region, one of the planet's greatest environmental treasures.[249] Largely to service power-hungry mining and industrial companies, the Brookfield consortium was building the world's longest (2,000 kilometres) high-tension power line from a series of then-yet-unapproved dams in Patagonia to Chile's central and northern industrial centres. The dams were expected to flood 60 square kilometres, lead to a loss of fertility downstream and destroy a number of different species. But it's the power lines that were likely to have the most damaging effect on the environment. The power line to Santiago could unlock a slew of hydroelectric and industrial projects throughout Patagonia.[250]

"This kind of project could never be implemented in a full-fledged democracy," explained Juan Pablo Orrego of Ecosistemas. "Our country is still under a constitutional, political, and financial checkmate to democracy which was put in place during the [Pinochet] military dictatorship and empowers the private sector."[251]

Colombia

In the latter part of the first decade of the 21st century Canada seemed closest diplomatically to Latin America's most repressive state, despite the growing and widespread move to the left among the vast majority of the region's governments. A July 2007 visit to Colombia by the Canadian Prime Minister was described by the Economist magazine as giving President Alvaro Uribe "a vote of confidence at a time when he [was] being assailed both in Washington and at home."[252] At the time, Uribe's government was plagued by a scandal tying numerous top officials to Colombia's brutal paramilitaries. Dozens of Uribe-aligned congresspeople were implicated and the president's cousin was among those who had been thrown in jail.

Under Uribe's stewardship Colombia's already poor human rights record deteriorated. In August 2008 the Los Angeles Times reported that "in 2007 there were 329 extrajudicial killings by the Colombian military and police, an increase from 223 in 2006. A June 2007 study found that of 900 cases of alleged murder involving uniformed soldiers and police only four had won convictions. Extrajudicial killings by Colombian military and police over a five-year period ending June 2006 was 50 percent higher than during the preceding comparable period."[253]

Between 2002 and 2007, 13,634 Colombians were killed in the country's civil war, up 67 percent from the previous five years. According to a human rights report presented to the U.N. in September 2008, the state was responsible for the majority of the human rights violations either directly or through government support for paramilitary groups. The report also noted that despite a widely publicized demobilization more than 9,000 paramilitaries remained active in the country.[254]

Uribe's terrible human rights record did not stop Harper from signing a free-trade agreement with Colombia (not yet ratified as this book went to press). It did, however, give pause to much of the U.S. political class. To pressure Democratic congressman who opposed a trade agreement with Colombia, President George W. Bush trotted out Harper's diplomatic support for Uribe. "I like to quote Prime Minister Stephen Harper," Bush said. "He said the biggest fear in South America is not the leader in Venezuela, but the biggest fear for stability is if the United States Congress rejects the free trade agreement with Colombia." Bush misquoted Harper. What he actually said was "Colombia needs its democratic friends to lean forward and give them a chance at partnership and trade with North America.... [I am] very concerned that some in the United States seem unwilling to do that... if the U.S. turns its back on its friends in Colombia, this will set back our cause far more than any Latin American dictator could ever hope to achieve."[255] In May 2008 Michael Michaud, leader of U.S. congressional Democrats opposed to a free-trade agreement with Colombia, responded to Harper and Bush. "I don't buy Prime Minister Harper's argument," Michaud told a reporter. "The president of Colombia, if he wants to truly treat the workers fairly and deal with labour rights and low standards, he can pretty much do that now. He doesn't need a trade agreement to deal with that."[256] In a letter to all four political parties seven Democratic members of Congress warned Canada against a free trade agreement with Colombia.

Harper's support for the Colombian president put more than just diplomatic pressure on the Democrats. The Canada-Colombia accord gave Canadian farmers preferential access to the USA's third largest market for wheat exports in Latin America, increasing pressure from farm lobbyists on opponents of a U.S.- Colombia free-trade accord. This pressure on American opponents of an FTA was one reason Uribe desperately wanted to sign a trade deal with Canada.

The Canada-Colombia trade agreement was opposed by most of that country's organized peasantry and labour. Embassy magazine reported that the "vast majority — about 80 percent — of Colombian goods already enter Canada tariff-free. So then who will benefit?... Canadian exports to Colombia are charged an average 12 percent tariff. Agricultural goods, in particular, are hit with 80 percent tariffs. With a free trade agreement, Canadian farmers will be able to inundate Colombian markets with subsidized meat, fruits, vegetables and grains. It doesn't take a rocket scientist to realize that this will not have the positive impact the Conservatives are advocating, but could in all likelihood severely damage Colombia's agricultural industry. And when that happens, guess what Colombian farmers will turn to? Another crop: drugs."[257]

Ottawa's trade deal with Colombia was part of a long-standing push to liberalize that country's economy. In 1997 Ottawa began an $11 million project to re-write Colombia's mining code. CIDA worked on the project with a Colombian law firm, Martinez Córdoba and Associates, that represents multinational companies, and the Canadian Energy Research Institute (CERI), an industry think-tank based at the University of Calgary.[258] They spent a couple years canvassing mining companies to find out what the industry wanted from new mining regulations. A representative from Greystar Corp., which was involved in the effort for nearly two years, explained how they provided "input that reflected the mining industry's point of view as to what was important in such legislation to encourage mining."[259]

Once completed the CERI/CIDA proposal was submitted to Colombia's Department of Mines and Energy and became law in August 2001. "The new code flexibilised environmental regulations, diminished labour guarantees for workers and opened the property of afro-Colombian and indigenous people to exploitation," explained Francisco Ramirez, president of SINTRAMINERCOL, Colombia's State Mine Workers Union.[260] "The CIDA-backed code also contains some articles that are simply unheard of in other countries," added Ramirez. "If a mining company has to cut down trees before digging, they can now export that timber for 30 years with a total exemption on taxation."[261] The new code also reduced the royalty rate companies pay the government to 0.4 percent from 10 percent for mineral exports above 3 million tonnes per year and from 5 percent for exports below 3 million tonnes. In addition, the new code increased the length of mining concessions from 25 years to 30 years, with the possibility that concessions can be tripled to 90 years.[262]

Canadian officials were happy with the results. According to CIDA's summary of the project, "Canadian energy and mining sector companies with an interest in Colombia will benefit from the development of a stable, consistent and familiar operating environment in this resource-rich developing economy." Or as Maclean's put it, "from the beginning, the aim [of CIDA's mining project] was far from altruistic."[263]

Canadian energy corporations also benefited from these CIDA-backed liberalization efforts. Canadian companies received 73 percent of new exploration contracts after the implementation of a CIDA-supported petroleum legislation reform, part of the larger reforms to resource regulations.[264]

Canadian assistance has been used to reform the country's non-resource sector as well. In 1995, CIDA provided a $4 million grant to "contribute to the liberalization process of the telecommunications sector in Colombia."[265] Ottawa-based Destrier Management Consultants used the money for training seminars, workshops and advisors. Within a few years Canadian companies operated Colombia's leading cellular phone provider and installed a large proportion of the country's phone lines.[266] Asad Ismi explained that in 2003 Brampton-based "Nortel Networks helped bring about the liquidation of

TELECOM, Colombia's biggest telecommunications company, and the likely privatization of its successor. ... With the privatization, however, 10,000 unionized telecommunications workers lost their jobs that year, and over 70 trade unionists were murdered by paramilitaries for demonstrating against the privatization."[267] On top of pushing a liberalization agenda Ottawa gave direct support to Nortel's operations in Colombia. In 2003 EDC provided Nortel with a $300 million line of credit for its Colombian operations.[268] Nortel was one of many companies EDC supported in that country.[269] A February 1997 Foreign Affairs report cited Colombia as EDC's largest market for its Foreign Investment Insurance policies, "particularly in the oil and gas and telecom sectors."[270]

EDC was involved in Colombia despite widespread state-sponsored human rights violations. In fact, Colombia's instability explains EDC's ties to that country. In 1997, Foreign Affairs noted that "the on-going decertification of Colombia by the United States, which has frozen export credits from the U.S. export-import bank, has opened opportunities for Canadian financial entities such as the EDC and Canada's private banks."[271] By 2007 Canada had some $6 billion invested in Colombia, mostly in the resource and service sectors.[272] During his 2007 trip Harper told reporters, "Canadian expertise complements Colombian economic strength in areas such as mining, engineering, and oil and gas."[273] More than 20 oil and gas companies from Alberta were active in the country in 2009.[274] Canadian companies, for instance, ran Colombia's most important oil pipeline and its two largest natural gas pipelines.[275]

Canadian investment in Colombia, especially in the resource sector, was intimately tied to human rights abuses. A study on "The Presence of Canadian Petroleum Companies in Colombia," found that "an avalanche of new contracts and new Canadian companies" entered Colombia in 2000 "at a moment when the internal conflict has intensified particularly in traditional, indigenous-occupied areas, and where resistance to their projects is significant."[276]

In the late 1990s Calgary-based Enbridge operated the OCENSA pipeline jointly with Toronto-based TransCanada Pipelines. Both companies owned a 17.5 percent share of the pipeline along with shares held by British Petroleum, Total and The Strategic Transaction Company. Until 1997 the OCENSA consortium contracted Defence Systems Colombia (a British firm) for security purposes. According to Amnesty International: "What is disturbing is that OCENSA/DSC's security strategy reportedly relies heavily on paid informants whose purpose is to covertly gather intelligence information' on the activities of the local population in the communities through which the pipeline passes and to identify possible 'subversives' within those communities. What is even more disturbing is that this intelligence information is then reportedly passed by OCENSA to the Colombian military who, together with their paramilitary allies, have frequently targeted those considered subversive for extrajudicial execution and disappearance. ...The passing of intelligence information to the Colombian military may have contributed to subsequent human rights violations." Amnesty added that OCENSA and DSC purchased military equipment for the notoriously violent 14th Brigade of the Colombian army.[277]

In the late 1990s another Canadian resource company, Conquistador Mines, was accused of spurring human rights violations in Colombia. A 1997 Canadian union and church delegation to Colombia concluded that "the presence of Conquistador Mines and its interest in the south of Bolivar appears to have encouraged the murder of local community leaders and the massive displacement of peasant miners and their families."[278]

Two other Canadian companies, BFC Construction and Agra-Monenco, were linked to human rights violations in the northeastern department of Córdoba. With $18.2 million from EDC the companies' Urra dam submerged over 7,400 hectares, including old-growth forest as well as the lands and homes of 411 families, all of whom were without individual legal land titles, only having collective indigenous land rights. About 2,800 people were forcibly resettled to make way for the Canadian companies' project and a further 70,000 people were directly impacted. Predictably the community resisted the dam. According to Amnesty International, six indigenous people protesting the project were killed and ten additional members of the community were disappeared by paramilitary and guerrilla forces.[279]

While Canadian investors contributed to Colombia's dirty war, so did Canadian arms manufacturers. In the late 1990s the Department of National Defence sold 33 Huey helicopters to the U.S. State Department, which added machine guns and sent them to the Colombian police and military.[280] The Huey sale followed a decision by Ottawa to allow Bell Helicopter Textron Canada (BHTC) to sell 12 helicopters directly to the Colombian air force and police. "The Chrétien government has approved a $65-million deal under which a Mirabel, Que., company will sell transport helicopters labelled as 'civilian aircraft' to Colombia's armed forces. Under the secret accord between Bell Helicopter Textron (Canada) and the Colombian defence ministry" that country's military got 12 Bell-212 helicopters, a type of aircraft that was "widely used by the U.S. military in the 1970s in counter-insurgency operations in Vietnam."[281] Not only did Ottawa allow helicopter sales to Colombia's military, it promoted them. A February 1999 "guide for Canadian exporters and investors issued by the Canadian embassy in Bogota provides details of how the Canadian government is promoting new opportunities and further sales in the aviation field to Colombia's police and armed forces."[282]

As part of its "role in the fight against drug traffickers" Canada also supplied intelligence gathering equipment to Colombia in the early 1990s.[283] In 1990 Canada began a $2 million program to provide intelligence equipment and bomb detectors to the Colombian Departamento Adminitrativo De Securidad. At that time Colombia's leading news magazine, Semana, suggested that Canada was working with the U.S. in a hegemonic project in the region.[284]

According to one author, Canada also sent soldiers to Colombia. Nous étions invincibles, a book by a former JTF2 soldier, describes his mission to the Colombian jungle to rescue NGO and church workers "because FARC guerillas threatened the peace in the region."[285] The Canadian soldiers were unaware that they were transporting the son of a Colombian leader, which prompted the FARC to give chase for a couple days. On two different occasions the Canadian forces came under fire from FARC guerrillas.[286] Two Canadian soldiers were hit in the firefight and immediately after the operation one of the wounded soldiers left the army with post-traumatic stress disorder.[287] Ultimately the Canadians were saved by U.S. helicopters, as the JTF2 mission was part of a U.S. initiative.[288]

Venezuela

The contrast is stark between Ottawa's relations with Colombia, the region's worst human rights abuser, and Venezuela, the government most aggressively combating social inequity. Since electing a government led by Hugo Chavez in 1998, Venezuela has been on the receiving end of U.S.-backed attempts to destabilize it and Canada tacitly supported the U.S. campaign to replace the government of Venezuela.

In April 2002 a military coup took Chavez prisoner and imposed an unelected government. It only lasted two days, before popular demonstrations, a split within the army and international condemnation returned the elected government. While most Latin American leaders condemned the coup, Canadian diplomats were silent. "In the Venezuelan coup [of] 2002, Canada maintained a low profile, probably because it was sensitive to the United States ambivalence towards Venezuelan president Hugo Chavez."[289]

It was particularly hypocritical of Ottawa to accept the coup. Only a year earlier, during the Summit of the Americas in Québec City, Jean Chrétien's Liberals made a big show of the new Organization of American States "democracy clause" that was supposed to commit the hemisphere to electoral democracy.

Eight months after the coup, the Venezuelan opposition renewed its campaign to oust Chavez by sabotaging the oil industry and closing their businesses. In the midst of the upheaval, Foreign Affairs Minister Bill Graham simply asked both sides to resume dialogue, never stating Canada's opposition to any government that gained power undemocratically. But, growing social reforms in Venezuela increased Ottawa's ire. While the NDP called on the Liberal government to invite Chavez for an official visit, the president was passed over in favour of the leader of a U.S.-funded opposition group.

In January 2005, Foreign Affairs invited Maria Corina Machado to Ottawa. Machado was in charge of Súmate, an organization at the forefront of anti-Chavez political campaigns. Just prior to her invitation, Súmate led the unsuccessful campaign to recall Chavez through a referendum in August 2004. Before that, Machado's name appeared on a list of people who endorsed the 2002 coup, for which she faced charges of treason. She denied signing the now-infamous "Carmona decree" that dissolved the National Assembly and Supreme Court and suspended the elected government, the Attorney General, Comptroller General, governors as well as mayors elected during Chavez's administration. It also annulled land reforms and increases in royalties paid by oil companies.

Canada also helped finance Súmate. According to disclosures made in response to a question by NDP Foreign Affairs critic Alexa Mcdonnough, Canada gave Súmate $22,000 in 2005-06.[290] Minister of International Cooperation José Verner explained that "Canada considered Súmate to be an experienced NGO with the capability to promote respect for democracy, particularly a free and fair electoral process in Venezuela."[291]

Canadian government-funded NGOs have also been involved in "democracy promotion" work in Venezuela. Ottawa's favourite Latin American think tank, the Canadian Foundation for the Americas (FOCAL) received $95,000 from the U.S. government's National Endowment for Democracy to do "democracy promotion" work in Venezuela.[292]

In October 2006 Canada sided with the U.S. in a diplomatic row with Venezuela over the Western Hemisphere's Security Council seat. The U.S. and Canada backed the notorious human rights violator Guatemala, while Venezuela was seen as a protest vote by developing countries fed up with U.S. policy.

When Chavez was reelected with 63 percent of the vote two months later, 32 members of the OAS supported a resolution to congratulate him on the victory. Ottawa was the only nation to join Washington in opposing a message of congratulations for an election monitored by the OAS.[293] Just after Chavez's reelection U.S. Assistant Secretary of State for Hemispheric Affairs, Thomas Shannon, called Canada "a country that can deliver messages that can resonate in ways that sometimes our messages don't for historical or psychological reasons."[294] Seven months later, Harper toured South America, "to show [the region] that Canada functions and that it can be a better model than Venezuela," in the words of a high-level Foreign Affairs official.[295] During the trip, Harper and his entourage made a number of comments critical of the Venezuelan government.

If Ottawa were serious about its stated goal of fighting global poverty, one would assume that Venezuela's successes on this front would be lauded. Instead, both Liberal and Conservative governments have been antagonistic towards a country that has significant economic relations with Canada (Venezuela sells oil to eastern Canada). Ottawa's antagonism towards Chavez is motivated by a desire to support Washington, but is also being driven by Canadian business interests. In 2001 the Venezuelan National Guard seized Vancouver-based Vanessa Ventures' gold project, prompting the company to spend "seven years and hundreds of thousands of dollars in legal fees on nearly a dozen legal proceedings before unsympathetic Venezuelan courts to claim more than $181-million it says it invested in the mining camp."[296] In early 2007 Venezuela forced private oil companies to become minority partners with the state oil company, prompting Calgary-based PetroCanada to sell its portion of an oil project.[297] And "Gold Reserve Inc. has seen its share price get punished by the uncertainty surrounding mining projects in that country and the possibility that Hugo Chavez's government will take over their deposits."[298] But the move that received the most attention from the business press was the government's legal maneuvers over the Las Cristinas gold mine, Venezuela's largest gold deposit. The stock of Toronto-based Crystallex, which had the rights to operate Las Cristinas, plunged and in December 2008 "Crystallex International filed a letter with Venezuela's government claiming that the country's denial of approvals to mine the Las Cristinas gold deposit goes against a treaty between Canada and Venezuela."[299]

In a August 2007 letter to the Financial Times headlined "Stop Chavez' Demagoguery Before it is Too Late", leading Canadian capitalist, Peter Munk wrote: "Your editorial 'Chavez in Control' was way too benign a characterization of a dangerous dictator — the latest of a type who takes over a nation through the democratic process, and then perverts or abolishes it to perpetuate his own power ... aren't we ignoring the lessons of history and forgetting that the dictators Hitler, Mugabe, Pol Pot and so on became heads of state by a democratic process? ... autocratic demagogues in the Chavez mode get away with [it] until their countries become totalitarian regimes like Nazi Germany, the Soviet Union, or Slobadan Milosevic's Serbia ... Let us not give President Chavez a chance to do the same step-by-step transformation of Venezuela."[300] Earlier, Munk, who heads Barrick, the world's largest gold mining company, was quoted by the Canadian Press saying he'd prefer to invest in the (Taliban controlled) western part of Pakistan than in Venezuela or Bolivia. "If I had the choice to put my money in one of the Latin American countries run by (Bolivian President) Evo Morales or Venezuelan President Hugo Chavez — I know where I'd put my buck," said Munk, referring to moves to nationalize resources to the detriment of foreign investors.[301]

Beyond seeing Venezuela's reforms as a threat to their profit-making possibilities and as an example that might be replicated elsewhere, Munk and other leading Canadian businessman had ties to Venezuela's elite. The country's richest man, Gustavo Cisneros was a member of Barrick Gold's International Advisory Board. Cisneros also had ties to Québec's most prominent family, the Desmarais. Les Voltigeurs de Québec, the Canadian Army's oldest French-speaking regiment, named Cisneros an international friend. On hand for the celebration was Jean Chrétien as well as Power Corporation's André Desmarais, who is also a member of Les Voltigeurs.[302]

Discussion

No other region in the world provides a clearer example of Canadian corporate integration with U.S. interests than Mexico, Central and South America. Just as Canadian capitalists back home are partners with U.S. and other foreign-owned corporations — not junior partners, but owners of key sectors of the economy — they play a similar role from Mexico to Chile. Mirroring the Canadian economy, in most respects Canadian-based corporations act independently in this region, even competing with U.S.

interests. But the bigger picture is one of integration in a wider capitalist system. James Petras and Morris Morley describe it this way: "The U.S. imperial state provides an umbrella under which to operate. In so far as Canadian capital depends on the same kind of social and political conditions to reproduce itself, it benefits from this U.S. umbrella and hence is reluctant to criticize its benefactor."[303]

Canadian corporations are major investors throughout the USA's backyard with $117.2 billion invested in 2007 and $125.3 billion in 2006.[304] For their part, Canadian mining companies owned more than 1,300 mineral properties in Latin America.[305] In so far as Canadian capitalism is integrated with U.S. capitalism, and is dependent upon its military, political and diplomatic shield, Ottawa will act in concert with Washington to thwart the region's desire to back away from "free" market economics and U.S. dependence.

In the current political environment across the region this may just be a losing strategy. As governments move to the left, it would seem to offer opportunities for Canada to differentiate itself from the U.S.. Instead, Ottawa has joined the U.S. in its growing isolation. In mid-December 2008, for example, leaders from 33 Latin American and Caribbean nations met for a two day "mega summit" in Brazil to discuss regional economic and political integration. Unlike meetings of the Organization of American States, Cuba was invited to this summit. But, "the United States and Canada were notably not invited to the summit convened by Brazilian President Luis Inacio Lula da Silva, which to [Venezuelan president Hugo] Chavez signified 'the start of a new era... the United States doesn't rule here anymore.'"[306]

The extent to which Canadian-owned corporations and government policy have soured this country's image in South and Central America is significant and growing. While ordinary Canadians have long understood the meaning of the term "Ugly American" few of us are familiar with the "Ugly Canadian."

Chapter Notes

1   Northern Shadows, 19
2   Canada in the European Age, 485
3   Anatomy of Big Business, 139
4   Canada in the European Age, 486
5   Canada in the European Age, 486
6   Our Generation Vol 10 #4, 36
7   Our Generation Vol 10 #4, 37
8   Imperialism, Nationalism and Canada, 64
9   Canadian Gunboat Diplomacy, 30/84
10 Globe and Mail Dec 1 2006
11 La Jornada Jan 23 2008
12 La Jornada Jan 23 2008
13 Latin America Working Group Letter #45, 15
14 Enquetes sur les services secret, 123
15 Vancouver Sun Jan 6 1994
16 Canadian Forum Mar 1994
17 http://teaching.quotidiana.org/our/2006/chiapas/nafta.html
18 Discovering the Americas, 132
19 Discovering the Americas, 132
20 Discovering the Americas, 132
21 Discovering the Americas, 132
22 McGill Daily Oct 4 2007
23 http://www.fleetstreetinvest.co.uk/commodities/mining/can-us-stop-mexicos-mining-boom-00080.html)
24 Montréal Gazette Mar 5 2008
25 La Jornada July 2008
26 http://www.dominionpaper.ca/articles/1632
27 Le Devoir Aug 24 2007
28 La Jornada Apr 30 2007
29 Dominion paper mining issue 2008
30 McGill Daily Oct 4 2007
31 From Telegrapher Titan, 387
32 Global Mission, 306
33 A Dynamic Partnership, 87; Canada and the Commonwealth Caribbean, 280
34 Canada Commonwealth Caribbean, 289
35 Canada Commonwealth Caribbean, 290
36 Canada Commonwealth Caribbean, 290
37 The Caribbean Basin, 106
38 The Caribbean Basin, 106
39 Global Mission, 636
40 Corporate Imperialism, 103; The Caribbean Basin, 106
41 Nationalization of Guyana's Bauxite, 106
42 Last Post Vol 1 #4
43 Last Post Vol 1 #4
44 Corporate Imperialism, 166

45 Imperialism, Nationalism and Canada, 64
46 Nationalization of Guyana's Bauxite, 206
47 Globe and Mail Dec 22 1982
48 Globe and Mail Dec 22 1982
49 Canadian Journal of Development Studies 1995, 69
50 Conflicts of Interest, 80
51 Conflicts of Interest, 80
52 Conflicts of Interest, 22; Vancouver Sun Mar 16 1990
53 Montréal Gazette Nov 21 2006
54 This Magazine Nov 1998
55 http://upsidedownworld.org/main/content/view/854/49/
56 http://upsidedownworld.org/main/content/view/854/49/
57 http://www.republic-news.org/archive/149-repub/149_mychalejko.htm
58 National Post Nov 26 2007
59 http://ecuador-rising.blogspot.com/2007_08_01_archive.html
60 http://www.minesandcommunities.org/article.php?a=180
61 http://www.miningwatch.ca/index.php?/Ecuador_en/Ascendant_community_relns
62 Ottawa Citizen July 27 2007
63 Upside Down World Apr 8 2008
64 Ottawa Citizen Jan 18 2007
65 http://www.miningwatch.ca/updir/Ecuador_Analysis_final.pdf
66 Ottawa Citizen Oct 6 2007
67 Montréal Mirror Oct 11 2007
68 http://www.corriente.com/news/news.php
69 Dominion paper mining issue 2008
70 Dominion paper mining issue 2008
71 <http://www.miningwatch.ca/updir/Ecuador_Analysis_final.pdf>
72 <http://www.miningwatch.ca/updir/Ecuador_Analysis_final.pdf>
73 upsidedownworld.org May 5 2008
74 http://www.focal.ca/publications/focalpoint/fp0608/?article=article2&lang=e
75 http://upsidedownworld.org/main/content/view/1320/49/
76 http://www.dominionpaper.ca/articles/2054
77 http://upsidedownworld.org/main/content/view/1575/1/
78 Montréal Gazette Mar 8 2007
79 Le Devoir Nov 14 2006

80　McGill Daily Oct 4 2007; http://embassymag.ca/page/view/.2007.january.31.Peru

81　Ottawa Citizen Feb 19 2008

82　http://www.amazonwatch.org/newsroom/view_news.php?id=1679

83　http://towardfreedom.com/home/content/view/1452/64/

84　National Post May 11 2006

85　Reuters March 7 2005

86　Community Rights and Corporate Responsibility, 62

87　Community Rights and Corporate Responsibility, 61

88　http://www.miningwatch.ca/index.php?/Peru/Tambogrande_case_study

89　www.chinaview.cn Dec 20 2008

90　Third World Quarterly Vol 29 #1 2008, 69

91　Embassy magazine Jan 2008

92　upsidedownworld.org July 1 2008

93　Nous étions invincibles, 161

94　Discovering the Americas, 221

95　Community Rights and Corporate Responsibility, 77

96　Community Rights and Corporate Responsibility, 77

97　Community Rights and Corporate Responsibility, 76

98　http://64.233.169.132/search?q=cache:S5_4WVAgb8MJ:www.oag-bvg.gc.ca/internet/English/att_9629xe11_e_5818.html+ percentE2percent80 percent9C22+Canadian+firms+received+spin-off+benefits+from+the+Bolivian+Oil+and+Gas+Project&hl=en&ie=UTF-8

99　Impasse in Bolivia, 119

100　Impasse in Bolivia, 119

101　http://www.corpwatch.org/article.php?id=14452

102　http://colombiasupport.net/news/2007_09_01_archive.html

103　miningwatch.ca Mar 21 2005

104　Narcosphere.narconews.com Sept 30 2007

105　New Socialist Nov 2005

106　À bâbord Apr 2005; New Socialist Nov 2005

107　http://www.miningwatch.ca/index.php?/Goldcorp/Koehl_billions

108　http://embassymag.ca/page/view/.2005.june.15.canada_guatemala

109　http://www.miningwatch.ca/index.php?/Skye/Cook_letter

110　This Magazine Mar 2007

111　Latin America Working Group Letter Vol 5 #1, 4

112　Northern Shadows, 127; The Big Nickel, 77

113　Northern Shadows, 127

114　À bâbord Apr 2005

115　This Magazine Mar 2007; Northern Shadows, 130

116　Northern shadows, 148; Canada, Latin America, and the New Internationalism, 202

117　Northern Shadows, 149

118　Northern Shadows, 149

119　Northern Shadows, 178

120　Human Rights and Canadian Foreign Policy, 174

121　International human rights and Canadian foreign-policy, 365/416; Canadian Churches and Foreign Policy, 121

122　Between War and Peace in Central America, 193

123　Between War and Peace in Central America, 219

124　Northern Shadows, 98

125　Discovering the Americas, 35

126　Discovering the Americas, 35

127　Discovering the Americas, 40

128　Northern Shadows, 100

129　Northern Shadows, 38

130　The Big Nickel, 67

131　Northern Shadows, 31

132　Anatomy of Big Business 140

133　Northern Shadows, 47

134　Canadian Gunboat Diplomacy, 31

135　Northern Shadows, 51

136　Canadian Gunboat Diplomacy, 36

137　Northern Shadows, 61

138　Northern Shadows, 59

139　Northern Shadows, 56

140　Northern Shadows, 48

141　Discovering the Americas, 122; Human Rights and Canadian Foreign Policy, 174

142　Between War and Peace in Central America, 206

143　Northern Shadows, 196; Latin America Working Group Letter Vol X #1

144　Between War and Peace in Central America, 102 and Latin America Working Group Letter Vol X #1

145　Latin America Working Group Letter Vol X #1

146　Latin America Working Group Letter Vol X #1

147　Canada and the Crisis in Central America, 79

148　Upside Down World May 28 2007

149　http://www.dominionpaper.ca/articles/2369

150　National Post July 4 2008

151　Reuters July 3 2008

152　Between War and Peace in Central America, 236

153 International human rights and Canadian foreign-policy, 403

154 Discovering the Americas, 117

155 Discovering the Americas, 117

156 Discovering the Americas, 118

157 Discovering the Americas, 121

158 http://en.wikipedia.org/wiki/Sandinista

159 Discovering the Americas, 121

160 Discovering the Americas, 119

161 International human rights and Canadian foreign-policy, 423

162 International human rights and Canadian foreign-policy, 419

163 Discovering the Americas, 123; Between War and Peace in Central America, 107

164 Official Secrets, 250

165 This Magazine June 1988; Northern Shadows, 219

166 This Magazine June 1988

167 Canadian Bilateral Aid policy in Neoliberal Nicaragua, 14

168 Northern Shadows, 164

169 Canadian Dimension Jan 1979

170 Canadian Dimension Jan 1979

171 Northern Shadow, 67

172 Northern Shadow, 81

173 Northern Shadow, 83

174 Northern Shadow, 85

175 Northern Shadows, 89

176 Conflicts of Interest, 298

177 Ottawa Citizen Dec 20 1989

178 Canada and the Crisis in Central America, 27

179 Killing Hope, 312

180 Discovering the Americas, 193

181 Windsor Star Dec 22 1989

182 Costa Rica-Great Britain Arbitration, 133

183 Costa Rica-Great Britain Arbitration, 47; Northern Shadow, 43

184 Canadian Gunboat Diplomacy, 30

185 Northern Shadows, 11

186 Northern Shadows, 93

187 Brazil and Canada in the Americas, 31

188 The Brass Ring, 33; Brascan Ltd, 12; Last Post Mar 1973 Vol 3 #2

189 Canada Among Nations 2002, 264; The Brass Ring, 33

190 Last Post Mar 1973 Vol 3 #2

191 Brazil and Canada in the Americas, 37

192 Brazil and Canada in the Americas, 35

193 The Multinational Corporations and Brazil, 91

194 Last Post Mar 1973 Vol 3 #2

195 The Multinational Corporations and Brazil, 99

196 Last Post Mar 1973 Vol 3 #2

197 The Multinational Corporations and Brazil, 99

198 Imperialism, Nationalism and Canada, 56

199 The Multinational Corporations and Brazil, 93; Brascan Ltd, 2

200 Last Post Mar 1973 Vol 3 #2

201 The Multinational Corporations and Brazil, 100

202 But not in Canada, 261

203 Last Post Mar 1973 Vol 3 #2

204 The Multinational Corporations and Brazil, 92

205 Latin America Working Group Letter, Vol iv #2 "The Dark Side of the 'Light'"; Discovering the Americas, 96

206 Discovering the Americas, 42

207 Latin America Working Group Letter Vol iv #2

208 Last Post Mar 1973 Vol 3 #2

209 Last Post Mar 1973 Vol 3 #2

210 The Multinational Corporations and Brazil, 94

211 Latin America Working Group Letter Vol iv #2

212 Latin America Working Group Letter Vol iv #2

213 Last Post Mar 1973 Vol 3 #2

214 The Brass Ring, 41

215 Brazil and Canada in the Americas, 44

216 Brazil and Canada in the Americas, 44

217 Brazil and Canada in the Americas, 46

218 Brazil and Canada in the Americas, 47

219 Perpetuating Poverty, 64; Latin America Working Group Letter Vol 7 #1/2, 33

220 Latin America Working Group Letter, Vol iv #5/6, 25; Discovering the Americas, 86

221 Discovering the Americas, 88

222 Northern Shadows, 136

223 Towers of Gold, 192

224 Discovering the Americas, 83

225 Northern Shadows, 136

226 Discovering the Americas, 89

227 Perpetuating Poverty, 158

228 Canada, Latin America, and the New Internationalism, 195

229 Latin America Working Group Letter Vol 5 #4/5, 22

230 Last Post June 1977

231 Last Post Sept 1977 Vol 6 #4

232 Unlikely Allies, 9

233 Latin America Working Group Letter Vol iv #5/6, 22

234 Last Post Vol 7 #2 Nov 1978; Latin America Working Group Letter, Vol 5 #4/5, 36

235 Latin America Working Group Letter, Vol 5 #4/5, vi

236 Human Rights and Canadian Foreign Policy, 177

237 http://www.asadismi.ws/pinochet.html

238 http://www.asadismi.ws/pinochet.html

239 New York Times July 30 2006

240 Community Rights and Corporate Responsibility, 100

241 http://www.tcgnews.com/santiagotimes/index.php?nav=story&story_id=14096&topic_id=15

242 Barrick's Dirty Secrets http://www.corpwatch.org/article.php?id=14466

243 http://www.corpwatch.org/article.php?id=12447

244 http://www.miningwatch.ca/index.php?/Chile_en/Diaguita_Accord

245 http://www.corpwatch.org/article.php?id=12447

246 Toronto Star July 19 2007

247 http://www.policyalternatives.ca/MonitorIssues/2001/11/MonitorIssue1685/

248 http://www.halifaxinitiative.org/index.php/Action_Alert_Arch/ART3ea814926cb29

249 Globe and Mail May 5 2007

250 Globe and Mail May 5 2007

251 http://www.straight.com/article-123599/canadian-pensioners-to-pave-patagonia

252 http://www.mcgilldaily.com/view.php?aid=6861

253 LA Times Aug 21 2008

254 Le Monde Sept 27 2008

255 Canadian foreign-policy Vol 14 #3 fall 2008

256 Bloomberg May 7 2008

257 Embassy magazine Apr 23 2008

258 IPS Oct 22 2007

259 Maclean's July 1 2006

260 IPS Oct 22 2007

261 IPS Oct 22 2007

262 IPS Oct 22 2007

263 Maclean's July 1 2006

264 The Profits of Extermination, 41

265 CCPA Monitor Dec 2000

266 http://www.asadismi.ws/colombia.html

267 http://www.policyalternatives.ca/MonitorIssues/2004/10/MonitorIssue1673/

268 http://www.halifaxinitiative.org/updir/PolicyBrief-EDCandHR.pdf

269 http://www.halifaxinitiative.org/updir/PolicyBrief-EDCandHR.pdf

270 http://groups.yahoo.com/group/ColombiaUpdate/files/Asad percent20Ismi/

271 Canadian Corporations and Social Responsibility, Page 126

272 Embassy Magazine Oct 8 2008

273 http://www.torontohispano.com/entretenimiento/comunidad/2007/harper_colombia_jul07/main.shtml

274 http://www.dominionpaper.ca/articles/2475

275 http://www.asadismi.ws/colombia.html

276 http://www.asadismi.ws/colombia.html

277 http://www.policyalternatives.ca/MonitorIssues/2000/12/MonitorIssue1689/

278 http://www.tao.ca/~asadismi/colombiareport.html; Third World Quarterly Volume 29, Number 1, 2008, 79

279 Canadian Dimension May 20 2000; La Presse Mar 23/24 2007

280 Canadian Dimension May 2001

281 Ottawa Citizen June 8 1994

282 This Magazine Mar 2000

283 Discovering the Americas, 221; Montréal Gazette Sept 5 1989

284 A Dynamic Partnership, 101

285 Nous étions invincibles, 137

286 Nous étions invincibles, 137

287 Nous étions invincibles, 144

288 Nous étions invincibles, 143

289 Promoting Democracy in the Americas, 100

290 http://www2.parl.gc.ca/HousePublications/Publication.aspx?DocId=2314066&Language=E&Mode=1&Parl=39&Ses=1

291 http://www2.parl.gc.ca/HousePublications/Publication.aspx?DocId=2314066&Language=E&Mode=1&Parl=39&Ses=1

292 Bush versus Chavez, 73

293 Toronto Star Dec 15 2006

294 Toronto Star Dec 15 2006

295 Le Devoir July 12 2007

296 Globe and Mail Oct 29 2008

297 Financial Post Magazine May 2008

298 National Post Nov 27 2008

299 http://www.mineweb.com/mineweb/view/mineweb/en/page34?oid=74089&sn=Detail

300 Financial Times Aug 22 2007

301 Canadian Press May 4 2006

302 Le Soleil May 13 2007

303 Northern Shadows, 228

304 http://www.canadianbusiness.com/managing/strategy/article.jsp?content=20090316_10005_10005

305 Canadian foreign-policy Vol 14 #3 fall 2008

306 http://www.venezuelanalysis.com/news/4053

East Asia

Two factors motivating Canadian foreign policy — direct corporate self-interest and a partnership within the U.S.-led empire — were well illustrated in Latin America. East Asia in the decades after World War Two provides an example of just how integrated Canadian policy has been with our southern neighbour when acting in a theatre of overriding U.S. concern.

Canadian policy towards East Asia was strongly affected by the Chinese revolution. Mao's 1949 Communist Party victory, which united a foreign-dominated China, frightened U.S. policymakers and supporters of capitalism. They saw the revolution as a challenge to both particular corporate interests — many foreign companies had investments in China — and to the Washington-led capitalist economic system more generally. In hindsight Chinese "communism" might be better described as a form of nationalism using communist rhetoric, but at the time it was seen as an existential threat. Fighting this "communism" helps to explain Canadian policy during the Korean and Vietnamese wars as well as this country's support for Suharto in Indonesia.

China

Ottawa tacitly supported Japan's brutal 1931 invasion of Manchuria China that left 20,000 dead. "Whatever may be thought of the moral or ethical rights of the Japanese to be in and to exercise control over Manchuria their presence there must be recognized as a stabilizing and regulating force," noted the Canadian diplomat who opened the first Canadian mission in Japan, Hugh Llewellyn Keenleyside.[1] Six years later the Canadian ambassador to China, Randolph Bruce, told the Toronto Star that Japan's invasion of Nanking, to the west of Manchuria, was "simply an attempt to put her neighbour country into decent shape, as she has already done in Manchuria."[2] Some 20,000 women were raped and tens of thousands of Chinese killed in the six weeks after Japan entered Nanking. Yet Canadian officials in the region, who received reports regarding the massacres, were more worried about Japan's sinking of the USS Panay and HMS Ladybird then the human rights situation.[3]

Canadian diplomats viewed China as a weak and divided country subject to communist influence. On the other hand, they were impressed by Japan's ability to keep order in East Asia.[4] Through Ottawa's accession to Anglo-Japanese military and commercial treaties Canada and Japan were imperial allies and most favoured trading partners.[5] "A certain fascination with imperialism — both British and Japanese — lingered [in Ottawa] throughout the period."[6] Support for Japanese imperialism went beyond diplomatic circles. Believing it would make their work easier, Canadian missionaries, who received federal government money through the Board of Foreign Missions, supported Japan's intervention into Manchuria.[7] Canadian missionary E.O. Fraser wrote that: "Japan is suppressing the bandits alright, and Manchuria will be better for it. The Chinese officials have been replaced by other Chinese who are favourable to the real rulers, and there are Japanese advisors with them, so things will smooth down, and trade will be much advanced in Manchuria."[8] Québec-based Missions Étrangère claimed that Japan's seizure of Manchuria was "pour proteger leur nationaus et metre l'ordre dans le pays."[9] For their part, many Chinese saw Canadian missionaries as imperialists.[10] Chinese peasants, according to *Cross Culture and Faith*, demanded to know of the Canadians "are you Christians or imperialists?"[11]

Canadian missionaries were a significant force in China. Some claim that in proportion to their size and resources, Canadian churches sponsored more missionaries in China than any other country.[12] By 1919 there were almost 580 Canadian missionaries in China with Canadian Methodist, Presbyterian and Anglican churches operating 270 schools and 30 hospitals.[13] The missionaries also worked to shape Canadian policy through "missionary statesmanship."[14] In the *Christian Guardian*, Albert Hinton, explained "it is a tragic mistake to divorce the missionary and the maker of foreign-policy."[15]

The business community also reinforced Ottawa's support for imperialism. Echoing the Financial Post, Canadian Business demanded the government ignore "the socialist group" advocating an arms embargo of Japan for its role in China.[16] "Canadian business, untroubled by diplomatic concerns, promoted trade with Manchuria and the rest of the Japanese empire. Japan's wartime footing revived the interest of Canadian exporters."[17]

On the eve of World War Two, Japan was the third largest importer of Canadian non-ferrous metals.[18] Canada was Japan's chief supplier of nickel, a militarily important commodity.[19] Japan imported 9,000 tons of Canadian nickel in 1937, 10,000 tons in 1938 and 7,000 tons in the first half of 1939 alone.[20]

Throughout the mid- to late-1930s leftist organizations, peace groups, and self-styled "friends of China" called for an economic and military boycott of Japan to end Canada's complicity with Japanese expansionism.[21] The Trades and Labour Congress condemned Ottawa's support for a "fascist dictatorship" in China.[22]

Of course once World War Two began Japan quickly turned from ally to enemy. Suddenly Ottawa was willing to send thousands of Canadian troops half way across the world to stop Japanese expansionism. Demonstrating a flagrant disregard for the lives of those in the armed forces, in the fall of 1941 Ottawa sent 1,975 troops to defend Hong Kong, even though the mission was doomed from the outset. Officialdom was distracted by imperial rivalry. "Hong Kong constituted an outpost which the Commonwealth intended to hold" read an External Affairs message to London in response to a request for troops.[23] Nearly a third of the Canadian troops deployed to Hong Kong perished in a futile effort to stop Japan's conquest of the British colony.

A number of Chinese-Canadians were covertly sent into China during World War Two partly because "whenever the Japanese capitulated, it would be useful to have on hand a team to enter Hong Kong promptly to help reestablish the British writ there."[24] By January 1945 there were also 3,100 Canadian airmen serving in Southeast Asia with the Royal Air Force or Royal Canadian Air Force.[25]

After the Second World War Canada sided with Chiang Kai-Shek's Kuomintang against Mao's Communists. Once again the missionary community took the side of imperialism's defenders. "The vast majority of Canadian missionaries supported Chiang Kai Shek personally, and in varying degrees still supported his regime" into the 1950s.[26] Canadian missionaries even supported the U.S. and British naval presence. "I'm not prepared to work here without some protection for my wife and children. When the gunboats go, I go," explained Dr. C. B. Kelly.[27]

Ottawa aided the Kuomintang by sending 170 planes and providing $60 million in export credits between 1945 and 1948.[28] The money was granted even though some members of the Liberal cabinet opposed taking sides in the Chinese Civil War.[29]

In a bizarre move, Ottawa sent a naval vessel to China in 1949 as the Communists were on the verge of victory.[30] According to *Canadian Gunboat Diplomacy*, the boat was sent too late to stop the Kuomintang's defeat and was not needed to evacuate Canadians since British boats could remove them. The objective, it seems, was to demonstrate Canada's growing might to its allies, the U.S. and U.K.[31]

Upon seizing power, Mao's government was met with hostility from Ottawa. A November 1949 External Affairs memo to Prime Minister Saint Laurent complained that "China must now be regarded as a potential enemy state and would probably side with Russia in the event of a general war."[32] During the 1950-53 Korean War Ottawa voted for a U.N. resolution branding China an aggressor, but China sent soldiers only after hundreds of thousands of hostile troops, including Canadians, approached its border.[33] For years Washington used this resolution to justify opposing China's entry to the U.N.

Despite British recognition of the Chinese government in 1950 Ottawa refused to recognize China until 1970 and did not support China's accession to the U.N. until then.[34] As late as 1965 Prime Minister Pearson told the CBC "if there is a division of opinion in your own country on a particular type of foreign policy, such as recognition of Red China ... then it seems to me the reaction of the United States becomes even more important. If you can't make up your own minds ... then you should be very careful about not getting into trouble with your friends."[35] Pearson was ignoring Canadian opinion. As early as 1961, a Gallup poll found that a growing majority of Canadians favoured seating China at the U.N.[36] Of more importance than public opinion was the fact that U.S. rapprochement with China began the same year as Canada finally recognized the Communist government.

Eight years after Canada began diplomatic relations with China the Chinese "formerly invited" Montréal-based Power Corporation President Paul Desmarais to organize a delegation of Canadian business leaders to China.[37] This 1978 trade and investment mission was part of an effort by the Chinese government to liberalize its economy. Ottawa supported China's moves towards a more capitalist oriented economy. "In 1979, in response to the Chinese annunciation of the 'Four Modernisation Plan,' Canada, through the Export Development Corporation, extended a $2 billion line-of-credit to China. Up to that time this was the largest line-of-credit ever awarded to a foreign country. ... It is interesting to note that this further cementing to the Canada-China economic relationship happened at a time when the Chinese leadership was in the midst of clamping down on the Xidan Democracy Wall Movement."[38]

A decade later the story was much the same. Lobbying by the Canadian business community and support within the federal government for Chinese economic reforms made it difficult for Brian Mulroney's Conservatives to oppose the Tiananmen Square massacre that left between 200 and 3,000 peaceful protesters dead. "Canadian foreign policy is nothing short of hypocrisy," a letter to the Toronto Star noted. "They go all out to condemn China's inhuman behaviour, but fall short of taking action for fear of losing the billion dollar trade we have with them."[39]

Ottawa never implemented serious economic sanctions against China in response to the Tiananmen Square massacre. The Paul Desmarais led China Trade Council (with 120 corporate members) convinced the Mulroney government to ignore calls for sanctions.[40] "Influencing Mulroney's views of China was his close relationship with Paul Desmarais, the Chief Executive Officer of Power Corporation and the principle founder of the Canada-China Trade Council."[41]

One could argue that human rights violations at Tiananmen Square were relatively limited compared to the social, cultural and environmental destruction wrought by the Canadian-supported Three Gorges dam. It was one of the biggest projects the world has ever seen. Environmentalists condemned the dam's impact on the region's ecosystem. With a thousand square kilometers submerged in water, 1.4 million people were displaced, many of whom were expected to be relocated again.[42] As with many other ecologically and socially devastating dams, Canada played a part in advancing the Three Gorges project. "Many Western governments including the U.S., initially refused to support China's plan to build the world's largest hydroelectric dam," noted the Wall Street Journal in 2007. "Canada was the first country to break ranks and back the massive project."[43]

Alongside China's Ministry of Water, Resources and Electric Power, CIDA financed a 1988 feasibility study of the Three Gorges Dam.[44] The study was done by a consortium that included Acres International, SNC Lavalin International, as well as B.C. Hydro International and Hydro-Québec International.[45] The Vice President of CIDA's professional services branch, Peter Hanes, stated "our private sector is living up to its potential in the Three Gorges Project in China, the world's biggest ever power development. By working closely together, with some support from CIDA, a number of our leading consultants and utilities have good prospects of winning hundreds of millions of dollars worth of business for Canada."[46]

Hanes was right. In 1997, General Electric Canada won a $160 million contract to supply turbines and generators for the dam.[47] Agra-Monenco, Fuller FL Smidth Canada and Acres International also won millions of dollars in Three Gorges work.[48] EDC provided as much as $1.5 billion in credits for dam-related work. While EDC jumped head first into financing the Three Gorges Dam, the U.S. Export-Import Bank concluded the project was "not consistent" with its environmental guidelines.[49]

Korea

As in China, Ottawa supported Japanese imperialism in Korea prior to World War Two. The Canadian diplomat who opened the first Canadian mission in Japan, H. L. Keenleyside, argued that Korea should become a Dominion within the Japanese empire.[50] Following Ottawa, Canadian missionaries in Korea mostly supported the Japanese and opposed resistance to occupation. "During the 1930s Canadian missionaries stood apart from the mainstream of the foreign missionary movement and the Korean Presbyterian church who both relished resistance to the Japanese colonial regime."[51] Most of the 200 Canadian missionaries were hostile to Korean Communists despite a widespread belief in the country that they were the forefront of the liberation struggle.[52] Even during World War Two the United Church of Canada failed to support Korean independence, fearing this might prevent Canadian missionaries from returning if Japan maintained control after the war.[53] Japan, of course, didn't maintain control of Korea after World War Two. Instead, the country fell under U.S. and Soviet influence.

After the war the U.S. wanted the (Western dominated) U.N. to take responsibility for Korea. The Soviets objected to the U.N.'s 1947 decision to involve itself in Korean affairs, claiming the international organization had no jurisdiction over post-war settlement issues (as the U.S. argued for Germany and Japan). For its part, Canada participated in the U.N.'s 1947 commission supervising elections in South Korea. Canada was also among the first countries to recognize the South, the Republic of Korea, in 1949.[54] Ottawa's decision to become involved in Korea was highly contentious within the cabinet.

The official story is that the Korean War began when the Soviet-backed North invaded the South. The U.S. and its allies then came to the South's aid. As is the case with most official U.S. history the story is incomplete, if not downright false. "The best explanation of what happened on June 25 [the day the war began] is that [South Korean President] Syngman Rhee deliberately initiated the fighting and then successfully blamed the North, eagerly waiting for provocation, took advantage of the southern attack and, without incitement by the Soviet Union, launched its own strike with the objective of capturing Seoul. Then a massive U.S. intervention followed."[55]

The background to the war is that Washington feared the outcome of Koreans deciding their own fate, which is why the U.S. spurned a 1947 proposal from Moscow to immediately withdraw all foreign troops from the country.[56] Instead the U.S. supported a brutal dictatorship in the South that pursued an unpopular policy of dividing the country.[57] And while the

Soviets had little involvement with "southern attacks ... the U.S. organized and equipped the Southern counterinsurgent forces."[58]

About 27,000 Canadian soldiers fought in the three-year Korean War and eight Canadian warships deployed to the country between 1950 and 1955.[59] Beginning the U.S.-intervention-equals-Canadian-aid pattern, Ottawa sent $7.25 million to South Korea on March 31st 1951, the third largest amount pledged by any government.[60] A major principle of Canadian foreign aid has been that where the USA wields its big stick, Canada carries its police baton and offers a carrot. During the Korean War the south of that country was a major recipient of Canadian aid and so was Vietnam during the U.S. war there. (The major recipient of Canadian aid in 1999-2000 was the former Yugoslavia; Iraq and Afghanistan were the top two recipients in 2003-2004; in 2008-2009Afghanistan and Haiti were Nos. 1 and 2. One could call it the "intervention-equals-aid" principle.)

Korea was also Canada's first foray into U.N. peacekeeping/peacemaking and it was done at Washington's behest.[61] U.S. troops intervened in Korea and then Washington moved to have the U.N. support their action, not the other way around. The U.N. resolution referred to "a unified command under the United States."[62] "The finishing touch," wrote I. F. Stone, "was to make the 'United Nations' forces subject to [U.S. General] MacArthur without making MacArthur subject to the United Nations."[63]

Ottawa focused on making the military operation more palatable to Canadians. Instead of searching for peace, or even a U.N.-controlled force, Canadian diplomatic activity at the U.N. "was directed to the more modest objective of changing the wording of the American text in such as way as to reinforce the impression that the United Nations was the genuine parent of the response to the North Korean attack and hence to establish that the command really was a United Nations agent."[64] In August 1950 Prime Minister St. Laurent tried to sell the mission to Canadians by claiming the intervention in Korea was not a war but a "police action intended to prevent war by discouraging aggression."[65]

Canada's intervention in Korea was no police action. After pushing the North Korean troops back to the 38th parallel, the artificial line that divided the north and south, the U.N. force moved to conquer the entire country. U.N. troops pushed north even after the Chinese made it clear that they would intervene to block a hostile force from approaching their border. It's not surprising that the U.S.-led force continued north since the intervention in Korea was partly designed to undermine the Chinese Communist government, which took power only a year earlier.

Millions died in the Korean War, including two million North Korean civilians, 500,000 North Korean soldiers, one million Chinese soldiers, one million South Korean civilians, ten thousand South Korean soldiers and 95,000 U.N. soldiers (516 Canadians).[66] "The monstrous effects on Korean civilians of the methods of warfare adopted by the United Nations — the blanket fire bombing of North Korean cities, the destruction of dams and the resulting devastation of the food supply and an unremitting aerial bombardment more intensive than anything experienced during the Second World War. At one point the Americans gave up bombing targets in the North when their intelligence reported that there were no more buildings over one story high left standing in the entire country ... the overall death toll was staggering: possibly as many as four million people. About three million were civilians (one out of every ten Koreans). Even to a world that had just began to recover from the vast devastation of the Second World War, Korea was a man-made hell with a place among the most violent excesses of the 20th century."[67]

Canadian troops denigrated the "yellow horde" of Koreans and Chinese they fought. One Canadian colonel wrote about the importance of defensive positions to "kill at will the hordes that rush the positions."[68] Crimes committed by Canadian troops, even against allied South Koreans, largely went unpunished. Canadian troops found guilty of murdering or raping Korean civilians were usually released from prison within a year or two after legal experts and civilian judges in Ottawa reviewed their cases. In one disturbing example, a half dozen Canadian troops who beat South Korean soldiers and then raped and killed two South Korean women barely spent any time in jail.[69] "The Canadian military justice system," Chris Madsen explained, "showed astounding lenience towards these men's criminal actions."[70]

Vietnam

As was the case in China and Korea, blunting the de-colonization process was the primary aim of Canadian policy in Vietnam after World War Two. Before Washington's large-scale military buildup in Vietnam, Ottawa supported France's move to maintain control over its former colony. At the end of 1952 Ottawa supported a French attempt to accord "recognition to Vietnam, Cambodia and Laos as associated States of Indo-China within the French Union in accordance with the terms of agreements between France and the respective states."[71] When the NATO Council concluded that France's war in Indochina was in "the fullest harmony with the aims and ideals of the Atlantic community," Norway and Denmark opposed this position. Ottawa endorsed it.[72]

Between 1950 and 1954, $61.3 million worth of Canadian arms, bullets, aircraft and engines were used by the French in Indo-China.[73] "[External Affairs Minister] Lester Pearson believed that France's war against communism in Indo-China deserved Canada's support, but Louis St. Laurent and Minister of Defence Brook Claxton worried about how the Canadian public would react to sending Canadian military supplies to help France retain its colonial position in South East Asia. ... the Canadian cabinet approved the transfer of the Canadian equipment without any such restrictions by agreeing to send Mutual Aid equipment to France itself. ... the French were told that what they did with the supplies after their arrival in France was of no concern to the Canadian government."[74]

Before Washington decided to launch a full-scale intervention in Vietnam both U.S. Secretary of State John Foster Dulles and President Dwight Eisenhower called Prime Minister St. Laurent and External Affairs Minister Lester Pearson to inquire about their views regarding the matter. The Canadian politicians were even asked their opinion about a possible nuclear strike in support of the French. Both St. Laurent and Pearson told the American officials they had little opinion on the matter.[75]

Through the International Control Commission Ottawa played an important role in supporting U.S. aggression in the region. Canada represented the West, Poland represented the Eastern bloc and India was the non- aligned member on the commission. "Confidential documents reveal that the Canadian delegation on the International Control Commission (ICC) from 1954-72, acting on Ottawa's instructions, willingly played a coordinated part in Washington's strategy of bolstering South Vietnam in defiance of the Geneva accords."[76] The third Canadian commissioner to serve in Vietnam, Bruce Williams explained "that Canada's main concern in Vietnam is not the fulfillment of the Geneva agreements per se, but the maintenance of peace in south east Asia as a method of thwarting communist ascendancy in the area."[77] In fact, by recognizing South Vietnam on December 20, 1955, Ottawa broke the Geneva Accords, which were designed to peacefully reunify the country.[78]

Ottawa helped blunt ICC condemnation of Washington's troop buildup in the South as well as their bombing of North Vietnam.[79] Canadian ICC officials also acted as U.S. spies. Brigadier Donald Ketcheson, admitted that he "regularly furnished the CIA with information about [North Vietnamese] troop movements."[80] External Affairs was "unofficially" aware, but "looked the other way."[81] "Washington regarded [Canada's ICC Comissioner J. Blair] Seaborne as its eyes, ears and mouth in Hanoi. Aside from transmitting U.S. messages, he was instructed to bring back political intelligence on the level of war weariness among the North Vietnamese, on the state of their economy, on the respective influence of the Russians and the Chinese and on possible divisions among the leaders."[82]

Seaborne received "instructions" from Washington to convey a carrot-and-stick policy to the North Vietnamese.[83] "By allowing Seaborne to carry U.S. ultimatums to Hanoi," *Snow Job* concludes, "the government accepted an active role in the unfolding of this escalation scenario. Once the bombings had begun, Ottawa tried to excuse them by again harping on North Vietnam's aggression in the South."[84]

Unwilling to heed the calls of a growing antiwar movement, in June 1965 External Affairs Minister Paul Martin blamed the North for war in Vietnam, even drawing a parallel with Nazi expansionism. "If this form of indirect aggression is allowed to succeed there will be incalculable consequences for world peace. … suffice it to say that if North Vietnam succeeds in taking over the whole of Vietnam by force, if the rest of the world is prepared to sit back and see this happen, saying feebly that, after all, it is only a domestic rebellion so why not accept the inevitable, we would in my judgment, be guilty of an error of the same nature as the mistakes at Munich, and before that, in the League of Nations. Aggression is aggression, whether it takes place in Europe, Ethiopia or in Vietnam."[85] At Philadelphia's Temple University two months earlier Prime Minister Pearson argued that "the situation cannot be expected to improve until North Vietnam becomes convinced that aggression, in whatever guise, for whatever reason, is inadmissible and will not succeed."[86] The above quote is from Pearson's famous "anti-war" speech, probably the most often cited example of a Canadian leader opposing U.S. militarism.

Contrary to what we're now told, Canadian politicians' statements about the war in Vietnam were overwhelmingly supportive of the U.S. "Ottawa denied the indigenous character of the struggle, accused Hanoi of aggression, subscribed to the Domino theory, blamed Peking for the popular insurrections in South East Asia, white washed the regime in Saigon, and absolved it of its responsibilities towards the Geneva Accords, and invoked article 51 of the United Nations charter to exonerate the United States."[87]

Ottawa did not only provide ideological support for the U.S. intervention in South East Asia, but "at every stage of its involvement in Vietnam, Canada gave active support to the United States and its policies."[88] Canadian material aid, mostly through the Free World Assistance Program, was extended to one side, South Vietnam, of a country engaged in a civil war.[89] The former administrator of the Canadian aid program, Liberal MP David Anderson, admitted to an External Affairs Committee in December 1968 that, "a good portion of our aid was strictly for political purposes that were of no value to the people in the area concerned."[90] *Quiet Complicity* notes: "Canadian aid was an integral part of U.S. counter-insurgency efforts aimed at maintaining South Vietnam within the western sphere of influence."[91]

As the U.S. military buildup in Vietnam grew, Canadian weapons sales to the U.S. doubled between 1964 and 1966, peaking in 1967.[92] Between 1965 and 1973, Canada sold $2.5 billion worth of war materials to the Pentagon.[93] "American planes [that dropped rockets and napalm on North Vietnamese towns or southern villages] were often guided by Canadian made Marconi-Doppler navigation systems and used bombing computers built in Rexdale, Ontario. The bombs could have been armed with dynamite shipped from Valleyfield, Québec; polystyrene, a major component in the napalm, was supplied by Dow Chemical. Defoliants came from Naugatuck chemicals in Elmira, Ontario, and air-to-ground rockets were furnished by the Ingersoll Machine and Tool Company. On the ground, American infantry and artillery units were supplied by De Havilland Caribou built at Milton, Ontario. Less lethal Canadian products included Bata boots for the troops and the famous green berets of the Special Forces which came from Dorothea Knitting Mills in Toronto … Canadian arsenals Ltd, a Crown Corporation, sold small arms, fill for artillery shells, mines, bombs, grenades, torpedo warheads, depth charges and rockets."[94]

Backed by a significant protest movement across the country the NDP's Tommy Douglas urged the Liberals to follow Sweden's example by ending weapons sales to the U.S. until there was peace in Vietnam.[95] Those who supported continued arm sales often responded to protesters demands by claiming that Canadian weapons were not central to the U.S. war effort. According to its opponents, a weapons ban would harm Canada's economy while Washington would simply procure armaments elsewhere. This line of argument may have been correct, but it's pretty clear that "Canadian nickel, aluminum, iron ore, and steel were essential to the U.S. war machine … it was no coincidence that these exports rose dramatically during the height of the Vietnam conflict in the 1960s."[96]

Canada's abundant resources as well as its vast landmass aided the U.S. military effort in Southeast Asia. B-52 bombers did practice bombing runs in Saskatchewan and Alberta while the U.S. tested chemical weapons (agents orange, purple and blue) at CFB Gagetown.[97] A 1968 U.S. Army memorandum titled "defoliation tests in 1966 at base Gagetown, New Brunswick, Canada" explained: "The department of the army, Fort Detrick, Maryland, has been charged with finding effective chemical agents that will cause rapid defoliation of woody and Herbaceous vegetation. To further develop these objectives, large areas similar in density to those of interest in South East Asia were needed. In March 1965, the Canadian ministry of defense offered Crops Division large areas of densely forested land for experimental tests of defoliant chemicals. This land, located at Canadian forces base Gagetown, Oromocto, New Brunswick, was suitable in size and density and was free from hazards and adjacent cropland. The test site selected contained a mixture of conifers and deciduous broad leaf species in a dense undisturbed forest cover that would provide similar vegetation densities to those of temperate and tropical areas such as South East Asia."[98]

Even though Canada didn't officially go into battle, an estimated twenty to thirty thousand Canadians served in the U.S. military during the war. According to official statistics, 111 died.[99] "During the Vietnam War, the Canadian government did not discourage the enlistment of Canadians in the American forces. No Canadians were prosecuted for violating the foreign enlistment act in joining to fight in Vietnam."[100] Towards the end of the U.S. war, two Canadian destroyers, HMCS Terranova and Kootenay, were sent to Southeast Asia to support Canadian forces serving on the International Commission of Control and Supervision.[101]

Even after the U.S. pulled out, Ottawa worked to isolate Vietnam. Largely to check the influence of Vietnam, Ottawa supported the Association of Southeast Asian Nations (ASEAN). "Canada endorsed diplomatically, the establishment of ASEAN in 1967 as a regional mechanism ... in face of the threat of Vietnamese expansionism." Just after the U.S. pulled out of Vietnam, "Ottawa committed to support financially and morally the anti-Communist Association of Southeast Asian Nations consisting of Indonesia, Malaysia, Thailand, the Philippines and Singapore. According to the minister of External Affairs 'it stands with democracy' even though when the minister made his comments the Thai government had overthrown an elected government in 1973 and the Generals in Indonesia killed a million after a coup d'etat in 1965 and the Philippines was operating under martial law."[102]

A decade after the U.S. pulled out of Vietnam an interchurch delegation complained that External Affairs still showed "no signs of deviating from the policy of the isolation of Vietnam."[103] It wasn't until 1990 that Ottawa opened a diplomatic mission in Hanoi.[104] Once Vietnam began to follow IMF prescriptions and agreed to pay debts the South incurred to the U.S. during the war, Ottawa's relations with Vietnam improved.

Philippines

As U.S. national banks were not allowed to establish foreign branches until 1914, "the CIBC [Canadian Imperial Bank of Commerce] acted for the U.S. government after the U.S. came into possession of the Philippines following the Spanish-American war."[105] Other Canadian corporations such as Sun Life and the Bank of Nova Scotia also began investing in this quasi U.S. colony at the turn of the last century.[106]

Nearly two decades into the pro-Western Ferdinand Marcos dictatorship Prime Minister Pierre Trudeau visited Manila in 1983.[107] Displaying a certain sympathy for the kleptocratic dictator, CIDA only stopped its bilateral assistance two years before Marcos's 1986 downfall.[108] After a popular rebellion brought Marcos down, Ottawa immediately restarted its aid program. Did this indicate Ottawa's support for the popular movement or was something else afoot? Unfortunately, likely the latter. Canadian aid to post-Marcos Philippines was used to push structural adjustment programs.[109] The "Philippines Assistance Program was made contingent upon further efforts by the Philippines on effecting policy reforms pertaining to the macroeconomic framework embodied in the IMF agreement and to the Medium Term Public Investment Program. ... It was even indicated that additional Canadian assistance for a Philippine Assistance Program could only be foreseeable were some very fundamental adjustment measures implemented."[110]

On top of providing aid contingent upon economic reform, Canada was a member of the Consulative Group for the Philippines, which was organized and chaired by the neoliberal-oriented World Bank.[111] Part of Ottawa's support for World Bank initiatives was assistance for its Natural Resource Management/Environment sector policy analysis, an endeavour to reform the country's mining regulations.[112]

Post-Marcos Canadian aid was used to reform the country's economy in the interests of foreign investors and to support right-wing organizations. In the late 1980s millions in Canadian aid flowed to the Negros region's elite who were blocking much-needed land reform, sometimes with paramilitary violence. "Instead of helping the poorest of the poor, it [CIDA] has funded efforts to keep the peasantry in its place," explained an October 1988 This Magazine article. "And there's compelling evidence that our aid dollars have played a role in a dirty war that rivals the worst of the Marcos dictatorship."[113] Project applications for $11 million in Canadian aid were reviewed by a committee put together by the governor of Negros that consisted largely of the land-owning elite. The biggest single chunk of funding, $1.7 million, was allocated to organizations dominated by planters, "a veritable rogue's gallery of the far right." Canadian aid was channeled through landlord foundations accused of "educating against land reform."[114]

Another CIDA-funded organization was "known to accuse workers who refuse to sign up for Kabalaka [a right wing land owning group] projects of being members of the New People's Army."[115] While Canadian aid was supposed to be used for the "transformation of existing social structures" the money largely went to preserve unequal relationships in Negros. And even after public criticism, both in Canada and the Philippines, CIDA continued its projects in Negros. "Canada and the U.S. will continue to send aid to the impoverished island of Negros despite threats by communist rebels to attack projects funded by both countries," reported the Vancouver Sun in April 1988.[116] In fact, CIDA continued dispersing money after the project's planned conclusion in 1990.

CIDA money also went to a group called In Hand, which produced goods for K-Mart amongst others. They paid assembly line workers an average of $1.50 for a 10 hour day while In Hand board of directors and managers all received almost $700 a month. On CIDA's books In Hand was known as "self-reliance".[117]

Two decades later Canadian aid to the Philippines continued to be criticized by progressive forces in that country. During an April 2008 tour, organized by a Canadian solidarity group, Filipino Congressman Crispin Beltran complained that "President Gloria Macapagal-Arroyo is strongly supported by the current Canadian government, even through direct military assistance to a military that is engaged in political killings."[118] Ottawa provided about $20 million in aid annually to the Arroyo government, which was increasingly brutal and corrupt.

Beginning in 1997 a number of Filipino military personnel were trained in Canada every year under the Military Training Assistance Program. In August 2008 the Ottawa Citizen reported that Canada would send personnel to the Philippines to train the country's special forces and other units in the use of chemical and biological "defence" equipment.[119] DND trained the Filipino military even though its guidelines barred military support "to countries that are involved in armed conflict or whose governments have a persistent record of human rights violations."[120] The Filipino army had been at war with the New People's Army for nearly four decades and in 2002 the southern Philippines became a "new front" in the "War on Terror" with thousands of U.S. troops deployed, targeting armed Muslim movements such as the Moro Islamic Liberation Front (MILF) and the Abu Sayyaf group. At the same time there were widespread political killings, many linked to government forces, across the Philippines. From 2001-2008 there were more than 800 political assassinations, including 100 unionists.[121]

While Canadian aid to Arroyo's government was criticized by some Filipinos, so too was Ottawa's support for Canadian miners responsible for environmental damage and human rights abuses. On the southern Filipino island of Mindanao Calgary-based TVI Pacific operated a particularly damaging open pit gold and silver mine. Pollution from the mine caused dangerous increases in mercury, arsenic, cyanide and lead levels in the area. Not concerned with the health of the people around its mine the company also disregarded the traditional leadership structure and sacred sites of the local indigenous population, the Subanon. TVI's actions caused the Subanon's gukom — their traditional judicial authority — to declare TVI guilty of crimes against the Subanon and their territory.[122] A 2007 report on TVI's activities said that the mine has "deprived thousands of small-scale miners of their livelihood" and "contributed to a militarization of the area" that has had a "negative impact on the ability of the Subanon to enjoy the human right to security and the human right to housing."[123]

Frustrated with the mine's damage to their community, local demonstrators regularly clashed with the 160-person Special Civilian Armed Force Geographical Active Auxiliary (SCAA), a force paid by the mining company but trained and armed by the national military. "We have become TVI's private army," an unnamed SCAA told a Canadian research group. "We took part in demolitions and have sacrificed a lot."[124]

Canadian diplomatic support for TVI's mine was notable. "Two ambassadors have visited the site, and have praised the company as a responsible miner. ... In a controversial move, the Canadian International Development Agency (CIDA) channelled funds earmarked for local initiatives through the mining company between 2003 and 2005. The funds were meant to be used to buy goats for local women. The CIDA personnel in the Canadian Embassy in Manila were well aware of the long-standing conflict in Mindanao when, in June 2003, they approved the program financed by the Canada Fund for Local Initiatives. ... According to CIDA, the money was channelled through the mining company's community development officer because the local community did not have the capacity to administer the program. In the course of the project, the local people made embassy officials aware of the specific human rights allegations against the mining company."[125]

From the southern island of Mindanao to the central Filipino island of Marinduque Canadian mining companies laid waste to the country's ecosystem. Between 1975 and 1991 Vancouver-based Placer Dome's Marcopper Mine dumped more than 200 million tonnes of mine tailings directly into the shallow waters of Calancan Bay.[126] The constant leakage covered coral reefs, seagrasses and the bottom of the bay with 80 square kilometres of tailings. A dam holding back tonnes of the Marcopper mine's toxic sludge burst in 1993, contaminating a river and killing two villagers.[127] Three years later, on March 24, 1996, another huge tailings spill filled the 26-kilometre-long Boac River with 3-4 million tonnes of metal-enriched and acid generating waste.[128] A U.N. investigative team that visited the site shortly after the 1996 spill noted that "it is evident that environmental management was not a high priority for Marcopper."[129] Twelve fishing villages around the bay had their livelihood severely affected for at least 27 years by the Canadian-owned mine. A large portion of the tailings were exposed in the bay and toxic waste regularly blew into nearby villages, which locals called "snow from Canada."[130] The tailings also leached metals into the bay and were suspected to be the cause of the lead contamination found in children from villages around the bay. In 1998 the government declared a state of calamity because of lead contamination suffered by Calancan Bay villages.[131]

After the 1996 Boac River disaster, Placer Dome promised to plug the tunnel, clean up the river and its seashore in addition to compensating the affected people. But, in 1997 Placer Dome divested from Marcopper through a wholly owned Cayman Island holding company and then left the Philippines entirely a couple years later. Filipino Congressman Edmund Reyes explained in 2002: "Just before Christmas, Placer Dome fled our country like a thief in the night. Their mine managers have a criminal indictment against them, Placer has refused to attend a Congressional Inquiry looking into their conduct and they have ignored a direct order by our Secretary of the Environment and Natural Resources to save lives on my island. ... Placer Dome's track record has made us wary of dealing with Canadian mining companies. This company gives Canada a black eye."[132]

It is interesting to note that for the first 17 years of the project, until he was deposed in 1986, former Philippine dictator Ferdinand Marcos held 49 percent of the mine's shares.[133] The Canadian Pension Plan, for its part, invested over $350 million into the Marinduque mine.[134]

Papua New Guinea

Canadian mining companies were also under fire in Papua New Guinea. On July 22, 2008, Barrick Gold's security guards killed a teenaged boy, Ibson Umbi, from a village located metres from its open pit copper and gold operation in the remote Engan province.[135] Between 1996 and 2006 police and security guards at Barrick's Porgera mine in Papua New Guinea killed 14 villagers and wounded hundreds, according to a local association. The company claimed its security force, numbering between 400 and 500, only killed eight people for trespassing.[136] Another 3,000 to 4,000 people were jailed for trespassing.[137] For their part, locals maintain their right to traditional alluvial mining so they don't consider entering Barrick's "property" trespassing. Working conditions at the mine are atrocious, causing dozens of deaths. Some 2,000 miners have also been injured because of unsafe working conditions. There is a sharp divide between local employees and foreigners. Locally hired employees receive low wages while management personnel are employed on a fly-in-fly-out basis. As of July 2007 all departmental managers were white and of non- Papua New Guinea origin.[138]

The mine disrupted the area's social order, increasing alcoholism, crime and rape. Along with social disorder, the mine caused significant ecological destruction with 40,000 tonnes of waste dumped into the area's main river every day (14.6 million tonnes annually).[139] At Barrick's May 2008 annual general meeting in Toronto Jethro Tullin, from the Porgera Landowners Association, demanded: "Mr. [CEO Peter] Munk, you have destroyed our land, our water, our safety and our ability to feed ourselves. We know that we can no longer live on our ancestral land. We know that we must leave our place so that our children can have a future. But now your company — Barrick — is refusing to offer us fair terms for our relocation…. When will Barrick agree to move the more than 5,000 families who live within your mine lease in a way that is fair and will provide us an opportunity to be healthy, to feed our families, and to educate our children?"[140] In February 2009 Norway's Ministry of Finance decided the country's pension fund would no longer invest in Barrick due to the company's actions at the Porgera mine.[141]

Backed by Barrick Gold and a number of other Canadian mining companies, Vancouver's Nautilus Minerals explored off the coast of Papa New Guinea. "We are leading the mining industry into the deep oceans," boasted Scott Trebilcock, vice-president of business development at Nautilus.[142] The company hoped to be the world's first company to commercially explore the ocean floor for gold and copper. But, mining in the South Pacific Sea poses a serious threat to fragile ecosystems drawing significant protest from local communities. Even the journal Science chimed in, calling for the seafloor to be protected from mining.[143]

Indonesia

Just as it did with the French in Vietnam, Ottawa supported Dutch colonialism in Indonesia. Canada opposed a 1948 U.N. resolution calling for the withdrawal of Dutch troops from Indonesia and continued to sell weapons to the Netherlands as they put down anticolonial resistance.[144]

Indonesia finally gained independence in 1949 but that didn't stop growing numbers of its population from demanding further social change. With the Communists in control of China and an insurgency raging in Vietnam, Washington worried that Indonesia might also choose an independent path. In 1965 Major General Suharto began to wipe out some 500,000 "Communists" and then overthrew democratically elected president Sukarno. Ottawa responded by selecting Indonesia as the main Asian country outside of the Commonwealth to receive Canadian aid.[145] "The domestic political stability achieved by Suharto after the ouster of Sukarno in 1966, together with a pronounced tilt in foreign policy towards the West, made Indonesia an attractive target in the eyes of [Canadian] policymakers."[146] Beginning in 1968, Canadian aid (mostly bilateral) rose rapidly from a little under a million to nearly $7 million in 1971-2 and then between 1975 and 1996 Canadian aid to Indonesia grew ten-fold.[147] By the mid-1990s Canada was providing Indonesia with tens of millions of dollars in assistance annually.[148]

Canadian aid helped the kleptocratic Suharto dictatorship consolidate control. It also helped Canadian investors.[149] An Inco mine on the island of Sulawesi, which displaced the indigenous Karonsi Dongo community of Soro wako, received significant support from Ottawa. EDC provided more than $50 million in financial guarantees and CIDA provided $38 million over ten years to a Guelph University project located near Inco's mine.[150] On November 14, 1994, Prime Minister Jean Chrétien met Suharto and the same day Inco received a 17-year contract extension for its mine.[151]

Canada's largest investor in Indonesia, Inco, spent $2.3 billion in the country between 1968 and 1995.[152] By 1981 Canada was Indonesia's third largest foreign investor.[153] A single Jean Chrétien led Team Canada business delegation to Indonesia netted more than $2 billion in agreements and by the mid-1990s, Canadian companies had more than $5 billion invested in the country.[154] In the early 1980s Canada even tried to sell Indonesia a Candu nuclear reactor.[155]

As relations between Ottawa and Suharto improved, Canada embraced Indonesia's 1975 invasion of East Timor. Against world opinion, in 1980 Canada changed its vote on annual General Assembly resolutions condemning Indonesia's invasion of East Timor from abstain to No.[156] During Pierre Trudeau's 1983 visit to Indonesia, an External Affairs official said "we do not have a view on whether the Indonesian invasion [of East Timor] was a good or bad thing."[157] When Jack Whittleton, Canada's ambassador to Indonesia, visited East Timor in 1987 he went with the Indonesian foreign minister and the main candidate in East Timor for the pro-Indonesian government party.[158] The extent to which Ottawa accepted Indonesia's jurisdiction over East Timor became clear when a 1993 CIDA programs in Asia map showed East Timor as Indonesia's 27th province.[159]

In November 1991 the Indonesian army slaughtered 200 peaceful protesters in what became known as the "Dili massacre." International outrage prompted many countries to cut off assistance to Indonesia. "Canada's response to that event was to blink, suspend $30 million in new aid projects for three years, but maintain its annual donation of $35-40 million in bilateral (government-to-government) assistance. In fact, CIDA reports 'ODA [Overseas Development Assistance] from Canada to Indonesia, including that channeled through international organizations, totaled $69.7 million in 1991/92'."[160]

Worried about protests by the East Timor Action Network and other anti-imperialist groups General Suharto considered cancelling his attendance at the 1997 Asia-Pacific Economic Cooperation (APEC) summit in Vancouver. Foreign Affairs Minister Lloyd Axworthy sent a letter to the Indonesian dictator making it clear that Canadian authorities would do their utmost to block protesters from embarrassing him. RCMP documents released after the police crack down on anti-APEC protesters show that the Prime Minister's office was indeed worried about embarrassing Suharto.[161]

Throughout Indonesia's brutal occupation of East Timor Ottawa let Canadian weapons makers sell their wares to the Indonesian army. "Since the invasion of East Timor and the deaths of up to 200,000 ethnic East Timorese, Canada has pumped more than a third of a billion dollars in military exports into Indonesia, an outlaw state repeatedly condemned by the United Nations."[162] The federal government supported Canadian weapons makers participation in trade fairs and trade missions to Indonesia and Ottawa even sponsored a military trade fair in Jakarta.[163] Indonesia's campaign of violence after the East Timorese voted for independence in late 1999 prompted Ottawa to finally ban military sales to that country. But, it was only a half measure. The Chrétien government exempted a military training simulator, worth more than $100 million, to be shipped to the Indonesian airforce.[164]

When Indonesian control over East Timor collapsed, foreign troops were sent to the country, including JTF2. Canada's special forces were sent to pave the way for a larger U.S. military contingent. Former JTF2 officer Denis Morisset writes that Canadian troops oversaw a small village where "the poor villagers were terrorized by our presence."[165]

It was not just Canada's foreign policy elite, corporations and military that supported Indonesia, despite its appalling human rights record. Even Canadian universities were "bought off", according to one author. In a chapter titled Partnership in an Evil Action: Canadian universities, Indonesia, East Timor and the question of international responsibility, *Bound by Power* documents how Canadian academics minimized the importance of Indonesian human rights violations in East Timor.[166] The book suggests that academic complicity is partly explained by the millions of dollars worth of Canadian aid money that went to universities for projects in Indonesia, including $38 million for a University of Guelph project. More generally, CIDA is active on campuses through initiatives such as the Higher Education Cooperation Plan.[167] In 1998, Canada's development agency boasted that it had relations with 50 universities and 60 colleges across the country. McGill University's Office of International Research is one example. Beginning in 1998 it received $10.5 million for a 10-year civil society and peace-building program in the Middle East.[168]

CIDA cherishes the influence it has within academia. In the late 1980s the Universities and Colleges of Canada, which represents the country's institutions of higher education, tried to develop a more stable source of funding for its international endeavours, but CIDA blocked the move to create a new government agency to fund universities' international partnerships. The aid agency preferred that the universities stay dependent.[169]

Canadian universities were also reluctant to challenge Canadian support for Indonesia's genocide in East Timor because of their ties to Canadian corporations active in the country. In March 1991 Carleton University's Public Interest Research Group (OPIRG) showed a documentary about East Timor titled *Buried Alive*. Indonesian officials called Carleton President Robin Farquhar to complain about the film. Farquhar called OPIRG's Jane Beauchamp, to tell "her the Indonesian government was unhappy about the film. … The Embassy officials were obviously correct in thinking they could expect a sympathetic response from Carleton's president. Perhaps they were influenced by the fact Carleton had just accepted a $750,000 donation from their own biggest Canadian investor, Inco."[170]

Discussion

Carleton's president was right to be concerned about Inco's reaction if she were seen to be sympathetic to critics of Suharto. When Laurentian University in Sudbury, Ontario offered mining critic, Joan Kuyek, an honourary degree in 1995 Inco threatened to withdraw its $3 million grant to the university.[171] A longtime critic of Canadian mining companies Kuyek was a director at Mining Watch and editor of *Community Rights and Corporate Responsibility*, a book about Canadian resource companies operating abroad. This brings up an important point. Canadian mining firms active internationally are major donors to Canadian universities. Here is a short list of some recent donations:

• In 2005 Inco donated $20 million to Memorial University in Newfoundland for an "Inco Innovation Centre".[172]

•In 2006 Goldcorp gave $1.5 million to the University of Ottawa for a Goldcorp Chair in Economic Geology.[173]

• In early 2007 fourteen B.C. mining companies gave the University of British Columbia more than $20 million, including $5 million from Goldcorp alone, for its School of Earth and Ocean Sciences.[174]

• In 2007 Ian Telfer, the former CEO of Goldcorp and current chair of its board of directors, gave $25 million to the University of Ottawa School of Management (it's now called the Telfer School of Management).[175]

• Since 1993 Joseph Rotman, who has sat on Barrick Gold's board since its inception, has given $36 million to the University of Toronto's School of Management (now Joseph L. Rotman School of Management). Rotman also sits on U of T's top decision-making body while another member of Barrick's board, Marshall Cohen, chairs the board of Toronto's other large university, York.[176]

• Mining magnate Seymour Schulich, an associate of Peter Munk, has probably been the leading private donor to universities across the country from the Schulich School of Engineering at the University of Calgary to the Schulich School of Medicine and Dentistry at the University of Western Ontario along with the Schulich School of Business at York and the Schulich Library of Science and Engineering and Schulich School of Music at McGill.[177]

Most of this mining money is not going to university departments directly shaping Canadian foreign-policy. Still, major donations usually buy influence, especially when combined with positions on university decision-making bodies, as is often the case. But, on occasion mining magnates do directly shape the study of international relations. Barrick Gold founder and chairman Peter Munk, for instance, provided nearly $10 million through a foundation set up to spread "liberty, freedom and free enterprise" to build the Munk Centre for International Studies at the University of Toronto.[178] Munk, we should recall, had strong political views including support for Chile's Augusto Pinochet and opposition to Venezuela's Hugo Chavez, as well as a personal interest in Canadian policy towards numerous countries in which Barrick operated. Asked why he appointed former Prime Minister Brian Mulroney to his board, Munk told Peter C. Newman: "He has great contacts. He knows every dictator in the world on a first name basis."[179]

Beyond the mining sector, wealthy individuals provide significant sums for the study of international affairs. In September 1999 media mogul Izzy Asper gave $2 million to the University of Manitoba, then the largest donation in the university's history, for an Asper Chair in International Business and Trade Law.[180] A year earlier the University of Manitoba received a million dollars from Montréal billionaire, Stephen Jarislowsky, to "create Canada's first chair in Middle East and North African studies."[181] Jarislowsky has endowed at least 15 chairs at Canadian universities in the sciences and humanities. Prominent pro-Israel family, the Bronfmans, provided $2 million to the University of Toronto in 1997 to create an Andrea and Charles Bronfman Chair in Israeli Studies. "Fifty years after its rebirth, the miracle of modern Israel is of broad interest," said Charles Bronfman. "Andy and I are happy that students at the U of T will have the opportunity to delve into the social, political and economic revolutions that have taken place within this remarkable society."[182]

The billionaire founder of Research in Motion, Jim Balsilllie, provided the most important support for the study of international affairs at Canadian universities. "Balsillie has donated over $130 million to launch three new institutions: the Balsillie School of International Affairs; the Centre for International Governance Innovation (CIGI); and the Canada International Council."[183] Embassy magazine reports that Balsillie wants to make CIGI "not unlike the Brookings Institute," the liberal imperialist Washington-based think tank on whose international advisory board he sits. Trying to drum up support for the CIC among the corporate sector, Balsillie wrote a commentary for the Globe and Mail Report on Business. He explained that "in return for their support, contributing business leaders would be offered seats in a CIC corporate senate that would give them influence over the research agenda and priorities of the new council."[184]

From the Chinese Revolution to the Korean War, to the American War in Vietnam, to Suharto's slaughter of half a million people in Indonesia, and beyond, there has always been a war of ideas. One side brings massive resources to that war. Incredibly, that side doesn't always win.

Chapter Notes

1   The Dominion and the Rising Sun, 40
2   The Dominion and the Rising Sun, 152
3   The Dominion and the Rising Sun, 167
4   The Dominion and the Rising Sun, 88/91
5   The Dominion and the Rising Sun, 2
6   The Dominion and the Rising Sun, 200
7   Canada in Korea, 61; Cross Culture and Faith, 82
8   Canada in Korea, 61
9   The Dominion and the Rising Sun, 65
10   A Worldly Mission, 54
11   Cross Culture and Faith, 107
12   Saving China, 85
13   Saving China, 85; A Worldly Mission, 53
14   A Worldly Mission, 122
15   A Worldly Mission, 123
16   The Dominion and the Rising Sun, 161
17   The Dominion and the Rising Sun, 145
18   The Dominion and the Rising Sun, 181
19   The Dominion and the Rising Sun, 158
20   The Dominion and the Rising Sun, 183
21   The Dominion and the Rising Sun, 74/155
22   The Dominion and the Rising Sun, 159
23   Canada and Japan, 95
24   Cross Culture and Faith, 130; War and Peacekeeping, 26; Canadians Behind Enemy Lines, 186
25   Canadians Behind Enemy Lines, 201
26   Saving China, 312
27   Saving China, 207
28   Saving China, 290; Alliance and Illusion, 32; Reluctant Adversaries, 29
29   The Worldly Years, 33
30   Reluctant Adversaries, 136
31   Canadian Gunboat Diplomacy, 90
32   Outposts of Empire, 59
33   Radical Mandarin, 263
34   Canadian Foreign Policy: 1945-2000, 136
35   Reluctant Adversaries, 122
36   Reluctant Adversaries, 86
37   Explaining the Canadian Response to the Tiananmen Square Massacre, 124
38   Explaining the Canadian Response to the Tiananmen Square Massacre, 130
39   Explaining the Canadian Response to the Tiananmen Square Massacre, 201
40   Explaining the Canadian Response to the Tiananmen Square Massacre, 207
41   Explaining the Canadian Response to the Tiananmen Square Massacre, 124
42   Wall Street Journal Feb 6 2009
43   Wall Street Journal Dec 31 2007
44   Aid and Ebb Tide, 247
45   Damning the Three Gorges, 9
46   Damning the Three Gorges, 10
47   Canada Among Nations 1998, 158
48   This Magazine Jan 2004
49   This Magazine Mar 2000; Canadian Forum Mar 1997
50   The Dominion and the Rising Sun, 54
51   Canada in Korea, 69
52   Canada in Korea, 63
53   Canada in Korea, 47
54   The Diplomacy of Constraint, 205
55   Korea, 121
56   Korea, 84
57   Korea, 77/88
58   Korea, 89
59   Canadian Foreign Policy: 1945-2000, 53; Canadian Gunboat Diplomacy, 136
60   Canadian Foreign Policy, 319
61   Canada in Korea, 73
62   Killing Hope, 49
63   Killing Hope, 49
64   Diplomacy of Constraint, 68
65   Blood on the Hill, 33
66   Korea, 133
67   Cold War Canada, 391
68   Far Eastern Tour, 90
69   Another Kind of Justice, 110
70   Blood on the Hills, 177
71   Quiet Complicity, 44
72   Partner to Behemoth, 80
73   Quiet complicity, 43
74   Towards a Francophone Community, 31
75   The Worldly Years, 91
76   Quiet Complicity, 4
77   Quiet Complicity, 119
78   Quiet Complicity, 129
79   Quiet complicity, 108
80   Quiet Complicity, 195
81   Snowjob, 18
82   Snowjob, 57
83   Snowjob, 57
84   Snowjob, 84
85   Quiet Complicity, 49
86   Quiet Complicity, 197
87   Quiet Complicity, 48
88   Snow Job, 185
89   Quiet Complicity, 81; Unknown Warriors, 30
90   Quiet Complicity, 81
91   Quiet Complicity, 4

92 Arms Canada, 61
93 Making a Killing, 3; Quiet Complicity, 4
94 Snow Job, 121
95 Making a Killing, 8
96 Snow Job, 122
97 Quiet Complicity, 204-205
98 Quiet Complicity, 205
99 Alliance and Illusion, 213
100 Unknown Warriors, 33
101 Canadian Gunboat Diplomacy, 137
102 Canadian Dimensions 1976
103 Rain-dancing, 63
104 Rain-dancing, 59
105 Nationalization of Guyana's Bauxite, 173
106 Canada and the Philippines, 46
107 Partnering and health development, 105
108 Canada and the Philippines, 13
109 Canada and the Philippines, 60
110 Canada and the Philippines, 62
111 Canada and the Philippines, 18
112 Canada and the Philippines, 65
113 This Magazine Oct 1988
114 This Magazine Oct 1988
115 This Magazine Oct 1988
116 Vancouver Sun Apr 23 1988
117 This Magazine Oct 1988
118 Hour newspaper April 10 2008
119 Ottawa Citizen Aug 18 2008
120 http://www.dominionpaper.ca/articles/1526
121 http://en.wikipedia.org/wiki/Human_rights_in_the_Philippines
122 Grande Epoque Aug 6 2008
123 www.dd-rd.ca/site/ PDF/publications/globalization/hria/Philippines percent20-REPORT.pdf
124 www.dd-rd.ca/site/ PDF/publications/globalization/hria/Philippines percent20-REPORT.pdf
125 www.dd-rd.ca/site/ PDF/publications/globalization/hria/Philippines percent20-REPORT.pdf
126 This Magazine Mar 2000
127 http://www.minesandcommunities.org/article.php?a=4236
128 http://www.minesandcommunities.org/article.php?a=1445
129 www.miningwatch.ca <http://www.miningwatch.ca/> October 4, 2005
130 This Magazine Nov 2008
131 http://www.minesandcommunities.org/article.php?a=1445
132 http://www.miningwatch.ca/index.php?/Placer Dome/Philippine Congressman
133 http://www.minesandcommunities.org/article.php?a=4236
134 This Magazine Nov 2008
135 http://www.protestbarrick.net/article.php?id=304
136 Montréal Gazette June 4 2006
137 www.foei.org/en/publications/pdfs/Barrick final sml.pdf
138 www.foei.org/en/publications/pdfs/Barrick final sml.pdf
139 http://www.mpi.org.au/default_178.html
140 http://www.mpi.org.au/campaigns/indigenous/barrick agm/
141 http://www.protestbarrick.net/article.php?id=399
142 http://www.zendiving.com/forums/showthread.php?p=168132
143 Ottawa Citizen May 18 2007
144 Canadian Foreign Policy, 147
145 Aid and Ebb Tide, 74
146 Rain-Dancing, 39
147 Rain-Dancing, 40; Complicity, 157/174
148 Victoria Times-Colonist July 28 1995
149 Complicity, 189
150 Complicity, 169/189
151 http://www.miningwatch.ca/index.php?/Sulawesi/INCO_in_INDONESIA_A_
152 Complicity, 189
153 Pacific Challenge, 215
154 Complicity, 188
155 Globe and Mail Jan 14 1981
156 Complicity, 108
157 Ethics and the Formation of Foreign Policy, 94
158 Complicity, 142
159 Canadian Journal of Development Studies Vol XXVII #4 2006
160 Bound by Power, 222
161 http://www.peak.sfu.ca/the-peak/98-3/issue2/crackdown.html
162 Vancouver Sun Jan 10 1998
163 Complicity, 203/205
164 Mediathink, 20
165 Nous étions invincibles, 145
166 Bound by Power - Partnership in an evil action
167 Canada and Development Cooperation, 100
168 Canada and the Middle East, 119
169 Aid and Ebb Tide, 171
170 Bound by Power, 242
171 Community rights and corporate responsibility, 220
172 http://www.mun.ca/iic/about/

173 http://embassymag.ca/page/view/.2006. november.22.s2

174 Vancouver Sun, Jan 15 2008

175 McGill Daily Oct 4 2007

176 http://rotman.utoronto.ca/about/jrotman. htm

177 Titans, 130

178 Titans, 126/208

179 Titans, 192

180 Canadian Jewish News Sept 2 1999

181 Canadian Jewish News Oct 18 2007

182 Canadian Jewish News Dec 11 1997

183 Embassy magazine Feb 20 2008

184 Globe and Mail Sept 10 2007

Central and South Asia

This region is the location of Canada's most important military operation of the past half-century. South Asia is also where Canadian aid policy was developed. Taking a good look at what Canada has done in this part of the world gives us a glimpse into the thinking of military and foreign policy experts. Understanding the war in Afghanistan, and the justifications for it, is important for developing a citizen-based foreign policy: a vision of Canada's role in the world in opposition to the narrow, elite-controlled policy that our tax dollars currently fund.

Afghanistan

In one sense, Canada's participation in the 2001 invasion and subsequent occupation of Afghanistan was nothing out of the ordinary. In fact, Canada supported previous foreign interventions in that country. Canadians fought with the British Royal Air Force when they were "quelling what became known as the Third Afghan War in 1919."[1] One Canadian soldier fighting in Afghanistan in 2008 had a great grandfather who fought for the British there in the late 1800s.[2]

But, Canada has not always supported foreign interventions into Afghanistan. When the Soviet Union invaded Afghanistan in 1979 Ottawa's response was severe. Canada suspended diplomatic relations with the government in Afghanistan, cut off all assistance to that country, pulled out of an amateur sports exchange with the Soviet Union, boycotted the 1980 Moscow Olympics and "urge[d] more Third World countries to participate in the boycott."[3] Ottawa also cancelled or postponed official visits and implemented a series of economic measures against the Soviet Union.[4]

Why did the Soviets invade? Largely to prop up a pro-Communist regime and for their own geopolitical reasons. They claimed to have entered the country at the request of the Afghan government and that their 10-year occupation benefited women's rights.

The similarities between that invasion/occupation and the 21st century one are striking. Nikolai Lanine, a Canadian immigrant who fought for Russia in Afghanistan, explained: "A lot of Soviet citizens believed that they were helping in Afghanistan, and the life of many Afghanis was affected positively. I mean, you can debate numbers, but there were universities, colleges open. Women were going freely around Kabul without burkas, the ones who chose to. ... there was a very large body of Soviet soldiers, even draftees, who were believing in what they were doing. In fact in my unit, many officers were staying more than the two years of mandatory service they were required to do in Afghanistan. So, again, if I give you the same kind of approach we are using in Canada now [in evaluating the Soviet intervention], you would ask 'well look at the bigger picture, look at what the Soviet Union was doing in Afghanistan.' What I'm suggesting now is, this is the way Canadians should look at it."[5]

Canada's military presence in Afghanistan began in late 2001 when our special forces secretly invaded, alongside U.S. and British operatives.[6] In the first six months of their operations, members of JTF2 killed 115 Taliban or Al Quaida fighters and captured 107 Taliban leaders.[7] By early 2002 the British began having doubts about the tactics used by Canadian and American special forces. "The concern among the British was that the ongoing raids [by Americans and Canadians] were giving Afghans the impression that the coalition was just another invading foreign army that had no respect for the country's culture or religion."[8]

In April 2009, 2,800 Canadian soldiers continued to fight in the southern province of Kandahar alongside a number of RCMP and provincial police as well as an unknown number of Canadian Security Intelligence Service (CSIS) agents.[9] The Conservative government said troops would remain in Afghanistan until at least 2011 with some likely to remain beyond that point.[10] In November 2008 Defence Minister Peter "McKay hinted that Canadian troops might still have a role to play in Afghanistan after 2011 — the deadline set by Parliament for the end of the current combat mission."[11] The Ottawa Citizen reported that Canada's Afghanistan Procurement Task Force "is pushing ahead with its plan to buy aerial drones [by 2012] outfitted with weapons even as the Harper government is promising to pull troops out of Afghanistan in 2011."[12] In August 2007 the commander of U.K. forces in Kandahar's neighbouring province, Helmand, said it would take 30 years to win the counterinsurgency war.[13] As this book went to press, Ottawa appeared set to steadily increase the number of troops to 4,000 for the 2009 Afghan elections and then draw down to 1,000 soldiers after 2011.[14]

Canadian troops were part of the NATO-led International Security Assistance Force (ISAF), which "is not a U.N. force, but is a coalition of the willing."[15] Despite attempts to portray the situation otherwise, the invasion of Afghanistan "had no more U.N. authority than the war on Iraq," noted Osgoode Hall law professor Michael Mandel.[16] As was the case in Iraq, after the U.S. invaded, the Security Council was pressured to authorize the use of force to defend the installed Afghan government.[17] ISAF did not answer directly to U.S. operation Enduring Freedom — the U.S. mission in Afghanistan — but had to defer to it. This meant that the 30,000 non-American foreign troops in Afghanistan, including 2,800 Canadians, were effectively under American command.[18] Canadian forces, in fact, worked closely with those from the U.S. Along with the Dutch, British and French, Canadian troops fought side by side with the Americans in the violent south of Afghanistan.

In October 2001 the U.S. unilaterally invaded Afghanistan, launching air strikes in support of Northern Alliance rebels fighting the Taliban government. Portrayed as a battle against the misogynist Taliban, the foreign intervention benefited an equally unsavory assortment of warlords, many of whom were members of the Northern Alliance. According to a member of the Revolutionary Afghanistan Women's Association (RAWA), "it was the NA [Northern Alliance] who first — even before the Taliban — banned education for women, destroyed hospitals, schools, educational institutions, museums and cinema halls. They were the first who banned women from going out and imposed the veil on them."[19]

The former Northern Alliance continued to wield significant influence in the country years after the invasion. "Rather than being sidelined former rebel fighters and warlords were welcomed into the political system and have consolidated their power bases."[20] Individuals responsible for massive human rights violations during Afghanistan's mid-1990s civil war were prominent within the country's parliament. A January 2006 Economist headline described Afghanistan's parliament as "A place for warlords to meet."[21] U.S.-appointed Afghan president Hamid Karzai made a known war criminal, Abdul Rashid Dostum, national army chief of staff, and Ismail Khan, a fundamentalist misogynist warlord, minister of energy. Karzai made these moves, with U.S. backing, despite public opposition to war criminals taking office. A January 2005 survey of 6,000 Afghans found that 90 percent of the country wanted those guilty of war crimes excluded from public office.[22] (While supporting warlords, Karzai banned Communist parties and Communist activity in February 2002.[23])

Ottawa seemed to share a certain sympathy for the warlords. In March 2006 Maclean's reported on General Rick Hillier's "enormous respect for the warlords — even making allowances for those who profit from the poppy business." The magazine quoted the head of Canadian Forces saying, "I saw the finest leaders that I have ever had the opportunity to meet. They beat the Russians pretty fairly and squarely, at the end of the day they were responsible for thumping the Taliban and throwing them out, along with a significant number of Al-Qaeda folks."[24] The Canadian military even provided direct support to some warlords. Between January 2006 and March 2007, for instance, the Canadian military gave $1.14 million in contracts to a company bearing the same name as Goul Agha Sherzai, a former warlord who fought against the Taliban and who served as Kandahar's governor until 2005.[25]

From direct support to individual warlords, to fighting alongside a compromised Afghan government, Ottawa's claims of moral righteousness ring hollow. Canadian troops' actions in Afghanistan also belie claims of high-minded motives. In a letter to the Toronto Star Corporal Paul Demetrick, a Canadian reservist, claimed Canadian forces used white phosphorus (a chemical weapon, according to various groups) as a weapon against "enemy-occupied" vineyards in Afghanistan.[26] If Canada was "there to help" why did it take more than two-and-a-half years to investigate an incident where Afghan detainees appeared to have been beaten by Canadians forces?[27] In May 2007 Harper's Conservatives denied allegations that individuals detained by Canadians, and turned over to the Afghan army and prison system, were tortured. The denials came before officials even investigated the allegations and it was later revealed that the torture claims proved to be highly credible.[28] Numerous individuals given to the Afghan army by Canadian Forces were unaccounted for, perhaps lost in a prison system that does not keep good records or perhaps disposed of.[29] The mainstream (Western government financed) Afghanistan Independent Human Rights Commission said it couldn't properly monitor detainees Canada or other countries handed over to the Afghan authorities since they were barred from accessing the notorious detention cells of the intelligence service.[30]

Rather than being in Afghanistan for the good of the people, foreign armies spurred the insurgency. "Life is clearly more perilous because we are there," is how a 2007 Senate defence committee report described the violence engendered by the foreign occupation of Afghanistan.[31] Similarly, when the Globe and Mail interviewed 43 Taliban foot soldiers in Kandahar on why they joined the insurgency, 12 said their family members were killed in airstrikes and 21 said their poppy fields were targeted for destruction by anti-drug teams.[32]

Air strikes were the most common cause of civilian casualties. In 2008 at least 552 Afghan civilians died from air strikes, according to the U.N. In August 2008, "President Hamid Karzai said air strikes carried out in Afghan villages by U.S. and NATO troops are only killing civilians and that the international community should instead go after terror centers in Pakistan."[33] A week after Karzai made that statement 90 civilians, including 60 children, were killed in a single NATO bombing raid.[34]

Canada had no fighter jets in Afghanistan, but in early 2009 Canadian helicopters began launching night-time operations.[35] In addition, Canadian personnel operated the NORAD systems that supported U.S. bombings and Canadian troops regularly called in U.S. air strikes.[36]

In September 2006 Canadian forces spearheaded NATO's Operation Medusa aimed at Taliban strongholds in the Panjwaii and Zhari districts of Kandahar. This is how Corporal Ryan Pagnacco from Waterloo, Ontario, described the airstrikes: "After watching bomb after bomb drop on these targets, I wondered how anything could survive. I figured that when we went in, we'd be walking into a ghost town."[37] The Medusa offensive forced 80,000 civilians to flee their homes, resulted in hundreds of enemy combatant deaths and "at least 50 civilians were killed over several weeks of bombing."[38] In the air or on the ground, fighting in Afghanistan was a bloody job. U.S. captain Dan Kearney explained the horrors of fighting in the country. Describing one of his troops he explained, "Last tour, if you didn't give him information, he'd burn down your house. He killed so many people. He's checked out."[39] In May 2008 the U.N. special rapporteur on extra-judicial, summary and arbitrary executions, Philip Alston, denounced foreign forces for organizing informal groups of Afghan fighters who launched secret night raids with little concern for civilian casualties.[40] Six months after Alston made his comments the Afghanistan Independent Human Rights Commission, a group heavily reliant on Western government money, released a report highly critical of night raids, particularly in Kandahar province. "The combination of abusive behaviour and violent breaking and entry into civilians' homes in the middle of the night stokes almost as much anger and resentment toward PGF [pro-government forces] as the more lethal air strikes," the report concluded.[41]

On numerous occasions the Western press has reported on Canadian troops killing Afghan civilians. "Canadian soldiers have repeatedly killed and wounded civilians while on patrol in civilian areas," noted the New York Times in May 2007.[42] Leftover Canadian mortars were reported to have killed three children in February 2009, prompting a demonstration calling for "death to the Canadians."[43] In July 2008 Canadian soldiers killed a five-year-old girl and her two-year-old brother after their vehicle got too close to a convoy. The father said afterwards that "if I get a chance, I will kill Canadians."[44] (Because of an agreement between Kabul and Ottawa, Afghanis had no legal right for compensation if they are hurt or their property damaged by Canadian soldiers.[45])

Canadian armoured vehicles regularly fired warning shots at bikes, cars or trucks that got too close, often causing crashes, leaving Afghans injured or worse. In June 2006 France 2 TV showed unedited images of Canadian soldiers searching villages and houses, breaking down doors and interrogating residents. According to a report in La Presse, Canadian soldiers were shown telling villagers that it was not smart to join the Taliban because our soldiers are really good, they are well trained and good shots "and you will die".[46] Later on the video shows a Canadian commander saying "too bad for you if you don't want to tell us where the Taliban are hiding. We will come and kill them. We will drop many bombs and fire all over. Is this what you want? Well then continue telling us nothing."[47]

Government documents suggest Canadian forces waged an extremely active counterinsurgency campaign. Secret DND files show that Canadian troops fired an astounding 4.7 million bullets between April 2006 and December 2007, including over 1,650 tank shells and 12,000 artillery rounds.[48] Running low on ammunition, the Canadian military turned to the U.S. army for an emergency order of $14 million worth of bullets in late 2006 and then in the first five months of 2007 General Dynamic Ordnance and Tactical Systems Canada sold the military $46 million worth of bullets and mortars.[49]

Bullet manufacturers were not the only companies happy about Canada's involvement in Afghanistan. A company owned by the Prince Group, which controls notorious U.S. mercenary company Blackwater, received $850,000 to provide counter insurgency training to Canadian soldiers on their way to Afghanistan.[50] The private security industry has thrived in Afghanistan. In 2006-2007 Foreign Affairs spent at least $15 million on private security contractors in the country.[51] Saladin Security protected the Canadian embassy in Kabul, visiting dignitaries, as well as forward operating bases in Kandahar province.[52] With more than 2,000 "troops" in Afghanistan, Saladin's private army in the country was larger than all but a handful of NATO countries' armed contingents.[53] Another U.S.-based private security force, DynCorp International, had 2,500 contractors in the country.[54] Canadian Brigadier General Denis Thompson explained that "without private security firms it would be impossible to achieve what we are achieving here. There are many aspects of the mission here in Afghanistan, many security aspects that are performed by private security firms that which, if they were turned over to the military, would make our task impossible. We just don't have the numbers to do everything."[55]

Some security firms protecting Canadian installations have troubling histories. "The Canadian forces have hired a private security firm [Britain's Hart Security] in Afghanistan that once employed a former member of a South African military unit that assassinated opponents of the Apartheid regime."[56] Saladin's predecessor, KMS, trained and possibly equipped Islamic insurgents battling Russian forces in Afghanistan in the 1980s. The company also sent mercenaries into Nicaragua as part of the Iran Contra affair.[57]

Private security firms in Afghanistan operated under guidelines that practically guaranteed significant civilian casualties. After a Canadian officer was killed by a private security official in August 2008, Canadian Major Corey Frederickson explained that the "normal contact drill [for private security] is that as soon as they get hit with something then it's 360 [degrees], open up on anything that moves."[58] Describing the aftermath of the Canadian soldier's death, Stars and Stripes noted that "when questioned by Canadian and U.S. military officers, several of the Afghan security guards freely admitted opening fire on what they thought were Taliban fighters. But when informed that a Canadian soldier had been wounded, their stories began to change, and many never claimed to have fired all."[59] Despite the obvious social ills of a private, for-profit military, business boomed in Afghanistan. Kandahar city's "Commando District" was home to hundreds of well-armed men who earned about $300 a month for their services.[60]

Canadian companies also won themselves a piece of the booming business. Globe Risk, a Toronto-based security firm, had offices in Kabul and Kandahar while Montréal's Gardaworld had a company manager based in the country. Among other contracts, Gardaworld was hired by the U.N. to provide security, advice and logistical support during the 2005 parliamentary elections.[61]

The war was also good business for a number of other Canadian companies. In 2005, Rick Hillier told the Canadian Institute of Strategic Studies: "I think it's a Team Canada approach that we need ... we need private industry involved ... you want to come in and make money from us, build our camps, fulfill our contracts or do maintenance for us and then ten years later when everything is stabilized and secure you can come and start operating your business ... we need you there on Day 1. Take some risks with us on Day 1 as part of a team that we build ... with you supporting us and us being supported by you."[62]

At least 22 percent of the military's publicly declared costs in Afghanistan — $1.34 billion as of November 2007 — was spent on the Canadian Forces Contractor Augmentation Program (CANCAP).[63] Under CANCAP a company was reimbursed for all the costs it incurred and was paid two-three percent in general and administrative expenses and one percent in profit. It was then eligible for an eight percent performance incentive fee.[64]

In partnership with U.S. firm PAE, Montréal's SNC Lavalin had a ten-year contract worth as much as $700 million for construction and management of the Canadian military base in Kandahar.[65] There were at least 200 SNC-PAE employees who worked on the base but further details concerning the contract were hard to find. DND blocked Access to Information requests concerning its contract with SNC-PAE.[66] The military is tightlipped about its relations to private contractors in Afghanistan. "The defence department is keeping secret the names of dozens of companies that received almost $42 million worth of contracts in Afghanistan," reported the Ottawa Citizen.[67]

The military was not the only department outsourcing its operations in Afghanistan to private companies. CIDA, for instance, paid Development Works Inc. $5.1 million to run a "rapid village development plan" in Kandahar province. Nearly 40 percent of the contract was earmarked for professional fees.[68] Similarly, CIDA's $50 million "signature project" to repair the Dahla dam on the Arghandab River in the north of Kandahar province was given to SNC Lavalin.[69] (SNC planned to hire a significant number of private security operatives to protect the dam.)

The "benefits" of the war and occupation reached beyond companies working alongside the military or within the reconstruction industry — a small part of what Naomi Klein calls "disaster capitalism." The war improved the country's "investment climate" more generally. "Over the past four years," noted The Economist in April 2006, "Afghanistan has acquired new laws, including many aimed at securing a pleasant business-friendly society where human rights are upheld."[70] One Canadian who basked in the new climate was an Afghani Vancouverite who owned the country's biggest cellular phone company, Roshan.[71]

"Is mineral-rich Afghanistan the next mining hotspot?" asked a Financial Post headline in March 2008.[72] For its part, the Afghan government was "launching an ambitious campaign to woo foreign mining companies." In March 2007 Afghan Minister of Mines Abrahim Adel attended Toronto's Prospectors and Developers Association of Canada Conference.[73] Ottawa helped bring the Afghan minister and Canadian investors together. "Minister Adel," a Foreign Affairs invitation to the conference promised, "will speak about the tremendous mining opportunities in Afghanistan, including details on a number of projects. He welcomes the opportunity to meet with Canadian companies."[74] At the time Vancouver-based Hunter Dickinson was one Canadian mining company already prospecting in the country.

But, direct benefits to companies or individuals were too small to make the money spent by Canada in Afghanistan make sense from an economic perspective. So what else can explain Ottawa's eagerness for engaging in a violent counterinsurgency campaign in Afghanistan that cost over 110 Canadian lives and billions of dollars? It seems clear that pressure from Washington was the main reason Canada was fighting. "Washington's reactions tended to be the exclusive consideration in almost all of the discussions about Afghanistan. ... The political problem, of course, was how to support Washington in its war on terror without supporting the war in Iraq. The answer to the problem was the so-called 'Afghan solution.'"[75] Former Foreign Affairs Minister Bill Graham explained "there was no question, every time we talked about the Afghan mission, it gave us cover for not going to Iraq."[76]

But what were Washington's objectives in Afghanistan? Occupying the country added to U.S. influence in the Caucasus region, improving the U.S. geostrategic position vis-à-vis Russia and China. Afghanistan also borders Iran and U.S. military bases in the country could facilitate an attack on that country. As well, Afghanistan has non-military geostrategic value as an energy corridor. The U.S. wants a gas pipeline through Turkmenistan, Pakistan and India to bypass Iran and Afghan territory is necessary for that endeavour. Canada endorsed this pipeline project. In November 2006, a parliamentary secretary, Canada's high commissioner to India, the director of the Afghanistan task force in Foreign Affairs and the first secretary for aid and development attended a regional conference on Central Asian energy issues. The conference's final statement pledged: "Countries and organizations will assist Afghanistan to become an energy bridge in the region and to develop regional trade through supporting initiatives in bilateral/multilateral cross-border energy projects. ... Work will be accelerated on [the] Turkmenistan-Afghanistan-Pakistan-India gas pipeline to develop a technically and commercially viable project."[77] A primary aim of this pipeline was to isolate Iran, which was negotiating a $7.5 billion pipeline with Pakistan and India to supply those countries with Iranian gas, according to a June 2008 Canadian Centre for Policy Alternatives report.[78] The report claims southern Afghanistan needed to be cleared of insurgent activity for the pipeline project to go ahead as scheduled. "Nobody is going to start putting pipe in the ground unless they are satisfied that there is some reasonable insurance that the workers for the pipeline are going to be safe," explained Howard Brown, Canada's representative for the Asian Development Bank, which financed the project.[79]

Good for business and U.S. geopolitical designs, the war also benefited those who argue that Canada should spend more on its military and project more than its good name to the world. By further militarizing Canada, the Afghan war was likely to have long-term effects on Canadian foreign policy. In June 2008 the Conservative government announced a plan to spend $490 billion on the military over the next 20 years. By 2012 the military was supposed to double to 75,000 soldiers and 35,000 reserves.[80]

Just as the war required an increase in the size of the military, it also created demand for new military purchases. For example, despite an international ban, DND purchased laser weapons for use in Afghanistan.[81] "The Canadian Forces are spending $27 million over the next three years to buy equipment for a new military spy unit" needed in Afghanistan.[82]

In 2006 the military created the Special Operations Command to oversee the newly created Canadian Special Operations Regiment, a special operations aviation squadron and an expanded nuclear, biological, chemical and radiological response unit.[83] JTF2, which "has outgrown its Ottawa base," was to be overseen by Special Operations Command. JTF2 was relocating at a cost of $340 million after having doubled from 300 to 600 men since 2002.[84] By the end of 2010, Canadian Special Operations Command was to be responsible for about 2,300 personnel. The advantage of special operations forces is that they operate in almost total secrecy. "Deniability," according to a March 2002 speech by Major B. J. Brister, is why the federal government prefers special operation forces.[85]

Still, many citizens did not support a military buildup so Foreign Affairs preferred to focus public attention on Canadian aid to Afghanistan rather than the war. Many supporters of Canada's intervention, including numerous NGO workers, seemed to make a strong distinction between our military role and "aid" to Afghanistan. But, as seen elsewhere, Canadian aid has often been closely associated with military intervention. More than two years before Afghanistan's October 2004 presidential election Canadian aid was going to prop up the U.S.-installed Afghan government. The person in charge of aid at the Canadian embassy in Kabul, Nipa Banerjee, explained how CIDA played a role in "helping the government to establish its authority and securing the community and getting the community's support."[86]

For the military, aid is part of its counterinsurgency operations. "It's a useful counterinsurgency tool," is how Lieutenant-Colonel Tom Doucette, commander of Canada's provincial reconstruction team, described CIDA's work.[87] Development assistance, for instance, was sometimes given to communities in exchange for information on combatants. Reconstruction aid was an important part of what the Canadian army called "three block war." "Our military could be engaged in combat against well-armed militia in one city block, stabilization operations in the next block and humanitarian relief and reconstruction two blocks over," explained the Paul Martin government's 2005 International Policy Statement.[88]

The army began to train troops in foreign "reconstruction." One hundred Canadian troops from Québec City went to Belize in August 2008 to work on humanitarian projects. The objective of the training was to teach soldiers how to do humanitarian work in an unfamiliar environment. The organizer told a reporter "when we go to a country like Belize, we can negotiate, find a common ground, just like in Afghanistan."[89]

What Ottawa calls "aid" has also been used to co-opt non-governmental organizations. Just after leaving her position as head of CIDA in Afghanistan, Nipa Banerjee explained, in a column for Policy Options magazine, that Canadian aid is used to gain NGO support for the Afghan mission.[90]

Rights & Democracy, often described as an NGO despite having been created by Parliament in 1988 and receiving its budget from Ottawa, was one group that vigorously defended the mission for Ottawa. Echoing the official description of the Canadian mission, Rights & Democracy "has urged the Security Council to increase the peacekeeping forces to at least 30,000 and to deploy peace troops throughout the country with instructions to disarm warring factions."[91] In 2002 Rights & Democracy's Women's Rights Fund for Afghanistan opened an office in Kabul with $500,000 from CIDA. Vancouver researcher Harsha Walia explained the one-sided nature of the Women's Rights Fund: "A 'non-partisan' Afghanistan backgrounder on the website of the Fund highlights only the historic abuse of women by the Taliban and characterizes the current period as one of 'ongoing conflict' without any mention of foreign forces in the country."[92]

In February 2009 Rights & Democracy organized a Montréal conference with Afghanistan's minister for women's affairs. CIDA, SNC Lavalin and Rio Tinto Alcan sponsored the event. By December 2007 the federal government had given Rights & Democracy $5 million for its Afghan work.[93] Some of this was channeled to other groups, such as Canadian Women for Women in Afghanistan, which used feminism to justify imperialism. (CIDA provided more than $500,000 directly to Canadian Women for Women in Afghanistan.[94]) In a January 2009 Ottawa Citizen Commentary headlined "The cultural relativists can't excuse evil" Lauryn Oates, president of Canadian Women for Women in Afghanistan, argued against those opposing Canada's mission in Afghanistan.[95] An earlier piece by Oates in the Globe and Mail was titled, "Don't share a table with the Taliban."[96]

In 2007 CIDA gave $575,000 to a group called Peace Build.[97] This was in addition to money from Foreign Affairs and a Crown corporation, IDRC. Peace Build was a network of NGOs that was a "moderate" counterweight to the more activist-oriented (and less financially dependent) Canadian Peace Alliance.

In addition to money, government influence is felt through the jobs provided to people from the NGO world, and vice versa. Peace Build's founder Peggy Mason, a former Foreign Affairs officer, was but one example. Scott Gilmore was another member of the foreign service to establish an NGO, Peace Dividend Trust, active in Afghanistan.[98] There is a tradition of this sort of movement. Bill McWhinney, the executive secretary of Canada's first major NGO, CUSO, from 1962-1966, became president of CIDA in 1982-1983. Similarly, the head of CIDA at the end of 2008, Margaret Biggs, was director of research at the North-South Institute from 1976 to 1985.[99] A CIDA-funded NGO, the United Nations Association of Canada sees developing future foreign service employees as an important part of its mandate. The organization's spokesperson, Kathryn White, described their Young Junior Professionals program to Embassy magazine: "These Canadian kids were sought after, they had skills, they were comfortable working in multi-ethnic environments and so on. It builds a relationship, it builds future young diplomats."[100] When the Conservatives cut CIDA's internship program in 2008 Liberal Party CIDA critic Keith Martin complained that this would harm the aid agency. "This is a breeding ground for CIDA workers and it allows young people to get the experience they need."[101]

The back and forth between NGOs and the federal government has the effect of stifling criticism of Canadian foreign-policy, be it in Afghanistan or elsewhere. It can be hard to criticize former or future colleagues. Most important, if working for the government is a possible career choice it is professionally dangerous to be highly critical of Canadian policy. It is also crucial for NGOs to have contacts in Ottawa and diplomatic circles as NGO proposals are routinely cleared through the Canadian mission in the country concerned.[102]

"Government funding, policies and procedures for NGOs, more than any other single factor, have determined the pattern of Canadian NGO activity," said Ian Smiley, one of Canada's most prominent spokespersons for development NGOs.[103]

Of course many people who work for NGOs claim to be critical of the government. Some have demanded that resources spent on the military component of Canada's intervention be diverted towards an increase in aid, but is it realistic to think that Ottawa would provide nearly $300 million a year in aid to Afghanistan if there were no Canadian troops in that country? This much is clear: Canadian aid was designed to consolidate the military occupation of Afghanistan. Any improvements this aid might bring to the living conditions of Afghanis were incidental, something that might be useful for propaganda purposes.

And it's not just "aid" agencies and NGOs that were engaged in propaganda efforts aimed at Canadians. DND also worked hard to shape public opinion regarding the Afghan war and military activities more generally. Tens of millions of dollars were spent on advertising alone. For example, between April 1 and September 30, 2006, the federal government spent $15.5 million on military publicity, compared to only $2.35 million on projects for the Ministry of Environment.[104] DND also had a variety of less direct means to influence the media landscape. To build relations with the media, DND created a vast network of individuals paid to produce press releases, befriend journalists or perform a wide variety of other media-related activities. According to CBC's The National, DND employed 500 public relations officers and spent $23 million annually spinning the Afghan war.[105] After perusing official documents concerning the military's media strategy James Laxer wrote: "At what are called 'message events' where journalists are updated on developments in Afghanistan, officials from Foreign Affairs, National Defence and the Canadian International Development Agency are to present the government line following 'dry runs' to make sure the briefing motivates journalists to adopt what is called the 'desired sound bite.'"[106]

In February 2007 Walrus magazine ran a lengthy article about the Journalist Familiarization Course, which prepares reporters going to Afghanistan to be embedded with Canadian troops. The article explained: "At Meadford [training grounds] I also learned this: it's hard to be objective when you're hurtling backward through the air. We'd entrusted the soldiers with our safety and in return we'd hoped to impress them with our courage. There was an exhilarating sense that we were all in this together — and it was only nine in the morning on our first day ... I can only imagine how difficult it would be to stay objective if your life actually depended on the soldiers around you."[107]

When the Pentagon began training reporters in 2003 it provoked outrage. Yet the Journalist Familiarization Course was barely noticed in Canada. The same can be said for the rules governing those gathering news in Afghanistan. Journalists have been expelled from Kandahar airfield for breaking Canadian Forces' rules, which include publishing information the military does not want released. "At the Kandahar airfield Canadian military public affairs officers threatened journalists with expulsion from the installation if they dare to write about special forces operating from the base. Some reporters were even told not to look in the direction of the JTF2 compound as they walked by."[108] On February 12, 2002, a Toronto Star reporter was expelled from a military base in Afghanistan after reporting on JTF2 night operations as well as the guard towers around a prisoner detention centre.[109] "Canadian military officials removed four journalists accompanying troops on an Afghanistan operation earlier this year [2006] after complaints from allies, newly released documents show."[110] Two weeks before this incident, Canadian officers denied a request from a Dutch journalist for a five-day visit to Kandahar airfield after "investigating the comfort level of the Dutch" and learning the Dutch Ministry of Defence did not support it.[111] The Canadian army also made it extremely difficult for independent journalists to stay at their base in Kandahar.[112]

There were also a variety of more subtle ways in which the military influenced what we learned about their work. In November 2008 Le Devoir's military affairs reporter Alec Castonguay received the Conference of Defence Associations' Ross Munro Media Award, along with $2,500. Combat Camera, a DND program that provided media organizations with video footage and photographic stills of Canadian military engagements, offered the army another mechanism to influence the media.[113]

In 2006 DND invested $9 million in university training.[114] The same year the Canadian Defence Academy helped numerous colleges and community colleges add military diplomas and programs formerly provided at the Royal Military College in Kingston.[115] In addition, the Canadian Defence Academy Press published books on the military.

In February 2008 it was reported that DND's Security and Defence Forum (SDF) gave $580,000 to York University, $630,000 to UQAM, $630,000 to Wilfrid Laurier, $655,000 to the University of Laval, $680,000 to McGill, $680,000 to UBC, $680,000 to the University of Manitoba, $680,000 to UNB, $780,0000 to Carleton, $780,000 to Dalhousie, $780,000 to the University of Calgary and $1.480 000 to Queen's.[116] For some departments this military money makes up a large portion of their entire budgets. The University of New Brunswick's Gregg Centre for the Study of War and Society received a quarter of its yearly funding from the military.[117] While individual departments received sizable sums from the military so did some individual academics. One Canadian professor received an $825,000 SDF grant in which DND expected the professor to "conduct outreach activities with the Canadian public … and Parliament about security and defence issues."[118] A May 2008 Walrus magazine article noted that "when DND needs a kind word in Parliament or the media —presto! — an SDF-sponsored scholar often appears, without disclosing his or her financial link."[119]

In March 2007 Interpress Service reported: "Can Canadians have a fair debate on their military mission in southern Afghanistan when so many of the sources quoted in the domestic press are bankrolled by the Department of National Defence (DND)? That's the worry of peace studies experts who point out that a disproportionate number of those quoted by the media or penning op-eds on foreign affairs hail from the 14 defence, international studies and military history programmes across the country receiving DND dole-outs."[120] In addition to military affairs, DND money shapes foreign-policy studies more generally. Peter Langille, a University of Western Ontario professor, told IPS that DND "has a near monopoly over discussion and programmes not only of defence issues, but also IR [international relations studies] within Canadian academe."[121]

The mechanism of influence was rarely to pressure those receiving its money to toe the DND line. Rather some are funded and others are not. For instance, McMaster University in Hamilton had a Centre for Peace Studies for 17 years but as of 2008 had yet to find the money to hire a single faculty member. (Of course government ministries hiring academics to promote wars is nothing new. During the Boer war Ottawa commissioned Steven Leacock, a McGill professor and famous author, to tour the empire as an "imperial missionary."[122])

The military is not even shy about spending tax dollars to shape public opinion. "It is the responsibility of the Department of National Defense to build and maintain a constituency for defence among Canada's citizens," noted a headline in the Journal of Conference of Defence Associations Institute.[123] Former chief of the defence staff, General R. M. Withers, explained: "In its attempts to place the facts before the public, DND has done a great deal of good, honest work. Prompt, professionally compiled press announcements; the creation of a speakers bureau; an endowment of chairs of strategic studies at universities; the production of special videos; the provision of expert testimony to parliamentary committees; the support given associations and organizations such as the Conference of Defence Associations and the Canadian Institute of Strategic Studies."[124]

India

Long before Ottawa set aside $2 billion in aid to Afghanistan, geopolitical considerations were the primary motivation for disbursing foreign assistance. With Mao's triumph in China in 1949, Canada began its first significant (non-European) allocation of foreign aid through the Colombo plan. The Colombo plan's primary aim was to keep the former British Asian colonies, especially India, within the Western fold.

External Affairs Minister Lester Pearson told the 1950 Colombo conference that "Communist expansionism may now spill over into south East Asia as well as into the Middle East.... If South East and South Asia are not to be conquered by Communism, we of the free democratic world must demonstrate that it is we and not the Russians who stand for national liberation and economic and social progress."[125] Two years later Prime Minister Louis St. Laurent was even more explicit about the carrot and stick approach to defeating "Communism." In September 1952 St. Laurent explained "in South East Asia through the establishment of the Colombo plan not only are we trying to provide wider commercial relations but we are also fighting another Asiatic war against Communism in the interests of peace, this time with economic rather than military weapons. We Canadians know that in the struggle against Communism there are two useful weapons, the economic and the military. While we much prefer to use the economic weapons as we are in the Colombo plan, we know that we may have no choice but to use the military weapons as we have been forced to do in Korea."[126] In other words, if some of India's post-colonial population had not set their sights on a Communist solution to their troubles — with the possibility of Soviet or Chinese assistance — Canada probably would not have provided aid.

(The Colombo plan was later extended to Africa and the Caribbean amidst fears the British Empire's former territories would follow wholly independent paths or fall under the influence of the Communist bloc. Once newly independent countries joined the Commonwealth, such as Ghana in 1958, they also began to receive Canadian aid.)

During the early Cold War years aid underpinned Canada's "special relationship" with India, which was aimed at keeping the world's second most populous nation within the Western fold. Or as Pearson put it, "one of the jobs of a Canadian in New Delhi would be to help disabuse Indians of their more extreme prejudices against the United States."[127]

It worked. Canadian influence over India, the largest recipient of Canadian Colombo plan aid, was apparent at the International Control Commission (ICC) for Vietnam, created in 1954 to oversee the implementation of the Geneva Accords that ended the First Indochina War with the partition of Vietnam. At the ICC Poland represented the Eastern bloc, Canada represented the West and India was supposed to be neutral. But, more often than not, India sided with Canada in support of the U.S. military buildup in South Vietnam, despite India's history of colonial domination. Canadian and U.S. aid to India, which dwarfed anything Poland, Vietnam or the USSR was offering, played no small role in India's stance. It wasn't until the totally one-sided nature of Canada's position on the ICC and U.S. aggression became unbearably flagrant that India moved closer to Poland's position. "It was largely because of Indochina" that the focus of Canadian aid shifted from India. Or less diplomatically, "that Canadian goodwill and encouragement towards India was transformed into bitterness and distrust."[128]

The broad rationale for extending foreign aid was laid out at a 1968 seminar for the newly established Canadian International Development Agency. This day-long event was devoted to discussing a paper titled "Canada's Purpose in Extending Foreign Assistance" written by Professor Steven Triantas of the University of Toronto. Foreign aid, Triantas argued, "may be used to induce the underdeveloped countries to accept the international status quo or change it in our favour." Aid provided an opportunity "to lead them to rational political and economic developments and a better understanding of our interests and problems of mutual concern." Triantis discussed the appeal of a "'Sunday School mentality' which 'appears' noble and unselfish and can serve in pushing into the background other motives … [that] might be difficult to discuss publicly."[129]

A 1969 CIDA background paper, expanding on Triantas views, summarized the rationale for Canadian aid: "To establish within recipient countries those political attitudes or commitments, military alliances or military bases that would assist Canada or Canada's western allies to maintain a reasonably stable and secure international political system. Through this objective, Canada's aid programs would serve not only to help increase Canada's influence within the developing world, but also within the western alliance."[130]

Aid is also used to turn taxes into corporate profits both directly and indirectly. The government may call it foreign aid, but a central aim of CIDA has always been to help Canadian companies expand abroad. For example: "As a result of suggestions made by Alcan (and long discussions in Ottawa and Lagos) the Canadian International Development Agency... agreed to make a substantial 'soft' loan to the Nigerian government [in the early 1970s]. This was for an amount of $1.6 million for 50 years at a low interest rate. As the agreements provided, the Nigerian government in turn would undertake to lend the money at a higher interest rate, for ten years, to Alcan Nigeria to be used mainly to finance the training of a new workforce of Nigerians to operate the [Alcan] plants at Port Harcourt, where jobs and rebuilt industry were needed. Since this was a new concept (CIDA loans government-to-government for the aid of private industry) it took long negotiations, and the sympathetic support of the Canadian High Commissioner and the Trade Commisioner in Lagos."[131]

The program that best exemplifies CIDA's aim of turning taxes into profits is CIDA-INC. Established in 1978, CIDA-INC provides grants for investors to finance feasibility and starter studies in poorer countries.[132] Companies only repay public money they receive if they secure a contract worth $5 million, or export that amount of goods. An internal audit found that between 1978 and 2005 CIDA-INC disbursed $1.1 billion to Canadian businesses and that of 8,138 projects funded only 972 were implemented.[133] "Some companies were using the CIDA-INC program as a cash cow, sending in project proposals with no intention of ever following through."[134]

Through exhibits and seminars supported by CIDA-INC the business community benefited from taxpayer-funded information-gathering efforts. The aid program also provided financial and logistical support for firms seeking contracts from the World Bank and other multilateral agencies.[135]

But, CIDA-INC is just one piece of a larger aid puzzle designed to make sure Canadian companies benefit from tax dollars. Initially all Canadian aid was tied, meaning it had to be spent on Canadian-produced goods or services.[136] In 1970 the percentage of tied aid dropped to 80 percent and in 2008, even after four decades of criticism, a little less half of all Canadian aid was still tied.[137] At 43 percent Canada's tied aid was significantly higher than most rich countries. It's seven percent in Belgian, 11 percent in Denmark, six percent in France, eight percent in Germany, five percent in Japan, zero percent in Ireland, zero percent in Norway, zero percent in the U.K. Only

Austria reported a higher proportion of tied aid, according to one study that excluded the U.S.[138] In fact, CIDA diligently breaks down the number of Canadian jobs created, how many businesses receive contracts as well as the number of universities and colleges that benefit from Canadian aid.[139]

Tied aid has also helped Canada deal with surplus commodities and products. With an abundance of grain produced on the prairies food aid is the commodity most often tied to Canadian exports.[140] $15 million of the first $25 million Ottawa gave to India was Canadian food aid. In 1958 Prime Minister John Diefenbaker explained "in view of the fact that we have in Canada a tremendous surplus of wheat, we would naturally hope, if not expect, that these countries would take a large share of wheat and flour under the Colombo Plan."[141] By 1971 CIDA was the main cash customer of the Canadian Wheat Board.[142]

CIDA was not only concerned with the excess produced by the family farmer. Major corporations such as Bombardier have also sold unwanted products with CIDA's help.[143] Regarding Bombardier in the 1980s, the company's Senior Vice President Yvon Turcot recalled: "I traveled with them to foreign countries where they sold their locomotives and the only contracts they got were from CIDA. Nobody would buy except the governments of emerging nations, financed by CIDA on favourable terms."[144]

An important way in which aid was structured to benefit Canadian business was by channeling funds to sectors where Canada had a technological advantage. CIDA prioritized sectors where Canadian companies led the field and were well-positioned to win future contracts. "Canada will continue to offer its assistance in sectors such as transport and communications where Canadian expertise and technology are appropriate and competitive," noted the Liberals' 1970 White Paper.[145]

With Canadian industry well equipped to build hydro dams, our aid flowed freely to that sector. During the 1950s almost a third of all Canadian Colombo plan aid and close to two thirds of capital assistance was taken up by India's Kundah hydro development, and the Warsak Hydro and Irrigation Scheme in Pakistan (as well as steam locomotives).[146] Both of these projects destroyed their respective area's ecosystems. The Chamera was another controversial Canadian-backed dam in India heavily financed with Canadian assistance.

Aid helped develop international investment opportunities for Canadian companies. Former External Affairs diplomat Michel Dupuy told the Empire Club in 1977: "By establishing Canadian technology and expertise in the developing countries on whatever terms we grant them, we are laying the groundwork for repeat business and for expansion of Canadian trade in the future."[147]

Assistance through Canadian non-governmental organizations often had a similar effect. Explaining the rationale for developing CIDA's Business and Industry Program, particularly the Canadian Executive Service Organization (CESO), former CIDA president Maurice Strong explained: "Canada did not have the same relationship that many big countries had with the developing world ... many developing country people were familiar with big U.S. corporations or had gone to major U.S. universities and colleges. ... of course, the former colonial powers, like France and the Netherlands, had cadres of people who had been actively on their side in the developing world. ...so there were natural linkages between the developing countries and the other major countries offering development assistance. Canada had far fewer of those relationships. So, we felt we needed to take special measures to introduce industry into the development process."[148]

Montréal mining company SEMAFO provides an example. SEMAFO was an outgrowth of Benoit La Salle's work for CIDA financed Plan Canada, a subsidiary of Plan International, "one of the world's largest development organizations, working in more than 65 countries worldwide on critical issues affecting millions of children."[149] La Salle told an interviewer that SEMAFO "was created in 1995 during my first visit to Burkina Faso as part of a mission with the NGO-Plan. I am the president of the administration council of Plan Canada and a director of Plan International. So, after the Plan organized visit to Burkina Faso provided me an opportunity to get close with national authorities, I decided to create SEMAFO to participate in the development of Burkina Faso's mining industry."[150] In another interview, La Salle said "[in my position at Plan] I was able to meet [African] presidents, prime ministers and functionaries" whom he now does business with.[151]

Mongolia

Beginning in 2005 the Financial Post, the business section of the National Post, began to press Ottawa to increase diplomatic relations with Mongolia. "Ottawa should open a full-fledged embassy with a career diplomat in the capital city of Mongolia, Ulan Bator, immediately," demanded columnist Diane Francis.[152] In her column Francis quoted Ivanhoe Mining's chairman, Robert Friedland. "The U.S. is here with an embassy," said Friedland. "Why is Canada ignoring a country that wants close relations and the only truly democratic country in Asia that needs our help? Why is Canada kissing Fidel Castro's ass in Cuba? It's hypocrisy."[153]

Julian Dierkes, a professor at the Institute of Asian Research at UBC, added her voice to calls for greater Canadian diplomatic representation in the most sparsely populated country in the world. "Mongolia is one of the few countries where Canada is the 800 pound gorilla," Dierkes told the Financial Post in April 2007.[154] "It's the biggest investor, and everyone looks to Canada for leadership... [but] there's still no embassy or diplomatic representation, which is really terrible. And so the initial enthusiasm for Canadian involvement in mining has been tempered somewhat by the lack of government involvement in any of this."[155] A year later, the business press reported that "Canada will establish a new trade mission in Ulaanbaatar, Mongolia, this year to help Canadian companies active in the region's mining sector."[156] Three months after that the Canadian trade mission was expanded to full embassy status.[157] Canadian diplomatic representation in Mongolia was necessary because, according to Canada's Minister of Trade, "there have been some policy issues including taxation, control and investment regulations that have put Canadian companies in the region in an extremely challenging position."[158]

Which Canadian companies? As of July 2008, 25 Canadian mining companies were active in the country.[159] But Ottawa's biggest concern was Vancouver-based Ivanhoe Inc's copper and gold project in the Gobi desert. This $3 billion project "was the major campaign issue" in Mongolia's 2008 election.[160] In April 2006 at least 3,000 people marched against foreign mining in Mongolia's capital with protesters burning an effigy of Ivanhoe's Robert Friedland.[161] The ire directed towards Friedland was partly because of comments he made in 2005. Friedland explained his Mongolian venture to an investor's conference this way: "So we're coming in from outer space and landing at Oyu Tolgoi ... And the nice thing about this: there's no people around; the land is flat, there's no tropical jungle; there's no NGOs. We're only 70 kilometres from the Chinese border. It does not snow here. You've got lots of room for waste dumps."[162]

The company took heat for loaning $50 million to the government in exchange for tax concessions.[163] To counter popular opposition Ivanhoe flew dozens of Mongolians to the Oyu Tolgoi site, created a lobbying group called the Minerals and Mining Development Foundation and forged an alliance with the Mongolian National Mining Association.[164] The company also convinced some major international political figures to lobby the Mongolian government. In early 2008 Friedland got former U.S. Secretary of State James Baker to trek to Mongolia on Ivanhoe's behalf.[165] Entrée, a Canadian company partly owned by Ivanhoe that also had a concession in the Gobi Desert, hired Michael Howard, a British MP and former leader of the Conservative Party, for his political contacts in the country.[166]

Canadian officials also joined the lobbying campaign. The company added Howard Balloch, Canada's former ambassador to China (who was also responsible for Mongolia and North Korea), to its board of directors.[167] A Globe and Mail Report on Business headline described a January 2008 trip by Minister of International Trade David Emerson to Mongolia: "Emerson to push for Ivanhoe deal in Mongolia."[168] Ottawa's lobbying efforts were also facilitated by the millions of dollars Canada provided in aid to Mongolia since the late 1990s. Included in this aid to Mongolia was regulatory advice concerning the mining sector.[169]

Kazakhstan

Near Mongolia, Canadian miners, U.S. politicians and the local government forged mutually beneficial bonds in Kazakhstan. A January 31, 2008, front page New York Times article reported: "Late on Sept. 6, 2005, a private plane carrying the Canadian mining financier Frank Giustra touched Kazakhstan. ... Accompanying Mr. Giustra on his luxuriously appointed MD-87 jet that day was a former president of the United States, Bill Clinton. ...[the] two men were whisked off to share a sumptuous midnight banquet with Kazakhstan's president, Nursultan A. Nazarbayev, whose 19-year stranglehold on the country has all but quashed political dissent.

"Mr. Nazarbayev walked away from the table with a propaganda coup, after Mr. Clinton expressed enthusiastic support for the Kazakh leader's bid to head an international organization that monitors elections and supports democracy. Within two days, corporate records show that Mr. Giustra also came up a winner when his company signed preliminary agreements giving it the right to buy into three uranium projects controlled by Kazakhstan's state-owned uranium agency, Kazatomprom. The monster deal stunned the mining industry, turning an unknown shell company into one of the world's largest uranium producers ... Just months after the Kazakh pact was finalized, Mr. Clinton's charitable foundation received its own windfall: a $31.3 million donation from Mr. Giustra that had remained a secret until he acknowledged it last month. The gift, combined with Mr. Giustra's more recent and public pledge to give the William J. Clinton Foundation an additional $100 million ... In February 2007, a company called Uranium One agreed to pay $3.1 billion to acquire UrAsia. Mr. Giustra, a director and major shareholder in UrAsia, would be paid $7.05 per share for a company that just two years earlier was trading at 10 cents per share. ..."

There were 35 Canadian energy companies operating in Kazakhstan in 2005 and by 2008 Canadian mining investment in that country totalled over $2 billion.[170]

Discussion

Canada's military mission in Afghanistan provides a window into how aid was used to co-opt NGOs into Ottawa's elite-based foreign-policy objectives. The reach of military propagandists extended into the halls of academia. Even though most Canadians opposed Canada's role in Afghanistan, our tax dollars were used to sell us on a military adventure doomed to failure. The foreign policy and military establishment, hand-in-hand with the corporate elite, acted in their self-interest. Ordinary Canadians were largely shut out of controlling what was done in our name.

Chapter Notes

1   Canada's Flying Gunners, 25
2   Globe and Mail Jan 2 2008
3   Globe and Mail Apr 23 1980; Globe and Mail Jan 21 1980
4   Diplomatic Missions, 58; Globe and Mail Jan 15 1980
5   CBC Sounds Like Canada July 11 2007
6   Unexpected War, 10
7   Canada in Afghanistan, 86
8   Shadow Wars, 112
9   Ottawa Citizen Oct 28 2008
10 Globe and Mail Apr 16 2007
11 Ottawa Citizen Nov 2008
12 Ottawa Citizen Sept 17 2008
13 The Observer Aug 5 2007
14 National Post Feb 9 2009; http://www.edmontonsun.com/Comment/2009/02/13/8375796-sun.html
15 Ottawa Citizen Mar 17 2008
16 Ottawa Citizen Mar 17 2008
17 Ottawa Citizen Mar 17 2008
18 Ottawa Citizen Mar 17 2008
19 http://www.counterpunch.org/rawa03022004.html
20 LA Times Apr 29 2007
21 Economist Jan 7 2006
22 Economist Jan 21 2006
23 http://www.counterpunch.org/sonali03282005.html
24 Maclean's Mar 20 2006
25 Ottawa Citizen Nov 19 2007
26 Toronto Star Oct 8 2008
27 Globe and Mail Sept 23 2008
28 Le Devoir May 28 2007
29 La Presse Mar 15 2007
30 Globe and Mail Apr 24 2007
31 http://www.thestar.com/News/article/181030
32 Globe and Mail Mar 24 2008
33 Associated Press Aug 10 2008
34 http://www.msnbc.msn.com/id/26742540/
35 La Presse Feb 23 2009
36 The Canadian Forces and interoperability, 99
37 http://mostlywater.org/canada_peacekeeper_or_warmonger
38 New York Times Nov 27
39 New York Times Magazine Feb 24 2008
40 Financial Times May 16 2008
41 Globe and Mail December 23 2008
42 New York Times May 13 2007
43 Canadian Press Feb 24 2009
44 National Post Aug 1 2008
45 Canadian Press July 10 2006
46 La Presse June 22 2006
47 La Presse June 22 2006
48 Ottawa Citizen Feb 7 2008
49 Ottawa Citizen Nov 21 2007
50 Toronto Star Aug 27 2008
51 Le Devoir Oct 24 2007
52 Ottawa Citizen Nov 22 2007
53 Globe and Mail Oct 22 2007
54 http://www.bizjournals.com/washington/stories/2007/12/10/daily4.html?ana=from_rss
55 Montréal Gazette Aug 10 2008
56 Montréal Gazette Dec 3 2007
57 Montréal Gazette Dec 3 2007
58 National Post Aug 12 2008
59 National Post Aug 12 2008
60 Ottawa Citizen Nov 19 2007
61 Ottawa Citizen Nov 22 2007
62 Too Close for Comfort, 87
63 Ottawa Citizen Nov 20 2007
64 Ottawa Citizen Nov 20 2007
65 Ottawa Citizen Nov 19 2007
66 Ottawa Citizen Nov 21 2007; Canada in Afghanistan, 94
67 Ottawa Citizen Nov 19 2007
68 Ottawa Citizen Sept 19 2006
69 Ottawa Citizen Jan 12 2009
70 The Economist Apr 15 2006
71 L'actualite Oct 1 2005
72 National Post Mar 5 2008
73 Globe and Mail Mar 9 2007
74 nowtoronto.com 24 Mar 2008
75 Ottawa Citizen Mar 17 2008
76 Unexpected War, 65
77 http://www.policyalternatives.ca/documents/National_Office_Pubs/2008/A_Pipeline_Through_a_Troubled_Land.pdf
78 http://www.policyalternatives.ca/documents/National_Office_Pubs/2008/A_Pipeline_Through_a_Troubled_Land.pdf
79 http://www.globalresearch.ca/index.php?context=va&aid=9640
80 Ottawa Citizen Feb 1 2007
81 Canwest News Service July 11 2008
82 CBC News May 26 2008
83 National Post Dec 18 2006
84 Ottawa Citizen Dec 4 2006; Aug 27 2008
85 Shadow Wars, 175; Ottawa Citizen Aug 6 2006
86 McGill International Review Fall 2004
87 Globe and Mail May 22 2006
88 International Policy Statement Apr 2005

89   Le Soleil June 9 2008
90   Globe and Mail June 6 2008
91   http://www.dd-rd.ca/site/media/index.
php?id=505&subsection=news
92   Countercurrents.org Oct 7 2006
93   Montréal Gazette Dec 14 2007
94   http://74.125.45.132/search?q=cache:
B2_S5MTHAYYJ:www.acdi cida.gc.ca/cidaweb/
acdicida.nsf/En/NAT-36111441 M38+Canadian+
Women+for+Women+in+Afghanistan+Rights+a
nd+Democracy&hl=en&ct=clnk&cd=8&gl=ca
95   Ottawa Citizen Jan 28 2009
96   Globe and Mail Nov 3 2006
97   National Post Aug 28 2008
98   Ottawa Citizen Jan 7 2007
99   Aid and Ebb Tide, 196
100 http://embassymag.ca/html/index.
phpdisplay=story&full_path=/2008/july/30/
ngo_community
101 http://embassymag.ca/html/index.
phpdisplay=story&full_path=/2008/july/30/
ngo_community
102 Bridges of Hope?, 4
103 Bridges of Hope?, 4
104 La Presse Dec 22 2006
105 Ottawa Citizen June 4 2008
106 Globe and Mail July 22 2008
107 Walrus Feb 2007
108 Shadow Wars, 109
109 Shadow Wars, 109
110 Canadian Press Dec 30 2006
111 Canadian Press Dec 30 2006
112 Trente Dec 2007
113 Ottawa Citizen Sept 21 2006
114 Ottawa Citizen Oct 13 2006
115 Ottawa Citizen Oct 13 2006
116 Globe and Mail Feb 21 2008
117 Concordia Link Sept 2 2008
118 Globe and Mail Feb 21 2008
119 Walrus May 2008
120 IPS Mar 2 2007
121 IPS Mar 2 2007
122 Canadian Relations to South Africa, 29
123 Journal of Conference of Defense
Associations Institute Jan 1990
124 Journal of Conference of Defence
Associations Institute Jan 1990, 18
125 Ties that Bind, 153
126 In the Interests of Peace, 50
127 More Than a Peacemaker, 40
128 Peacekeeping in Vietnam, 264
129 Aid and Ebb Tide, 87
130 Policy Options Sept 2008

131 Global Mission, 1380
132 Human Rights and Canadian Foreign
Policy, 206
133 Embassy Magazine Mar 26 2008
134 Embassy Magazine Mar 26 2008
135 Development and Debt, 54; Aid and Ebb
Tide, 22
136 Canadian International Development
Assistance Policies, 8
137 http://www.actionaid.org.uk/100061/
africa_tells_the_g8__do_no_harm_and_
deliver_on_your_promises.html
138 Canadian Journal of Development Studies
xxvii 2007
139 Canada Among Nations 1998, 155
140 Canadian International Development
Assistance Policies, 80
141 Latin America Working Group Letter Vol 5 #6
142 Latin America Working Group Letter Vol 5 #6
143 Canadian International Development
Assistance Policies, 187
144 Silent Partners, 46
145 Conflicts of Interest, 57
146 Aid and Ebb Tide, 35
147 Perpetuating Poverty, 99
148 Aid and Ebb Tide, 70
149 http://plancanada.ca/NetCommunity/
Page.aspx?pid=922
150 http://www.fasopresse.net/article.
php3?id_article=10442
151 La Presse June 2008
152 National Post Aug 11 2005
153 National Post Aug 11 2005
154 National Post Apr 11 2007
155 National Post Apr 11 2007
156 AFP Apr 18 2008
157 Canadian Press July 27 2008
158 Canadian Press 30 May 2008
159 La Presse July 27 2008
160 National Post July 2 2008
161 Ottawa Citizen Apr 19 2006; Wall Street
Journal Jan 4 2007
162 www.minesandcommunities.org Sept 14 2006
163 Globe and Mail July 26 2004
164 Globe and Mail Sept 15 2006
165 Maclean's Mar 17 2008
166 National Post June 6 2007
167 PR Newswire Mar 14 2005
168 Globe and Mail Jan 9 2008
169 According to Ted Menzies, parliamentary
secretary to the Minister of Finance
170 http://embassymag.ca/page/view/
kazakhstan-12-10-2008

Africa

The extent to which ordinary Canadians are lied to and excluded from meaningful control of our country's foreign policy is revealed by comparing the reality of Canada's involvement in Africa with the myth. There is a stark difference between what Africans have experienced at the hands of our diplomats and corporations and what most Canadians believe this country stands for. According to the mainstream media, Canada's relations to Africa include feeding starving people, heroic, if not often successful, peacekeeping and valiant attempts to speak out against genocide. But is that the essence of our foreign policy, as experienced by ordinary Africans?

On balance, we have certainly not been a force for good. Rather, another question must be asked: Has Canada helped to underdevelop Africa? That is the most important question of this section.

South Africa

The late 1800s were a time of growing imperialism both in Britain and Canada. Canada's 1898 Christmas stamp showed a world map with a vast British Empire boldly coloured in red and the statement: "We hold a vaster empire than has been."[1] Also in 1898, descendants of Dutch settlers, the Boers, found themselves at odds with British imperial interests in the southern tip of Africa. About 2,700 Canadians headed to Africa to defend the empire. At least 270 Canadian soldiers were killed or died of disease during the four-year war.[2] "Bold headlines, sensational and often fabricated news stories, incendiary editorials, carefully selected letters to the editor, poems and cartoons were all used to portray the [British] Uitlanders as suffering servants of empire besieged by cruel and crafty people, determined to destroy the last vestige of British power in South Africa."[3] Imperial minded businesses also encouraged enlistment. Soldiers who enlisted to fight "were showered in gifts from private donors and commercial corporations."[4]

The war was devastating for the Boers. As part of a scorched-earth campaign the British-led forces burned their crops and homesteads and poisoned their wells.[5] Tens of thousands of Boers were rounded up and sent to concentration camps. Twenty-eight thousand (mostly children) died of disease, starvation and exposure in these camps.[6]

"Canadian troops became intimately involved in the nastier aspects of the South African war."[7] Whole columns of Canadian troops participated in search, expel and burn missions.[8] "Organized columns of troops descended upon areas still offering resistance and destroyed farms in those vicinities on the slightest pretext."[9] Canadian forces killed thousands of Boer cattle and looting was commonplace.[10] One Canadian soldier wrote home, "as fast as we come up the country ... we loot the farms." Another wrote, "I tell you there is some fun in it. We ride up to a house and commandeer anything you set your eyes on. We are living pretty well now."[11] There are also numerous documented instances of Canadian troops raping and killing innocent civilians.[12]

Similar to World War One, militaristic-minded Canadians claimed the battles in South Africa were a sign of nationhood, a declaration "to the world that a new power had arisen in the West."[13] And, also similar to World War One, few commentators discuss what motivated the war. "Although imperialists had made much of the Boer maltreatment of the Blacks, the British did little after the war to remedy their injustices."[14] The real reason for the war: Thirty miles south of Pretoria, the Boer capital, large quantities of gold were found in 1886. The Prime Minister of the Cape Colony, Cecil Rhodes, and British mine owners wanted to get their hands on the loot.

For a half-century after the Boer War, South Africa was a British colony. After independence the Boer descendents — who considered themselves oppressed because of British conquest — imposed a system of legal racial discrimination known as apartheid. In his 2007 book former Canadian diplomat Robert Calderisi describes a trip to South Africa during apartheid: "It was an unusual trip for a Canadian. South Africa had been expelled from the British Commonwealth in 1961 for its racist policies and Canada had broken off all economic ties with it. The two countries still had diplomatic relations, but they were strained, as it was a Canadian Prime Minister, [John Diefenbaker] who had led the charge to punish South Africa."[15] The description is hardly accurate.

Contrary to popular understanding, Canada mostly supported apartheid in South Africa. First, by providing it with a model. South Africa patterned its policy towards Blacks after Canadian policy towards First Nations. "South African officials regularly came to Canada to examine reserves set aside for First Nations, following colleagues who had studied residential schools in earlier parts of the century."[16]

Canada also supported South African apartheid through a duplicitous policy of publicly opposing the country's racist system yet continuing to do business as usual with this former British Dominion. It's true that in 1961 John Diefenbaker's Conservative government called for South

Africa to be expelled from the British Commonwealth. But this position was not a moral rebuke of apartheid. "Nothing has been more constant in Diefenbaker's approach than his search for a tolerable way of averting South Africa's withdrawal," commented an External Affairs official at the 1961 Commonwealth meeting where South Africa left the organization.[17]

Diefenbaker pushed for South Africa's exclusion in an attempt to save the Commonwealth. The former British colonies — notably in South Asia and Africa — threatened to leave the Commonwealth if South Africa stayed. This would have been the death of the British Empire's Commonwealth. Diefenbaker's lack of principled opposition to apartheid helps explain his refusal to cancel the 1932 Canada-South Africa trade agreement.[18] Later, Ottawa opposed attempts to expel South Africa from the U.N. and abstained on a Nigerian resolution to remove South Africa from the International Labour Organization, despite the country's systematic oppression of black workers.[19] The Department of Energy, Mines and Resources even included South African officials in secret mid-1970s negotiations to establish a uranium cartel and until 1979 Canada provided preferential tariff rates to the apartheid regime.[20]

Widely viewed as a progressive internationalist, Pierre Trudeau's government sympathized with the apartheid regime not the black liberation movement or nascent Canadian solidarity groups. Throughout Trudeau's time in office, Canadian companies were heavily invested in South Africa, enjoying the benefits of cheap black labour. The federal government's 1970 White Paper recognized that Canadian corporations were in South Africa because of the "better than normal opportunities" for economic returns.[21] A Falconbridge official explained to a parliamentary committee "in fact the whites are in the … senior positions and the blacks in junior positions. I am not denying that. That is just the way it is in South Africa … the system automatically segregates the jobs … there is no question of whether you want to or whether you do not want to. It is a law."[22]

In October 1982 the Trudeau government delivered 4.91 percent of the votes that enabled Western powers to gain a slim 51.9 percent majority in support of South Africa's application for a billion-dollar IMF credit. Sixty-eight IMF members opposed the loan as did 121 countries in a non-binding vote at the U.N. General Assembly. Five IMF executive directors said South Africa did not meet the standards of conditionality imposed on other borrowers.[23] The Canadian minister of finance justified support for the IMF loan claiming that "the IMF must be careful … not to be accused of meddling in the internal affairs of sovereign states."[24] A few months later,

Ottawa opposed IMF funding for Vietnam because of its occupation of Cambodia.[25]

Officially, the Trudeau government supported the international arms embargo against South Africa. But his government mostly failed to enforce it.[26] As late as 1978 Canadian-government financed weapons continued to make their way to South Africa.[27] Canadair (at the time a Crown company) sold the apartheid regime amphibious water bombers, which according to the manufacturer, were useful "particularly in internal troop-lift operations."[28] (The official buyer was the South African forestry department.) In the early 1970s the Montréal Gazette discovered that the RCMP trained South African police in "some sort of liaison or intelligence gathering" instruction.[29] As apartheid came to an end, it was discovered that Canada had assisted South Africa in developing its capacity to manufacture nuclear weapons.[30] Describing a 155 mm gun that could fire up to 42 kilometres, "the world's most advanced artillery technology, developed by a Canadian company with Canadian government assistance played a major role in strengthening South Africa's defence capabilities and in wreaking havoc in the region."[31]

Supporters of apartheid would say anything to slow opposition to this cruel system. At a 1977 Commonwealth meeting, Trudeau dodged press questions on post-Soweto South Africa suggesting that Idi Amin's brutal regime in Uganda should be discussed along with southern Africa.[32] For its part, the Globe and Mail argued in 1982 that "disinvestment would be unwittingly an ally of apartheid" since foreign investment brought progressive ideas.[33] During this period Canada's representative to the U.N., Michel Dupuis, denounced a call for mandatory sanctions by the Security Council against South Africa. This plan, Dupuis explained, "would probably put an end to United Nation's efforts and could indefinitely delay progress towards Namibian independence" — a country occupied by South Africa.[34]

But, Canadian officials did come up with a way to avoid criticism of their policy toward South Africa. In the 1970s Ottawa increased aid to African states as a way to mitigate their criticism of Canada's economic and political relations with the apartheid system. "The government has concluded that Canadian interests would be better served by maintaining its current policy framework on the problems of southern Africa, which balances two policy themes [social justice and economic relations] of importance to Canadians. The government intends, however, to give more expression to the social policy theme. To this end the Canadian government will make available further economic assistance to black African states of the area to assist them to develop their own institutions and resources."[35]

Apartheid South Africa's brutality crossed borders and so did Canadian support. Ottawa refused to recognize the legal authority of the Council for Namibia, a body established by the U.N. General Assembly to govern the territory. Canada also voted against a 1973 U.N. resolution giving observer status to the South West Africa People's Organization, the main Namibian liberation movement.[36]

At odds with a Canadian-backed U.N. resolution that declared South Africa's presence illegal, Ottawa conceded South Africa's jurisdiction over Namibia and the Department of Industry, Trade and Commerce spent public money promoting economic relations with Namibia.[37] In 1971 Falconbridge partnered with the South African government in a Namibian silver-copper mining company, Oamites.[38] Falconbridge paid taxes to South Africa and received credits from Ottawa for these payments to the apartheid regime. The issue of taxes was highly political since not taxing Canadian firms operating in Namibia implied recognition of South Africa's mandate over that country.[39]

A crown corporation, El Dorado Nuclear Ltd., processed uranium from mines in Namibia, which contravened a 1970 U.N. resolution against trade with Namibia.[40] Eldorado obscured the origins of its Namibian uranium by falsely labeling it South African, which made it difficult for countries such as Japan to observe the U.N. Security Council decree opposing the exploitation of Namibian natural resources.[41] For a time Ottawa was even more lenient than Washington toward South Africa's occupation of Namibia. When the U.S. passed regulations to deter corporate involvement in Namibia, some U.S. companies opened holding companies in Toronto to take advantage of Canadian policy.[42]

The President of the South West African People's Organization of Namibia, S. Nuyoma explained: "The people of Namibia strongly condemn the policies of the Canadian companies working with the cooperation of American and British companies who are mercilessly exploiting Namibian natural resources. Especially, we strongly condemn the Canadian companies like Falconbridge and Etosha Petroleum ... [that] employ African slave labour. The Canadian-American companies are not only helping the South African government to perpetuate white supremacy, economic exploitation and the permanent enslavement of the African people of Namibia, but also support South Africa through providing capital, goods and industrial aid. We therefore appeal to the people and government of Canada, who believe in freedom and human equality, to demand an immediate withdrawal of all Canadian companies now operating in and exploiting Namibia."

After decades of protest by Canadian unions, churches, students and others, Brian Mulroney's Conservative government finally implemented economic sanctions on South Africa in 1986. The Conservatives only moved after numerous other countries had already done so. "The record clearly shows that the Canadian government followed rather than led the sanctions campaign."[43] Unlike Canada, countries such as Norway, Denmark New Zealand, Brazil and Argentina also cut off diplomatic ties to South Africa.[44] Even U.S. sanctions, due to an activist Congress, were tougher than those implemented by Ottawa.[45]

From October 1986 to September 1993, the period in which economic sanctions were in effect, Canada's two-way trade with South Africa totaled $1.6 billion — 44 percent of the comparable period before sanctions (1979-1985).[46] Canadian imports from South Africa averaged $122 million a year during the sanctions period.[47]

Canada did business with the apartheid regime and opposed the liberation movements. Ottawa's relationship with the African National Congress (ANC) was initially one of hostility and then ambivalence. Canada failed to recognize the ANC until July 1984 and then worked to moderate their direction.[48] In an August 1987 letter to the Toronto Star, Foreign Affairs Minister Joe Clark explained the government's thinking: "Canada has been able to develop a relationship of trust with the ... African National Congress that it is hoped has helped to strengthen the hand of black moderates."[49]

With apartheid's end on the horizon, Ottawa wanted to guarantee that an ANC government would follow pro-capitalist policy, contrary to the wishes of many of its supporters. The man in charge of External Affairs' South African Taskforce said that Ottawa wanted an early IMF planning mission to the country to ensure that the post-apartheid government would "get things right" from the start.[50] One author notes: "The Canadian state has entered fully in the drive to open South Africa to global forces and to promote the interests of the private sector."[51]

Ottawa's policy towards apartheid South Africa was controversial among Canadians. There was an active solidarity movement that opposed Canadian support for the racist regime. Ottawa did not enjoy being criticized and the federal government tried to use its influence to minimize opposition. One way it accomplished this was by encouraging the creation of new non-governmental organizations more amenable to its policy. During apartheid "CIDA secured creation of the South African Education Trust Fund because it did not think the strong NGOs already active vis-à-vis South Africa sufficiently sensitive to Canadian foreign policy concerns."[52] (In another part of the globe, the Asia Pacific and Thai-Canada Foundations were also partly created by CIDA.[53])

Many NGOs receiving government assistance began to self censor on South Africa.[54] For example, "CIDA specified that CUSO could not use CIDA funds to criticize Canadian foreign policy or to draw parallels between struggles against oppression in developing countries [particularly in Southern Africa] and struggles by powerless groups in Canada ... CIDA ... wanted 'development education' to emphasize Canada's contribution to technical assistance in developing countries and to defend the case for 'foreign aid.'"[55] According to CIDA, CUSO's French language equivalent, SUCO, strayed too far from its founding principles, which was to send educated Canadians to volunteer in poor countries. In the late 1970s and early 1980s SUCO began to draw links between struggles in southern Africa and Canada as well as other politically sensitive topics. CIDA responded to this political turn by chopping all funding in March 1984.[56] The organization's capacity to function basically disappeared overnight.

Tanzania

Since its 1961 independence Tanzania has been a major recipient of Canadian assistance. Ottawa was concerned that this former British colony, led for two decades by socialist leaning Julius Nyerere, would develop an independent path. In 1967 External Affairs Minister Paul Martin Sr. argued that "had Canada not extended aid [to Tanzania], China and perhaps one or two other Communist countries would have. I am satisfied beyond doubt that, had we not given it, we would have made a serious mistake."[57] By 2007 Ottawa had contributed more than a quarter billion dollars in aid to Tanzania.[58] Part of this went to the Canadian Armed Forces Advisory and Training Team Tanzania, a program that brought a hundred Canadian military advisors to that country between 1965 and 1970.[59] It was "a Canadian squadron leader, Peter Partner, [who] drafted Tanzania's national Defence Act, framed appropriate regulations and a code of service discipline and trained the country's [Judge Advocate General] JAG-in-waiting."[60]

Some Canadian aid to Tanzania drew criticism. The Tanzania-Canada Wheat Program was one of the more controversial programs. This 1970s "frontier development" project displaced the indigenous (nomadic) Barabaig people from their tribal lands so others could farm wheat.[61] "Economic interests, not political considerations determined the extent and nature of Canadian aid to Tanzania. Large-scale, capital intensive technologically sophisticated schemes not only provide a market for Canadian goods and services, but also offer jobs, travel, training and access the means for private accumulation of wealth for Tanzanian officials. An alliance is thus struck between Tanzanian bureaucratic elites and western capital."[62]

Canadian relations with Tanzanian officials were very successful. Up to 2009, Canada was the leading foreign investor in the country, with Barrick Gold alone investing more than $1 billion in four Tanzanian mines since 1999. But there is some question as to whether Canada's role in Tanzania has been good for most Tanzanians. Mining companies were paying the government a measly three percent royalty rate. Despite hundreds of millions of dollars being taken out of the ground the government received only $28 million from mining each year.[63] A 2008 report into foreign mining in the country explained: "A very small circle of people in Tanzania — an elite clique consisting of government ministers, some donors and mining companies — has determined the fate of the country's rich natural resources in a way that is entirely unaccountable. ... The governments of South Africa, Canada and Britain must begin to challenge the role of the gold mining companies in Tanzania in terms of their impacts on local and national development."[64]

Far from challenging Canadian resource companies, Ottawa has worked to consolidate and improve the situation for Canadian investors. In June 2008 the High Commission "energetically intervened in Tanzanian parliamentary affairs to ensure that the country's politicians rejected the conclusions of the Presidential Mining Sector Review Committee on revisions of the mining sector."[65] The review recommended that a larger proportion of profits created by higher mineral (mostly gold) prices be retained by the government.

"Canadian mining interests abroad," Embassy magazine noted in March 2008, "are at the root of the government's recent push to sign investment protection agreements with developing countries, a drive that now includes Tanzania."[66] This move followed from a November 2007 visit to Tanzania by Stephen Harper, who met representatives of Barrick Gold as well as 10 other Canadian resource firms operating in that country. According to Harper, the meeting was to discuss "the general business climate [and] what the government of Canada can do to assist in building our investments here."[67]

Harper's meeting with Canadian resource companies was controversial. Days before meeting with Harper, Barrick declared illegal a strike at one of its Tanzanian mines and was looking to replace a thousand striking miners.[68] But Tanzanians' displeasure towards Barrick went beyond its labour practices. Just prior to Harper's visit the company received a sweetheart concession at its new Buzwagi mine. Barrick signed the agreement with the government in London, not Dar-es-Salaam, so Parliament was unable to look at the deal despite its responsibility to review all mining contracts. About the same time Barrick was accused of tax evasion on imports worth up to two billion TShillings ($1.5 million).[69] A report into the small amount of money that the Tanzanian government received from mining noted: "Barrick does not state in its financial reports on its website how much in taxes and royalties it pays to the Tanzanian government" despite being "listed as a company supporter of the Extractive Industries Transparency Initiative, the purpose of which is to improve transparency of company tax payments."[70]

Barrick's North Mara mine in Tanzania displaced thousands of artisanal miners, peasant farmers and their families since operations began in 2001.[71] From July 2005 to late 2008 security operatives at the mine were linked to seven violent deaths. Mine critics claim it's part of a strategy to silence them.[72] In December 2008 Mwita Mang'weina and some friends were engaged in an argument with Barrick security when one of the guards shot Mang'weina, who was unarmed at the time. This incident caused an uproar within the community, which immediately took up stones, overpowered mine security (who then fled), and attacked the mine, setting fire to millions worth of equipment … the killing of a local boy [in July 2005] sparked a similar uprising that resulted in the destruction of mine equipment and the subsequent detention of over 200 villagers."[73]

In 1999 Barrick bought a Canadian-owned mine in Tanzania with a disturbing human rights record. Vancouver-based Sutton played an important role in displacing thousands of small-scale miners from their livelihoods in August 1996. There were also allegations (hotly denied) that 52 miners were buried alive at the Bulyanhulu mine when the army filled the mine holes during evictions. Denied by the mining sector and Tanzania's government, the deaths were reported by Amnesty International (annual reports from 1997 to 1999).[74] A mission to Tanzania in 2001 by the Council of Canadians, Mining Watch Canada and Amnesty International found: "The intensity and seriousness in the telling of the stories of the alleged evictions, violence and brutality of the police and mining officials, the level of detail, as well as the willingness of the Bulyanhulu residents to take significant risks to their own personal safety to come and speak with us, impressed the members of the mission, as did the willingness of apparently 250 others who waited several hours for us to arrive in Bulyanhulu. The mission members thought that these factors lent weight to the credibility of the allegations."[75] Mission members called for an independent international investigation into the allegations of mass murder in the Bulyanhulu pit. Appeals for an investigation into the evictions were made to Liberal foreign affairs ministers John Manley, Pierre Pettigrew and Bill Graham, but all rejected calls for an inquiry.[76]

Through Access to Information laws Probe International obtained boxes of heavily censored correspondence from the Canadian high commissioner in Tanzania concerning the evictions. The documents detail a Canadian diplomat actively pressuring Tanzanian officials to clear Sutton's concession of small-scale miners. "Sutton [censored words] is ready to go to stock market [censored words] but cannot / not do so in absence of Tanz govt action to remove 7,000/10,000/ illegal miners..." said a report to Foreign Affairs in December 1995.[77] Later, the High Commission reported back to Ottawa, "Sutton has appealed to High Court for panel hearing. We do not / not believe that judicial action on injunction need impede action by govt to resolve situ[ation]."[78]

The Canadian high commissioner pressed Sutton's case despite a Tanzanian judge concluding that a special three-judge panel needed to decide the case. "I found no provision made for compensation and/or resettlement of the indigenous people," read the judge's ruling. For a time, the court ruling (as well as an upcoming election) stopped the Tanzanian government from removing the miners. But Canadian pressure grew as the estimated size of the Bulyanhulu mine's deposits increased. The high commissioner discussed the issue directly with the Tanzanian prime minister and president. In a memo to the president of Tanzania, the high commissioner noted the "Vancouver, Calgary and Toronto stock exchanges have become the leading sources of exploration capital in the resource sector.... It will be important, therefore, that outstanding problems relating to title and to illegal activities be quickly removed." The "illegal activities" that concerned the high commissioner were the area's residents and small-scale peasant miners who had dug for gold since it was discovered in 1976.[79]

To advance Sutton's interests, the High Commission published a special supplement in the Tanzanian press and the high commissioner appeared in a half-hour TV interview. "In short, with this full court press," the Canadian High Commission wrote in a memo to Ottawa: "the decision makers will be fully aware of how important this mining sector, Cdn participation, and rule of law is to their economy."[80] After the evictions the high commissioner explained to Foreign Affairs: "In most cases there is a will on the part of the Tanzanian government to facilitate solutions [to the problems of foreign mining companies with peasant miners] regardless of legal or resource constraints. The new mining legislation should deal with current problems."[81]

Congo

In the early 1890s Halifax native William Stairs led a 1,950 man mission to conquer the resource-rich Katanga region of the Congo on behalf of Belgium's King Leopold II.[82] (A Canadian missionary, William Faulknor, was also in Katanga at the time of Stairs' mission.[83]) "The principal aim of Stair's expedition was to get Msiri, the ruler of Garengaze, to submit to the authorities of the Congo Free State, either by persuasion or by force. Furthermore, Stairs hoped to discover mineral deposits capable of profitable exploitation and also to engage in exploration leading to useful geographical discoveries west of Tanganyika."[84] Investigating the area's suitability for European settlement and for raising domestic animals were other aims of the mission.[85]

Stairs was extremely racist. In mid-1891 he wrote: "What value would it have [the land he was trying to conquer] in the hands of blacks, who, in their natural state, are far more cruel to one another than the worst Arabs or the wickedest whites."[86] A couple months later his diary noted: "I suppose that it's because of their love of filth and their laziness that most of the time they [his African troops] refrain from washing their milk pots."[87]

Stairs was barbarous. He regularly severed hands and reportedly collected the head of an enemy.[88] Stairs diary noted: "this morning I cut off the heads of the two [Wasangora] men [we shot last night] and placed them on polls one at each exit from the bush into the plantation." A few months later Stairs wrote: "Every male native capable of using the bow [and arrow] is shot, this of course we must do. All the children and women are taken as slaves by our men to do work in the camps."[89] Stairs admitted to using slaves even though Leopold's mission to the Congo was justified as a humanistic endeavour to stop the Arab slave trade.[90]

Stairs found official Canadian support for his mission. Though he died in the Congo Stairs' exploits were lauded in Ottawa when Senator W.J. Macdonald moved "a parliamentary resolution expressing satisfaction for Stairs' manly conduct." After an earlier mission in Africa the mayor of Halifax gave Stairs a steel sword and a civic reception attended by the Lieutenant-Governor. A military band played "Here the Conquering Hero Comes."[91]

The British Army's Royal Engineers gave Stairs a leave to conquer Katanga. They did so because he was working to colonize the Congo on behalf of Leopold and the British preferred Belgian control over the area rather than French possession.[92] Like many other Canadians who helped colonize Africa in the late 1800s, Stairs was trained at the Royal Military College (RMC) in Kingston, Ontario. Two brass plaques were erected in Stairs' honour at the RMC despite the fact that under King Leopold II ten million Congolese were killed from 1891 to 1906.[93]

The Belgians continued an unmerciful pillaging of the country's resources through the late 1950s and some Canadian interests joined in. In December 1957 the Royal Bank (with eight other banks) financed a $40 million World Bank loan to the Belgian colony.[94] In addition, a Montréal registered company, Sudkat, had six of its board members who also sat on the board of Union Minière parent company Société Générale. Two also sat on the board of Union Minière, a massive mining company infamous as the real power in the Congo.[95] Ghana's first president Kwame Nkrumah explained: "The full picture shows a large Canadian bank, linked at home with Sogemines Ltd. which is owned by the Société Générale the owners of the Union Minière, lending money to build roads in the Congo (to the undoubted benefit of Union Minière interests who have other more profitable uses for their money) while Union Minière profits find their way back through the Société Générale into Sogemines and interests connected with the Royal [Bank] and other banks."[96]

Patrice Lumumba's election as prime minister in 1960 threatened Belgium's, particularly Union Minière's, plan to maintain control over the newly independent country's resources. Belgium worked to weaken the Congolese prime minister and Ottawa sided with the Belgians. When the impoverished Congo asked Ottawa for support, in August 1960, Prime Minister Diefenbaker responded that Canada could not help "as Canada, in a stage of great development, needed capital itself."[97]

To undermine Lumumba, Belgium and Union Minière backed a secessionist movement in the resource rich eastern province of Katanga. Having faith in the international organization, Lumumba requested a U.N. force to halt the eastern rebellion. A total of 1,900 Canadians served in the Congo from 1960 to 1964.[98] Initially, however, Canadian troops were rejected by the Congolese authorities.[99] Lumumba expressed a desire for "considerations of nationality and race" in the U.N. force.[100] For his part, the Soviet ambassador to the U.N., Vasily Kuznetzov, explained: "As is known, Canada is a member of the NATO military block which also includes Belgium which has committed an aggression against the independent Congo. In these conditions the dispatch of Canadian troops, or of troops of any other state belonging to a military bloc of which Belgium is a member, would constitute nothing but assistance to the aggressor from his military ally."[101]

The Soviets were right. The archives suggest that Ottawa "shaped policy in a manner that offered some support for Belgian actions. They were consistently concerned with the impact of Canadian policy on their ally."[102] Secretary of State for External Affairs Howard Green told Belgium's Canadian ambassador that Ottawa "would do all [it] could to avoid making the situation more difficult for the Belgian government."[103]

Despite initially being rejected, Ottawa persisted and the Canadian military became one of the more active members of ONUC (Organisation des Nations Unies au Congo).[104] For a time Canadian Brigadier General Jacques Dextraze was major chief of state for the U.N. mission.[105] Canadian troops within the U.N. force were concentrated in militarily important logistical positions.[106] They played a major part in controlling Congolese airspace, for instance.[107] "At headquarters, which operated in both French and English when sufficient bilingual officers could be found, the Canadians handled everything from telephones to phones to dispatch riders. Indeed, to read Canadian messages to Ottawa, it often seemed as if Canadians were running everything. ... by 1962, Canadians held sixteen positions on ONUC's staff, where they were the only officers able to speak to the Congolese employees and government officials."[108]

The U.N. mission to the Congo facilitated a major injustice and Canada actively participated in this crime against the Congolese people through its efforts to undermine Prime Minister Lumumba. On one occasion Canadian troops, mistaken for Belgian forces, were beaten by government soldiers. Lumumba accused the Canadians of provoking the incident by refusing to identify themselves and complained that the "unimportant" affair had been "blown up out of all proportion ... so that [U.N. head Dag Hammarskjold] could influence public opinion."[109]

Canada supported the U.N. secretary general's controversial anti-Lumumba position. "Canada's objective in this conflict was to generate support for Hammarskjold and ONUC in every possible way."[110] Ottawa supported Hammarskjold despite the fact the U.N. secretary general sided with the Belgian-backed secessionists against the central government.[111] "The [U.N.] Secretary General went to Katanga province in the Congo and telegraphed directly [secessionist leader] Moise Tchombe to discuss the terms 'for deploying United Nations troops to Katanga.' No country, even Belgium, had officially recognized Katanga's independence. Yet by this action the Secretary General sent a very bad signal by implicitly implying that the rebellious province could somehow be regarded as sovereign to the point that the U.N. chief administrator could deal with it directly."[112] (An External Affairs memo described Ottawa's thinking on Katanga. "An independent Katanga, working with the neighbouring British colonies, could serve as a bulwark against the 'major threat to Western interests' that the Lumumba government was becoming."[113])

The U.N. head also worked to undermine Lumumba within the central government. When President Joseph Kasavubu dismissed Lumumba as prime minister, which was of debatable legality and opposed by most of the country's parliament, Hammerskjold publicly endorsed the dismissal before the Security Council. Lumumba tried to respond to his dismissal by broadcasting to the nation, but U.N. forces blocked him from accessing the main radio station.[114] U.N. forces, allegedly working with the CIA, undermined Lumumba in other ways.[115] They prevented Lumumba's forces from flying into the capital from other parts of the country and closed the airport to Soviet weapons and transportation equipment when Lumumba turned to Russia for assistance.[116]

Ghanaian president Kwame Nkrumah, who Canada would help overthrow a few years later, described the U.N.'s complicity in Lumumba's murder: "Somewhere in Katanga in the Congo … three of our brother freedom fighters have been done to death. … about their end many things are uncertain, but one fact is crystal clear. They have been killed because the United Nations whom Patrice Lumumba himself as Prime Minister had invited to the Congo to preserve law and order, not only failed to maintain that law and order, but also denied to the lawful government of the Congo all other means of self-protection. History records many occasions when rulers of states have been assassinated. The murder of Patrice Lumumba and of his two colleagues, however, is unique in that it is the first time in history that the legal ruler of a country has been done to death with the open connivance of a world organization in whom that ruler put his trust … instead of preserving law and order, the United Nations declared itself neutral between law and disorder and refused to lend any assistance whatsoever to the legal government in suppressing the mutineers who had set themselves up in power in Katanga and South Kasai. When, in order to move its troops against the rebels, the government of the Congo obtained some civilian aircraft in civilian motor vehicles from the Soviet Union, the colonialist powers at the United Nations raised a howl of rage while, at the same time maintaining a discreet silence over the buildup of Belgian arms and actual Belgian military forces in the service of the rebels ... when Lumumba [after Casavubu's coup] wished to broadcast to the people explaining what happened, the United Nations in the so-called interest of law and order prevented him by force from speaking. They did not, however, use the same force to prevent the mutineers of the Congolese army from seizing power in Leopoldville and installing a completely illegal government ... the United Nations sat by while the so-called Katanga government, which is entirely Belgian controlled, imported aircraft and arms from Belgium and other countries, such as South Africa, which have a vested interest in the suppression of African freedom. The United Nations connived at the setting up, in fact of an independent Katanga state, though this is contrary to the Security Council's own resolutions. Finally, the United Nations, which could exert its authority to prevent Patrice Lumumba from broadcasting, was, so it pleaded, quite unable to prevent his arrest by mutineers or his transfer, through the use of airfields under United Nations control, into the hands of the Belgian-dominated government of Katanga."[117]

After conspiring to eliminate Lumuba, the U.N. helped imprison Antoine Gizenga, formerly Lumumba's deputy prime minister.[118] With the country's progressive forces weakened by Lumumba's death and Gizenga's imprisonment, Katanga's secessionists were no longer useful to the Western powers and the U.N. proceeded to violently suppress them despite supporting the same movement while Lumumba was in power. At least 300 U.N. soldiers died fighting to maintain the Congo's territorial integrity.[119]

The major beneficiaries of U.N. operations in the Congo were foreign resource companies and Western geopolitical interests. The leading Congolese beneficiary of the U.N. mission was Joseph Mobutu who ran the country for three decades. "Mobutu learned to trust the Canadian officers. This trust was of inestimable value in arranging ceasefires between Congolese and U.N. forces, negotiating the release of prisoners as well as liasing between U.N. and Congolese authorities. Mobutu, who became president of the Democratic Republic of Zaire, visited Canada in May of 1964. At that time, he thanked those Canadian officers who had contributed so much to the maintenance of the unity of the country."[120]

While Canada had a hand in Mobutu's rise, Ottawa's support also helped keep Mobutu in power. Between 1985 and 1989 alone Canada provided almost $140 million in assistance to the Congo.[121] In 1990, "Canadian taxpayers contributed $52.95 million to Zaire: almost $16 million went direct to [Mobuto's] corrupt regime."[122] When Mobutu's henchmen slaughtered up to 150 university students on May 11, 1990 (the "Lubumbashi massacre") Ottawa barely protested.[123] For nearly three decades Canada supported the brutal dictator.

Then, Canada also helped get rid of Mobutu. Famous for his corruption and brutality, Mobutu remained in office until 1997 when Joseph Kabila's forces pushed him out. Mobutu had become an embarassment and with the end of the Cold War and weakening of Russia's influence, Washington decided it would no longer allow the French to dominate large parts of Africa. After a May 1995 Afro-American summit Ron Brown, Secretary of Commerce, explained: "America is going to be demanding of Africa's traditional partners, starting with France. We are no longer going to leave Africa to the Europeans."[124] Similarly, on an October 1996 visit to Africa, U.S. Secretary of State Warren Christopher noted: "The time is up when Africa could be divided into spheres of influence, when foreign powers could consider whole groups of countries to be reserved for them. Today Africa needs the support of all its friends rather than the exclusive patronage of a few."[125]

Almost never discussed in North America is the geopolitical interests that spurred the Rwandan genocide. Rwanda was viewed as an important staging ground for control over central Africa's big prize, the Congo's mineral resources worth an estimated $300 billion.[126] "Mobutu continued to favour French, Belgian and South African companies over those from the United States and Canada. A safe platform was needed from which an attack could be launched on Mobutu and his French and Belgian mining benefactors. That platform would be one of the poorest and most densely populated tinder boxes in Africa — Rwanda."[127] Ottawa, with many French-speaking soldiers, diplomats and businesspeople at its disposal, played its part in bringing the formerly Francophone-dominated Rwanda into the U.S. orbit.

In 1990 an army of mostly exiled Tutsi elite, the Rwandan Patriotic Forces (RPF), invaded Rwanda from neighbouring Uganda. According to the hard-to-believe official story, 4,000 Ugandan troops "deserted" to invade Rwanda, including many who were in important positions within the Ugandan government. Its leader, Paul Kagame, who was head of intelligence for the Ugandan government, was trained by the U.S. military at Fort Leavenworth Kansas.[128] The RPF captured control of the country in mid-1994 after widespread killings. The RPF's rise to power was tied to economic hardships brought on by the low price of coffee and foreign-imposed economic adjustments. No longer worried that poor coffee producers might turn towards the Soviet Union, in 1989 the U.S. withdrew its support for the International Coffee Agreement, an accord Ottawa was never enamoured with. The price of coffee tumbled, devastating Rwanda's main cash crop. Largely because of the reduction in the price of coffee the government's budget dropped by 40 percent.[129] When Rwanda went in search of international support the IMF used the country's weakness to push economic reforms at the same time as donors demanded political reforms. One author notes that "political adjustments were pushed on Rwanda at the same time that Canada required Rwanda to adopt a structural adjustment approach to its economy."[130] As in so many other places, IMF structural adjustment brought social instability.

In the years leading up to the genocide Canada began tying its aid to a democratization process despite the country being under assault from a foreign-supported guerrilla group, the RPF. Ostensibly, because of human rights violations, Ottawa cut millions in aid to Rwanda. Prime Minister Brian Mulroney wrote three letters in the early 1990s to Rwanda's President Juvénal Habyarimana, criticizing his human rights record and his slow pace on peace negotiations with the RPF.[131] On December 6, 1991, Foreign Affairs wrote Ed Broadbent, the head of its arm's length human rights organization Rights & Democracy, telling him to visit Rwanda and to begin a program in that country.[132] After a visit to Rwanda, in January 1993, Broadbent gave a press conference in Brussels claiming Habyarimana was directly responsible for a genocide (more than a year before the mass killings began).[133] Rights & Democracy was quick to criticize Habyarimana's rights record, but it failed to recognize the context: a civil war organized, armed and financed by its neighbour Uganda (with quiet support from Washington).[134]

The RPF benefited from the role Canada played in weakening the Habyarimana government. Ottawa also played a more direct part in Paul Kagame's rise to power. Taking direction from Washington, Canadian General (then Senator) Romeo Dallaire commanded the U.N. military force for Rwanda. According to numerous accounts, including his civilian commander on the U.N. mission, Jacques-Roger Booh Booh, Dallaire aided the RPF. In his book *Le patron de Dallaire parle*, Booh Booh, a Cameroon diplomat, claims that Dallaire had little interest in the military actions of the RPF despite reports of summary executions in areas controlled by the RPF.[135] After a peace agreement RPF soldiers were regularly seen in Dallaire's office, with the Canadian commander describing the Rwandan army's position in Kigali. This prompted Booh Booh to wonder if Dallaire "also shared MINUAR (the U.N. mission to Rwanda) military secrets with the RPF when he invited them to work in his offices."[136] Finally, Booh Booh says Dallaire turned a blind eye to RPF weapons coming across the border from Uganda and he believes the U.N. forces may have even transported weapons directly to the RPF.[137] Dallaire, Booh Booh concludes "abandoned his role as head of the military to play a political role. He violated the neutrality principle of MINUAR by becoming an objective ally of one of the parties in the conflict."[138]

In his own book, published in 2003, six years after Kagame unleashed a horror in the Congo, Dallaire wrote that "my guys and the RPF soldiers had a good time together" at a small cantina.[139] Dallaire then explained: "It had been amazing to see Kagame with his guard down for a couple of hours, to glimpse the passion that drove this extraordinary man."[140] Dallaire's relationship to the RPF contravened U.N. guidelines that called on staff to avoid close ties to individuals, organizations, parties or factions of a conflict.[141]

Some commentators have even suggested the U.N. military force, which was in charge of airport security in Kigali, helped the RPF shoot down the plane carrying both Rwandan President Juvénal Habyarimana and Burundian President Cyprien Ntaryamira on April 6, 1994. That event sparked the Rwandan genocide and provided the instability necessary for the RPF's rise to power.

Canadian Supreme Court Justice and head of the International Tribunal for Rwanda Louise Arbour refused to investigate evidence implicating the RPF in shooting down Habyarimana's airplane, according to French government investigators and the National Post.[142] "The documents [from the International Tribunal for Rwanda released in 2009] also establish that the U.N. prosecutor and former Canadian Supreme Court Justice, Louise Arbour, knew that Kagame had assassinated the former President in 1997, but refused to act despite the recommendation of a former FBI agent; an Australian Queen's Prosecutor; and U.N. Gen. Dallaire's own Chief of Military Intelligence. First she refused to prosecute, then shut down the investigation team completely."[143] When the International Tribunal for Rwanda prosecutor who took over from Arbour, Carla del Ponte, began to investigate the RPF's role in shooting down Habyarimana's plane the British and Americans had her removed from her position.

Dallaire did not support the RPF on a personal whim. During the worst of the Rwandan conflict, Canadian military aircraft continued to fly into Rwanda from neighbouring Uganda, the country that sponsored the RPF.[144] Were they bringing weapons? "A sizable contingent of JTF2 [Canadian special forces] had been deployed into Africa. To provide additional 'security' for the U.N. mission in Rwanda, MacLean and his team had set up an 'advanced operational base' in Uganda. From there they would launch long-range, covert intelligence patrols deep into Rwandan territory."[145]

After the Canadian-backed RPF took power in Rwanda they helped Joseph Kabila's rebels launch an attack on Zaire (Congo). A few months after launching his invasion from neighbouring Uganda and Rwanda, in September 1996, "Kabila sent a representative to Toronto to speak to mining companies about 'investment opportunities.'" According to Dale Grant, editor of Defence Policy Review, this trip "may have raised as much as $50 million to support Kabila's march on the capital of Kinshasa."[146] A number of Canadian companies signed deals with Kabila before he took power. First Quantum Minerals, which now has former Prime Minister Joe Clark on its board, signed three contracts worth nearly $1 billion.[147] With Brian Mulroney and George Bush on its board, Barrick signed a deal with Kabila for a gold concession in northeast Congo.[148] Heritage Oil — with known mercenary, Tony Buckingham, as a board member — also made an agreement with Kabila over a concession in the east of the country, which Kabila's army didn't yet control.[149] Resources fueled the war. Analysts even believe the zig-zag progression of Kabila's rebels was based on the location of minerals.[150]

Canadian NGO worker Carole Jerome described Ottawa's motivation for leading a U.N. mission into the Congo during this period. "Mining was what it was about. Zaire is the mother load of gold, cobalt, copper and potash. For decades under President Mobutu, it had largely been the preserve of French interests. With Mobutu's fall, British, American and Canadian companies had an eye on the prize. Tenke Mining, based in Vancouver, paid $30 million for copper and cobalt rights to Mobutu's successor Laurent Kabila. No less a personage than George Bush Sr. had a vested interest. American Barrick [now Barrick Gold], the gold and mining giant of which he sits on the board along with Brian Mulroney, holds enormous mining concessions in Haut Zaire. Unconfirmed reports say that Barick made a deal with Kabila in Lubumbashi in February, long before Kabila came to power with his final assault in Kinshasa. I was told this by a U.N. officer, but have not confirmed it. Other Canadian, British and South African mining companies did the same. They paid for his war and this war was run from the American embassy in Kigali strictly for the benefits of American and allied business interests. This is not some paranoid theory of mine. Laurent Kabila and his deputies announced the licensing agreements at a press conference and proudly confirmed they would pay for his war. In turn, Washington had absolutely no desire to go in and stop the carnage wrought by Kabila. Instead, it prevailed upon the Canadians to lead this doomed mission."[151] Others confirm this analysis: "The plan expressed clearly by the White House at the time was to use the Rwandan army as an instrument of American interests. One American analyst explained how Rwanda could be as important to the USA in Africa as Israel has been in the Middle East."[152]

In late 1996 Ottawa led a short-lived U.N. force into eastern Zaire that was supported by U.S. transport planes, intelligence overflights and satellite imagery.[153] The mission was opposed by that country and welcomed by Uganda, Rwanda and Kabila's rebels. Much to the dismay of the government of Zaire, General Maurice Baril, the Canadian multinational force commander, met Kabila in eastern Zaire during the guerrilla war. The book *Nous étions invincibles* provided a harrowing account of a JTF2 operation to bring Baril to meet Kabila. The convoy came under attack and was only bailed out when U.S. Apache and Blackhawk helicopters attack the Congolese. Some thirty Congolese were killed by a combination of helicopter and JTF2 fire.[154] Some say Canada's mission to the Congo was designed to camouflage Rwanda's invasion (whose troops supported Kabila) and the massacre of Hutu refugees and Congolese.[155] The official story is that Prime Minister Jean Chrétien decided to organize a humanitarian mission into eastern Zaire after his wife saw images of exiled Rwandan refugees on CNN. In fact, Washington proposed that Ottawa, with many French speakers at its disposal, lead the U.N. mission. The U.S. didn't want pro-Mobutu France to gain control of the U.N. force.[156] Ultimately, the complete U.N. force was not deployed because U.N. peacekeepers, some argued, would "slow down or prevent Kabila's triumph, and therefore should not be sent into the field."[157]

After successfully taking control of the Congo in mid-1997 Kabila turned on his Rwandan allies, demanding they leave the country. This prompted a full-scale invasion by Rwanda, which unleashed an eight-nation war. In late 2008 RPF proxies, with direct support from Rwanda, once again launched a full-scale war in eastern Congo.

It's widely accepted that millions have died in the violence largely unleashed by Rwanda. A January 2008 study by the International Rescue Committee blamed the conflict for 5.4 million Congolese deaths since 1998. Despite the millions killed in the Congo and a terrible domestic human rights record, Canada provided tens of millions of dollars in assistance as well as diplomatic support to the RPF. After Rwandan proxies once against displaced hundreds of thousands of people in eastern Congo in late 2008

Sweden and the Netherlands suspended some aid to Rwanda.[158] Ottawa did or said little about the Rwandan-backed killing in the Congo.

In late 2007 Kagame came to Canada to receive an honourary doctorate from the University of Sherbrooke. During the Rwandan president's trip University of Québec in Montréal Professor Emmanuel Hakizimana wrote: "Is Canada denying justice for the victims of Paul Kagame under pressure from Rwanda's powerful allies, Great Britain and the U.S., who do not want to see their protégé brought before justice? Or is to protect the interests of Canadian mining companies in the Great Lakes region?"[159]

(In a rare critical look, an August 2007 Toronto Star commentary headlined "No freedom for press in Rwanda" succinctly described the repressive nature of Kagame's government which "ordered the summary firing of the Sunday editor of the country's only daily for publishing an unflattering photo of the president ... the president's office only wants their man shown in command and in the middle of the photo ... All this happened days after a fledgling new newspaper, called The Weekly Post, was shut down by the government after its first issue."[160])

In October 2004 Canada-Australian Anvil Mining provided logistics to troops that massacred 50 in eastern Congo.[161] The Canada Pension Plan had $20 million invested in Anvil, which provided trucks to transport Congolese soldiers and then to dump the corpses in mass graves. The military operation in Kilwa "had been made possible thanks to the logistical efforts provided by Anvil mining," a Congolese military commander told U.N. military investigators.[162] "They requested assistance from Anvil for transportation," the head of Anvil noted. "We provided that transportation so that they could get their soldiers down to Kilwa." After responding to a question about Anvil providing vehicles to the army, he said, "so what?"[163]

Ten Canadian companies were implicated in a 2002 U.N. Security Council investigation titled "Report on the Illegal Exploitation of Natural Resources and other Forms of Wealth in the Congo." All 10 were accused of violating Organization for Economic Cooperation and Development guidelines. Some of the Canadian companies were alleged to have bribed officials for access to land. U.N. investigators accused one Canadian company of offering a hundred million dollar "down payment" to the state — "cash payments and shares held in trust for government officials. The share offer to those officials was premised on a sharp rise in its share price once it was announced that it had secured some of the most valuable mineral concessions in the Democratic Republic of the Congo."[164] Despite the serious allegations against Canadian companies Ottawa refused to investigate the mining industry's role in the Congo. Worse still, Canada's U.N. ambassador defended the companies, saying: "The alleged violations were not specified" and that "the OECD ethical principles are voluntary, not compulsory."[165]

"Ottawa responded to the report by exercising 'its clout in the U.N. on behalf of the Canadian companies cited for complicity in human rights violations in the Congo.' An informed source said the Canadian government exercised its clout in the U.N. on behalf of a Canadian company cited for complicity in human rights violations in the Congo. 'Canada has strong representation in the U.N.. They imposed on the Security Council to review [the 2002] report,' he said."[166]

Reportedly, First Quantum Minerals, with a former prime minister and longtime foreign affairs minister, Joe Clark, as special adviser for African affairs, lobbied Ottawa to demand a review of the U.N. report.[167] Clark, who led the Carter Center's delegation of election observers that gave Congo's 2007 presidential election its stamp of approval, has long lobbied for Canadian corporate interests in the Congo.[168] "With regard to the increasingly active role played by the DFAIT [Foreign Affairs], one may cite the recent visit of Mr. Kibassa-Maliba, Minister of Mines of the Democratic Republic of the Congo who was in Canada March 7-14, 1998 in order to meet representatives from the Canadian mining sector at the annual meeting of the Prospectors and Developers Association of Canada (PDAC). This mission was hosted jointly by the Canadian corporate interests and DFAIT. Key figures in the organization of this visit were the Right Honourable Joe Clark, who was instrumental in preparing the meeting with the NGOs, and the engineering firm Watts, Griffiths McOuatt, which acted as coordinators of the Canada mission on behalf of the federal government. The mission illustrates what appears to be a growing and pro-active involvement of the Canadian government in the creation of conditions favourable to the promotion of Canadian mining and financial interests in Africa."[169]

Clark is not the only former prime minister engaged on behalf of Canadian companies in the Congo. One commentator told Democracy Now radio in January 2008 that almost every prime minister since Pierre Trudeau (Clark, Mulroney, Martin, Chrétien) "has left office and profited from the natural resources of the Congo while the Congolese people suffer."[170] In March 2005 the Globe and Mail reported: "Mr. Chrétien flew into Kinshasa, the capital of Democratic Republic of Congo, for a series of meetings with political leaders of the African nation, which is emerging from the chaos of a civil war that left millions dead over the past decade. For the Congolese, who described Mr. Chrétien as Canada's 'honourary prime minister,' it was a big deal. As one Canadian businessman recalls being told by a Congolese colleague a few weeks before the visit, 'I hear that one of your prime ministers is coming here.'"[171]

In 2009 Canadian companies continued to feed the fighting in the Congo. With more than $2 billion in investments, numerous Canadian mining firms were active in the Congo, primarily in the volatile east of the country.

Ghana and Structural Adjustment Programs

To foster growth in the Commonwealth and to maintain a united western alliance against the Soviet bloc Canada initiated a small technical assistance program for Ghana in 1958.[172] External Affairs Minister Sidney Smith warned the House of Commons that unless Ottawa stepped into help, "these underdeveloped countries … may be prone to accept blandishments and offers from other parts of the world."[173] As part of its aid efforts, Canada began training Ghana's military in 1961 just as the country removed its British commanders. "From 1961 to 1972, the Canadian Armed Forces Training Team Ghana, consisting of up to 30 officers helped construct the Ghanaian armed forces."[174] Canada's Military Training Assistance Program assisted the armies of newly independent Commonwealth countries. These training missions were designed to "generate stability and foster a pro-West orientation," notes military historian Sean Maloney.[175] "These teams consisted of regular army officers who, at the operational level, trained military personnel of these new Commonwealth countries to increase their professionalism. The strategic function, particularly of the 83-man team in Tanzania, was to maintain a Western presence to counter Soviet and Chinese bloc political and military influence."[176]

Six years after first assisting Ghana's military this Canadian-trained army overthrew President Kwame Nkrumah, a leading Pan Africanist. Washington and London were leading backers of the coup. Direct ties between Canadian military trainers and those responsible for Nkrumah's ouster have yet to be documented, but Ottawa definitely gave its blessing to the coup. "Canada's presence became precarious as the militant factions in Ghana began seeing in a Western trained army a threat to Nkrumah's pro-Communist swing. The Canadian position became increasingly difficult because of its inability to establish an identity independent from that of the British due to similarities in language, uniform, military custom and professionalism. This precarious position was exacerbated by the military necessity for a close working relationship with the British, Canadian dependence upon the British Joint Services Training Team for support in the areas of dependents' schools and medical treatment, as well as the political similarities between these two countries. Whereas in the early 1960s Canada had a convincing self-image of a neutral nation untainted by a colonial past, and despite their original welcome in 1961, members of the ruling CPP tended to identify Canadian aid policies, especially in defence areas, with the aims of the U.S. and Britain. Opponents of the Canadian military program went so far as to create a countervailing force in the form of the Soviet equipped, pro-communist President's Own Guard Regiment. The coup on 24 February 1966 which ousted Kwame Krumah and the CPP was partially rooted in this divergence of military loyalty. The Western orientation and the more liberal approach of the new military government was welcomed by Canada."[177]

Just after Nkrumah was overthrown Canada sent $1.82 million worth of flour to Ghana and offered the military regime a hundred CUSO volunteers.[178] Despite severing financial assistance to Nkrumah's government, immediately after the coup the IMF restructured Ghana's debt (Canada contribution was an outright gift).[179] From 1966 to 1969 The National Liberation Council, the military regime, received as much aid as during Nkrumah's entire time in office. Ottawa gave $22 million in grants and loans, the fourth major donor after the U.S., U.K. and U.N.[180]

Canada provided diplomatic support for the coup as well. The day after Nkrumah was overthrown External Affairs Minister Paul Martin responded to questions about Canada's military training by saying there was no change in instructions. In response to a question about recognizing the military government he said "in many cases recognition is accorded automatically. In respective cases such as that which occurred in Ghana yesterday, the practice is developing of carrying on with the government which is taken over, but according no formal act until some interval has elapsed. We shall carry on with the present arrangement for Ghana. Whether there will be any formal act will depend on information which is not now before us."[181] Less than two weeks after the coup Martin told the military government that Canada intended to carry on normal relations.[182] Six months after overthrowing Nkrumah, the coup's leader General Joseph Ankrah made an official visit to Ottawa as part of a trip that also took him through London and Washington.[183]

Canadian aid played a part in putting the "right" Ghanian officials in place. It was also used to guarantee desired policy. Ghana was one of the first countries where CIDA openly pushed a Structural Adjustment Program (SAP). A 1987 CIDA memo explained, "approximately 35-40 percent of cash flow for the next five-year period will be transferred as unstructured program aid to support balance of payments ... all elements under this theme will be tied to satisfactory performance by Ghana under an internationally accepted SAP."[184]

Ghana was but one of many places where Canadian aid promoted neoliberalism. In the late 1980s and early 1990s, "CIDA began to work closely with the Department of Finance in the formulation of Structural Adjustment Programs by providing inputs into the Policy Framework Papers, the blueprints for economic reform that were prepared for the IMF in close consultation with the World Bank."[185] After five years as Executive Director of the IMF, in 1989, Marcel Massé again became president of CIDA. "He quickly concentrated the bilateral [aid] program on encouragement and underwriting of structural adjustment, in close cooperation with the IMF and the World Bank."[186] Massé explained that "CIDA has taken the leap of faith and plunged into the uncharted seas of structural adjustment ... structural adjustment figures among the priorities for Canadian Development Assistance."[187]

Ottawa was a major proponent of the World Bank's shift towards neoliberal policies in the early 1980s.[188] Canada was also one of the first western countries to provide financing for an IMF structural adjustment plan in the mid-1980s.[189] In 1986-87 Canada gave $250 million to subsidize a $515 million commercial rate loan to the IMF's Enhanced Structural Adjustment Facility, an IMF fund that placed high levels of conditionality on loans. As part of its support for the IMF's neoliberal push, in 1989 alone, Ottawa actively supported SAPs in Bangladesh, Guyana, Jamaica, Nepal and the Philippines.[190] Since the mid-1980s, billions of dollars worth of Canadian "aid" has supported structural adjustment programs.[191]

Getting countries to reform their economies along neoliberal lines has always taken a carrot and stick. Usually SAP promotion consists of making money available to countries that follow the rules, but Canadian policymakers have also been known to use the stick. "In the mid-1980s, CIDA terminated food aid shipments to Tanzania because it had failed to reform agricultural policy as proposed by donors. More recently, it stopped food aid to Sri Lanka because of its poor performance in structural adjustment."[192] Rather than aid people, structural adjustment programs have contributed to the continued impoverishment of most Africans. SAPs have worsened poverty and inequality across the continent, but they have benefited foreign mining companies by liberalizing mining laws. By 2007 Africa was home to hundreds of Canadian mining investments worth $14.7 billion US.[193] This was a huge increase in Canadian mining investment across the continent. Up from about a quarter billion dollars in 1989, Canadian mining assets in Africa (before the late 2008 commodities crash) were projected to reach $22 billion by 2010.[194] A single Canadian-owned coal mine and energy complex in Botswana, the largest private-sector investment in Africa, was expected to cost $9.5 billion upon completion.[195]

In 2006 eight in ten Ghanaian mines were Canadian owned.[196] With Canadian corporations having interests in almost 100 properties across the country, some have come under fire. "Canadian mining companies are in the forefront of the destruction of some of Ghana's rich forest reserves," explained Abdulai Darimani. "[Canadian owned mine] Bonte is a typical case of how the nation is being raped of its natural resources only to be abandoned after they are completely exhausted."[197]

Canadian mining sites have certainly witnessed social upheaval. At TSX-listed Golden Star's surface mine in the centre of Prestea, a city of 40,000 in the western part of Ghana, "riots occurred when two young men were shot dead by security forces. In June 2005, more riots occurred as the Prestea community gave the authorities of Golden Star 21 days to cease all operations that were destroying their environment. Once again, seven people were injured as shots were fired at the demonstrators."[198]

Free market reforms were designed to reduce the state's role in economic life. But cuts to social services can be devastating for society's most vulnerable. For this reason donors that push laissez-faire economics often couple their push for reforms with aid to NGOs that provide social services. In the 1980s, Ottawa began to finance social investment funds to alleviate the effect of SAPs.[199]

As part of its support for Ghana's 1987 SAP CIDA gave $8.4 million dollars to UNICEF's Plan of Action to Mitigate the Social Costs of Adjustment.[200] A former president of CIDA, Margaret Catley-Carlson, explained to the Ghanaians: "We know that if you take on this [IMF] program of reform it will cost you. Your food prices are going to shoot up, and in the urban areas that is going to be very destabilizing. So we will put in some food aid and help you out over this very difficult period."[201] (In early 1989, in an another example of the close relationship between NGOs and government, CIDA financed a small NGO fact-finding mission to Guyana to investigate ways of dealing with the expected social hardships of a Canadian backed SAP.)[202]

The process of withdrawing the state through structural adjustment programs resulted in ever-growing dependence on nonstate actors. "In many third-world and transition countries, international or local NGOs are taking over the role of the state in providing welfare, health and sanitation."[203] For its part, Ottawa asked the NGO sector to "undertake tasks previously performed by governments, such as the delivery of significant portions of humanitarian and development assistance."[204] With a hint of pride, Jeanine Cudmore, an employee of the CIDA-funded Social Enterprise Development Foundation, explained in April 2007 that in northern Ghana "the government relies on NGOs."[205]

Niger

An April 2007 Montréal Gazette business article headlined "Local Miner a Major Force in Niger," reported on the close relations between SEMAFO and the then prime minister of Niger. "We work very closely with [then Prime Minister Hama Amadou]... We're part of his budget every year. He knows us," La Salle told the Gazette.

La Salle then described how the prime minister helped his company break a strike at the mine. "We went to court, we had the strike declared illegal and that allowed us to let go of some of the employees and rehire some of them based upon a new work contract. It allowed us to let go of some undesirable employees because they had been on strike a few times," he said.[206] SEMAFO's preferred prime minister seems also to have been involved in activities not quite as "legal" as firing striking workers. Prime Minister Amadou was arrested in June 2008 on corruption charges stemming from two unrelated incidents and was awaiting trial.[207] The bitter strike led to a parliamentarian inquiry regarding environmental damage caused by the mine, lack of benefits for local communities and treatment of miners. "The wages are very low," explained Mohammed Bazoum, chairman of Niger's main opposition party. "The population is not benefiting at all from this gold."[208] The largest industrial project in Niger since the 1960s, SEMAFO had 600 workers at its Samira Hill mine.[209] By early 2009 Canada was the second biggest foreign investor in Niger after France.[210]

Another Canadian resource company operating in Niger also put its political connections to good use. Calgary-based TG World Energy, the Globe and Mail reported, "hired Mr. [Jean] Chrétien last year [2004] to help it get out of a pickle in the impoverished African nation of Niger."[211] TG's rights to explore 18 million acres of Niger's wilderness for oil and gas were revoked by the government, which felt TG hadn't invested enough prospecting. Niger then awarded the concession to a subsidiary of the China National Petroleum Corp. The Calgary company sued Niger's government and went to arbitration with the Chinese firm. "It also asked Mr. Chrétien to intervene. ... The former prime minister spoke with officials of China National Petroleum during a trip to Beijing and then in March of 2004, he flew into Niamey, the Niger capital. In normal circumstances, the best TG World could have hoped to get on its own was a meeting with the Energy Minister. But Mr. Chrétien managed to snag a meeting with the President."[212] Chrétien's lobbying led to a new agreement between TG World, Niger and the Chinese, which saw the company's stock increase from 8 cents to above $1 within a year.

(Niger was not the only place where Chrétien used his reputation to advance Canadian corporate interests. In 2004 alone he visited Gambian dictator Yahya Jammen to discuss offshore petroleum concessions for Calgary's Buried Hill Energy; met Turkmenistan's autocratic President Saparmurad Niyazov in Ashkhabad to discuss Buried Hill projects; went to China on two different occasions with Canadian corporate representatives.[213])

There are no laws against former Canadian politicians using their international contacts to lobby for Canadian companies. "Mr. Chrétien appears to be well within Ottawa's conflict-of-interest rules for former ministers — which are largely aimed at stopping ex-politicians from lobbying the Canadian government and are silent about such activities involving foreign governments."[214]

Sudan

Having established control over Egypt, in 1884 the British military moved to put down a Sudanese Arab rebellion against Egyptian rule. The Canadians who fought in Sudan went under the British flag. But, Prime Minister "Sir John A McDonald looked on favourably as a force of nearly 400 officers and men was recruited under British auspices for services on the Nile."[215] Ottawa prepared to help the British raise a thousand-man battalion if further reinforcements were needed in Sudan.[216]

One hundred and ten years after Britain's invasion of Sudan Foreign Affairs Minister Lloyd Axworthy defended the U.S.'s illegal bombing of the Al-Shifa pharmaceutical facility in August 1998, which was supposed to be producing chemical weapons. It wasn't.[217] Echoing U.S. Secretary of State Madeleine Albright's statement that "we have a legal right to self-defence," Axworthy said "when you come into this very murky and very dangerous area of dealing with terrorism, nations have a right to defend themselves."[218] The bombing left millions of people without medicines and is thought to have caused a large number of unnecessary deaths.[219]

Just after Ottawa supported the U.S. bombing of Sudan, Calgary-based Talisman Oil was heavily criticized for exacerbating southern Sudan's civil war. To mollify growing protests Axworthy sent a senior foreign policy advisor on Africa, John Harker, to investigate "the alleged link between oil development and human rights violations, particularly with respect to the forced removal of populations around oilfields and oil related development." The October 1999 federal government-sponsored investigation found that "Talisman was clearly adding to the suffering of the Sudanese people."[220] The government report continued: "there has been and probably still is, major displacement of civilian populations related to oil extraction. Sudan is a place of extraordinary suffering and continuing human rights violations, even though some forward progress can be recorded, and the oil operations in which a Canadian company is involved add more suffering."[221] Talisman and other oil companies built an airstrip owned by the Sudanese government, which was used as a base for bombing raids on the southern Sudanese.[222] Talisman also serviced broken military trucks, provided electricity lines to the army's barracks and piped water to army camps.[223] "Talisman provided expertise, China provided manpower, and Sudan provided army and loyal militias who not only protected the pipeline and facilities, but also aggressively cleansed the oil fields of people."[224] Beyond providing direct support to the Sudanese government's military campaign Talisman officials justified the army's actions. After the government bombed a Norwegian relief agency in the south, the head of Talisman claimed "the SPLA [Southern guerrillas] puts its camps next to Norwegian hospitals."[225]

As domestic pressure mounted on the Liberal government to take action against Talisman, the company played the nationalist card. The Calgary-based company argued that it offered important opportunities for Canadians to work in a major head office and that if Ottawa refused to support them, they would relocate.[226] Axworthy buckled under corporate pressure. Even after the Harker report found Talisman guilty of supporting the Sudanese government's brutal tactics, Axworthy described Talisman as "a positive force for change in Sudan."[227] And with prodding from the company, Canada opened an embassy in Khartoum.[228]

But, in 2003 Talisman finally pulled out of Sudan. The decision was sparked by mounting criticism from humanitarian groups as well as moves by the U.S. Congress to block investments in Sudan and a U.S. court case against Talisman for complicity with human rights abuses.[229] Despite Talisman's questionable record in Sudan, Ottawa sent a letter to the U.S. Federal District Court in June 2007 defending the company.[230]

A number of smaller Canadian energy companies working in Sudan in the late 1990s hired private security firms. U.S.-based, Airscan, provided surveillance and security services to Calgary's Arakis Energy and it was reported that notorious South African mercenary outfit, Executive Outcomes, also protected Canadian oil interests in the country.[231]

In 2008 the only foreign-operated mine in Sudan was run by Montréal-based La Mancha. The Canadian company owned 40 percent of the Hassai GoldMine in northeastern Sudan with the government owning the majority stake. Defending its ties to the Sudanese regime, a company spokesperson told the Montréal Gazette that a Canadian company ensures "some basic standards" in terms of environmental protection and human rights.[232]

Somalia

On March 4, 1993, Canadian troops fired into a crowd of between 50 and 300 Somali demonstrators, killing one of the protesters and disabling at least two.[233] Later in the day, two Somalis lured near the Canadian base were shot in the back, one fatally, by Canadian soldiers. The survivor claimed "instantly my companion was shot and he fell to the ground on the spot and as I looked at him I was shot too. My companion managed to move before me. At that time an armed man, you know, from the Canadian forces came out of the camp. Luckily, I fell under a shallow cliff and he could not see me. What he did was that, he followed the other man and shot him on that spot, the face. Over there on his front body part. And I saw the shot clearly. Some other forces ran out of the camp after him, and when he started to come running after me, the other forces held him by the hand and stopped him."[234]

The most disturbing incident of Canadian abuse in Somalia took place two weeks later. A sixteen-year-old, Shidane Abukar Arone, was tortured to death while dozens of other members of the Airborne Regiment knew what was happening.[235] As many as 80 soldiers heard Arone's screams, which lasted for hours.[236] "What is evident more than anything else is how absolutely unremarkable the violence seemed to be to the men who enacted it, witnessed it, or simply heard that it was happening."[237]

The Somali mission brought to light a disturbing level of overt racism within the military. Corporal Matt Mackay, a self confessed neo-Nazi who said he quit the white supremacist movement two years before going to

Somalia, gleefully reported "we haven't killed enough N- yet." Another Canadian soldier was caught on camera saying the Somalia intervention was called, "Operation Snatch Nig-nog." Yet another soldier explained how Somalis were not starving; "they never were, they're lazy, they're slobs, and they stink."[238]

Canadian military leaders in Somalia believed the natives had to be kept in line, often through violence.[239] The problem for the U.S. and its allies was that many (if not most) Somalis did not see the U.N. intervention, which was sanctioned as a peace enforcement rather than peacekeeping mission, as a humanitarian endeavour.[240] (Chapter VII of the U.N. charter has only been used in Korea, Iraq and Somalia.) At the time of the intervention The Nation magazine referred to Somalia as "one of the most strategically sensitive spots in the world today: astride the Horn of Africa, where oil, Islamic fundamentalism and Israeli, Iranian and Arab ambitions and arms are apt to crash and collide."[241] In 1993 Project Censored Canada found the prospects for extracting oil in Somalia the most under-reported Canadian news item that year.[242]

Somalia became a scandal for the Canadian military. Details of disgusting training rituals and racism within the force were widely derided, leading to the disbandment of the Airborne Regiment. But few individuals in positions of authority were punished. The Canadian forces commander in Somalia, Serge Labbé, was found to have "failed as a commander" by a public inquiry into the mission. He claimed with no evidence that the two victims shot in the back by Canadian troops were "trained saboteurs" and it was alleged at the Somalia inquiry "that he offered a case of champagne to the first soldier who killed a Somali."[243] Despite his actions in Somalia Labbé's career flourished. He received important NATO positions in the Balkans and Turkey. In Afghanistan he commanded Canada's 15-officer Strategic Advisory Team in Kabul, which worked closely with the government on national planning issues.[244] General Rick Hillier's last act as chief of defence staff in mid-2008 was to quietly promote Labbé to brigadier general, which was backdated to top up his salary for seven years. Military analyst Scott Taylor summarized Labbé's post-Somalia career: "All in all, he had the sort of high-flying career of adventure that most officers can only dream of. Now he's a brigadier-general, pockets bulging with wads of back pay, heading into an even more lucrative retirement."[245]

Once again demonstrating the armed intervention equals aid principle, Canada significantly increased its aid to Somalia in the early 1990s. But after Canadian troops pulled out it all but disappeared.[246] The relationship developed between NGOs and the military in Somalia foreshadowed what later took place in Afghanistan. *Canadian Naval Operations in the 1990s* explains: "The working relationships developed between the NGOs and the Canadian navy while operating in Somalia signified a new relationship that could affect Canada's influence and position in the international system. NGOs have become integral players in the managing of crisis and conflict, and the establishment of good relationships with them could affect Canada's future position in crisis responses. The Somalia operation was a success in that it laid important foundations in the NGO/Canadian navy relationship."[247]

In December 2006 the U.S. once again intervened militarily in Somalia. After the Islamic courts won control of the country in the fall of 2006, American forces launched air attacks while Ethiopian troops invaded to install a government operating in exile. Ottawa quietly supported this aggression, in which thousands were killed and hundreds of thousands displaced. Canada's support for foreign intervention in Somalia did not go unnoticed. When a group calling themselves Mujahedin of Somalia abducted a Canadian and Australian in October 2008 they accused Canada and Australia of "taking part in the destruction of Somalia."[248] They demanded a change in policy from these two countries.

Canada provided Ethiopia with significant assistance. It received $108 million in aid in 2004-05 and slightly smaller amounts over following years.[249] Ottawa did not make aid contingent on Ethiopia withdrawing its forces from Somalia and the federal government's public comments on the situation in Somalia broadly supported Ethiopian/U.S. actions. When prominent Somali-Canadian journalist Ali Iman Sharmarke was assassinated in Mogadishu in August 2007 Foreign Affairs Minister Peter Mackay only condemned "the violence" in the country. He never mentioned that the assassins were identified as pro-government militias with ties to Ethiopian troops.[250]

Throughout 2007 and 2008 when the U.S. launched periodic airstrikes in Somalia, Ottawa added its military presence. At various points during 2008, HMCS Calgary, Iroquois, Charlottetown, Protecteur, Toronto and Ville de Québec all patrolled off the coast of Somalia.[251] In the summer of 2008 Canada took command of NATO's Task Force 150 that worked off the coast of Somalia.[252] The National Post described Task Force 150's roots: "As U.S.-led forces prepared to invade Afghanistan, a coalition armada assembled in the Arabian Sea. Six Canadian warships, including the hulking, 36-year-old Iroquois, sped to the region. Over the intervening seven years, the mission shifted from supporting the Afghanistan war to aiding the 2003 invasion of Iraq. More recently, the force — which is under the regional command of U.S. Naval Forces Central Command in Bahrain — has taken on the broader, less tangible task of providing security and stability across an area that's more than six million square kilometres in size. Inexorably, CTF-150, which was created to fight terrorists, found itself chasing pirates [near Somalia]."[253]

There was some dispute as to whether the Canadian vessels near Somalia were simply concerned about pirates. To quote extensively from the Dalhousie University's J.L. Granatstein Postdoctoral Fellow at the Centre for Military and Strategic Studies, Patrick Lennox:

"Drug-peddlers and pirates weren't the entire reason for the significant sea presence that Canada had established for almost four months in this region. Thinking in broader terms about the strategic relevance of the Arabian Sea quickly reveals a number of compelling reasons for Canada's contribution to CTF 150 this summer.

"The Arabian Sea is a region of the Indian Ocean bounded to the east by India, Pakistan and Iran, to the north by the United Arab Emirates and Oman, and to the west by Yemen, the Maldives, and Somalia. This 'Arc of Instability' consists of more than two million strategically-vital square nautical miles, and contains two of the world's five most important oil choke points —Babel-Mandeb between Yemen and Djibouti, and the Strait of Hormuz between the most northern part of UAE and Iran. With the 'return of history' brought on by China's rise, Russia's rebound, India's awakening, Iran's ambition, and the ongoing and seemingly intractable conflicts in Iraq and Afghanistan, the geopolitical centre of gravity has shifted east decisively. This has made the Arabian Sea some of the most important maritime real-estate on the planet. Accordingly, the United States has positioned its Fifth Fleet — the world's premiere naval force — in the region; established a base in Djibouti, and maintained and upgraded bases in Qatar and Bahrain in support of three separate command structures which cover these waters and those that extend further into the northern-most point of the Persian Gulf. These commands, which are known by number – CTF 150, 152, and 158 – are all ultimately under the strategic guidance of United States Naval Forces Central Command (NAVCENT), which is personified at the moment by Vice Admiral William E. Gortney. CTF 150 is the largest of the three areas of responsibility by a long shot, and even extends into the Red Sea, all the way up to the Suez Canal. The economies in the Arabian Peninsula and, indeed, the broader system of economic globalization on the whole, would suffer significantly were the sea lanes of communication throughout the CTF 150 area of responsibility to become unserviceable. Approximately 50 percent of the world's oil production and 95 percent of the Far East trade to Europe transits these waters. Yet Babel-Mandeb is surrounded by political instability in Yemen and Somalia, and, to this day, Iran threatens to blockade Hormuz in response to the possibility of Israeli air strikes against its nuclear facilities. With 3.3 million barrels of oil crossing Babel-Mandeb and 17 million crossing Hormuz each day, the global economy depends heavily on the maintenance of these waters as reliable and secure avenues for commerce. Securing these central supply lines from disruptive forces is, accordingly, the stipulated mandate of CTF 150. There is, however, arguably a great deal more at stake than securing these sea lanes for commerce. The maintenance of the status quo international system, which is based primarily on the preponderance of American power, depends on the constant presence of a dominant American led armada in the area of our concern. A critical mass of western and western-allied warships in the Arabian Sea and Persian Gulf results in a critical absence of rival warships in these waters. Were Chinese, Russian, and Iranian hulls to command these sea lanes, it would mark a significant shift in the distribution of power in the international system. At its most fundamental and essential level, then, CTF 150 is about sea presence and commanding the commons. Accordingly, CTF 150 comprises ships and air assets from the navies of France, Denmark, Germany, Britain, Pakistan, Singapore, Japan (which only supplies gasoline free-of-charge to the coalition members and does not partake in any of the operations), Canada, and, of course, the U.S.

"Beginning with Operation Apollo which was Canada's initial naval contribution to the Afghanistan campaign, Canada has put 25 ships into the Arabian Sea since 9/11. In doing so it has accomplished a number of related ends which, while perhaps less immediately tangible than drug busts and foiling pirates, go far beyond either of these in terms of realizing the country's interests abroad. First, maintaining a presence in the Arabian Sea demonstrates to governments in the region that Canada is committed to security and development here, where Canadian soldiers are dying at an alarming rate, and where chaos seems to loom around the corner of each day's news cycle. Second, this sea presence demonstrates to our closest allies and to the rest of the world that we are an engaged maritime nation with a capable and professional navy willing to step up and even take the lead in making substantial contributions to security and development in an area critical to global stability. Finally, such a demonstration could, in the future, open opportunities for Canadian diplomats to fulfill a role they have traditionally relished: being the world's innovative problem-solver. With this region much like a leaky dam in constant need of a fix, Canadian foreign-policy makers should not discount the role of pride and influence that can be demonstrated when our diplomats are employed in solving significant problems on the world stage. Moreover, having naval assets forward deployed to this region acts as a multiplier for the realization of Canada's diplomatic and economic objectives."[254]

In early 2008 Le Devoir reported that one aim of the HMCS Toronto's four month trip around Africa, particularly off the coast of Nigeria and Somalia, was to develop a situational knowledge of these countries territorial waters.[255] How knowledge of these countries coast lines will be used was not made entirely clear. But it certainly was not to strengthen these countries sovereignty, according to Embassy magazine. "During the voyage, the fleet sailed at a distance of 12 to 15 miles off the African coast, just beyond the limits of sovereign national waters. The NATO fleet did not inform African nations it would soon be on the horizon. This, [Canadian] Lt.-Cmdr. [Angus] Topshee says, was an intentional move meant to 'keep options open.' 'International law is built on precedent,' he says. 'So if NATO creates a precedent where we're going to inform countries, we're going to operate off their coastline, over time that precedent actually becomes a requirement.'"[256]

La Francophonie

In 1965 France signed cultural agreements with Québec. Three years later, in a more significant move, Gabon invited Québec to an international conference of Francophone countries. Ottawa flipped out, diplomatically speaking. According to Ivan Head, then Prime Minister Pierre Trudeau's principal advisor on foreign affairs, the Gabonese invitation to Québec was "one of the most serious threats to the integrity of Canada that this country has ever faced … It contains the seeds of the destruction of Canada as a member of the international community."[257] Ottawa immediately severed diplomatic relations with Gabon and "issued some not so subtle reminders to other francophone African states that Québec was unlikely to be able to match federal development assistance programs."[258]

Since that time one objective of Canadian aid has been to weaken Québec's sovereignty movement and Ottawa has worked hard to channel Québeckers and Québec nationalism into its overall foreign policy agenda.

The "Federal government has given more aid to French-speaking countries in an attempt to diffuse Québec nationalist initiatives in this area and to try to redirect them through the national entity."[259] In the late 1960s Canada began to expand its aid to francophone nations as a way to placate Québec nationalists. In 1963-64, Canada granted $300,000 in aid to Francophone countries. "Aid to these states increased thirteen fold for 1964-65 from $300,000 to $4 million; allocations nearly doubled again for 1965-66 ... By 1967-68 over $12 million had been allocated for Francophone Africa."[260] Aid to the Francophonie was designed to convince Québec nationalists that Ottawa was sympathetic to francophone culture. Aid was intended as "an outward looking expression of the bilingual character of Canada."[261] In addition, Québec, unlike other provinces, explicitly provides development assistance to project the province's dominant linguistic heritage.[262]

(Despite the fact that French is a colonial language usually spoken by the elite, hundreds of millions of Canadian aid dollars have been spent to promote French. Aside from Québec is there any place in the world where French is the language of the oppressed? Haiti provides the clearest example of the — unintended? — consequences. Canadian Development Assistance to Haiti explains the country's importance to French Canada: "As the only independent French-speaking country in Latin American and the Caribbean, Haiti is of special importance for the preservation of the French language and culture." But most Haitians don't speak French, they speak Creole. French is the language of Haiti's elite and language has served as a mechanism through which they maintain their privilege (maybe 10 percent of Haitians speak French). A Québecois group in Haiti almost invariably reinforces the influence of French in that country. Whether conscious or not, a French-focused foreigner in Haiti has taken (at least linguistically speaking) a side in the country's brutal class war. While the linguistic/class French/Creole divide is particularly striking in Haiti it exists in most former French colonies. For instance, after Algeria won its independence there were moves to Arabize the country. At the same time Canadian aid to that country was often channeled through French-speaking Canadians. This stunted moves towards strengthening Arabic.)

Québec-based businesses have also benefited from Ottawa's focus on French-speaking Africa. One of Québec's leading proponents of the French language and former head of CIDA, Paul Gérin-Lajoie, played a major role in using the aid agency to build Québec-based companies. "PGL [Paul Gérin-Lajoie] expanded CIDA's commercial base in French-speaking Canada through active use of the contract approval process to build up Québec-based suppliers and consultancy firms, especially SNC and Lavalin."[263] Gérin-Lajoie's underling, Maurice Strong, continued this pattern when he took charge of CIDA. Much to the dismay of External Affairs "Strong hired SNC...to manage offices on behalf of CIDA in Francophone African countries where there was no Canadian diplomatic representation."[264] SNC's vice president of development Jack Hahn described their plan to enter Algeria in 1968: "They might be interested in North American technology offered in French."[265]

Algeria

Ottawa aided France in its war to stop Algeria from gaining independence, a fight that saw 700,000 killed and two million displaced from 1954 to 1962. Between 1950 and March 1960, the Canadian government provided $127,679,000 in military equipment to France under NATO's Mutual Aid Program, which was supposed to deter Soviet aggression in Western Europe.[266] "Even with 400,000 troops in Algeria, in autumn 1956, Canada continued to provide the French military with extensive gifts of armament. ... From 1955 to 1958, Canada gave France mutual aid that included 300,000 rounds of 20mm ammunition, 1 million rounds of .303 ammunition, trucks, dynamite, sub-machine guns, 90mm shells, pistols, and Harvard training aircraft ... Given that a majority of the French army was stationed in Algeria all these years, the St. Laurent government could not ignore the embarrassing probability that most of this equipment was probably being used against the nationalist movement in Algeria."[267]

The St. Laurent government was fully aware that France used Canadian weapons against Algeria's independence movement. To allow France to use Canadian equipment in Algeria, the federal government modified the Defence Appropriation Act, which required Canadian mutual aid supplies to be used to defend western Europe.[268] Ottawa also supported the French diplomatically. The federal government conceded when France demanded that Algeria be included in NATO even though it was a colony and was outside the North Atlantic region. In 1955, when African and Asian states tried to have the Algerian conflict debated at the U.N., Canada opposed the move.[269] Four years later Canada's U.N. delegation was still instructed to vote with France on Algeria.[270]

Ottawa's support for French colonialism in Algeria included pressuring the media. When Paris complained in 1959 about the CBC's coverage of Algeria (they interviewed a National Liberation Front representative in New York and two Algerian students in Montréal) External Affairs offered to consult the network concerning events in France and Algeria.[271]

Angola, Mozambique and Guinea Bissau

In addition to supporting the British and French, Ottawa also supported Portuguese colonialism in Africa. In the late 1950s, when many African countries won their independence, "Canada quite openly adopted an explicitly pro-Portuguese, pro-colonial stance, supporting Portugal's contention that it alone was competent to determine the status of its dependent territories."[272]

As late as December 1973 Canada voted against a U.N. resolution that directly challenged Portugal's claim to represent Angola, Mozambique and Guinea Bissau at the international body.[273] On September 24, 1973, the African Party for the Independence of Guinea and Cape Verde (PAIGC) declared an independent state of Guinea Bissau. Ottawa refused to recognize the new state, implicitly recognizing Portuguese sovereignty over the area. Ninety governments granted recognition to Guinea Bissau before the fall of the Salazar Caetano dictatorship in Portugal. But, Canada only recognized Guinea Bissau once it was clear that the new Portuguese government was about to do so.[274]

As Portugal waged brutal wars against the liberation movements in its African colonies Ottawa opposed U.N. resolutions calling upon members to stop trading with Portugal and investing in its colonies.[275] "Canada opposed anything that smacked of action against Portugal and aggressively harped upon the advisability of 'non-violence' in a situation which had never known anything else but violence and where all peaceful routes had been tried by the Africans and rejected by the Portuguese."[276]

During the wars of liberation in Angola, Mozambique, and Guinea Bissau, Canada greatly expanded its economic ties to these colonies.[277] Canadian trade officials busied themselves promoting the incentives Portugal offered in its "overseas provinces."[278] Canada's most controversial economic relationship to the colonies was Alcan's sale of aluminium rods to the Portuguese for the Cabora Bassa Dam.[279] Along with Toronto-based Reynolds, Alcan won contracts to provide rods "only after several other potential suppliers backed out because their governments were unwilling to face the pressures of being known as a breaker of the economic sanctions against Rhodesia."[280] A U.N. General Assembly resolution condemned the Cabora Bassa scheme as "contrary to [the] vital interests of the people of Mozambique" and described it as a "plot designed to perpetuate the domination, exploitation and oppression of the peoples of this part of Africa and southern Rhodesia, and which would lead to international tensions." The resolution passed 85-11 with Canada voting against.[281]

Canada's complicity in Portuguese colonialism went beyond diplomatic and economic support. Ottawa also provided military assistance to the Portuguese. On a number of occasions Canadian technologies were found in Portuguese armaments, including parts made by Computing Devices of Canada and Aviation Ltd in the wreckage of a Fiat G-91 fighter, shot down by PAIGC.[282] "Through uncritical acceptance of the NATO connection, which married the arsenal of the west to Portuguese colonial purposes, Canada made itself, willy-nilly, a partner of the Portuguese." Ottawa saw no problem with NATO weapons going to Portugal, refusing to support the Dutch and Scandinavian countries attempts to end these arms sales.[283]

Not long after Angola won its independence from Portugal, apartheid South Africa invaded. In an important display of international solidarity Cuba came to Angola's defence. Thousands of Cuban troops, most of them black, voluntarily enlisted to fight the racist South African regime. Contrary to Western claims, Cuba decided to intervene in Angola without Soviet input (Washington knew this at the time).[284] Cuba's intervention helped halt South Africa's invasion.

This successful military victory by black forces also helped bring down apartheid in South Africa. The famous township rebellion in Soweto took place three months after South Africa's initial defeat in Angola.[285] The ANC noted "their [the South African army's] racist arrogance shrank when our MPLA [Popular Movement for the Liberation of Angola] comrades thrashed them in Angola."[286] For its part, the Rand Daily Mail warned that the legacy of Angola was "the blows to South African pride. The boost to African nationalism which has seen South Africa forced to retreat."[287] In a similar vein another South African analyst observed "whether the bulk of the offensive was by Cubans or Angolans is immaterial in the colour-conscious context of this war's battlefield, for the reality is that they won, are winning, and are not white: and that psychological edge, that advantage the white man has enjoyed and exploited over 300 years of colonialism and empire, is slipping away. White elitism has suffered an irreversible blow in Angola and Whites who have been there know it."[288] Ottawa freaked out, diplomatically speaking. Trudeau stated: "Canada disapproves with horror [of] participation of Cuban troops in Africa" and in May 1978 Trudeau announced that CIDA would terminate its small aid program in Cuba as a result.[289]

Discussion

Canadian corporations, particularly mining companies, are major players across the African continent. Leaving aside South Africa, Canadian miners dominate the industry across the continent.[290] This is not unlike Latin America where Canadian investors dominate many countries' resource sectors. In Africa, however, Canadian capital operates more independently. Companies based in Canada dominate mining in countries within French, British and U.S. spheres of influence. Since no one country dominates the region Ottawa has greater room to maneuver. Canadian corporations and diplomats have a greater degree of independence in Africa than in most parts of the world. And what is the result?

It would be hard to argue that Canada's relations with Africa proves that, if given the independence to act as we want, Canada will be a force for good. Rather, Canada's role in Africa demonstrates that this country's foreign affairs is seldom determined by ordinary Canadians. Narrow corporate interests and the foreign policy establishment usually look out for themselves, not the impoverished. Our tax dollars are used to create profits for the few rather than to act as good neighbours. And then our tax dollars are often spent to distort what has been done in Canada's name.

How many Canadians would vote for a foreign policy that keeps Africa undeveloped, except as it benefits a few corporations? Yet, that has been the reality of Canadian policy.

Chapter Notes

1   War and Peacekeeping, 39
2   Painting the Map Red, 429
3   Painting the Map Red, 38
4   Canada and Imperialism, 251; Painting the Map Red, 59; Canada in Afghanistan, 109
5   Empire to Umpire, 23
6   The Boer War and Canadian Imperialism, 15
7   Another Kind of Justice, 31
8   Painting the Map Red, 263
9   Canadian Military Journal Summer 2005
10   Painting the Map Red, 194
11   Painting the Map Red, 232
12   Painting the Map Red, 448
13   Painting the Map Red, 111
14   Painting the Map Red, 389
15   Trouble with Africa, 38
16   The Ambiguous Champion, 16
17   Ambiguous Champion, 27
18   Canadian Relations to South Africa, 170
19   Ambiguous Champion, 28
20   Ambiguous Champion, 67
21   Ambiguous Champion, 52
22   Ambiguous Champions, 97
23   Ambiguous Champion, 88
24   Human Rights and Canadian Foreign Policy, 175
25   Ambiguous Champion, 89
26   Ambiguous Champion, 122
27   Ambiguous Champion, 117
28   Ambiguous Champion, 119
29   Canada Accomplice in Apartheid, 8
30   Ambiguous Champion, 104
31   Ambiguous Champion, 110
32   Ambiguous Champion, 41
33   Ambiguous Champion, 48
34   The Ambiguous Champion, 84
35   Canadian Development Assistance to Tanzania, 41
36   Ambiguous Champion, 63
37   Ambiguous Champion, 64; Last Post Vol 1 #3
38   Ambiguous Champion, 65; Canadian Multinationals, 111
39   Canadian Foreign Policy: Contemporary Issues and Themes, 116
40   Canadian Relations to South Africa, 181
41   Ambiguous Champion, 67
42   Ambiguous Champion, 66
43   Ambiguous Champion, 194
44   Ambiguous Champion, 194
45   Ambiguous Champion, 194
46   Ambiguous Champion, 261

47   Ambiguous Champion, 265
48   Ambiguous Champion, 125
49   Democratizing Southern Africa, 34
50   Ambiguous Champion, 202
51   Ambiguous Champion, 202
52   Canadian International Development Assistance Policies, 101
53   Canadian International Development Assistance Policies, 101
54   Ambiguous Champion, 186
55   Ambiguous champion, 127
56   Land of Lost Content, 307
57   Half a Loaf, 222
58   Toronto Star Nov 27 2007
59   In the Eye of the Storm, 243
60   Another Kind of Justice, 119
61   Conflicts of Interest, 141; Canadian Dimension Sept 1993
62   Conflicts of Interest, 154
63   http://www.africafiles.org/article.asp?ID=19218
64   http://www.africafiles.org/article.asp?ID=19218
65   <http://thesouthernafrican.com/index.php?option=com_content&view=article&id=3078 percent3Aafrica-canada-the-mining superpower&catid=2 percent3Amining&Itemid=50&limitstart=2>
66   Embassy magazine Mar 19 2008
67   Ottawa Citizen Nov 27 2007
68   Toronto Star Nov 27 2007
69   http://www.africafiles.org/article.asp?ID=13512
70   http://markcurtis.files.wordpress.com/2008/10/goldenopportunity2nded.pdf
71   http://www.dominionpaper.ca/articles/2385
72   Barrick's Dirty Secrets
73   http://www.dominionpaper.ca/articles/2385
74   http://www.theperspective.org/bulyanhulu.html
75   http://www.miningwatch.ca/index.php?/Tanzania_en/What_Really_Happened
76   http://khalidmagram.blogspot.com/2007/07/canadas-barrick-gold-in-tanzania.html
77   http://www.zmag.org/znet/viewArticle/11193
78   http://www.zmag.org/znet/viewArticle/11193

79 http://www.zmag.org/znet/viewArticle/11193
80 http://www.zmag.org/znet/viewArticle/11193
81 http://www.zmag.org/znet/viewArticle/11193
82 Victorian Explorer, 37
83 African Exploits, 314
84 Victorian Explorer, 39
85 Victorian Explorer, 39
86 Victorian explorer, 187
87 Victorian Explorer, 197
88 African Exploits, 386
89 Building Liberty 217
90 African Exploits, 323
91 African Exploits, 304
92 African Exploits, 305
93 African Exploits, 394; Canada's RMC, 119
94 Anatomy of Big Business, 156
95 Neo-colonialism the Last Stage of Imperialism, 207
96 Anatomy of Big Business, 158
97 Anatomy of Big Business, 161
98 Meeting Each Other Half Way, 1
99 Canadian Dimension Mar 1966
100 The Assassination of Lumumba, 15
101 Peacekeeping, 158
102 A role for Canada in an African Crisis, 88
103 A role for Canada in an African Crisis, 91
104 Canada and the World Order, 98
105 Canadian Defence Quarterly Aug 1992, 15
106 In the Eye of the Storm, 227
107 Canadian Defence Quarterly Aug 1992, 14
108 War in Peacekeeping, 219
109 Peacekeeping, 161
110 Canada and U.N. Peacekeeping, 121
111 Defense in the Nuclear Age, 81
112 Africa in the United Nations system 1945 – 2005, 97
113 A role for Canada in an African crisis, 83
114 Killing Hope, 158
115 The Canadian Way of War, 304
116 The evolution of U.N. peacekeeping, 321
117 The Assassination of Lumumba, 149
118 Killing Hope, 160
119 Killing Hope, 159
120 In the Eye of the Storm, 227
121 Ottawa Citizen June 28 1990
122 Ottawa Citizen June 28 1990
123 Ottawa Citizen June 28 1990
124 <http://www.taylor-report.com/Rwanda_1994/index.php?id=ch15>
125 www.taylor-report.com/Rwanda
126 Montréal Gazette Nov 13, 2006
127 Genocide and Covert Operations in Africa, 94
128 http://en.wikipedia.org/wiki/Paul_Kagame
129 Peacemaking in Rwanda, 27
130 The Path of a Genocide, 189
131 Path of a Genocide, 191
132 Path of a Genocide, 192
133 Path of a Genocide, 195
134 Path of a Genocide, 195
135 Le Patron de Dallaire Parle, 70
136 Le Patron de Dallaire Parle, 161
137 Le Patron de Dallaire Parle, 71/95
138 Les Secret de la Justice Internationale, 127
139 Shake Hands with the Devil, 327
140 Shake Hands with the Devil, 156
141 Shake Hands with the Devil, 164
142 The Lion, the Fox and the Eagle, 357
143 http://www.globalresearch.ca/index.php?context=va&aid=12139
144 Tested Mettle, 186
145 Tested Mettle, 196
146 Genocide and Covert Operations in Africa
147 Noir Canada, 68
148 Genocide and Covert Operations in Africa, 301
149 Noir Canada, 126-138
150 Noir Canada, 61
151 Future Peacekeeping, 41
152 The Congo, 179
153 Canadian Military Journal Spring 2001, 15
154 Nous étions invincibles 158; Genocide and Covert Operations in Africa, 215
155 Rwanda, crimes, mensonges et étouffement de la vérité, 81
156 CBC Fifth Estate Nov 18 1997; L'action humanitaire du Canada, 293
157 The International Dimension of Genocide in Rwanda, 155
158 http://radiokatwe.com/Uswidimekatausaidia081218.htm
159 http://www.ledevoir.com/2007/04/10/138837.html
160 Toronto Star Aug 14 2007
161 Montréal Mirror June 22 2006
162 Montréal Mirror June 22 2006
163 Montréal Mirror June 22 2006
164 U.N. Security Council 2002 http://www.insiderzim.com/novdec02drcplunder.html
165 http://www.dominionpaper.ca/articles/2198
166 Montréal Mirror June 22 2006

167 Montréal Mirror June 22 2006
168 Montréal Gazette Nov 2 2006
169 http://www.ddrd.ca/site/publications/index.php?id=1277&page=3&subsection=catalogue
170 Democracy Now Jan 23 2008
171 Globe and Mail March 5 2005
172 Canada and the Third World, 61; Ties that Bind, 154
173 Perpetuating Poverty, 57
174 In the Eye of the Storm, 242
175 Policy Options Sept 2008
176 Policy Options Sept 2008
177 Deceptive Ash, 63
178 Ghana and Nkrumah, 129/143
179 Ghana and Nkrumah, 149
180 Deceptive Ash, 64
181 CIAA Vol V #2
182 CIAA Vol V #3
183 Ghana and Nkrumah, 175
184 Canadian International Development Assistance Policies, 219
185 Canada's International Policies, 188
186 Canadian International Development Assistance Policies, 99
187 Canada's International Policies, 188
188 Canadian International Development Assistance Policies, 34
189 Canadian Foreign Policy, 358
190 Canadian International Development Assistance Policies, 222
191 Development and Debt, 56
192 Canadian International Development Assistance Policies, 75
193 http://www.ethicalcorp.com/content.asp?ContentID=6325
194 http://thesouthernafrican.com/index.php?option=com_content&view=article&id=3078 percent3Aafrica-canada-the-mining-superpower&catid=2 percent3Amining&Itemid=50&limitstart=2; National Post Mar 1 2008
195 National Post Mar 1 2008
196 Le Devoir Nov 14 2006
197 http://www.miningwatch.ca/updir/Africa case study.pdf
198 http://www.modernghana.com/news2/191779/1/ghana-when-silence-is-golden.html
199 Canadian International Development Assistance Policies, 280
200 Aid and Ebb Tide, 260; Mosaic or Patchwork, 22
201 Human Rights and Canadian Foreign Policy, 182
202 Canadian Journal of Development Studies Vol 72 1995
203 Guardian Weekly Jan 26 2007
204 Foreign Policy Vol 8 #1 118
205 Montréal Gazette Apr 10 2007
206 Montréal Gazette Apr 16 2007
207 Reuters June 24 2008
208 Globe and Mail Feb 9 2009
209 Globe and Mail Feb 9 2009
210 Globe and Mail Feb 9 2009
211 Globe and Mail Mar 5 2005
212 Globe and Mail Mar 5 2005
213 Noir Canada, 257; http://embassymag.ca/issue/archive/2006/2006-09-20
214 Globe and Mail Mar 5 2005
215 Canada in British Wars, 7; Canada and the Commonwealth Caribbean, 279
216 http://www.irpp.org/events/archive/nov00/maloney.pdf
217 http://www.doublestandards.org/sudan.html
218 Windsor Star Aug 25 1998
219 http://www.harvardir.org/articles/909/
220 Making A Killing, 268
221 Foreign Policy Vol 8 #3, 41
222 Making A Killing, 262
223 Foreign Policy Vol 8 #3, 41
224 Making A Killing, 264
225 Making A Killing, 248
226 Making A Killing, 270
227 Foreign Policy Vol 10 #1, 114; Canada's Global Engagements and Relations with India, 82
228 Making A Killing, 272
229 Making A Killing, 288
230 Montréal Gazette June 12 2007
231 Foreign Policy Vol 11 #2, 2; Genocide and Covert Operations in Africa, 228
232 Montréal Gazette July 2008
233 Dark Threats and White Knights, 77
234 Dark Threats and White Knights, 78
235 Dark Threats and White Knights, 4
236 Dark Threats and White Knights, 97
237 Dark Threats and White Knights, 115
238 Dark Threats and White Knights, 4
239 Dark Threats and White Knights, 93
240 Dark Threats and White Knights, 136
241 The Nation Dec 21 1992
242 Democracy's Oxygen, 132
243 Montréal Gazette July 25 2008
244 CBC News Mar 8 2007; Tested Mettle, 97; Uncivil War, 40
245 Embassy magazine Aug 6 2008
246 Canada and Missions for Peace, 92

247 Canadian Naval Operations in the 1990s, 164

248 http://vigilantejournalist.com/blog/archives/421

249 National Post Nov 2007

250 Alternatives 2007

251 <http://www.thestar.com/News/Canada/article/542646>

252 National Post Sept 15 2008

253 National Post Sept 15 2008

254 Diplomat and International Canada Nov 2008

255 Le Devoir Jan 24 2008

256 http://www.maritimeterrorism.com/2008/02/06/modern-pirates-are-high-tech-and-dangerous/

257 The Politics of Canadian Foreign Policy, 327

258 The Politics of Canadian Foreign Policy, 327

259 Fire Proof House to Third Option, 526

260 Deceptive Ash, 229

261 Canadian Development Assistance to Senegal, 49

262 The Politics of Canadian Foreign Policy, 316

263 Aid and Ebb Tide, 131

264 Aid and Ebb Tide, 67

265 SNC, 152

266 Towards a Francophone Community, 57

267 Towards a Francophone Community, 38

268 Towards a Francophone Community, 38

269 Towards a Francophone Community, 32

270 Towards a Francophone Community, 53

271 Towards a Francophone Community, 51

272 Words and Deeds, 77

273 Words and Deeds, 80

274 Words and Deeds, 85

275 Words and Deeds, 80

276 Words and Deeds, 79

277 Words and Deeds, 8

278 Words and Deeds, 12

279 Canada and the Third World, 75

280 Words and Deeds, 28

281 Words and Deeds, 35

282 Words and Deeds, 65

283 Words and Deeds, 68

284 Three Nights in Havana, 193

285 Conflicting missions, 346

286 Conflicting missions, 346

287 Conflicting missions, 346

288 Conflicting missions, 346

289 Three Nights in Havana, 242

290 http://thesouthernafrican.com/index.php?option=com_content&view=article&id=3078 percent3Aafrica-canada-the-mining-superpower&catid=2 percent3Amining&Itemid=50&limitstart=2

Canada in International Alliances

Canada participates in a wide variety of international alliances. NATO, NORAD, the U.N., WTO and IMF/World Bank are among the most important. What role does Canada play in these important bodies? Does Ottawa argue for the rights of ordinary people? Does it use its wealth and clout to help improve the economies of poor countries? Or, is maintaining the international status quo its prime objective?

The United Nations

At the end of the Second World War, Canada was probably the most important middle power. But instead of working for a more just planet Ottawa committed its new-found status towards an undemocratic world order. At the United Nations founding convention in the spring of 1945 Ottawa abstained on an Australian motion that did not include a veto for permanent members of the Security Council, which denied the Australians the backing they needed to carry the meeting. Ottawa then declared its support for the Big Five Security Council veto. "Canada Switches to Back Big 5 Veto," blared the front page of the New York Times.[1] Five medium and smaller countries followed Ottawa's lead and the rest is history.[2] Canada's approach at the U.N.'s founding convention was "designed with the interests of the United States and Great Britain in mind."[3] Pearson is said to have asked the U.S. delegation whether it would sign the charter without the veto. The U.S. refused, so Ottawa voted for the veto.[4]

Over the years Ottawa and Washington's position on the structure of the U.N. have been remarkably similar. In 1974, for instance, a proposal to extend the authority of the General Assembly (at the expense of the Security Council) was adopted 86-2 with 25 abstentions. Ottawa joined Washington in opposing the proposal.[5] During a June 2006 meeting on U.N. budgetary reform, Ottawa sided with the U.S., Australia and New Zealand against much of the world.[6] Those U.N. budget discussions were largely based on differing views of the organization: The South wanted the U.N. to focus on development while the North prefered an emphasis on peacekeeping.[7] Ottawa and Washington's voting pattern at the U.N. have also been remarkably similar.[8] From the early 1950s to the early 1970s, Canada co-sponsored more U.S. General Assembly resolutions than any other country.[9]

Ottawa has usually opposed moves to use the U.N. to overcome global inequity. "In general, Canada has not favoured efforts by developing countries to establish new international machinery with the aim of redistributing wealth in their favour."[10] In 1966, for instance, the General Assembly launched the U.N. Capital Development Fund to compete with the World Bank, but over the next five years Canada, along with France, Japan, the U.K. and U.S. opposed every General Assembly resolution regarding the fund.[11] "The Canadian government [has] been distinctly cautious to date in its attitude towards the various schemes for accelerating capital development in the underdeveloped countries by grants and long-term low-interest loans that have been advocated by delegates from those countries at United Nations meetings."[12]

IMF/World Bank

Ottawa has opposed U.N.-backed financial institutions largely because they undermine the World Bank and IMF where Canada has significant clout.[13] Canada has a permanent (constituency-based) seat on the 24-member IMF executive board. Moreover, Ottawa played an important role in the creation of the World Bank and IMF. During the 1944 Bretton Woods, New Hampshire negotiations to establish post-World War Two international financial institutions Britain and the U.S. disagreed. The U.K. wanted financial institutions that would help indebted nations access loans. Washington (and Wall Street), on the other hand, wanted financial institutions that would favour creditors. Ottawa supported Washington's basic outline for the fund. It simply proposed to make a larger pool of capital ($8 billion US) available.[14] "They [Canada] were sensitive to the American desire for a fund with a limited liability. They had to be, for increasingly there was every likelihood that Canada too would emerge from the war as a creditor in current account."[15] In fact, when the IMF was founded Canada was the world's second biggest creditor, after the U.S.[16]

Canada's proposal ultimately won out and most of the world suffered as a result. A member of Canada's Bretton Woods delegation, Wynn Plumptre, explained: "It is true ... that the [post-war] international institutions, largely fashioned in Washington, were designed to serve the international interests of the United States. The charge that they could in many respects be considered as the creatures of American 'capitalist imperialism' can in a sense be accepted. It does not follow, however, that their establishment and operation were contrary to Canadian interests as perceived at the time or subsequently by Canadian governments."[17]

Since the founding of the IMF and World Bank, Ottawa has generally supported the status quo, a situation where Europe and North America control a disproportionate number of votes. In 1974, for instance, Canada opposed the Group of 77's demand for a greater voice in the IMF and World Bank.[18] Five years later, when third world states unanimously pressed the IMF for less stringent loans, Ottawa rejected the request. Finance Minister John Crosbie stated: "Continuing balance of payments deficits by developing countries means their economic policies are wrong ... some stringent methods of economic self discipline are required."[19] More recently, Canada sided with Bush-administration-appointed World Bank president Paul Wolfowitz at a time when most of the organization's members wanted to fire him for his corrupt practices and right-wing policies. "Its [Canada's] endorsement of Mr. Wolfowitz is in keeping with a long tradition of siding with the United States at the World Bank," noted the Globe and Mail.[20]

Group of Seven and World Trade Organization

Organizations such as the IMF/World Bank, as well as the World Trade Organization, draw much of their clout from the Group of Seven (G7). Canada is the smallest and least colonially tainted G7 country. Yet this country's political elite maintains a strong disposition towards Canada's place among the world's powers. Ottawa prefers to work with the great powers instead of the Nordic states and The Netherlands. By doing so Ottawa prioritizes its ties to the G-7 over the more progressive position of mid-sized rich countries.[21] "Participation in the G7 has clearly linked Canada with the [free market] policies being pursued by the other members of the club and in turn, distanced the country from the policies and activities of other middle powers."[22]

Over the past two decades Ottawa has been a leading proponent of international agreements designed to strengthen the hand of international capital. "The Canadian team developed the contours of what would eventually become the agreement establishing the World Trade Organization."[23] Canada's highly transnational business class was enamoured with its U.S. (and Mexican) trade agreement and wanted to expand investor rights accords to the whole world.[24]

At the December 1996 Singapore ministerial meeting of the WTO Canada worked hard to advance investment guarantees. Ottawa was also a strong proponent of the failed Multilateral Agreement on Investment (MAI), which would have extended the investment components of NAFTA (particularly the notorious Chapter 11) to dozens of countries. With opposition to investment agreements growing, especially in the South, Canada began trying "to portray their demands for rules to more fully protect investors in a more development oriented way."[25] Ottawa began to produce reports to prove that countries with investor-friendly regulations were more likely to develop because of increased investment flows.

Significant amounts of Canadian aid dollars have been used to help poor countries adopt trade/investment agreements. Between 1995 and 2002 Canada provided $38 million in trade-related technical assistance to Eastern Europe.[26] Ottawa gave a few million dollars to the Advisory Center on WTO law in Geneva and the International Trade Center in Geneva, while the $7 million given to the Joint Integrated Technical Assistance Program was "for training in technical assistance for trade negotiations, implementation of WTO agreements, policy formulation and market development."[27]

Ottawa has spent tens of millions of dollars to promote "trade" agreements in Africa. The Program for building African Capacity for Trade (PACT) was an $8 million project to reinforce "free" market economics.[28] The same can be said for CIDA's support for the African Trade Policy Center and the $10 million in Canadian assistance to the New Partnership for African Development (NEPAD) Infrastructure Project Preparation Facility.[29] This money was earmarked partly to promote public-private partnerships in water and sanitation, transportation, energy etc.[30]

Canada works for pro-capitalist reforms in poor countries, but usually works with the world's powers in international trade forums. At the WTO the U.S., Japan, Europe and Canada regularly prepare joint plans that are then brought to the negotiating table. That was the case at the October 2006 WTO meeting in Cancun, Mexico where a Canada-European Community-U.S. negotiation paper was circulated.[31] "At the United Nations, GATT [the precursor to the WTO], UNCTAD [United Nations Conference on Trade and Development] and the North-South dialogue, Canada's representatives have generally supported the position of the industrialized nations and (more particularly that of the U.S.) against the position of the Third World Nations on matters of trade, aid, debt relief and monetary structures."[32]

Below is a sample of instances when Ottawa sided with the rich against the poor in international forums:

• "Canada has followed the United States' lead in resisting ICA [International Coffee Agreement] coffee price increases, has refused to countenance participation in CIPEC [Canadian Industry Program for Energy Conservation], and has opposed, in so far as possible, the formation of new cartels such as the IBA [International Bauxite Agreement]. In practice, Canada's role in policy areas critically affecting Africa has thus reflected concerns to maintain low-cost raw material imports, rather than concern for social justice."[33]

• In the mid-1980s "Canadian negotiators tended to neglect the interests and needs of poorer countries in sugar negotiations."[34]

• Canada delayed payment of its annual assessment to the Food and Agricultural Association after the West's candidate lost in 1987.[35]

• In the 1970s Canada resisted a producer organization for iron put forward by a number of poorer producers of the material.[36]

• During the 1970s Ottawa helped block a copper agreement supported by the South at the IPC [Interated Program for Commodities], believing that copper producers in Canada would be better off without an international agreement.[37]

• The 1974 U.N. conference on the Law of the Sea began with a plea from the poorer nations of the world, especially those which possess little or no access to the sea. Ottawa was not convinced and instead pushed to extend the area defined as a country's coastal waters. The Minister of the Environment and Fisheries, Jack Davis, admitted "we have the world's biggest continental shelf, we are taking over these great resources, making them ours ... with very little effort and very little attention." The minister's comments prompted this reply: "Considering that Canadians per capita were already richer in acreage and resources than any other nation, it is difficult to recall a parallel, for greed, to Mr. Davis's proud boast."[38]

• At an April 2002 meeting of the United Nations Commission on Human Rights Canada was the only country to vote against the human right to water (37 countries voted yes and 15 abstained).[39] In 2008 once again "Canada emerged as the pivotal nation behind recent maneuvers to block the United Nations Human Rights Council from recognizing water as a basic human right."[40]

• In 2002 Canada refused to sign the British-led Extractive Industries Transparency Initiative, which was designed to reduce foreign resource companies' capacity to avoid paying taxes and royalties to poorer countries.[41]

• In September 2006 La Presse reported that Ottawa refused to sign onto a plan to abolish the export of toxic materials. The issue was then in the news after sixteen people died in Cote d'Ivoire and tens of thousands fell ill when a ship full of toxic waste was dumped in the country's harbour.[42]

• Documents leaked to the press in 2005 indicated that Canadian officials went to a convention on biodiversity with instructions to "block consensus" on extending the moratorium on genetically modified organisms and were told to try to end the de facto international moratorium on "terminator gene" technology.[43]

• In early 2008 the International Assessment of Agricultural Knowledge proposed a plan to help small-scale farmers improve production and marketing of their stock. The U.S., Australia and Canada refused to endorse it.[44]

• In January 2005 Canada sided with the U.S., U.K., Japan and Australia in maintaining that no protocol of the International Covenant on Civil and Political Rights or International Covenant on Economic, Social and Cultural Rights should be developed that enhances economic, social and cultural rights. Ottawa joined the U.N. High Commissioner for Human Rights committee that was developing an optional protocol, but Canadian officials tried to hinder the process from the inside.[45]

• In 2007 Ottawa opposed the U.N. declaration on the rights of indigenous peoples. According to Amnesty International, Canada lobbied African, Asian and Latin American governments to vote against the U.N.'s indigenous rights charter.[46] It was later revealed that Canada also tried to block a declaration on the rights of indigenous people at the Organization of American States.[47] The failure of the U.N. declaration on the rights of indigenous peoples was an "important victory for Canadian mining companies since most of their current and future projects are on inhabited lands, and removing the people who stand in the way of their investments is a principal aim of Canadian policy in the developing world."[48] (In 2007 the "U.N. Committee on the Elimination of Racial Discrimination encouraged Canada to take legal or administrative actions to prevent transnationals registered here from negatively affecting the rights of indigenous peoples outside Canada."[49])

• At a number of environmental conferences, Ottawa was cited by environmental groups and other countries' diplomats as a major obstacle to initiatives such as the Kyoto protocol. In late 2008 "the Climate Action Network ... named Canada the country most active in blocking, stalling or undermining the U.N. climate negotiations in Poland."[50] At a 2006 U.N. climate change conference in Nairobi, Canada repeatedly received the "fossil of the day" award handed out by environmental groups to the country doing the most to hinder negotiations.[51] "Canada killing European effort to cut emissions" and "Canada blocking [Commonwealth] consensus on climate change," explained front page Globe and Mail headlines concerning two different international meetings in 2007.[52] In January

2009 Canada failed to attend the founding convention of the International Renewable Energy Agency[53]

• In November 2006 Ottawa helped block a U.N. agreement to ban bottom trawling. This fishing method uses a giant net weighted down by steel gates that is dragged along the ocean floor to scoop up bottom feeders.[54] This practice is universally condemned by environmentalists since the nets kill nearly everything in their path. The same week Ottawa opposed the trawling ban, the Ottawa Citizen reported that the federal government had protected less than one half of one percent of Canada's territorial oceans. This is less than the world average and far off Ottawa's commitment to protect ten percent of this country's ocean space by 2012.[55]

• In 2003 Canada refused to sign the Commonwealth Code of Practice for the international recruitment of health workers.[56] When Libyan officials asked Canada's College of Physicians and Surgeons to disallow the licensing of specialist doctors that Libya funds at a cost of upward of $500,000 to train in Canada, a number of provinces rejected the request.[57] More than 3,000 of Canada's foreign-trained doctors have come from low income countries — primarily South Africa and India.[58]

• In October 2006 Canada successfully convinced the Rotterdam Convention to postpone a decision to place chrysotile asbestos on its list of dangerous products.[59] Even after widespread media attention of the hazards of Canadian asbestos in the lead-up to the next Rotterdam convention meeting Ottawa once again opposed adding asbestos to its list of dangerous products in October 2008. "Canada got others to do their dirty work for them. The first speakers were our biggest customers," said NDP MP Pat Martin.[60] For the past half century Canada has been a leading exporter of asbestos and continues to be the world's second largest exporter after Russia.[61]

NATO

Established in 1949, NATO was part of Cold War hysteria, but the roots of the organization lie in age-old European conflict and the British rivalry with Russia in the late 1800s. (See appendix.) Some believe NATO was a Canadian idea. At the U.N. General Assembly in September 1947 External Affairs Minister Louis St. Laurent warned the floor that if the Security Council's veto crisis was not resolved countries would establish a NATO-type organization.[62] Canada, along with Britain and the U.S., was part of initial NATO discussions in March 1948 and at the start of 2007, well-known military analyst J. L. Granatstein wrote that NATO is "the alliance to which Canada had devoted perhaps 90 percent of its military effort since 1949."[63]

Rather than a defence against possible Russian attack, NATO was largely conceived as a reaction to growing Communist sentiment in Western Europe, particularly in Italy and France. During Italy's 1948 elections Deputy Under-Secretary for External Affairs Escott Reid explained, "the whole game of the Russians is obviously to conquer without armed attack."[64] NATO planners feared a weakening self confidence in Western Europe and the widely held belief that Communism was the wave of the future.[65] George Kennan, the top U.S. government policy planner at the time of NATO's formation, considered "the communist danger in its most threatening form as an internal problem that is of western society."[66] Exactly how little NATO really had to do with any "Communist" threat is demonstrated by the fact that it continued to exist long after the demise of the Soviet Union. In fact, one could argue that its recent interventions in Afghanistan and Yugoslavia demonstrate that its real role is to project force in the interests of the U.S.-led empire.

NATO in Yugoslavia

Author Tariq Ali noted: "One goal of the war against Yugoslavia was to expand NATO to the very frontiers of the former Soviet Union. And that is what they did. The actual needs of the populations in that region were a secondary matter."[67]

During NATO's 78-day bombing of Serbia 18 Canadian CF-18 jets dropped 530 bombs in 682 sorties — approximately 10 percent of NATO's sorties.[68] "By the time the bombing came to an end, thousands more were dead, 600,000 were internally displaced and one million were refugees. Billions of dollars of property and infrastructure damage was inflicted and the region is now facing an environmental crisis due to the destruction of chemical plants and the effects of depleted uranium and cluster bombs."[69]

According to Osgoode Hall Law Professor Michael Mandel, "the first thing to note about NATO's war against Yugoslavia is that it was flatly illegal both in the fact that it was ever undertaken and in the way it was carried out. It was a gross and deliberate violation of international law and the charter of the United Nations."[70] Ottawa justified its bombing of Serbia as a humanitarian intervention to save Kosovars. Foreign Affairs Minister Lloyd Axworthy claimed that "NATO is engaged in Kosovo to restore human security to the Kosovars."[71] Contrary to the mainstream media's characterization of the campiagn, NATO's bombing of Yugoslavia spurred the ethnic cleansing they claimed to be curbing. Noam Chomsky writes: "The State Department's analysis showed that 'the crimes of Milosevic's willing executioners' were not a motive for the bombing: the crimes followed the bombing, according to the State Department's definitive case against Milosevic, and were precipitated by it, it is only rational to assume."[72] One of the few scholarly studies that tried to quantify and analyze those killed in Kosovo in the year before the bombing found that Serbs were to blame for 500 of 2000 killed. Robert Hayden, director of the Center for Russian and East European studies at the University of Pittsburgh, noted that "the casualties among Serb civilians in the first three weeks of the war were higher than all of the casualties on both sides in Kosovo in the three months that led up to this war, and yet those three months were supposed to be a humanitarian catastrophe."[73] Even "James Bissett, Canada's former ambassador to Yugoslavia, note[d] that up to March 24, when the Rambouillet accords collapsed, fewer than 2,000 people had died as a result of skirmishes in Kosovo between the Serbian army and the KLA [Kosovo Liberation Army]."[74]

NATO leaders claimed humanitarian motives for bombing Serbia but their actions were largely driven by frustration with Yugoslavia's failure to follow U.S. and Western European imposed economic and political changes. "It was Yugoslavia's resistance to the broader trends of political and economic reform — not the plight of Kosovar Albanians — that best explains NATO's war," wrote John Norris, assistant to Strobe Talbott, who was the U.S. official responsible for diplomacy during the war and who wrote a glowing introduction to Norris's book.[75]

Supreme Court Judge Louise Arbour, who presided over the Canadian-supported International Criminal Tribunal for the former Yugoslavia (ICTY), played an important role in justifying NATO's bombing of Serbia. Just prior to the bombing Arbour brought along the international media for a stunt where she claimed Milosevic was blocking her from investigating a massacre in the Kosovar village of Racak. Subsequent investigations into what happened at Racak were inconclusive despite widespread reporting of a Serbian massacre. This "massacre" was an important part of NATO's justification for bombing.

While quick to blame Serb leaders for human rights violations Arbour ignored evidence of Western leaders' crimes. "After a formal complaint against NATO leaders had been laid before the tribunal [ICTY] by a team of lawyers from Canada, the U.S., Britain and France, Arbour appeared before television cameras with one of the accused, British Foreign Secretary

Robin Cook, who made a great show of handing her a dossier of alleged Serbian war crimes. A week later, she attended a press conference with U.S. Secretary of State Madeleine Albright, herself the subject of two complaints of war crimes over the targeting of civilians. As she looked on rapturously, Albright announced that the U.S. was about to increase its funding for the Tribunal. Within days, indictments were issued against Yugoslav President Milosevic and four other Serb leaders."[76]

The ICTY was largely conceived as a means to prosecute Serbian leaders, not as a way to enforce humanitarian law in general. If the ICTY were genuinely concerned with human rights they would have vigorously prosecuted all sides in the civil war (Croatian, Serbian, Bosnian Muslim etc.) not to mention Clinton, Blair and Chrétien.

NATO in Eastern Europe

The breakup of Yugoslavia was attractive to NATO because it diminished Russia's sphere of influence. The same can be said for the western-backed "coloured" revolutions in Eastern Europe, U.S.-led initiatives that Ottawa supported. An in-depth Globe and Mail article headlined "Agent Orange: Our secret role in Ukraine," detailed some of the ways Canada intervened in the 2004-2005 Ukrainian elections. "Beginning in January 2004 — soon after the success of the Rose Revolution in Georgia, he [Canadian ambassador to the Ukraine, Andrew Robinson] began to organize secret monthly meetings of western ambassadors, presiding over what he called 'donor coordination' sessions among 20 countries interested in seeing Mr. [presidential candidate Viktor] Yushchenko succeed. Eventually, he acted as the group's spokesman and became a prominent critic of the Kuchma government's heavy handed media control. Canada also invested in a controversial exit poll, carried out on election day by Ukraine's Razumkov Centre and other groups that contradicted the official results showing Mr. Yanukovich [winning]."[77] The Canadian embassy gave $30,000 US to Pora, a leading civil society group active in the Orange Revolution.[78] In total Ottawa spent half a million dollars promoting "fair elections" in the Ukraine.[79] The ambassador promised the Ukraine's lead electoral commissioner a passport (Canadian citizenship) if he did "the right thing." The embassy paid for 500 election observers from Canada, the largest official delegation from any country (another 500 Ukrainian-Canadians came independently). Many of these election observers were far from impartial, according to the Globe.[80]

Boosted by its success in Ukraine's 2005 elections Ottawa continued to push against Russian influence in Eastern Europe. Federal government documents uncovered by Canwest in July 2007 explained that Ottawa was trying to be "a visible and effective partner of the United States in Russia, Ukraine and zones of instability in Eastern Europe."[81] During a July 2007 visit to the Ukraine, Foreign Affairs Minister Peter MacKay said Canada would help provide a "counterbalance" to Russia. "There are outside pressures [on Ukraine], from Russia most notably. ... We want to make sure they feel the support that is there for them in the international community."[82] As part of Canada's "counterbalance" to Russia MacKay announced $16 million in aid to support democratic reform in the Ukraine.[83]

The coloured revolutions in Eastern Europe are the most high-profile recent examples of "democracy promotion" at the service of Western aims. By 2007 nearly a fifth of CIDA's budget, some $600 million, was spent on initiatives directed towards "promoting democracy."[84] In 2004 the Canada Corps was established as "a new vehicle to strengthen Canada's contribution to human rights, democracy and good governance internationally" and in 2006 CIDA established both the Office of Democratic Governance and the Deployment for Democracy Development Mechanism.[85] The Harper government appointed a minister of state for democratic reform in October 2008 and was set to create a government institution entirely dedicated to "democracy promotion" as this book went to press.[86]

(The U.S. is, of course, the largest democracy promotion donor with the National Endowment for Democracy's Democracy Projects Database coordinating 6,000 projects worldwide. William I. Robinson argues that "democracy promotion" is an important aspect of modern imperialism. It's a change in U.S. policy from "earlier strategies to contain social and political mobilization through a focus on control of the state and governmental apparatus" to a process in which "the United States [and Canada] and local elites thoroughly penetrate civil society, and from therein, assure control over popular mobilization and mass movements."[87]

Peacekeeping

According to *The Canadian Peacekeeper*, the first Canadian peacekeeping mission was not Suez but rather in Korea (Suez was the fifth Canadian peacekeeping mission). Four million were killed in the Korean conflict.[88]

Peacekeeping has received a huge amount of media attention yet rarely do commentators discuss what motivated Ottawa's support for the Suez mission or peacekeeping more generally. Popularly viewed as a benevolent form of intervention, peacekeeping missions have generally been motivated by larger geopolitical interests. During the Cold War, the U.S. did not dispatch troops on peacekeeping missions, which made Canadian contributions particularly important. Contrary to popular understanding, Canadian internationalism has rarely been at odds with American belligerence. As far as I can tell, Canadian peacekeeping missions always received U.S. support. Military analyst J.L. Granatstein concurs: "Our peacekeeping efforts almost always supported western interests. Certainly this was true in the Middle East, the Congo, Cyprus, Vietnam and Bosnia too."[89] *Canada and the Early Cold War*, a book financed by Foreign Affairs, explains that "the more extreme version of this myth, which makes Lester Pearson into Herbert Evatt raging against Great Power dominance and transforms Canada's peacekeeping into neutralism or even pacifism, receives no support in the DCER [documents on Canadian external relations]."[90] Most often, peacekeeping was Canada's contribution to the Cold War. "During the Cold War, the United States, the United Kingdom and France, all permanent members of the Security Council, remained aloof in several difficult circumstances as a sort of plausible deniability. Canada was the West's champion in the Cold War U.N. arena."[91]

According to military historian Sean Maloney, "Every one of the U.N. peacekeeping and peace observation operations which Canada participated in from 1948 to 1968 were directly related to the Cold War game of position. When we look at the pattern of Canadian U.N. deployments during the first 20 years of the Cold War, a definite pattern emerges. Canada deployed forces overseas for nuclear crisis stabilization (UNEF I in the Suez 1956 affair), to prop up a U.N. effort to prevent Soviet intervention in the Third World (ONUC in the Congo) or to prevent a crisis involving NATO allies from escalating to the point where it could be exploited by the Soviets (UNFICYP in Cyprus) to gain an advantageous position against NATO. If the Americans used the CIA to wage a twilight war against Communist expansion in the Third World, Canada used U.N. peacekeeping deployments as surrogates to achieve Canadian aims in that fight."[92]

Coinciding with Ottawa's move away from peacekeeping was the growing clout of the Third World at the U.N. *The Canadian Way of War* explains that "By 1967 the sun was setting on the utility of the U.N. as a tool to contain communist influence ... decolonization was nearly over. This increased the number of Third World non-aligned states in the U.N., altering the character of the organization and its willingness to be used by the West."[93]

Since the end of the Cold War and the decline of the Soviet bloc's role in checking U.S. power there has been a resurgence of peacekeeping in the interests of Western imperialism. Yugoslavia and Haiti are two prime examples where Canada has played a significant role.

NORAD and U.S.-Canada military relations

While Ottawa has signed numerous military agreements with Washington (according to DND, there are 330 agreements and arrangements between the U.S. and Canadian militaries[94]), by far the most important U.S.-Canada military accord is the North American Aerospace Defence Command (NORAD). It provides aerospace warning, air sovereignty and defence for North America, but NORAD also allows the U.S. military to rely on Canadian support for a variety of politically unpopular military endeavours — from the attack on Iraq to the weaponization of space. Paul Martin's Liberals, for instance, claimed to oppose "missile defence" yet through NORAD Canadian military planners helped implement the project. "The Liberals have already given the United States exactly what it sought to begin with — full cooperation by NORAD in missile-defence work."[95]

Even beyond NORAD Canada has contributed to the U.S. neoconservatives's completely mad imperial project, otherwise known as missile defence. (It's called "missile defence" because it's designed to defend U.S. missiles when they use them in offensive wars.) The Canadian taxpayer-funded — about $1 billion — RADARSAT provides crucial satellite imagery for moves towards the weaponization of space.[96] An advanced space-based technology, RADARSAT can be used to gather "target data for first-strike U.S. and NATO attacks during 'theatre missile defence' engagements."[97]

Canada's support for the U.S. military takes a variety of forms. One way we help our southern neighbours is by providing them with training opportunities. In October 2007, for instance, DND sent five ships, two helicopters, a surveillance plane and more than 1,100 sailors to a training exercise to play the "opposing force" against a group of U.S. ships led by the aircraft carrier, USS Abraham Lincoln.[98] Between 1946 and 1963 "700 Canadian military personnel took part in almost 30 [Pentagon organized] nuclear weapons trials in the United States and the South Pacific."[99]

Canadian territory has also been used to test U.S. nuclear weapons. Beginning in 1952 Ottawa agreed to let the U.S. Strategic Air Command use Canadian air space for training flights of nuclear-armed aircraft.[100] At the same time, the U.S. Atomic Energy Commission conducted military tests in Canada to circumvent oversight by American "watchdog committees." As part of the agreement Ottawa committed to prevent any investigation into the military aspects of nuclear research in Canada.[101] Pierre Trudeau's government claimed to be suffocating the arms race but allowed the U.S. to test cruise missiles in Canada. The Mulroney government continued this policy.[102]

"The United States military tests weapons in Canada and it has done so for fifty years.... No matter how bizarre the weapon, no matter how dangerous the test, no matter how contrary the weapon to stated foreign policy objectives, Canada has never refused a single testing request from the United States. They have delayed in some cases, but a flat refusal has not been recorded."[103]

Feeding U.S. militarism has long been an aim of Canadian politicians and weapons manufacturers. When right-wing U.S. politicians slash social programs to boost the military's budget, Canada's arms industry celebrates. A 1983 Canadian Business magazine cover captured the sentiment: "Hail to the Hawks: Ronald Reagan's $200 billion-plus defence budget is good news for Canadian business."[104] Largely due to Reagan's weapons purchases, Canada exported two billion dollars worth of military commodities in the first half of the 1980s.[105]

All the way back in 1918 Prime Minister Robert Borden journeyed to Washington to promote munitions exports.[106] The 1940 Permanent Joint Board on Defence strengthened arms relations between the two countries and since signing the Defence Production Sharing Agreement in 1956 "it has been Canadian policy to reject the development of a Canadian defence industrial base in favour of linking up with the Americans as part of a North American defence industrial base."[107] Canada provides the Pentagon with a sophisticated arms production industry that is able to work to American specifications and enjoys close relations with American corporations. In recent years Canadian companies have sold an average of $1.5 billion worth of armaments to the U.S.[108] With most exports going to our southern neighbour, Canada is a major exporter of military equipment.

Ottawa also provides significant political and financial support to arms exports.[109] Foreign Affairs, DND and the Department of Regional Industrial Expansion all promote military exports. A Defence Programs Bureau was established in 1963 "in recognition of the need for a highly specialized industrial and trade-oriented branch within the Canadian government to promote the export of Canadian Defence products."[110] The Canadian Commercial Corporation, which was once called War Supplies Limited, draws Canadian suppliers and foreign buyers together.[111] The CCC is a Crown Corporation that "becomes the prime contractor" for the U.S.

Department of Defence whenever a Canadian firm makes a sale greater than $100,000 to the Pentagon. The CCC does more than $1.2 billion in business annually, 70 percent of which is weapons, weapons components and services to the Pentagon and NASA.[112]

Military manufacturers are among the most heavily subsidized Canadian corporations. As part of its supposed ideological opposition to corporate welfare, in 2007 the Conservatives abolished Technology Partnerships Canada, which dished out hundreds of millions of dollars in unrepaid loans to companies, including the arms industry. In place of Technology Partnerships Canada, the Conservatives established a subsidy program focused entirely on weapons and aerospace companies.[113] The move was a step back in time. TPC's predecessor was called the Defence Industry Productivity Program and it doled out nearly $2 billion to Canadian corporations.[114] According to the Coalition to Oppose the Arms Trade (COAT), Canadian arms suppliers received $5 billion in grants and unpaid loans from 1976 to 2006.[115]

Public money for arms manufacturers is so widely available that nine of the world's 10 biggest weapons companies have a Canadian subsidiary.[116] These multinational corporations have Canadian subsidiaries because this allows them to access subsidies made available by Ottawa and it also improves their chances of winning contracts with the Canadian military.

At $18 billion a year, Canada's military budget eats up 40 percent of the federal government's discretionary funding.[117] Adjusting for inflation, in 2007 Canada's defence spending was 2.3 percent higher than its Cold War peak during the Korean War in 1952-53.[118] In June 2008 the Conservative government announced a plan to spend $490 billion on the military over the next 20 years.

Discussion

The "defence establishment" or Canada's very own military industrial complex — the Armed Forces, arms manufacturers, DND-funded thinks tanks, etc. — has a self-interest in expanding Canadian militarism. For the people who profit from manufacturing weapons war is not a bad thing. For the people who are employed to justify Canada's support of U.S. military operations, their jobs depend on making pro-war arguments. The existence of a "defence establishment" is one factor that helps explain Canada's policy on the international stage. This is the subject of the next chapter.

Chapter Notes

1   The Middle Power Project, 138
2   Canadian Foreign policy Vol 13 #1 2006
3   The Middle Power Project, 142
4   The Middle Power Project, 138
5   A Foremost Nation, 165
6   La Presse June 29 2006
7   La Presse June 29 2006
8   Canada as an International Actor, 178
9   Canada as an International Actor, 172
10 A Foremost Nation, 167
11 A Foremost Nation, 167
12 Canada and the World Order, 123
13 A Foremost Nation, 162
14 Canada and the World Order, 50
15 Canada and the World Order, 50
16 Canadian Foreign Policy: Selected Cases, 2
17 Conflicts of Interest, 22
18 Canada and the World Order, 130
19 Latin American Working Group Labour Report Vol 3 #3 Nov 1979
20 Globe and Mail Apr 26 2007
21 Canada and the World Order, 133; Democratizing Southern Africa, 35
22 Canada and the World Order, 198
23 Canada and the World Order, 192
24 Canada and the World Order, 196
25 Readings in Canadian foreign-policy, 326
26 Canadian Journal of Development Studies Vol XXIII #3 2002
27 Canadian Journal of Development Studies Vol XXIII #3, 2002; Delivering Results, 12
28 Delivering Results, 12
29 Delivering Results, 14
30 Delivering Results, 12
31 Too Close For Comfort, 269; Canada Among Nations 1998, 157/245
32 Canadian Dimension June 1981
33 A Foremost Nation, 190
34 Canada and the Third World, 98
35 Canadian International Development Assistance Policies, 43
36 Canada as an International Actor, 155
37 Internationalism Under Strain, 30
38 Canada as an International Actor, 179/185
39 Too Close For Comfort, 269
40 Toronto Star Apr 2008
41 Les Affaires Dec 9 2006
42 La Presse Sept 26 2006
43 Dominion Foreign Policy issue, 22
44 http://www.monbiot.com/archives/2008/06/10/small-is-bountiful/
45 Human Rights and Democracy, 19
46 La Presse June 8 2007
47 Alternatives June 2008
48 Third World Quarterly Vol 29 #1 2008, 70
49 http://embassymag.ca/page/view/.2007.april.4.mackenzie
50 http://www.dominionpaper.ca/articles/2369
51 Montréal Gazette Nov 18 2006
52 Globe and Mail Dec 12 2007; Globe and Mail Nov 24 2007
53 Le Devoir Feb 7 2009
54 Ottawa Citizen Nov 24 2006
55 Ottawa Citizen Nov 20 2006
56 The Walrus June 2008
57 This Magazine May 2007
58 http://embassymag.ca/page/view/.2005.november.16.health
59 La Presse Oct 2006
60 Ottawa Citizen Oct 29 2008
61 http://www.twnside.org.sg/title/deadly-cn.htm
62 Canada and the Birth of Israel, 140
63 National Post Jan 1 2007
64 Canadian Dimension June 1981
65 Canadian Foreign Policy; Selected Cases, 32
66 Words and Deeds, 56
67 http://www.counterpunch.org/gb02262008.html
68 New Socialist Nov 2005; A Samaritan State, 54
69 Esprit de Corps Oct 1999, 13
70 Mediathink, 87
71 http://w01.international.gc.ca/minpub/PublicationContentOnly.asp?publication_id=374895&Language=E&MODE=CONTENTONLY&Local=False
72 New Generation Draws the Line, 99
73 Monthly Review Sept 2008
74 Esprit de Corps Oct 1999, 13
75 Monthly Review Sept 2008
76 Esprit de Corps Oct 1999, 13
77 Globe and Mail Apr 14 2007
78 Globe and Mail Apr 14 2007
79 Globe and Mail Apr 14 2007
80 Globe and Mail Apr 14 2007
81 Vancouver Sun July 19 2007
82 Vancouver Sun July 19 2007
83 Vancouver Sun July 19 2007
84 Vancouver Sun July 20 2007
85 Promoting Democracy in the Americas,

89; http://www.acdi-cida.gc.ca/ips

86 http://www.embassymag.ca/page/view/spreading_democracy-2-18-2009

87 Promoting Polyarchy: Globalization, U.S. Intervention and Hegemony

88 The Canadian Peacekeeper, 11/21

89 Canada and the New World Order, 21; Canada and U.N. Peacekeeping, xii

90 Canada and the Early Cold War, 85

91 Cold War by Other Means -1945-1970, xii

92 http://www.irpp.org/events/archive/nov00/maloney.pdf

93 The Canadian Way of War, 305

94 Canada Among Nations 2003, 139

95 Too Close for Comfort, 86

96 http://coat.ncf.ca/our_magazine/links/58/58.html

97 http://coat.ncf.ca/our_magazine/links/58/blurb-58.htm

98 Montréal Gazette Oct 22 2007

99 Toronto Star Sept 3 2008

100 Just Dummies, 208

101 Exporting Danger, 34

102 Canadian Foreign Policy: 1945-2000, Page 83; Just Dummies, 10

103 Just Dummies, 199

104 Holding the Bully's Coat, 168

105 Arms Canada, 17

106 Arms Canada, 33

107 Arms Canada, 68

108 A babords Oct 2006

109 Arms Canada, 100

110 Arms Canada, 102

111 Arms Canada, 101; Making a Killing, 8

112 http://paulmartintime.ca/mediacoverage/000008.html

113 La Presse Apr 3 2007

114 Financial Post Jan 11 2007

115 http://www.dominionpaper.ca/foreign_policy/2006/08/07/making_war.html

116 A babords Oct 2006

117 Arms Canada, 21; Montréal Gazette Oct 22 2007; Pacific Challenge, 95

118 Montréal Gazette Oct 22 2007

Why our foreign policy is the way it is and how to change it

In the preceding chapters Canada's role in world affairs has been revealed as consistently pro-empire (whether British, U.S.), pro-colonial (whether British, U.S., French, Portuguese, Dutch, etc.) and serving narrow corporate interests. In order to understand why this is so, we must trace the unbroken line of policy makers and the policy they made.

Canada has had a particularly close relationship to the world's leading imperial power from the British Empire to today's U.S. Empire. Before Confederation Canadians fought to defend British imperialism. India's anti-colonial rebellion of 1857 prompted the creation of the 100th Regiment, comprised of Canadian officers and men, but paid for by Britain.[1] 1,027 men were recruited in Canada, "the first occasion on which a regiment was raised in Canada for service abroad in the imperial interests."[2] General Frederick Middleton, who would later be a major figure in suppressing the North-West rebellion of 1885, participated in the British military campaign in India.[3]

After 1867 Ottawa regularly argued that it "was looking after British imperial interests in North America and that the country's material growth reinforced the British Empire. The construction of the Canadian Pacific Railway was especially justified as a British military route to the East."[4] Canada helped connect Britain to the Far East in a number of ways. In 1887 a graving dock capable of holding the largest British war ships in the Pacific was opened in Esquimalt, British Columbia.[5] Sandford Fleming, who represented Canada at the 1887 Colonial Conference in London, wanted the Dominions and Britain to build a state-owned Pacific cable from B.C. to East Asia and to secure a mid-Pacific Island as a way station.[6] "He hired a retired naval officer living in Ontario and sent him to Hawaii to raise the Union Jack over nearby Necker Island."[7] Hawaii nearly became Canadian property as part of this endeavour.[8]

A number of Canadian military institutions were established in large part to expand the British Empire's military capacity. Opened in Kingston, Ontario, in 1876, the Royal Military College was largely designed to train soldiers to fight on behalf of British colonialism.[9] One hundred and twenty years ago Sir Adolph Caron explained the RMC's usefulness for Canada. "There was a time, I remember, when Canada did not stand in the proud position which she occupies today in Great Britain. Our present position is due to the fact that our Royal Military College Cadets were able to take their places side by side with the men who had been trained in the [British] military service. It was also due to the fact that … [militia] teams which were sent to England showed not only that loyalty existed, but that Great Britain in her Canadian subject found men who were prepared to take their share in fighting her battles and who were able to fight these battles side by side with the best men that England could send to the front."[10]

For years the Indian Staff Corps — the British military's command in that country — offered one commission annually to the Royal Military College.[11] The RMC's Sergeant H.C. Freer served with distinction during Britain's quest to control Egypt in 1882.[12] A number of RMC-trained Canadians helped the British survey the railway route to Lake Victoria Nyanza in today's Uganda.[13] In the same part of the continent RMC graduate Colonel J.H.V. Crowe commanded an artillery division for General Jan Christiaan Smuts.[14] After serving in Bechuanaland Southern Africa from 1884-5, Huntley Brodie Mackay commanded the Royal Engineers in West Africa from 1887-9. "He [Brodie Mackay] won the RMC's first DSO [Distinguished Service Order] fighting tribes near Sierra Leone and then became acting administrator of the British East Africa Company."[15] Working alongside a number of other Canadians, Kenneth J.R. Campbell became British vice consul in western Africa's Oil Rivers District.[16] "These Canadian RMC cadets won fame for their contribution to the expansion of the British Empire when [in Campbell's words] 'Britain true to [her] instincts annexed the Oil Rivers, the largest and best share of that part of West Africa.'"[17]

"During the last years of [Queen] Victoria's long reign [1837 to 1901] her great empire increasingly offered young Canadians both challenge and adventure in its self-appointed mission to spread Christianity, commerce and civilization. No longer did the frontiers of Canada contain their ambitions: The completion of the transcontinental railway had seen to that."[18]

It will surprise some, but the Canadian elite has not always been on good terms with the U.S. business world. Many of Canada's (pre-Confederation) elite fled north after staying loyal to the British Empire during the U.S. war of independence. Known as United Empire Loyalists their descendents continued to be well represented among Canada's elite well after Confederation.[19] The Canadian Military Institute, for instance, boasted that most of its 500 members in 1910 were descendents of United Empire Loyalists.[20] Loyalists were usually unabashed supporters of British imperialism. G.M. Grant, a Loyalist descendent explained in 1891:

"The work that the British Empire has in hand is far grander than the comparatively parochial duties with which the [United] States are content to deal. Its problems are wider and more inspiring ... already our sons are taking their part in introducing civilization into Africa under the aegis of the flag, and in preserving the Pax Britanica among the teeming millions of India and Southeastern Asia."[21]

Often spurred by Loyalist descendents, imperial revelry gripped Canada in the late 1800s. Beginning in 1899 Ontario schools celebrated Empire Day.[22] By 1914 the Canadian Cadets, a paramilitary group that prepared the young to be imperial citizens, had 40,000 members, three times the size of its peer organization, the Boy Scouts.[23]

This late 1800s support for imperialism was propelled by a racist worldview. Imperial unity "derived part of its strength from the potency of Anglo-Saxon racism and social Darwinism."[24] One example is to be found in a 1899 Canadian Magazine Christmas message. The magazine complained that it was "difficult to write of 'Peace on earth, good-will towards men' when both branches of the Anglo-Saxon people are engaged in subduing inferior races." The editors then explained how the world would be secure "when the Boer and Filipino have been made to realize that the Anglo-Saxon race never errs, that it makes war only for the benefit of humanity."[25] Notice how at this early date some Canadian imperialists already saw both British and American militarism as "Anglo-Saxons subduing inferior races."

Canada's military has long been tied to this grand "Anglo-Saxon" project. Established in 1909 the Royal Canadian Navy and the Royal Naval College of Canada came out of London's Imperial conference on naval and military defence. That same year Ottawa agreed to standardize its weapons, ammunition and military equipment with those of Great Britain.[26] In fact, earlier military agreements with Britain were similar to today's accords with the U.S. Ties between the Canadian and U.S. military began in earnest in the 1950s, particularly after the Korean War. The three hundred agreements between the two countries seek to integrate Canada's military into the U.S. war machine. Moreover, Canadian weapons acquisitions are largely designed to be compatible with those of the U.S. "Maintaining interoperability [with the U.S.] is the key to the future relevance of the CF [Canadian Forces]," noted the chief of Defence Staff in his 2002 annual report.[27]

Canada's 2005 Defence Policy Statement claimed increased collaboration with the U.S. military will "not see the Canadian Forces replicate every function of the world's premier militaries." Rather, the Canadian Army "will fulfill roles that make Canada's interventionist capabilities relevant and credible."[28]

What does this military history tell us? That the people running Canada's armed forces have always looked to serve the needs of the most powerful military force of its time. They have, in fact, gloried in empire. And, our military has never been designed to be independent, or even to primarily serve the needs of Canadians. Instead, it has been integrated within the larger forces of an empire, first British and then U.S. Given this, is it any surprise that the people running the Canadian military, who have been educated within it, or those who receive funding from it, argue in favour of participating in U.S. wars? It would be a surprise if they did otherwise.

Just like the Canadian military, this country's business class is well integrated into the U.S. corporate world. Many leading Canadian CEOs sit on the boards of major U.S. corporations, think tanks, etc. Conversely, prominent U.S. businessman and politicians often have close relations with Canadian corporations. This elite integration, alongside Canadian economic integration with the U.S. more generally, drives much of Canada's support for U.S. foreign policy.

Support for British imperialism was also largely an economic calculation. At its annual meeting in 1898 the president of the Canadian Bankers Association exclaimed: "Are we not part and parcel of an empire that is worldwide ... can we do nothing to stimulate and encourage trade within the empire? ... of what use is the shedding of our best blood on the sands of Africa or on the snows of the Himalayas if nothing is to come of their sacrifice but military glory?"[29]

War contracts were the most direct economic benefit Canada gained from British conquest. Canada was contracted by the India Office in 1900, for example, to supply the British forces quelling the Boxer rebellion in China.[30] It wasn't only during times of war that Canada benefited from its membership in the British Empire. The Canadian economy was given a boost when U.S. companies established subsidiaries in Canada to gain access to the British Empire's protected market.[31] In addition, the business elite wanted Ottawa to be on good terms with England since this helped them tap into London's financial markets. Membership in the British Empire also helped Canadians invest in other countries. When Bermuda, for instance, prohibited "aliens" from banking without licence in 1920 it didn't include British subjects, allowing Canadians to gain influence over the country's banking sector.[32]

From its inception the Canadian foreign service reflected a bias towards economic concerns. There were trade commissioners, for instance, long before ambassadors.[33] By 1907 there were 12 Canadian trade commissions staffed by "commercial agents" located in Sydney, Capetown, Mexico City, Yokohama and numerous European and U.S. cities.[34]

Though less pronounced today there is still a clear bias towards business in diplomatic postings. The Canadian Trade Commissioner Service has over 150 offices in cities around the world, which are designed to expand Canadian investment and trade.[35] Canadian embassies are also oriented towards economic issues. According to a 1981 article, "embassy program staff spend more time on trade and industrial development matters (25 percent of time for all programs) than on any other concern (immigration, diplomatic relations and public affairs are distant second, third and fourth priorities)."[36] In many poorer countries Canadian embassies play a particularly active role promoting mining investment. "Canadian diplomatic missions in Africa spend much of their time making sure that mining companies and host governments are brought together and the companies are much praised by Canadian officials."[37]

Just like the structure of the foreign service, the background of foreign policy practitioners has strengthened the economic bias in Canadian policy. Often in the late 1800s diplomacy was conducted by wealthy individuals not employed by Ottawa. The owner of the Toronto Globe, George Brown, for instance, negotiated a draft treaty with the U.S. in 1874, while Sandford Fleming, the surveyor of the Canadian Pacific Railway, represented Canada at the 1887 Colonial Conference in London.[38] "Successive holders of this office [high commissioner in the U.K.] were distinguished not only by political influence and social prestige, but usually also by personal wealth."[39]

In 1931, when Ottawa officially became independent from Britain in foreign relations, External Affairs' initial batch of foreign service officers were all men and overwhelmingly white, Protestant, university graduates when higher education was for the wealthy (there were few French Canadians or Jews, let alone any Asians, Blacks or Aboriginal people).[40] Former businessmen have continued to play a preponderant role in shaping Canadian foreign policy. Even Canada's aid agency has been heavily influenced by former business executives. After a stint as president and COO of Bombardier, Robert Greenhill, became president of CIDA in May 2005 and one of CIDA's most influential leaders, Maurice Strong, was formerly president of Power Corporation.[41] "Maurice Strong, a businessman first and CIDA president afterwards has been concerned to increase the flow of private Canadian dollars abroad."[42]

Strong, and Ottawa more generally, have been successful. In 2007 Canada was the world's eighth biggest foreign investor and on a per capita basis, Canadians were the second largest foreign investors within the G7.[4344] Canadians had \$431 billion invested across the globe in 2002.[45] Canadians invest more abroad than foreigners invest in Canada and there is a net inflow of capital into Canada even after taking into consideration this country's so-called foreign aid.[46]

The mining sector provides the best example of Canadian capital's international prominence. In the first decade of the 21st century 60 percent of the world's mining companies were based in Canada and half of all equity financing for mineral exploration and development projects was raised by companies listed on Canadian stock exchanges.[47] Responsible for over \$50 billion in direct investment, there were a thousand Canadian mining companies operating outside this country. (Seventy-five Canadian oil and gas companies hold land in 69 developing world countries.[48]) Present in over a hundred countries, Canadian corporations operated 3,000 mineral projects abroad.[49] "Today Canadians are hewers of other people's wood, drawers of other people's water — and exploiters of other people's copper, oil and gold. Funny how those other people are usually of an, er, dusky hue."[50]

The mining industry is a powerful political player. Long an important engine of the Canadian economy, industry lobbyists are highly active in Ottawa. In February 2009 Embassy magazine cited Peter Munk, chairman and founder of Barrick Gold, as one of "the Top 50 People Influencing Canadian Foreign Policy." "The head of one of Canada's largest and most successful companies, which has operations all over the world, Mr. Munk is a major player in one of the few areas Canada can claim to be a world leader."[51]

Canadian taxation policy has enabled the mining industry. "Canadian legislation with respect to investment in Canada or abroad makes the tax burden on profits generated from minerals at least comparable to, if not less burdensome than, that in other mineral producing jurisdictions."[52] In addition, TSX information requirements were more lax than the New York Stock Exchange, especially concerning the environmental impact of a company's operations. The Mining Association of Canada boasted that TSX rules were "designed around the needs of the mining industry."[53]

The mining sector, which has a history of social and environmental abuse, also benefited from the Canadian judicial system. Unlike our southern neighbour, Canadian law does not allow criminal or civil suits against Canadian companies responsible for environmental and/or human rights violations abroad.

While mining is where Canada was most dominant it was not the only Canadian industry active in "developing" countries in 2009. Canadian banks have long been major international players and in early 2009 four of them were among the 10 largest North American Banks.[54] The big five banks generated about 40 percent of their sizable profits from international operations.[55] In November 1981 a Bank of Nova Scotia executive explained: "I don't know why Canadians are upset about bank profits. We've stopped screwing Canadians. Now we're screwing foreigners."[56]

Federal government policy is largely responsible for the banks' capacity for worldwide operations. Ottawa allowed the industry to become dominant and for a small number of institutions to dominate banking.[57] By way of example, the five largest banks in 1997 were also the largest in 1901.[58]

Beyond mining and banking, Montréal-based SNC Lavalin was the largest engineering company in the world in 2009 and probably Canada's preeminent "disaster capitalist" corporation. From reconstruction projects in Haiti to Chinese nuclear centres, to military camps in Afghanistan and pharmaceutical factories in Belgium, the sun never set on SNC Lavalin.[59] In Africa alone SNC Lavalin was involved in 430 projects in 37 different countries at the end of 2008.[60] SNC Lavalin has been one of the largest corporate recipients of Canadian "aid." SNC-Lavalin has entire departments dedicated to applying for CIDA, U.N. and World Bank funded projects. SNC's first international contract, in 1963 in India, was financed by Canadian aid and led to further work in that country.[61] In 2006 SNC was bailed out by the Canadian aid agency after it didn't follow proper procedure for a contract to renovate and modernize the Pallivasal, Sengulam and Panniyar hydroelectric projects in the southern Indian state of Kerala. A new state government demanded a hospital in compensation for the irregularities and SNC got CIDA to put up $1.8 million for the project.[62] (SNC-Lavalin initially said they would put $20 million into the hospital, but they only invested between $2 and $4.4 million.)

SNC Lavalin worked hard to build, according to the Financial Post, its "considerable lobbying power in Ottawa."[63] The President and CEO of SNC-Lavalin Group, Jacques Lamarre, was among Embassy magazine's list of 50 "Top People Influencing Canadian Foreign Policy." "Canada's largest engineering company is also one of the country's most active companies internationally. SNC-Lavalin works closely with the government on development … is active in more than 100 countries, and is always on the hunt for new projects overseas. As such, whoever is heading it is a major player in Ottawa."[64] Company officials were fairly explicit about the role

Canadian diplomacy played in their business. Regarding the Middle East, Paul Mariamo, SNC's senior vice president, explained: "We would love to see our prime minister or minister there often, promoting our product. We can fight companies, but we cannot fight governments. We need you to fight the governments for us: we cannot do it ourselves."[65] In another candid moment, president Jacques Lamarre described how the company benefits from Ottawa's lobbying. "The official support of our governments, whether through commercial missions or more private conversations, has a beneficial and convincing impact on our international clients."[66] Like many major corporations SNC makes a point of hiring people who have worked for the government. For example, Christiane Bergevin, who was running SNC-Lavalin's financing subsidiary in 2008, had SNC as her client when she worked at EDC.[67]

It is relatively common for mainstream commentators and even government officials to justify Canadian support for U.S. intervention on the grounds that that country is our leading trade partner. It's less common for Canadian politicians to state explicitly that foreign policy is designed by corporate interests, but some have. External Affairs Minister Mark MacGuigan said in a mid-1980 speech: "It is the role of the private sector to inject life and substance into economic relationships, and for this reason the Canadian government is encouraging a more explicit role for businessmen and business associations in shaping relationships and in influencing the form and conduct of foreign policy."[68]

Considering the history of our foreign affairs establishment and the self-interested lobbying of powerful corporations, is it a surprise that the Canadian government has acted the way it has around the world? There has certainly been no counterweight to the influence of business. Unions have not been powerful enough; churches have usually shared the dominant ideology of the day; the media has often been owned by the same business interests that are active around the world; many NGOs have been bought off by the government or corporations; few ordinary Canadians are informed about what is done in our name.

Fixing the problem

The first step to change is information. Canadians must be informed. Then, rather than simply criticize current and past Canadian foreign policy, it is important to suggest alternatives for the future.

A primary cause of Canada's poor behaviour around the world is allowing particular self-interest to take precedence over doing what's right.

As outlined in previous chapters, companies based in Canada engage in practices that would be illegal at home. Ottawa uses its resources to undermine foreign governments. Canadian companies profit from war and military buildup. Canadian "aid" is directed to rewrite laws to favour our corporations over the rights of citizens in the Global South. While the government talks about "democracy promotion" or "helping women" too often foreign policy and "aid" are used to enrich Canadians and curry favour with Washington. The rich and powerful do what they feel is in their self-interest. Of course, this is not surprising since that is exactly how the rich and powerful act inside Canada. The difference is they are unable to get away with as much bad behaviour since we are watching more closely and we have enacted laws to limit it. This is another way to say that the rule of law is weak in foreign affairs. There are few enforceable regulations governing the international behaviour of governments, corporations and other organizations.

Just as corporations and other special interest groups do inside Canada, these same groups work to reduce regulations governing their behaviour in foreign countries. The poorer, weaker and more desperate the country, the greater the likelihood they will be successful. The result is poor or non-existent environmental legislation, weak labour laws, low taxes, etc. Existing international laws, such as the Geneva Convention, are not enforced. Treaties, which are supposed to control the behaviour of governments, are frequently ignored. The international arena operates much like the lawless Wild West: Vigilante justice is imposed by those with the most or the biggest weapons; gunslingers go unpunished; the weak are at the mercy of the strong.

So, a primary task of Canadian foreign policy should be to encourage the rule of law in international affairs. Governments, corporations and other organizations must be held accountable. Already Canadian tourists can be sued here for abusing children overseas. Ottawa should pass legislation to allow Canadian corporations to be sued in this country for human rights violations and environmental devastation caused abroad. Legislation to this end already exists in "at least 125 countries", including the United States, and has been proposed here with Bill C-492.[69]

International treaties should be enforced. No one can be above the law. Just like the Magna Carta became the basis for our legal system because it limited the power of the king, so too will international law only be real when it applies to every country, even the wealthiest and most powerful. Canada must work towards that end. This means supporting existing international law and working towards expanding its range and effectiveness. It also means actively opposing those countries that claim to be above the law or refuse to obey it. Canada must ensure international law is applied equally to all.

It is important to note that this means our "friends" as well as our "enemies" must obey international law. Nothing undermines the law as much as when the most powerful act as if they are above judgment. Of course, when the country with the most powerful military in the world or other "allies" refuse to subject themselves to international law, we cannot send in our police, but we must, at a minimum, make our objection loud and clear. All too often in the past we have remained silent, or worse, joined in and justified the illegality.

While promoting international law and building institutions that can enforce it must be a central goal of Canadian foreign affairs, there are other specific policies that should also be priorities. Canada can be a force for good in the world by:

Encouraging peace in the world. Ottawa should pull out of NATO immediately. If there was ever any justification for this alliance, two decades after the Cold War it no longer exists. Ottawa should begin to evaluate whether its numerous military arrangements with Washington, including NORAD, are necessary.

Drastically reducing the size of the Canadian Armed Forces. Let's start with a 10 percent reduction in the military budget each year for the next five years. A Rideau Institute study released in the summer of 2008 found that 52 percent of Canadians want a reduction in military expenditures. 27 percent of those polled wanted programs to continue as planned and only 11 percent believed in greater military spending (10 percent had no opinion).[70] The truth, unpalatable as it may seem to some, is that there is only one nation on earth that could realistically invade Canada and that is the USA. This is not an argument for a military policy that views our neighbour to the south as a threat, rather that Canada follow an independent, neutral foreign policy path that works for world peace and justice for all. In the unlikely event that our country was facing a military threat, our best defence would be millions of people around the world who knew Canada was not their enemy. A pro-American, North American integrationist element of our political culture argues for junior-partner-to-the-U.S. status for our military. They push for Canada to become part of schemes to militarize space. They argue we must drastically increase military spending. In most respects they function as a Canadian branch plant of the U.S. military-industrial complex that President Eisenhower warned the world about in his last year in office. A critical element of any decent Canadian foreign policy must be opposing, rather than supporting this threat to world peace. If you buy the world's largest military force (the USA spends more than the rest of the world combined), war will inevitably follow.

Proclaiming that this country's armed forces will only be used abroad under a U.N. mandate passed by the 192 members of the General Assembly, not the Security Council. Numerous surveys show the vast majority of Canadians support real peacekeeping as the primary goal of our military.

Building democracy by supporting elected governments. Support for democracy must be real, not code for governments that kowtow to the rich and powerful. This means strengthening the capacity of governments to provide the same sorts of things we expect from our governments. People of all nations deserve governments that work to make their lives better. If citizens choose social democracy and an activist government that claims national resources should benefit society as a whole, it is their right. Should Canada be destabilized if we elect a socialist government? Too often "failed" states are created by the deliberate efforts of the rich and powerful. We have far too many examples of dictators put into place because corporations cared more about their profits than about democracy. Canadian aid should be targeted at strengthening democratic governments' ability to deliver services rather than supporting private charity. People become disillusioned with democracy when it does not deliver needed healthcare, education and social services. While Canada and other rich nations claim to favour democracy, all too often they undermine it by providing funds to groups that fight the popular will. In the name of avoiding corruption much "aid" is delivered through non-governmental organizations. This, in fact, can also undermine democracy by making the government irrelevant in the day-to-day lives of people.

Canadian foreign aid should help the poorest people in poor countries. It should not be tied to Canadian commodities or be used as a subsidy to Canadian investors. Based upon Canadian experience we know that improving public education, and ensuring it is free for all, is one of the best ways to help break the poverty cycle. Let's help poor countries build good public education systems. Another important way our governments made life better for poor people was by building public utilities that provided safe water, sewage, electricity and communication systems. Let's help poor countries do the same. Public health systems, including free healthcare for all, were also a key element in Canada's development. This too should be a prime objective of Canadian aid. Funds to improve housing, whether through low-interest loans to build private homes in poor neighbourhoods or to build public housing, would be another form of aid that Canadians would recognize as having done good here at home. And all this should be done with an eye on the environment. Perhaps we could benefit in Canada if our aid agency developed an expertise in building environmentally friendly infrastructure and other systems around the world.

Above all else it is key that Canadian aid should do no wrong. No more assistance to those trying to rewrite laws to benefit foreign business; no more support for reactionary elites; no more attempts to co-opt domestic groups; Canadian aid should no longer be used as a tool of geopolitics.

Most Canadians want an independent policy. This can be achieved by focusing on principles and building coalitions of nations willing to fight for those principles. Instead of looking to the G-7 Ottawa should build relationships with India, Brazil, Venezuela and other large, poorer countries. Simply siding with the USA because it is powerful and our largest trading partner, reinforces the reality that might makes right and undermines the rule of law. For example, going to war alongside the USA when it refuses to acknowledge international war crimes legislation undermines our credibility as a nation that supports the rule of law. For the first 80 years of Canada's existence we were a junior partner to Great Britain, assisting its imperial efforts when asked. Since the Suez crisis, instead of struggling to create an independent foreign policy, we have become a junior partner to the USA.

Canada should help the world reduce ethnic divisions and promote tolerance. We could target a proportion of our aid to those countries with the largest proportions of indigenous populations. This could accomplish at least two worthy goals: It would acknowledge domestic crimes; It could be integrated with programs that empower Canadian First Nations people. Another example might be a special focus on aid for Haiti, home of the world's first successful slave rebellion and the most impoverished country in the hemisphere. With a special claim on Canada's assistance due to our past bad behaviour, Haiti deserves to receive our highest per capita aid. As for other aspects of ethnic intolerance, Canada should make its objections known to every form of racism and intolerance, including any discrimination by our friends.

Canada should have a policy of promoting the equality of women and an end to gender-based discrimination. This can and should include the funding of advocacy groups in countries with particular problems. We should be up front about this and make every effort to ensure that the women's groups we are funding are not used as tools to undermine democratic governments. In the long term there is nothing that will undermine the cause of feminism more than using it as a way to justify imperialism. Poor and working class women and their needs should be the main target of our aid, rather than middle-class or elite feminists.

Finally, a key element of a just foreign policy must be to make sure that what we do abroad does not harm Canadian rights and freedoms. For example, when our country becomes entangled in wars that create resentment and blame, producing "blowback" in the form of people who want to do us harm, one result is pressure to undermine our rights in the name of security. The Golden Rule, versions of which exist in every culture and religion, is also apt in international affairs. Do Unto Others As You Would Have Them Do Unto You. In other words, before we send troops to another country to fight a war, we should ask ourselves: Is this something we would wish for Canada? Before we send aid to another country we should ask ourselves: Is what we are paying for, and the manner in which we are doing it, something that we would want to see in Canada? The greatest harm we can do to our rights and freedoms is to allow ourselves to do things in the international arena that would draw a penalty on our home ice. The history of empires proves that countries that tolerate human rights abuses and exploitation over there always end up bringing it home.

Some people argue that realism is the only proper basis for foreign policy. I believe realism can only be based on a firm foundation of principle. Of course compromise may sometimes be necessary. The world seldom works the way you want it to. But, if your guiding principles are "me first" and "get it while you can" then realism will be a tactic to those ends. If, on the other hand, your principles are to "empower others" and "we wish for others what we want for ourselves" then realism can work to make the world a better place.

Chapter Notes

1 Canada and Imperialism, 24
2 Canada's soldiers, 214; The Dominion partnership in Imperial defense; 127
3 http://library2.usask.ca/northwest/background/middletn.htm
4 Canada and Imperialism, 5; The Boer War and Canadian Imperialism, 8
5 Britain, Canada and the North Pacific, 353
6 Politics of Canadian Foreign Policy, 237
7 Britain, Canada and the North Pacific, 357
8 Our Generation Vol 10 #4, 13
9 Canada's RMC, 96
10 Canada's RMC, 159
11 Canada's RMC, 118
12 Canada's RMC, 74
13 African Exploits, 32
14 Canada's RMC, 200
15 Canada's RMC, 118; African Exploits, 60
16 Canada's RMC, 119
17 Canada's RMC, 119
18 African Exploits, 37
19 The Sense of Power, 86
20 The Sense of Power, 237
21 The Sense of Power, 223
22 Canada:1896-1921, 31
23 War and Society, 32
24 Canada and Imperialism, 66
25 The Sense of Power, 249
26 Making a Killing, 16
27 Canada Among Nations 2003, 142
28 IPS Jan 23 08
29 Our Generation Vol 10 #4, 10
30 The Boer War and Canadian Imperialism, 9
31 Imperialism, Nationalism and Canada, 24
32 The Banks of Canada in the Commonwealth Caribbean, 40
33 Diplomatic Missions, 133
34 The Politics of Canadian Foreign Policy, 236
35 http://www.infoexport.gc.ca/eng/offices-worldwide-map.jsp
36 Canadian Dimension June 1981
37 Africa's Blessing, Africa's Curse: The Legacy of Resource Extraction in Africa
38 The Politics of Canadian Foreign Policy, 237
39 Diplomatic Missions, 98
40 While Canada Slept, 122
41 International Leadership, 102
42 Half a Loaf, 182
43 http://www.rabble.ca/news/canadian-support-israel-signs-more-aggressive-international-posture
44 http://www.rabble.ca/news/canadian-support-israel-signs-more-aggressive-international-posture
45 http://www.chumirethicsfoundation.ca/files/pdf/CanValSec_VIDrohan.pdf
46 Canadian Multinationals, 169; Globe and Mail Sept 9 2006; Canadian Values in the World Community, 206
47 Too Close For Comfort, 285
48 http://embassymag.ca/page/view/.2007.april.4.mackenzie
49 Corporate Knights, July 2007; Montréal Gazette Nov 15 2006
50 This Magazine Jan 2004
51 http://www.embassymag.ca/page/view/top50-1-28-2009
52 http://www.6haynescapital.com/pdf/detail.cfm?id=90
53 This Magazine Mar 2007
54 http://www.gurufocus.com/news.php?id=49914
55 National Post Apr 19 2008
56 Towers of Gold, 183
57 The Banks of Canada in the Commonwealth Caribbean, 51
58 Canadian Corporations and Social Responsibility, 5
59 Actualites Dec 1 2006
60 Les Affaires Sept 6 2008
61 SNC, 131
62 Les Affaires June 30
63 Financial Post Nov 13 2006
64 Ottawa.http://www.embassymag.ca/page/view/top50-1-28-2009
65 Canada and the Middle East, 176
66 Canadian Corporations and Social Responsibility, 103
67 Globe and Mail June 21 2008
68 Perpetuating Poverty, 109
69 Canadian Dimension Oct 2008
70 La Presse Sept 29 2008

Appendix

One of the hardest parts of writing this book was deciding what to leave out. The difference between effectively making an argument and overwhelming the reader with detail can be difficult to judge when you have spent years researching material. I apologize to any reader who feels too many details were provided. For those who wish for more, I offer this appendix. In my research I came across many details that were a revelation, but just didn't fit into the main body of the book. They are presented here thematically, by chapter.

Belize

"Greedy BEL earns record profits, but threatens blackouts," read a May 2008 headline in Belize's Amandala newspaper.[1] The Newfoundland-based company, which has a monopoly on that country's electricity, wanted to pass the cost of rising oil prices to consumers despite an agreement with the government to maintain prices. Stan Marshall of Fortis Inc., the parent company, complained that "Belize has been the most frustrating jurisdiction I have ever experienced in my 30 years in the business." He then threatened "blackouts" prompting an emergency meeting of the Belizean cabinet.[2] The company's plans to expand at the start of this century also drew sharp criticism. To increase energy output, Fortis planned to construct a dam on the Macal River in western Belize — one of the last undisturbed rainforest valleys in Central America. The company's Chalillo Dam was expected to destroy 90 percent of the region's habitat of endangered species including the Jaguar, Scarlet Macaw, River Otter, Spider monkey and Belize's national animal the Tapir.[3] Fortis' expansion plans in Belize were supported by Canadian taxpayers. CIDA-INC provided the company with $466,000 for a feasibility report, which concluded that further studies were necessary so it was quickly shelved. According to CIDA documents, the aid agency then paid Agra Inc., a Toronto based engineering firm, to "justify construction of the Chalillo hydro dam in Belize."[4] Probe International found that Canadian companies were expected to win about $12 million in contracts from the project.[5]

Haiti

The ongoing occupation of Haiti described in Chapter 1 is just one of many foreign interventions into that country. For its part, Canada has a history of participating in interventions in Haiti. According to *Canadian Gunboat Diplomacy*, Canadian vessels have been sent to that country on a handful of occasions.[6] Beginning in May 1963 two Canadian naval vessels joined U.S., British and French warships that "conducted landing exercises up to the [Haiti's] territorial limit several times with the express purpose of intimidating the Duvalier government."[7] A year later HMCS Saskatchewan went to Haiti once again.[8] The 1963 mission was largely aimed at guaranteeing that Duvalier did not make any moves towards Cuba and that a Cuban-inspired guerilla movement did not seize power.[9] Ottawa's interest in Haiti during the mid-1960s was also prompted by the Royal Bank's stature as the country's only foreign bank, a Canadian-owned copper mine and 400 Canadian Catholic missionaries in the country. At one point Prime Minister Lester Pearson justified sending a naval vessel by noting that "if Canadian nuns or priests should be wounded or killed, it would be difficult to explain why the Canadian government had not ... taken some form of action."[10] In 1974 a Canadian warship was once again sent to Haiti. This time "Canadian naval vessels carried out humanitarian aid operations to generate goodwill with the Haitian government so that Haiti would support Canadian initiatives in la Francophonie designed to limit French interference in Canadian affairs."[11] In response to upheaval in the years after Jean Claude "Baby Doc" Duvalier's demise Canadian warships were again deployed in 1987 and 1988.[12]

The first allocation of Canadian aid to Haiti went through Catholic groups in 1968.[13] Four decades later a Press for Conversion investigation found that Ottawa-financed NGOs in Haiti were biased towards Christianity. (In 2009 Haiti probably had the largest concentration of Canadian missionaries anywhere in the hemisphere). These Canadian religious groups downplayed voodoo's significance despite the crucial role this domestic religion played in the Haitian revolution and the country's culture.[14] Through its aid program Ottawa supported Jean Claude Duvalier who took over after the death of his father in 1971. "CIDA has placed Canadian advisors as 'experts' in several Haitian ministries. One of the first projects undertaken by CIDA in 1973 was of this type, to be followed by five more over the next nine years."[15] *Spy Wars* describes one of the individuals working on a CIDA project. "[Hugh] Hambleton lived in true grandeur in the capital, Port-au-Prince, working closely with officials of the notoriously corrupt and brutal government of its dictator, 'Baby Doc' Jean-Claude Duvalier."[16]

By the late 1970s Canadian bilateral assistance to Haiti totalled just under $11 million.[17] Aid to Haiti during this period, notably ministerial advisors, supported the dictatorship. "It would be naive to pretend that this aid does not contribute to the support of the existing regime, at least in the short-run. It helps to legitimize the regime in the eyes of Haitians by demonstrating international approval and it generates projects and jobs, which the regime is careful to associate with itself as much as possible. To the extent that aid succeeds in mollifying popular discontent, it may serve to moderate sources of political opposition. For instance, by reducing financial pressure on the state, the provision of aid may facilitate regular and adequate payments of the armed forces."[18]

Towards the end of the 31-year Duvalier dictatorship Canadian aid financed two particularly contentious projects. The first was a hydroelectric dam in the Artibonite Valley to provide electricity largely for multinational corporations, which was scrapped after widespread peasant opposition. In 1983 Ottawa helped fund a U.S.-led pig eradication that wiped out the country's "Creole pigs." They were replaced with pigs from the U.S. Midwest that could not survive Haiti's harsh conditions.[19] Because pigs were the primary means for the peasantry to store wealth in case of emergency (to pay for school, baptisms or a funeral) the pig eradication devastated the countryside.

During the first coup against Jean-Bertrand Aristide (September 1991 to October 1994) Ottawa was generally supportive of the ousted president. At times, however, Ottawa used its good relations with Aristide to press U.S. demands. *Domestic Determinants of Foreign-Policy* notes that "[Mulroney's point person on Haiti Jim] Judd was to use Canada's good relationship with Aristide to pressure him to accept the Governor's Island follow-through, with which he [Aristide] was otherwise unhappy."[20] The Governor's Island's accords gave military officials responsible for the bloody coup immunity from prosecution and forced Aristide to accept a consensus prime minister.

Ecuador

In addition to the mining sector, Canadian companies have been active in Ecuador's oil industry. In the opening years of this century controversy engulfed an Ecuadorian oil pipeline led by Canada's largest natural gas producer, Calgary-based EnCana. The pipeline was built through an ecologically protected area and threatened the Siona nation's thriving sustainable eco-tourism industry. Construction of the pipeline failed to adhere to World Bank standards on environmental assessments, natural habitats, voluntary resettlement and indigenous peoples.[21] An investigation found that 92 percent of land owners who signed contracts to sell their land for the pipeline said they felt forced into doing so.[22] One author explained that the company "bought off community organization leaders by offering them salaries, scholarships and courses, so that they leave their own organization. … it became clear that one of the company's objectives was to demobilize the community that was trying to fight against the company's activities."[23] The company also militarized the area. EnCana "hired hundreds of private security personnel to guard its operations."[24] When a revolt against foreign oil companies in the largely indigenous Amazonian provinces broke out in March 2002, Ecuadorian armed forces used EnCana's airstrip and the company's trucks (with company drivers) to put down the protests. "The military attacked demonstrators with teargas and shot four people" while President Alfredo Palacio proclaimed a state of emergency, suspending human rights and the police made mass arrests.[25]

Iraq

Ottawa has long supported Western imperialism in Iraq. Canada played a small part in the British Empire's acquisition of Iraq from the Ottoman Empire. During World War One Canada's minister in London, Sir Edward Kemp, reported to the Prime Minister: "The imperial authorities were confronted with a difficult and hazardous situation. Owing to the demoralization and retirement of the Russian army in the Caucuses, which was operating on the eastern or right flank of the British army in Mesopotamia [modern-day Iraq]. … I was asked to furnish them with 15 level-headed Officers and 26 Non-Comissioned Officers, to cooperate with the British Officers and Officers from other Dominions in organizing a somewhat mixed and irregular army of different tribes and nationalities, which inhabit the territory to the North and East of the British Army. The population of this area is of a very mixed character, but to a considerable extent it is antagonistic to the Turk [Ottoman], and included in it is a certain number of Armenians."[26] A few dozen Canadian troops served in Mesopotamia from 1916 to 1919.[27] Canadians also fought to "hold the Batum-Tiflis-Baku-Krasnovodsk line to Afghanistan."[28]

In February 2000, when the U.S. and Britain bombed Iraq, Canada defended the assault. Chrétien claimed they had a duty to make Iraq respect the no-fly zone.[29] In 1998, Jean Chrétien said that "a military strike against Iraq would be justified to secure compliance with Security Council Resolution 687 and that Canada cannot stand on the sidelines at such a moment."[30] To aid U.S. airstrikes the Liberal government sent HMCS Toronto to the Persian Gulf as well as two Canadian Hercules air-to-air refueling aircraft.[31] Throughout the 1990s, Ottawa supported the murderous sanctions against

Iraq. To enforce sanctions, Ottawa provided a warship for most U.S. carrier battle groups patrolling the Arabian Gulf.[32] Art Eggleton, Minister of National Defence explained: "The Canadian Forces have been participating in the enforcement of U.N. sanctions against Iraq for the past ten years. Our contribution is important in promoting our national interests and is viewed as crucial by our allies. … This operation is extremely beneficial in ensuring our interoperability with our allies and particularly the United States. It will further strengthen our navy's relationship with the U.S. Navy and reaffirm our commitment to peace and stability in this region."[33]

Canadian destroyers were sent to the Persian Gulf to defend U.S./U.K. sanctions and to showcase Canadian vessels to the Kuwaiti navy. They used the HMCS Calgary "as a platform for SJSL [St. John's Shipbuilding Limited] Kuwait Offshore Missile Vessel proposals and for Ambassador [to Kuwait J. Christopher] Pool to promote Canadian industry and technology."[34] A military presence in the Middle East was viewed as a means of developing commercial relations, especially weapons sales.[35] "Canadian warships can serve as venues for trade initiatives, as examples of Canadian technology, and as visible symbols of Canadian interest in a country or region. In countries where relationships are built over time, as is the case with many Asian and Middle Eastern countries, a visit by a Canadian warship can be an important part of a dialogue that can lead to commercial opportunities for Canadian industry."[36]

Along with the U.S., U.K., France and Italy, Canada contributed significant military forces to the first Iraq war in 1991.[37] Ottawa dispatched two destroyers and a supply vessel, 24 CF-18 attack jets and 1,700 ground troops.[38] Offering its CF-18 jets, Canada was among a handful of coalition members to engage its forces in combat.[39] Initially part of a U.N. mandate, Canada's military operations went beyond what the U.N. authorized. The U.N. resolution allowed for attacks against Iraqi establishments in Kuwait while the U.S.-led forces bombed across Iraq.[40] The Canadian government, which spent $3 million a day in the first Gulf War, was hawkish in the lead-up to the conflict.[41] Foreign Affairs Minister Joe Clark explained that "the United Nations might not work, there might be veto … if there is a veto, we in Canada are prepared to discard the United Nations and we are prepared to take unilateral action."[42] Ottawa had little time or interest in waiting for sanctions or diplomacy to solve the crisis unleashed by Iraq's invasion of Kuwait. George H. W. Bush wanted to deepen the U.S. foothold in the region and Mulroney's Conservatives were prepared to contribute.[43] The first Gulf War was largely designed to reverse the Middle East's decolonization process, what Mark Curtis described as the open "rehabilitation of colonialism and imperialism."[44]

The war cost 20,000 Iraqi troops their lives and between 20,000 and 200,000 Iraqi civilians were killed in the fighting. "The coalition flew over 100,000 sorties, dropping 88,500 tons of bombs, and widely destroying military and civilian infrastructure. 11 of Iraq's 20 major power stations and 119 substations were totally destroyed, while a further six major power stations were damaged. At the end of the war, electricity production was at four percent of its pre-war levels. Bombs damaged all major dams, most major pumping stations and many sewage treatment plants, turning Iraq from one of the most advanced Arab countries into one of the most backward. Telecommunications equipment, port facilities, oil refineries and distribution, railroads and bridges were also destroyed."[45]

Some did benefit from the military action, however. In February 1992 Le Devoir reported that the Gulf War produced at least $100 million worth of contracts for Canadian arms merchants.[46] The Canadian Commercial Corporation actually set up a 24-hour telephone hotline to ensure that weapons "requests from allies wouldn't get snarled in red tape."[47] And once again, aid was motivated by geopolitical concerns rather than humanitarian ones. Canada provided $75 million for humanitarian and economic assistance to people in countries affected by the Gulf crisis.[48]

Saudi Arabia

The first Gulf war helped cement Canada's relations with the Saudi dictatorship and in 1992 the regime purchased $227 million worth of Canadian military equipment, mostly armoured vehicles.[49] "Canada has been a consistent and significant supplier of armoured vehicles to Saudi Arabia since the 1990s," according to Project Ploughshares.[50] By the mid-1990s the Saudis had purchased more than 1,600 light armored vehicles from Canada.[51] In 2004 alone Canada shipped $214 million worth of armoured vehicles to Saudi Arabia.[52] Ottawa only allowed armoured vehicle sales to Saudi Arabia because they were supposed to be for defensive purposes. That is, to keep the despotic regime in power.[53]

China

When the Harper government took power in 2006 they said they would change Canadian policy towards China. Previous governments, according to the ardently pro-business Harper, prioritized Canadian business interests, turning a blind eye to Chinese human rights violations. Harper was quoted by the Globe and Mail as saying he wouldn't "sell out" on human rights with China.[54] But one day earlier Minister of Natural Resources Gary Lunn was quoted in the business pages of the same paper saying: "I would like to encourage Chinese investment in Canada. Partnering with Canadian companies can help you secure the minerals and metals that China needs to fulfill its economic development. ... we invite Chinese mining companies to jointly explore and develop these and other deposits in Canada."[55]

To help Canadian investors, in June 2008, the Conservatives announced they were opening six new trade offices in cities across China.[56] The Harper government saw no problem with Pratt and Whitney selling Canadian-built engines for China's newest attack helicopter.[57] Nor did they stop Nortel from selling its highly advanced OPTera surveillance technology to China's security forces. Nortel also provided equipment used in China's surveillance architecture in Tibet, technology, that some said, would lead to the permanent militarization of the Tibetan plateau.[58] The Conservatives were happy to meet with the Dalai Lama but did nothing to stop Canadian companies from assisting China's further colonization of Tibet. Bombardier provided the Chinese with trains for its state of the art railway to Tibet and a number of Canadian mining companies (Continental Minerals, Hunter-Dixon and Inter-Citic Minerals) operated in the region.[59]

Harper's criticism of China was designed to appeal to Canadians who supported a human rights oriented foreign policy, but also to please the hawks in Washington. Harper's anti-Chinese comments reflected a worldview that longs for a divided and imperially dominated country like pre-1949 China. A weak China could increase the West's power and in the long term might benefit foreign investors. But in the short term there was a fundamental tension between the right wing geopolitical position represented in Harper's criticism of China and Canadian corporate interests. China was a large market and a great place to invest, which is why Nancy Hughes Anthony, president of the Canadian Bankers' Association, responded to Harper's comments by saying: "We are not the body that is going to judge China on the basis of any of its human rights record, and they may have comments for us on things that are happening in our domestic area."[60] Montréal's La Presse, which is owned by the founder of the Canada-China Business Council, Paul Desmarais, was also highly critical of Harper's attacks against China.[61]

Korea

When North Korea began testing nuclear weapons in the late 1990s the Canadian media barely reported on Canada's connection to the story:

Canada's nuclear sales to South Korea. Since 1973 Atomic Energy of Canada Limited (AECL) has provided four reactors to the Korea Electric Power Development Corporation. In September 1981 Prime Minister Trudeau even paid a visit to the AECL's Wolsung CANDU site in South Korea, which prompted negotiations for additional CANDU reactors. Between 1997 and 1999 three additional AECL CANDU units entered commercial operation at Wolsung. Pyongyang "criticized CANDU exports to South Korea for lowering South Korea's nuclear weapons acquisition threshold. For North Korea, nuclear exports were part of a series of provocative maneuvers made by the U.S. and South Korea."[62]

Vietnam

An April 2007 Vancouver Sun business section article had a picture with the cutline: "Students study sewing at Vietnam's Travinh University, which was set up with the help of Canadian community colleges and CIDA." The picture appeared to be women training to work in a clothing sweatshop. The article explained: "The role of the Canadian organizations was to create a community college that would graduate students that employers wanted to hire."[63]

In May 2008 Vancouver-based Asian Coast development Ltd. began building a $4.2 billion casino/tourism complex in southern Vietnam. Former Prime Minister Jean Chrétien was on hand for the groundbreaking ceremony. The project was controversial, however, since it was only for foreign tourists. Vietnam did not allow its citizens to gamble.

Cambodia

When Vietnam invaded Cambodia to topple Pol Pot's brutal Khmer Rouge in December 1978, Ottawa cut off its meager assistance to Vietnam, mostly contributions to the World Food Program.[64] Throughout the 1980s, Canada provided aid to the Cambodian political coalition that included the Khmer Rouge.[65] While Australia and the European Community withdrew their recognition of the Khmer Rouge beginning in February 1981 Canada joined ASEAN States in endorsing the coalition government that included the Khmer Rouge.[66] Ottawa had "what in essence was de facto support for Pol Pot and the Khmer Rouge."[67]

Myanmar

A dozen Canadian corporations were doing business in the first decade of this century with the military regime in Burma, including Ivanhoe, which had a 50-50 joint venture with Burma's state mining company. In

2005 alone, Ivanhoe paid the regime $5 million in royalties and the state-owned company $10 million in profit.[68] According to the Burma Campaign, Ivanhoe has "very close links to the junta. Its copper mine operating in Monywa generates $40 million for the junta. While Ivanhoe claimed to have sold its stake in the mine, the company received $6.6 million in a single quarter in 2007 from the unnamed trust it sold its stake to."[69]

Ivanhoe also claimed it consulted with Ottawa before initiating business with the Burmese military regime. Ivanhoe CEO Robert Friedland explained that "in 1996 representatives of the company met with officials of the Canadian government in Ottawa [and] at no time did the ...government advise us against investing in Myanmar [Burma] or attempt to dissuade us from doing business in the country."[70] In fact, as late as October 2007, the Canadian Pension Plan had $32 million invested in the company and Québec's public pension, the Caisse de depot et placement, controlled five percent of Ivanhoe's stock.[71]

Nepal

At the start of this decade Canadian aid to Nepal supported a monarchy facing a Maoist guerrilla insurgency. While CIDA's website claimed "neutrality" in the civil war, it blamed poverty and underdevelopment in the country on the "Maoist insurgency".[72] CIDA's 2004 Peace and Conflict Impact Assessment acknowledged that "CIDA will need to monitor whether its projects become Maoist targets because of linkages with government programs."[73] In 2004-05 Canada provided $10.4 million in development assistance to Nepal.[74] But Canadian support for the monarchy included more than development assistance. JTF2 special forces helped train the Royal Nepalese Army in counterinsurgency techniques. "The Canadian training team went to work in advising the RNA [Royal Nepalese Army] on tactics and the best use of its forces against the guerrillas. Two Royal Nepalese Army soldiers were also sent to Canada to attend mountain instructors courses — excellent training for the battles in which they would later take part. Another RNA officer was selected for Canadian military flying training while six others attended courses at Pearson peacekeeping center in Nova Scotia."[75] Regarding U.S. support for the Royal Nepal Army, Amnesty International claimed that such "assistance has enabled an increase in grave violations of international humanitarian and human rights law."[76]

Despite foreign opposition, in 2007 the Maoists won elections and dismantled the 200-year-old monarchy. As this book goes to press, they govern the country.

Zimbabwe

During the 1970s a number of major Canadian corporations had subsidiaries in white-dominated Rhodesia (now Zimbabwe).[77] Some of these companies continued to operate in Rhodesia even after it was prohibited by Canadian law yet the federal government did nothing.[78] Falconbridge's annual report, for example, discussed in detail the operations of its Blanket mine in Rhodesia.[79] Still, the parliamentary secretary to the Minister of Industry, Trade and Commerce claimed, "our record reveal no evidence that there are direct corporate ties between Falconbridge-Nickel Co. Ltd and Blanket mines [in Rhodesia]."[80]

Libya

The Mulroney government supported the U.S.'s April 1986 airstrikes on Libya designed to kill that country's president. Despite failing to kill Mohammed Gaddafi, the bombs left 37 people dead and 93 wounded.[81] Erik Nielsen, Brian Mulroney's deputy prime minister, said "Libya must end its support for extremists and its savage attacks against innocent and defenceless individuals throughout the world." Canada, Nielsen explained, accepted "the substantial body of evidence" that Libya was responsible for the bombing of a German discotheque frequented by American soldiers, which was the pretext for the U.S. airstrike.[82] Prior to the bombing Ottawa was the first country to impose sanctions on Tripoli following Ronald Reagan's decision to do so at the start of 1986.[83] Canada's Communications Security Establishment (CSE) planned to open a communications site in Algeria to help the U.S. National Security Agency (NSA) spy on Colonel Gaddafi's Libya.[84]

Kenya

In 2003, CIDA-INC gave Toronto-based Tiomin $391,000 for an environmental impact assessment study on a planned mine in Kenya.[85] Tiomin decided the terms of the study and hired a South African consulting company to administer the assessment. Kenyan environmental groups, including researchers at Kenyatta University in Nairobi, rejected the company-backed assessment. They criticized the assessment for underestimating the mine's likely environmental impacts, notably the quantity of sulphur dioxide emissions and exposure to radioactive elements in the earth. The area threatened by the mine is part of one of the world's 25 hotspots (areas of heavy biodiversity that are seriously threatened), according to Conservation International. The Kenyan coast, where Tiomin holds a 56 km² concession, is home to palm-fringed beaches, blue lagoons, magnificent coral beaches and ancient Arabic architecture. A variety of endangered species, including the only bands of Colobus monkeys on the East African coast and Kenya's last remaining herds of sable antelope, depend on the coast's fragile ecosystem. Alongside the animals that will lose their habitat Digo and Kamba farmers living in the area expect to be forced to flee to urban centres as their means of subsistence, notably coconut, cashew nut and mango groves, will be destroyed by the mine and accompanying development. The $225 million project, which will be the biggest mining venture in Kenya since independence, was under legal challenge in 2008. Tiomin did sign a sweetheart deal with the government that included a 50-per-cent reduction of the corporate tax rate for 10 years from the start of commercial production. The company would pay the Kenyan government a paltry 2.5 percent gross revenue royalty. Kenya's major paper, The Nation, reported accusations of bribery and corruption surrounding the mine. One website notes that "controversy has dogged the company since the day the announcement was made in early 1997. Since then, the issue has snowballed into what may be the biggest controversy since Kenya's independence."[86]

Nigeria

Richard Granier-Defferre, former Nigeria representative for TSX-listed Addax Petroleum, allegedly paid Nigeria's oil minister $10 million between 1993 and 1998 for drilling rights.[87] Granier-Defferre was also thought to have helped open bank accounts in Europe for the oil minister, Dan Etete, under dictator Sani Abacha, who looted as much as $3 billion from state coffers. According to a January 2008 Globe and Mail article, Etete was to stand trial in France for money laundering, part of a probe into kickbacks paid by oil companies for contracts. Adddax's man in Nigeria until 2000, Granier-Defferre, was to be tried as an accessory.[88]

International Criminal Court

Like the ICTY Canada played an important role in setting up the International Criminal Court (ICC). In 1998, Canada chaired The Like-Minded Group conference in Rome, which was key to forming a coalition of states that supported the ICC. Canada also paid for some developing countries to take part in the conference. And it was a Canadian, Philippe Kirsch, a senior diplomat, who presided over the ICC. While it's hard to disagree with the idea of a court to try human rights abusers that go unpunished in their home country, reality is more complicated. Simply put, the court is set up in the interests of the powerful. "The Security Council can refer cases to the ICC and block them even though some of its members were not signatories to the treaty. Additionally the Security Council can refer cases from non-signatory countries against the Law of Treaties which says countries cannot be bound by a treaty it has not signed. For these reasons India refused to sign the ICC."[89]

The ICC's bias towards the powerful includes its list of crimes. Employing poison gases, for instance, counts as a war crime, but the use of nuclear weapons does not.[90] Incredibly, aggression, the supreme international crime according to the Nuremberg Tribunal, is not covered under the International Court.[91] As Diana Johnstone points out, the ICC has been set up to administer "international" justice to internal conflicts, but only in countries too weak to resist its authority, or those not well enough connected to a major power.[92] It is unlikely that western allies, such as interim Haitian dictator Gérard Latortue or Rwanda's Paul Kagame (for his role in invading Rwanda or the millions killed in the Congo), will be sent to the ICC anytime soon. And it is even less likely that George Bush or Tony Blair will be indicted for their roles in Iraq, or Paul Martin for his role in Haiti. "The ICC is rapidly turning into a Western court to try African crimes against humanity," noted The Nation. "It has targeted governments that are U.S. adversaries and ignored actions the United States doesn't oppose, like those of Uganda and Rwanda in eastern Congo, effectively conferring impunity on them."[93] The first four investigations begun by the ICC were all in places where the U.S. does not oppose the course chartered by ICC investigators.[94]

Even worse than a court that reinforces the world's power imbalances, there is a strong possibility that NATO countries will justify future invasions on the grounds that a wanted fugitive is not being handed over to the ICC. "Rather than a court to keep the peace," Diana Johnstone writes, "the ICC could turn out to be — contrary to the wishes of its sincere supporters — an instrument to provide pretexts for war."[95] In October 2008 the Washington Post noted, "The [Bush] administration is emerging as an unlikely defender of the court in the face of efforts by Sudan and others to derail the prosecution" of that country's president, Omar Hassan Ahmad al-Bashir.[96] Will Washington justify invading Sudan on the grounds that Bashir is wanted by the ICC?

The roots of NATO

The North Atlantic Treaty Organization has its roots in the rivalry between Russia and Great Britain over Central Asia in the late 1800s. As an organization to paper over Western European divisions its roots are also to be found within Europe's inter-imperial struggles from the First World War to the Spanish Civil War through the Second World War and Cold War.

Inter-imperial rivalry in Europe prompted Canada's most significant foreign-policy endeavours. Nearly 60,000 Canadian soldiers died in World War One and another 150,000 returned home wounded.[97] An unknown number were killed by Canadian soldiers. After a 1916 battle, one Fifteenth Battalion diarist complained that too many Germans surrendered, but "some very useful killing was also achieved."[98]

The First World War had no clear and compelling purpose other than inter-imperial rivalry in Europe. It was a struggle for Eastern Europe and Asia's Caucasus region within the larger battle for global supremacy between up-and-coming Germany and the imperial powers of the day, Britain and France. Support for the British Empire was Ottawa's primary motive in joining the war. As Prime Minister Robert Borden saw it, the fight was "to put forth every effort and to make every sacrifice necessary to ensure the integrity and maintain the honour of our empire."[99] He even justified conscription as a way of preserving Canada's imperial standing.[100] This wasn't always popular. Ottawa feared the "danger of popular turbulence," according to the chief of the army.[101] Opposition to the war was greatest in Québec but even outside of that province the authorities were nervous. On Vancouver Island, for instance, prominent anti-war activist Ginger Goodwin was killed by a special constable tracking down conscientious objectors.

World War One reveals a schizophrenic Canadian mythology. Some believe Canada is the "peaceable kingdom" yet for many it gained nation status on the battlefields of one of the most absurd and destructive wars in history. "The view has often been expressed that Canada became a nation on the battlefield, Easter Monday 9 April 1917, when the Canadian Corps broke the German stranglehold on Vimy Ridge."[102] This sentiment is expressed in the titles of two books published in 2007: *Baptism of Fire: The second battle of Ypres and the forging of Canada, April 1915*, and *Victory at Vimy: Canada comes of age, April 9-12, 1917*. An April 2007 Globe and Mail article echoed this sentiment. "'It put Canadians on the map. It showed we actually do stuff. We became important. A great national achievement,' said Jeffery Bertrand, a 16-year old Grade 11 student who took part in an Ontario high school delegation that visited the 90-year anniversary of Vimy Ridge."[103] During the 90th anniversary commemoration, Prime Minister Harper drew a parallel between Canada's role in Afghanistan and World War One. "For these men and women, the terrain of Kandahar province looks as dangerous and desolate as Flanders field looked 90 years ago," Harper explained. "But those who wear the maple leaf on their uniform move forward against tyranny and fear with the same courage and determination that you did in your time and that the heroes of Vimy Ridge did before you."[104]

Russian Civil War

The First World War was particularly horrific for most Russians. Hundreds of thousands perished from the fighting and many more died from hunger and disease caused by the conflict. Bolshevism grew in response to this misery brought upon the country by a brutal Czar. The French, English and U.S. responded to the Bolshevik's rise to power by supporting the Russian monarchists (the whites) in their fight to maintain power. Six thousand Canadian troops invaded Russia.[105] Canadian gunners won "a vicious reputation amongst the Bolsheviks for the calm skill with which they used shrapnel as a short-range weapon against foot soldiers."[106] While a Canadian naval vessel supported the White Russians, Canadian pilots stationed near the Black Sea provided air support.[107]

The war against the Bolsheviks was initially justified as a way to reopen the war's Eastern Front (the Bolsheviks signed a peace treaty with Germany). Canadian troops, however, stayed after World War One ended. In fact, 2,700 Canadian troops arrived in the eastern city of Vladivostok on January 5, 1919, two months after the war's conclusion.[108] A total of 3,800 Canadian troops, as well as Royal Northwest Mounted Police and 697 horses, went to Siberia, which the Whites continued to control long after losing Moscow, St. Petersburg and most of the western part of the country. Ottawa maintained its forces in Russia after the conclusion of World War One partly to persuade the British that Canada merited inclusion in the Paris Peace conference that would divvy up the spoils of the war. Prime Minister Borden wrote: "We shall stand in an unfortunate position unless we proceed with Siberia expedition. We made definite arrangements with the British government on which they have relied ... Canada's present position and prestige would be singularly impaired by deliberate withdrawal."[109]

Ottawa also feared the rise of anti-capitalism. On December 1, 1918, Borden wrote in his diary that he was "struck with the progress of Bolshevism in European countries."[110] For their part, Canadian working class groups condemned the invasion of Russia as "for the benefit of the capitalist."[111] The Hamilton Daily Times wondered "are we sacrificing our soldiers...to validate Russian bonds held by foreign nations?"[112]

Ottawa hoped Canada's military participation would lead to economic opportunities in Russia after the revolution was defeated.[113] "Intimate relations with that rapidly developing country [Siberia]," Borden wrote, "will be of great advantage to Canada in the future. Other nations will make very vigorous and determined efforts to obtain a foothold and our interposition with a small military force would tend to bring Canada into favourable notice by the strongest elements in that great community."[114] Alongside its military force, Ottawa established a Trade Commission in Vladivostok and the Royal Bank opened an office in the city.[115] The Royal Bank convinced Canadian commanders to post eight soldiers around their branch. (After Canadian troops departed, British and American troops provided the bank's security).[116]

The allies invaded Russia to defend the status quo, much to the dismay of most Canadians who welcomed the Czar's demise and found it difficult to understand why Canada would support Russian reactionaries.[117] Opposition to the intervention was widespread even among soldiers. According to the Toronto Globe, 60-70 percent of the men sent to Siberia went unwillingly.[118] One artillery section even refused to obey orders.[119]

Throughout the 1920s and 1930s the West worked to isolate Moscow. Canada (and the U.S.) opposed a treaty to guarantee Russia's pre-war frontiers, which England had signed with Moscow.[120] Ottawa recognized the Bolshevik government in 1924 but ties were severed after the British cut off relations in mid-1927. London wanted to present a "uniformity of action" within the Commonwealth prompting J. S. Woodsworth, a progressive MP from Winnipeg, to denounce Ottawa for following the "lead of Great Britain and indirectly the behest of the oil kings ... [Royal Dutch Shell Company] when she severed relations with Russia."[121] Full diplomatic relations with Moscow would not restart until the late 1930s.

Spanish Civil War

After World War One and the invasion of Russia the next major historical event to shape what would become NATO was the Spanish Civil War. There the struggle between fascism and liberal democracy was thrust upon the world stage three years before the outbreak of World War Two. In Spain's 1936 national elections a left-wing coalition government won office. The church, landed gentry and big business immediately looked to overthrow the government with the help of General Francisco Franco, commander of Spain's overseas military. In this armed struggle, Franco was assisted by Hitler's Germany, Fascist Portugal and Mussolini's Italy. The Nazis gave

Franco's forces 43 million pounds worth of war material (600 planes, 200 tanks, highly effective artillery pieces) and sent 16,000 German men. "Spain functioned as a testing ground for Hitler's incipient war machine and was also something of a secret playground for the young pilots of Germany's Condor Legion."[122] Spain's neighbour, Portugal added 20,000 soldiers. The Italians provided the largest contribution to the fight against democratic Spain. They sent 75,000 soldiers, deployed 90 warships and the Italian air force launched more than 5,000 raids.[123]

The historical record is clear: Canada sided with the Fascists during the Spanish civil war. Ottawa refused repeated requests from Spain's elected government to sell it weaponry. During the same period, Canada found no fault supplying war materials to the Japanese army that occupied Korea and massacred the Chinese in Manchuria. When the Spanish government tried to build support for its cause by sending three elected representatives to Québec, Montréal's mayor cancelled the hall rented for the meeting.[124] The RCMP spied on the Spanish Solidarity Committee, which organized Canadians to cross the Atlantic to fight fascism. "Clothing workers in Toronto agreed to make suits on their own time and donate the profits to the Spanish Republic, something the RCMP apparently considered a security threat and duly reported."[125] It is suspected that the federal government pressured the Canadian Pacific Steam Ships Company to deny the Spanish Solidarity Committee spaces aboard their cross Atlantic vessels.[126] Most ominously, in April 1937, Ottawa passed the Foreign Enlistment Act designed to block Canadians from fighting on behalf of the Republican government. And after Prime Minister William McKenzie King met Hitler in the summer of 1937, he demanded a rigorous application of the act.[127]

Canadian officials claimed that "these youths are being sent to Spain, largely for the sake of gaining experience in practical revolutionary work and will return to this country to form the nucleus of a trained core."[128] Those who crossed the Atlantic had an alternate version: They sacrificed themselves in defence of an elected government and against the rising tide of fascism. The 1,448 Spanish veterans were later prevented from enlisting in the army during World War Two and in the mid 1980s, the survivors' request to be recognized as veterans of Canada's wars (with a pension) was denied.[129] As late as 1980 the RCMP still spied on the Spanish war veterans.[130] In 1970 the Canadian veterans applied for formal incorporation as a non-profit organization called Mackenzie-Papineau Batallion-Veterans of the International Brigades. An RCMP report into their request claimed "this organization would undoubtedly be used by the Communist Party of

Canada as a front organization to further their cause."[131] For its part, the Department of Consumer and Corporate Affairs noted: "We are somewhat concerned about the possible external political implications arising from the incorporation of such an association whose objectives are antagonistic to the existing regime in Spain. ... The incorporation of such an association seems to us inopportune at a time when our relations with Spain may be entering a new phase with that country's adoption of a more outward-looking policy. However, it is for you to determine whether these external political implications should have a bearing on the application before you."[132] On December 15, 1970, External Affairs denied the application. "The Canadian government so valued its relations with a squalid and fading dictator that it put Franco's concerns above those of its own citizens."[133]

World War Two

Canadian support for fascism in Spain (and Japan) in the years leading to World War Two should bedevil the notion that Canada joined the war to combat this perverse political system/ideology. Prime Minister MacKenzie King, in fact, was sympathetic to European fascism. In September 1936, King wrote that Hitler "might come to be thought of as one of the saviours of the world."[134] "The truth" according to King, "is Hitler and Mussolini, while dictators, have really sought to give the masses of the people, some opportunity for enjoyment, taste of art and the like and, in this way, have won them to their side."[135]

There is also a perception that Canada joined World War Two to defeat anti-Semitism. To the contrary, many Canadian leaders held anti-Semitic views. King said "I'm coming to feel that the democratic countries have allowed themselves to be too greatly controlled by the Jews and Jewish influence."[136] When King visited Germany in June 1937, he failed to mention (publicly or privately) the Nuremberg laws. In existence since mid-1935, these laws codified anti-Semitism in Germany.[137] Even in the face of terrible anti-Semitism in Europe, King opposed Jewish immigration to Canada. Nothing would be gained, King wrote in his diary, "by creating an internal problem in an effort to meet an international one [Nazi anti-Semitism]."[138] Fewer than 5,000 Jews were allowed into Canada from 1933-1945. Between the end of the war and 1948, Canada admitted only 8,000 more. "That record is arguably the worst of all possible refugee receiving states."[139]

Nazi expansionism's threat to British interests, not opposition to fascism or anti-Semitism, led Ottawa to war. "Canada went to war in September 1939 for the same reason as in 1914: because Britain went to war."[140] And once begun, the war was a huge boost to Canada's depressed economy. It also benefited Canada's world standing. On July 1, 1943, Mackenzie King proclaimed that "in the course of the present war, we have seen Canada emerge from nationhood into a position generally recognized as that of a world power."[141]

During the war, Canadian forces committed major humanitarian crimes. Most ominously, Canadian bombers helped destroy German cities. King "had no regrets about [British general in charge of bomber command Arthur] Harris' way of waging war against Germany's civilians."[142] According to Harris, "the destruction of German cities; the killing of German workers and the destruction of civilized life throughout Germany ... the destruction of houses, public utilities, transport and lives; the creation of a refugee problem on an unprecedented scale; and the breakdown of morale ... [These] are expected and intended aims of our bombing policy. They are not byproducts of attempts to hit factories."[143]

In 2007 controversy erupted over a Canadian War Museum exhibit that read: "The value and morality of the strategic bomber offensive against Germany remains bitterly contested. Bomber Command's aim was to crush civilian morale and force Germany to surrender by destroying its cities and industrial installations. Although Bomber Command and American attacks left 600,000 Germans dead and more than five million homeless, the raids resulted in only small reductions of German war production until late in the war."[144] Canadian war veterans campaigned successfully to change the exhibit's wording, despite numerous historians (including many of a distinctly pro-military bent) concluding that the description was accurate.

Just as during World War One, the Second World War was used to clamp down on undesirables. Numerous Communist publications were banned. The Communist Party was declared an unlawful association in the spring of 1940, and it stayed that way even after the USSR became a war ally.[145] "While Fascism was allowed virtually free rein in Canada, Communists found themselves running afoul of Québec's padlock law or Section 98 of the Canadian Criminal Code, which made it a punishable crime to be involved in an 'unlawful association.'"[146]

Cold War

Officially, NATO was a response to the Soviet Union's aggressive tendencies. But as we've seen, the Cold War can be traced to Canada and its allies invasion of Russia as well as attempts to isolate that country throughout the 1920s and 1930s. Canadian officials were fully aware that after the incredible destruction of World War Two the Soviets had little interest in fighting the U.S. or Western European countries. In 1945 Canada's ambassador to Russia, Dana Wilgress concluded that "the interests of the Soviet privileged class are bound up with the maintenance of a long period of peace." The Soviet elite, the ambassador continued, were "fearful of the possibility of attack from abroad" and "obsessed with problems of security."[147] Wilgress believed the Soviets wanted a post-war alliance with the U.K. to guarantee peace in Europe (with a Soviet sphere in the East and a U.K.-led West.[148]) In the face of Ambassador Wilgress' sober advice, Ottawa spouted Cold War hysteria. Prime Minister Mackenzie King responded to Churchill's famous March 1946 "Iron Curtain" speech by remarking that "it was the most courageous speech I have ever listened to, considering what we know of Russia's behaviour in Europe and in Asia since the war and what has been disclosed here in Ottawa."[149] For his part, Canadian ambassador to Washington Lester Pearson argued that "the USSR is ultimately bound to come into open conflict with western democracy."[150]

Canada's contribution to Cold War hysteria included the Canadian Psychological Warfare Committee, which continued after World War Two ended.[151] As part of the Psychological Warfare Committee, the CBC's International Service beamed Canadian information to the Soviet Union and other Eastern Bloc countries.[152] External Affairs, which was given a copy of the scripts used by commentators, had a liaison with CBC-IS, "particularly with the producers and broadcasters responsible for the various language programs intended for the 'other side'."[153] According to former Canadian ambassador to Czechoslovakia and Poland, and CBC-IS founder, Jack McCordick, the aim of CBC-IS was "to engage in psychological warfare against the communist regimes."[154] The U.S. and Britain pressed Ottawa to support CBC-IS as they felt it complimented the work of BBC International and Voice of America.[155]

Chapter Notes

1   Amandala May 23 2008

2   Globe and Mail June 3 2008

3   probeinternational.org/catalog/pi/images/ Belize/Belizeflyer.pdf

4   http://www.probeinternational. org/chalillo/news-and-opinion/foreign- interference-belize

5   Probe International and Natural Resources Defense Council Press Release August 8/2002

6   Canadian Gunboat Diplomacy - Maple Leaf Over the Caribbean

7   Canadian Gunboat Diplomacy, 151

8   Canadian Gunboat Diplomacy, 137

9   Canadian Gunboat Diplomacy, 151

10   Canadian Gunboat Diplomacy, 150

11   http://www.irpp.org/po/archive/jan01/ maloney.pdf

12   Canadian Gunboat Diplomacy, 138

13   Canadian Development Assistance to Haiti, 46/70

14   http://coat.ncf.ca/our_magazine/ links/63/63_11.htm

15   Canadian Development Assistance to Haiti, 52

16   Spy Wars, 172

17   Canadian Gunboat Diplomacy, 164

18   Canadian Development Assistance to Haiti, 40

19   Aiding Migration, 83

20   Domestic Determinants of Foreign Policy, 187

21   Community Rights and Corporate Responsibility, 120; This Magazine Sept 2003

22   Community Rights and Corporate Responsibility, 128

23   Community Rights and Corporate Responsibility, 122

24   Community Rights and Corporate Responsibility, 121

25   Community Rights and Corporate Responsibility, 121; New Socialist, Nov 2005

26   Allied Intervention in Russia, 43

27   Allied Intervention in Russia, 44

28   Allied Intervention in Russia, 44

29   In/Security, 355

30   Canada and the World Order, 209

31   In/Security, Page 354; The Canadian Forces, 24

32   Canada Among Nations, 121

33   War with Iraq, 36

34   War with Iraq, 35

35   War with Iraq, 46

36   Canadian Gunboat Diplomacy, 142

37   Canadian Foreign Policy, 387; Uncle Sam and Us, 387

38   Following the Americans to the Persian Gulf, 81

39   Canada and the World Order, 207

40   Weighing the Options, 51

41   Conflicts of Interest, 18

42   Canada and the Middle East, 90

43   Canada and the World Order, 208

44   http://auto_sol.tao.ca/node/3047

45   Wikipedia

46   Common Sense, 49

47   Common Sense, 49

48   Following the Americans to the Persian Gulf, 94

49   Empire to Umpire, 318

50   Montréal Gazette Jan 23 2008

51   Canadian Jewish News Sept 5 1996

52   Montréal Gazette Jan 23 2008

53   Arms Canada, 151

54   Globe and Mail Nov 16 2006

55   Globe and Mail Nov 15 2006

56   La Presse Jan 19 2008

57   Montréal Gazette Oct 18 2007

58   Globe and Mail May 30 2007

59   Concordia Link Apr 3 2007

60   Canwest Nov 28 2006

61   Le Canada face a l'Asie de l'Est, 94

62   http://www.dominionpaper.ca/foreign_ policy/2006/12/08/sanctionin.html

63   Vancouver Sun Apr 9 2007

64   Canadian International Development Assistance Policies, 246

65   Rain-dancing, 79

66   Rain-dancing, 60

67   Rain-dancing, 60

68   Ottawa Citizen Nov 4 2006

69   Montréal Gazette Oct 5 2007

70   CCPA Monitor Mar 2001

71   McGill Daily Oct 4 2007

72   http://www.countercurrents.org/sa- walia071006.htm

73   http://www.countercurrents.org/sa- walia071006.htm

74   http://www.dominionpaper.ca/foreign_ policy/2006/10/28/canadian_a.html)

75   Canada's Secret Commandos, 66

76   Countercurrents.org Oct 7 2006

77   Imperialism and the National Question, 86

78 The Ambiguous Champion, 34
79 Canadian Dimension, Vol 12 1977
80 Canadian Dimension, Vol 12 1977
81 In/Security, 349; Ottawa Citizen Jan 25 1986
82 Toronto Star Apr 18 1986
83 Canada and the Middle East, 49; The Domestic Battleground, 198
84 Spy World, 141
85 http://www.miningwatch.ca/updir/Canadian_Cos_in_Africa_2001.pdf
86 http://www.towardfreedom.com/home/content/view/105/63/
87 <http://www.linternationalmagazine.com/article345.html>
88 Globe and Mail Jan 12 2008
89 The Nation Sept 29 2008
90 http://www.counterpunch.org/johnstone01272007.html
91 http://en.wikipedia.org/wiki/International_Criminal_Court
92 http://www.counterpunch.org/johnstone01272007.html
93 The Nation Sept 29 2008
94 The Nation Sept 29 2008
95 http://www.counterpunch.org/johnstone01272007.html
96 Washington Post Oct 12 2008
97 The Canadian Way of War, 169
98 Canada and the Two World wars, 145
99 Canada: 1896-1921, 212
100 Canada and the Transition to Commonwealth, 53
101 Empire to Umpire, 65
102 Empire to Umpire, 62
103 Globe and Mail Apr 5 2007
104 Globe and Mail Apr 9 2007
105 Canadians in Russia, 259
106 Canadians in Russia, 79
107 Canadian Gunboat Diplomacy, 81
108 Canadian-Soviet Relations, 16
109 Canada and the Soviet Experiment, 31
110 Canada and the Soviet Experiment, 29
111 Canada and the Soviet Experiment, 35
112 Canadians in Russia, 171
113 Empire to Umpire, 70
114 Canada and the Soviet Experiment, 27
115 Canadians in Russia, 229/242
116 Canadians in Russia, 243; Quick to the Frontier, 195
117 Canadians in Russia, 158
118 Canadian-Soviet Relations, 17
119 Canada and the Soviet Experiment, 35
120 Diplomacy of fear, 34
121 Partner to Behemoth, 13; Canadian-Soviet Relations, 103
122 Renegades, xiv
123 The Gallant Cause, Page 220; Renegades, xv
124 Canadian Dimension, Apr 8 1989
125 Renegades, 47
126 Canadian Volunteers, 11
127 The Gallant Cause, 128
128 Canadian Volunteers, 12
129 Canadian Volunteers, 203
130 Renegades, 180
131 Renegades, 179
132 Renegades, 179
133 Renegades, 180
134 None is Too Many, 37
135 None is Too Many, 37
136 Diplomacy of Fear, 132
137 The Gallant Cause, 128
138 None is Too Many, 17
139 None is Too Many, 66
140 Canada and the Two World Wars, 177
141 The Middle Power Project, 46
142 Maple Leaf Against Axis, 125
143 National Post Oct 10 2008
144 National Post Aug 30, 2007
145 Cold War Canada, 10
146 The Gallant Cause, xi
147 Alliance and Illusion, 46
148 Diplomacy of Fear, 48
149 Alliance and Illusion, 46
150 Diplomacy of fear, 167
151 In the Clutches of the Kremlin, 115
152 On the Road to Freedom, 99
153 The rise and Fall of a Middle Power, 39
154 On the Road to Freedom, 132
155 On the Road to Freedom, 132

Bibliography

A Dynamic Partnership: Canada's Changing role in the Americas. Jerry Haar and Edgar J Dosman, University of Miami North South Center (1993)

A Foremost Nation: Canadian foreign policy and a changing world. Norman Hillmer and Garth Stevenson, McClelland & Stewart (1977)

Africa in the United Nations system 1945–2005. Issaka K Soure, Adonis Abbey publisher (2006)

African Exploits: The Diaries of William Stairs, 1887-1892. Roy Mclaren, McGill-Queens University Press (1998)

Aid and Ebb Tide: A History of CIDA and Canadian Development Assistance. David R Morrisson, Wilfrid Laurier University Press (1998)

Aid as a Peacemaker: Canadian Development Assistance and Third World Conflict. Robert Miller, Carleton University Press (1992)

Allied intervention in Russia, 1918-1919: And the Part Played by Canada. John Swettenham, Ryerson Press (1967)

The Ambiguous Champion: Canada and South Africa in the Trudeau and Mulroney years. Linda Freeman, University Of Toronto Press (1997)

American British Canadian Intelligence Relations 1939-2000, David Stafford and Rhodri Jeffreys Jones, Frank Cass publishers (2000)

Anatomy of Big Business. Libbie Park and Frank Park, Lorimer (1973)

An Independent Foreign Policy for Canada?. Stephen Clarkson, Carleton University Press (1968)

Another Kind of Justice: Canadian Military Law from Confederation to Somalia. Chris Madsen, UBC Press (1999)

Arms Canada: The Deadly Business of Military Exports. Ernie Regehr, James Lorimer (1987)

A role for Canada in an African crisis: perceptions of the Congo crisis and motivations for Canadian participation. Daniel Galvin, University of Guelph Thesis (2004)

The Assassination of Lumumba. Ludo De Witte, Verso (2001)

A World Mission: Canadian Protestantism and the quest for a new international order, 1918 – 1939. Robert Wright, McGill Queen's University Press (1991)

The Banks of Canada in the Commonwealth Caribbean: Economic Nationalism and multinational enterprises of a medium power. Daniel Baum, Jay Praeger Publishers (1974)

Battlegrounds: The Canadian Military and Aboriginal Lands. P Whitney Lackenbauer UBC Press (2007)

Between Arab and Israeli. ELM Burns, Ivan Obolensky Inc. (1962)

Between War and Peace in Central America. Liisa North and CAPA Between the Lines (1990)

Beyond Mexico. Jean Daudelin and Edgar J Dosman, Carleton University Press (1995)

The Big Nickel: Inco at Home and Abroad. Jamie Swift, Between the Lines (1977)

The Boer War and Canadian Imperialism. Robert Page, Canadian Historical Association (1987)

Bound by Power: intended consequences. Jeffery Klaehn, Black Rose books (2006)

Brascan Ltd: A corporate background report. Roy E. Birkett, Royal Commission on corporate concentration (1976)

Brazil and Canada in the Americas. Rosana Borbosa, Canada Visiting Research chair in Brazilian studies (2007)

Bridges of Hope?: Canadian Voluntary Agencies and the Third World. Tim Brodhead and Brent Herbert-Copley and Anne-Marie Lambert, North-South Institute (1999)

Britain, Canada and the North Pacific: Maritime Enterprise and Dominion, 1778 –1914. Ashgate Variorum (2004)

Bronfman Dynasty: the Rothschilds of the New World. Peter C. Newman, McClelland & Stewart (1978)

Canada: 1896-1921. Robert Craig Brown and Ramsay Cook, McClelland & Stewart (1974)

Canada Accomplice in Apartheid: Canadian Government and Corporate Involvement in South Africa. Dick Fidler, Vanguard Publications (1977)

Canada Among Nations 1998: Leadership and Dialogue. Fenh Osler Hampson and Maureen Appel Molot, Oxford University Press (2002)

Canada Among Nations 2002. Norman Hillmer & Maureen Appel Molot, Oxford University Press (2002)

Canada Among Nations 2003. David Carment & Fen Osler Hampson & Norman Hilmer, Oxford University Press (2003)

Canada Among Nations 2004: David Carment, Fen Osler Hampson and Norman Hillmer. McGill-Queens University Press (2005)

Canada and British Wars. John S Ewart (1923)

Canada and Development Cooperation annual review 1975-1976. Canadian International Development Agency

Canada and Imperialism: 1896-1899. Norman Penlington, University Toronto Press (1965)

Canada and Palestine: The Politics of Non-Commitment. Zachariah Kay, Israel University Press (1978)

Canada and September 11th: Impact and Responses. Karim-Aly Kassam & George Melnyk & Lynne Perras, Detselig Enterprises Ltd. (2002)

Canada and the Birth of Israel: A Study in Canadian Foreign Policy. David J Bercuson University of Toronto Press (1985)

Canada and the Crisis in Central America. Jonathan Lemco, Praeger (1991)

Canada and the Early Cold War: 1943-1957. Greg Donaghy, Department of Foreign Affairs and International Trade (1998)

Canada and the Middle East: In Theory and Practice. Paul Heinebecker and Momani Bessma, Wilfrid Laurier University Press (2007)

Canada and the Middle East: The Foreign Policy of a Client State. Tareq Y Ismael, Detselig Enterprises (1994)

Canada and the New American Empire. George Melnyk, University of Calgary Press (2004)

Canada and the New World Order. Michael J Tucker, Irwin Publishing (2000)

Canada and the Philippines: The Dimensions of a Developing Relationship. Micheal Rudner. Captus Press (1990)

Canada and the Soviet experiment: Essays on Canadian encounters with Russia and the Soviet Union, 1900-1991. David Davies, Canadian Scholars' Press (1994)

Canada and the Two World Wars. Jack Granatstein & Desmond Morton, Key Porter Books (2003)

Canada and the Third World. Peyton V Lyon & Tareq Y Ismael, Maclean-Hunter Press (1976)

Canada and UN Peacekeeping: Cold War by Other Means, 1945-1970. Sean M Maloney, Vanwell Publishing (2002)

Canada as an International Actor. Peyton V Lyon and Brian Tomlin, W McMillan (1979)

Canada as a Principle Power: A study in foreign policy and international relations. David B Dewitt and John J Kirton, John, Willy and sons (1983)

Canada-Cuba relations: The Other Good Neighbour Policy. John M Kirk and Peter McKenna, University Press of Florida (1997)

Canada in Afghanistan: The War so Far. Peter Pigott, Dundurn Press (2007)

Canada in Egypt from Antagonism to Partnership. Louis Delvoie, Center for International Relations, Occasional paper 57 (August 1997)

Canada in the European Age, 1453-1919. R.T Naylor, New Star Books (1987)

Canada in Korea: perspectives 2000. RWL Guisso and Young-Sik Yoo, Centre for Korean Studies University of Toronto (2002)

Canada-Israel Friendship. Shira Herzog Bessin and David Kaufman, Canada-Israel Committee (1979)

Canada, Latin America, and the New Internationalism: A foreign policy analysis, 1968-1990. Brian JR Stevenson, McGill-Queen's University Press (2000)

Canada's Deadly Secret: Saskatchewan Uranium and the Global Nuclear System. Jim Harding, Fernwood Publishing (2007)

Canada's Department of External Affairs: The early years 1909-1946. John Hilliker (1990)

Canada's Global Engagements and Relations with India. Christopher Sam Raj and Abdul Nafey, Manak (2007)

Canada's International Policies: Agendas, Alternatives and Politics. Norman Hillmer and Fen Osler Hampson, Oxford University Press (2008)

Canada's relations with the Caribbean and Latin America. Di Sanza E, McMaster masters thesis (1978)

Canada's R.M.C: A history of the Royal Military College. Richard Arthur Preston, University of Toronto Press (1969)

Canada's Secret Commandos: the unauthorized story of JTF 2. David Pugliese, Esprit de Corps Books (2002)

Canada's Soldiers 1604-1954: The Military History of An Unmilitary People. George F. G. Stanley, the Macmillan Company of Canada (1960)

Canada's Pacific Naval Presence: Purposeful or Peripheral, Peter T Haydon and Ann L Griffiths, The Centre for Foreign Policy Studies (1999)

Canada, the "lessons" of peacekeeping and Central America. David G Taglund and Peter L Jones, Centre for International Relations Occasional paper #33 (May 1989)

Canadian Aid and the Environment. North South Institute (1981)

Canadian-Arab Relations: Policy and Perspectives. Tareq Y Ismael. Jerusalem International publishing house (1984)

Canadian Banks and Global Competitiveness. James Darroch, McGill-Queen's University Press (1994)

Canadian Bilateral Aid policy in Neoliberal Nicaragua: Accommodation and Alternatives. Cappa (1996)

The Canadian Caper. Jean Pelletier and Claude Adams, MacMillan of Canada (1981)

Canadian Churches and Foreign Policy. Bonnie Greene, James Lorimer and Company (1990)

Canadian Corporations and Social Responsibility. Michelle Hibler and Rowena Beamish, The North South Institute (1998)

The Canadian Defence Industry in the New Global Environment, Queen's University Press (1995)

Canadian Development Assistance to Senegal. Real Lavergne and Philip E. English North South Institute (1987)

Canadian Development Assistance to Haiti: An independent study. Philip E. English, North South Institute (1984)

Canadian Development Assistance to Tanzania: An Independent Study. Roger Young, the North South institute (1983)

The Canadian Forces and Interoperability: Panacea or Perdition?. Ann L Griffiths, Center for Foreign Policy Studies, Dalhousie University (2002)

The Canadian Forces: hard choices, soft power. Joseph T. Jockel, Canadian Institute of Strategic Studies (1999)

Canadian Foreign Policy: 1945-2000. Arthur E Blanchette, The Golden Dog Press (2000)

Canadian Foreign policy 1945-1954: Selected Speeches and Documents. RA Mackay. McClelland & Stewart (1970)

Canadian Foreign Policy: Contemporary Issues and Themes. Micheal Tucker, McGraw Hill (1980)

Canadian Foreign Policy: selected cases. Don Munton and John Kirton, Orentice Hall Canada inc. (1992)

Canadian Gunboat Diplomacy: The Canadian Navy and Foreign Policy. Ann L Griffiths & Peter T Haydon & Richard H Gimblett, Center for Foreign Policy Studies, Dalhousie University (2000)

Canadian International Development Assistance Policies: An Appraisal. Cranford Pratt, McGill-Queen's University Press (1994)

Canadian Missionaries, Indigenous Peoples: presenting religion at home and abroad. Alvin Austin and Jamie S. Scott, University of Toronto Press (2005)

Canadian Multinationals. Jorge Niosi, Between the Lines (1985)

Canadian Nuclear Weapons: The Untold Story of Canada's Cold War Arsenal. John Clearwater, Dundurn Press (1998)

The Canadian Peacekeeper. John Gardam, General Store Publishing House (1992)

Canadian Policy towards Nikita Kruschev's Soviet Union. Jamie Glazob, York University Thesis (May 1997)

Canadian Relations with South Africa: A Diplomatic History. Brian Douglas Tennyson, University Press of America (1982)

Canadians Behind Enemy Lines. Roy MacLaren UBC Press (2004)

Canadians in Russia, 1918 – 1919. Roy Maclaren, MacMillan Hunter Press (1976)

Canadian-Soviet Relations during the World Wars. Aloysius Balawyder. University of Toronto Press (1972)

Canadian Values in the World Community. Marsha P Hanen and David W Cassels, Sheldon Chumir Foundation for Ethics in Leadership (2005)

Canadian Volunteers: Spain 1936-1939. William C Beeching, Plains Research Center, University of Regina (1989)

Canadian-West Indian Union: a Forty-year Minuet. Robin W Winks, Athlone Press (1968)

The Canadian Way of War. Colonel Bernd Horn. Dundurn Press (2006)

The Caribbean Basin: An International History. David Bright & Stephen J. Randall and Graeme S. Mount, Routledge (1998)

The Changing Face of the Caribbean. Irene Hawkins, Cedar Press (1976)

Closely Guarded: A Life in Canadian Security and Intelligence. John Starnes, University of Toronto Press (1998)

Cold War and its Origins, 1917-1960. DF Flemming, Doubleday (1961)

Cold War Canada: The Making of a National Insecurity State, 1945-1957. Reginald Whitaker and Gary Marcuse. University of Toronto Press (1994)

Community Rights and Corporate Responsibility: Canadian mining and oil companies in Latin America. Lisa North & Timothy David Clark & Viviana Patroni, Between the Lines (2006)

Complicity: Human Rights and Canadian Foreign Policy. Sharon Scharfe, Black Rose Books (1996)

Conflicting missions: Havana, Washington, and Africa, 1959-1976. Piero Gleijeses, University of North Carolina Press (2002)

Conflicts of Interest: Canada and the Third World. Jamie Swift and Brian Tomlinson, Between the Lines (1991)

The Congo: plunder and resistance. David Renton & David Seddon & Leo Zeilig, Zed Books (2007)

Contradictory impulses: Canada and Japan in the Twentieth Century. Greg Donaghy and Patricia Roy, UBC Press (2008)

Corporate Imperialism: Conflict and Expropriation. Norman M.E. Girvan, Sharpe Inc (1976)

Cross Culture and Faith: the Life and work of James Mellon Menzies. Linfu Dong, University of Toronto Press (2005)

Dark Threats and White Knights: The Somalia Affair, Peacekeeping and the New Imperialism. Sherene H Razack, University of Toronto Press (2004)

Defense in the Nuclear Age: An Introduction for Canadians. Elm Burns, Irwin Clarke and Co. Ltd. (1976)

Delivering Results: Canada Fund for Africa. CIDA (2006)

Demonstration Elections: US Staged Elections in the Dominican Republic, Vietnam and El Salvador. Edward S Herman and Frank Brodhead, South End Press (1984)

Democratizing Southern Africa: Challenges for Canadian policy. Heribert Adam and Kogila Moodley, MOM Printing Ottawa. (1992)

The Diplomacy of Constraint: Canada, the Korean War and the United States. Dennis Stairs, University of Toronto Press (1974)

Diplomacy of fear: Canada and the Cold War - 941-1948. Dennis Smith, University of Toronto Press (1988)

Diplomatic Missions: The Ambassador in Canadian Foreign Policy. Robert Wolfe, School of Policy Studies (1998)

Discovering the Americas: The Evolution of Canadian Foreign Policy Towards Latin America. James Roschlin, University of British Colombia Press (1994)

The Domestic Battleground: Canada and the Israeli Conflict. David Taras and David H Goldberg, McGill-Queens University Press (1989)

Domestic Determinants of Foreign Policy: Newly Immigrated Ethnic Communities and the Canadian Foreign Policy-Making Process, 1984-1993. Roy Brent Norton, UMI Dissertation services (1999)

The Dominion Partnership in Imperial Defense, 1870-1914. Donald C. Gordon, Johns Hopkins Press (1965)

Dreamland: How Canada's Pretend Foreign Policy has undermined sovereignty. Roy Rempel, Break Out Education Network (2006)

Dual Allegiance: An Autobiography. Ben Dunkelman, Macmillan of Canada (1976)

Empire to Umpire: Canada and the World to the 1990s. Norman Hilmer and JL Granatstein, Copp, Clark, Longman Ltd. (1994)

Enquetes sur les services secret. Normand Lester, Les editions de l'homme (1998)

Envoys Extraordinary: women of the Canadian foreign service. Margaret K. Weiers, Dundurn press (1995)

The Ethnic Cleansing of Palestine. Ilan Pappe, One World Publications (2006)

Ethics and the Formation of Foreign Policy: A Case Study of Canadian Government Policy Toward Indonesia, 1970-1990. Derek MacCuish, Concordia University Thesis (April 1999)

The Evolution of UN peacekeeping: case studies and comparative analysis. William J. Durch, St. Martin's press (1993)

Explaining the Canadian Response to the Tiananmen Square massacre: a Comparative Examination of Canadian Foreign Policy. Paul Gecelovsky, Department of Political Science, University of Alberta (Spring 2000)

Exporting Danger. Ron Finch, Black Rose Books (1986)

Far Eastern Tour. Brent Watson, McGill Queen's University Press (2002)

Fire Proof House to Third Option: Studies in the Theory and Practice of Canadian Foreign Policy. John Saint Peter, University of Manitoba (1977)

Following the Americans to the Persian Gulf: Canada, Australia and Development of the New World Order. Ronnie Miller, Associated University Presses (1994)

Foreign Policy for Canadians. Mitchell Sharp (1970)

From Lebanon to the Intifada: the Jewish Lobby and Canadian Middle East Policy. Ronnie Miller, University Press of America (1991)

From Peacekeeping to Peacemaking: Canada's response to the Yugoslav Crisis. Nicholas Gammer, McGill-Queen's University Press (2001)

From Telegrapher to Titan: the life of William C. Van Horne. Valerie Knowles, Dundurn press (2004)

Future Peacekeeping: A Canadian Perspective. David Rudd and Jim Hanson and Adam Stinson, Canadian Institute of Strategic Studies (2001)

The Gallant Cause: Canadians in the Spanish Civil War, 1936 - 1939. Mark Zuehlki, Whitecap Books Ltd. (1996)

Genocide and Covert Operations in Africa 1993-1999. Wayne Madsen, Edwin Mellen Press (1999)

Ghana and Nkrumah. Thomas A. Howell and Jeffrey P. Rajasooria, Facts on File (1972)

The Globalizers: Development Workers in Action. Jeffrey T Jackson, John Hopkins University Press (2005)

Global Mission: The Story of Alcan Volume I. Duncan C Campbell, Alcan Publishers (1985)

Global Mission: The Story of Alcan Volume II and III. Duncan C Campbell, Alcan Publishers (1990)

Hesitant Engagement: Canada and South East Asian Security. Louis A. Delvoie, Queens University Press (1995)

The Hindrance of Military Operations Ashore: Canadian Participation in Operation Sharpguard, 1993-1996. Shawn M Maloney, Maritimes Security Occasional Paper Number 7. Center for Foreign Policy Studies Dalhousie University

Holding the Bully's Coat. Linda McQuaig, Doubleday Canada (2007)

Humanitarian Imperialism: Using human Rights to sell War. Jean Bricmont, Monthly Review (2006)

Human Rights and Canadian Foreign Policy. Robert O Mathews and Cranford Pratt, McGill Queen's University Press (1988)

Human Rights and Democracy: Issues for Canadian Policy and Democracy Promotion. Nancy Thede, IRPP Policy Matters Volume 6, Number 3 (May 2005)

The In-Between Time. Robert Bothwell and Norman Hillmer, Copp Clark (1975)

In Defence of Canada. James Eayrs, University of Toronto Press (1980)

The Indian elephant sheds its past. Wendy Dobson, CD Howe (June 2006)

In Good Faith: Canadian churches against apartheid. Renate Pratt Canadian corporation for studies in religion (1997)

In Harms Way: Serving the Greater Good. Bernd Horn, Canadian Defense Academy Press (2006)

Imperialism, Nationalism and Canada: Essays from the Marxist Institute of Toronto. Craig Heron, Between the Lines (1977)

Inside Canadian Intelligence: exposing the new realities of espionage and international terrorism. Dwight Hamilton, Dundurn Press (2006)

In/Security: Canada in the Post 9/11 World. Allen Seager and Alexander N Etherton and Karl Froschauer, Center for Canadian Studies, Simon Frasier University (2005)

International Human Rights and Canadian Foreign-Policy: principles, priorities and practice in the Trudeau era and beyond. Amynmohamed Sajoo, McGill thesis (1987)

Internationalism under Strain: The North-South Policies of Canada, the Netherlands, Norway and Sweden. Cranford Pratt, University of Toronto Press (1989)

International leadership: by a Canada Strong and Free. Mike Harris and Preston Manning, The Fraser Institute (2006)

In the Clutches of the Kremlin: Canadian-East European relations (1945-1962). Aloysius Balawyder. East European Monographs. Distributed by Columbia University Press (2000)

In the Eye of the Storm: A History of Canadian Peacekeeping. Fred Gaffen, Deneau and Wayne (1987)

In the Interests of Peace: Canada in Vietnam, 1954-1973. Douglas A Ross. University of Toronto Press (1984)

In the Name of Progress: the Underside of Foreign Aid. Patricia Adams and Lawrence Solomon, Probe International (1991)

Jamaica Under Manley: Dilemmas of Socialism and Democracy. Michael Kaufmann, Between the Lines (1985)

Just Dummies: Cruise Missile Testing in Canada. John Clearwater, University of Calgary Press (2007)

Key Issues for Canada's Foreign Policy. The North South Institute (1994)

Killing Hope: US Military and CIA Interventions Since WWII. William Blum, Common Courage Press (2004)

Korea: Division, Reunification, and US Foreign Policy. Martin Hart-Landsberg, Monthly Review Press (1998)

L'action humanitaire du Canada: Histoire concepts, politiques et pratiques de terrain. Yvan Conoir and Gérard Verna, Les Presse de Universite Laval (2002)

Land of Lost Content: A history of CUSO. Ian Smillie, Deneau publishers (1985)

The Lebanese Crisis: 1958. M.S Agwani, Asia Publishing House (1965)

Le Canada et Le Québec sur la scene internationale. P. Painchaud, Presses de l'Universite du Québec (1977)

Le Canada et le conflit Isrealo-Arab depuis 1947. Houchang Hassan-Wari, Harmattan (1997)

Le Canada face a l'Asie de l'Est. Gérard Hervouet, Nouvelle Optique (1981)

Lessons from the North: Canada's Privatization of Military Ammunition Production. Rand (2004)

Les secrets de la justice internationale: Enquêtes truquées sur le génocide rwandais. Charles Onana, Editions du boiris (2005)

Let's Die Living: Exploring the World with CESO. Vivienne Clarke, Simon and Pierre (1983)

Lies the Media Tell Us. James Winter, Black Rose Books (2007)

Making a Killing: Canada's Arms Industry. Ernie Regehr, McClelland & Stewart (1975)

The Making of the Arab-Israeli Conflict, 1947-51. Ilan Pappé, I.B. Tauris and Co. (1992)

Maritimes Security Occasional Paper, number 12. Center for Foreign Policy Studies, Dalhousie University (2002)

The Middle Power Project: Canada and the Founding of the United Nations. Adam Chapnick, UBC Press (2005)

More than a Peacemaker: Canada's cold war policy and the Suez crisis, 1948-1956. Nicholas Gafuik, McGill University Masters thesis (October 2004)

Mosaic or patchwork? Canadian policy toward Subsaharan Africa in the 1980s. Andrew Clark, The North South Institute (1991)

The Multilateral Development Banks: The Caribbean development Bank. Hardy Chandra, Lynne Rienner (1995)

The Multinational Corporations and Brazil: The Impact of Multinational Corporations in the Contemporary Brazilian Economy. Marcos Arruda & Herbert De Sousa & Carlos Aphonso, Latin American Research Unit (1975)

Nationalization of Guyana's Bauxite: the Case of Alcan. M Shahabuddeen, Guyana Ministry of Information (1981)

The Naval Service of Canada, Volume 1. GN Tucker. Military Affairs Volume 36 Number 32. Canadian Historical Review. Volume 62, number 4 (1981)

Noir Canada: Pillage, corruption et criminalite en Afrique. Alain Denault, Ecosociete (2008)

None is too many: Canada and the Jews of Europe, 1933-1948. Irving Abella and Harold Troper, Keiy Porter Books (2000)

Northern Shadows: Canadians and Central America. Peter McFarlane, Between the Lines (1989)

Nous etions invincibles: Temoignage d'un ex-commando. Dennis Morisette and Claude Coulombe, Editions Egitios JCL Inc. (2008)

Official Secrets: the story behind the Canadian Security Intelligence Service. Richard Cleroux, McGraw-Hill (1990)

On the Road to Freedom: Canadian – East European Relations, 1963-1990. Aloysius Balawyder, East European Monographs and distributed by Columbia University Press (2005)

On the Road to Kandahar. Jason Burke, Doubleday Canada (2006)

Outposts of Empire: Korea, Vietnam, and the Origins of the Cold War in Asia: 1949-1954. Steven Hugh Lee, McGill-Queens University Press (1995)

Pacific Challenge: Canada's Future in the New Asia. Eric Downtown, Stoddart (1986)

Pakistan-Canada Relations, 1947-1982: a brief survey. Azmi M. Raziullah, Quiad-i-Azam University (1982)

The Path of a Genocide: The Rwanda Crisis from Uganda to Zaire. Howard Adelman and Astri Shurke, Transaction (2000)

Partner to Behemoth: the military policy of a satellite Canada. John W. Warnock, new press (1970)

Paul Martin and Canadian Diplomacy. Ryan Touhey, University of Waterloo Centre on Foreign Policy and Federalism (2001)

Painting the Map Red: Canada and the South African War, 1899-1902. Carman Miller, McGill-Queens University Press (1993)

Le Patron de Dallaire Parle: con révelations sur derives d'un general de l'ONU au Rwanda. Jacques Roger Boohbooh, Duboiris (2005)

Pearson: his life and worlds. Robert Bothwell, MacGraw Hill Ryerson Limited (1978)

Peacekeeping: International Challenge and Canadian Response. Alistair Taylor, Canadian Institute of International Affairs (1968)

Peacekeeping in Vietnam: Canada, India, Poland and the International Commission. Ramesh Thakur, University of Alberta Press (1984)

Perpetuating Poverty: The Political Economy of Canadian Foreign Aid. Robert Carty and Virginia Smith, Between the Lines (1981)

Personal Policy Making: Canada's role in the adoption of the Palestine Partition Resolution. Eliezer Tauber, Greenwood Press (2002)

The Politics of Canadian Foreign Policy, Third Edition. Kim Richard Nossal, Prentice Hall Canada Inc. (1997)

The Politics of Candu Exports. Dwayne Bratt, University of Toronto Press (2006)

Profits in Politics: Beaverbrook in the Gilded Age of Canadian Finance. Gregory P. Marchildon, University of Toronto Press (1996)

The Profits of Extermination: How US Corporate Power is destroying Colombia. Francisco Ramirez Cuellar, Common Courage Press (2005)

Promoting Democracy in the Americas. Thomas Legler & Sharon F Lean & Dexter F Boniface. John Hopkins University Press (2007)

Quick to the Frontier: Canada's Royal Bank. Duncan McDowall, McClelland & Stewart (1993)

Quiet complicity: Canadian involvement in the Vietnam War. Victor Levant, Between the Lines (1986)

Radical Mandarin: The Memoirs of Escott Reid. University of Toronto Press (1999)

Rain-dancing: Sanctions in Canadian and Australian Foreign Policy. Kim Richard Nossal, University of Toronto Press (1994)

Readings in Canadian Foreign-Policy: classic debates and new ideas. Duane Bratt and Christopher kukucha, Oxford University Press (2006)

Reluctant Adversaries: Canada and the People's Republic of China, 1949-1970. Paul M Evan and Michael B. Frolic, University of Toronto Press (1991)

Renegades: Canadians in the Spanish Civil War. Micheal Peprou UBC Press (2008)

The rise and Fall of a Middle Power: Canadian Diplomacy from King to Mulroney Andrew. James Arthur, Lorimer and Co. (1993)

Saving China: Canadian missionaries in the middle Kingdom 1888– 1959. Alvin Austin, University of Toronto press (1986)

The Secret Army. David J Bercuson, Lester and Orpen Dennys (1993)

Seize the Day: Lester B Pearson and Crisis Diplomacy. Geoffrey AH Pearson, Carleton University Press (1993)

The Sense of Power: Studies in the Ideas of Canadian Imperialism 1867-1914. Carl Berger, University of Toronto Press (1973)

Shake Hands with the Devil: The Failure of Humanity in Rwanda. Romeo Dallaire, Random House Canada (2003)

Shifting priorities: The evolution of Canada's relations with French Africa, 1945-1968. Robin Stewart Gendron, University of Calgary Thesis (2001)

SNC: Engineering Beyond Frontiers. Suzane Lelande, Libre Expression (1992)

Snowjob: Canada, the United States and Vietnam [1954-1973] Charles Taylor, Anansi (1974)

Spy Wars: Espionage and Canada from Gouzenko to Glasnost. J. L. Granatstein and David Stafford, Key Porter Books (1990)

Spy world: inside the Canadian and American intelligence establishments. Mike Frost and Michel Gratton, Doubleday Canada Ltd. (1994)

Tested Mettle: Canada's peacekeepers at war. Scott Taylor and Brian Nolan, Esprit de corps books (1998)

Three Nights in Havana: Pierre Trudeau, Fidel Castro and the cold War. Robert Wright, Harper Collins (2007)

Ties that Bind: Canada and the Third World. Richard Swift and Robert Clarke, Between the Lines (1982)

The Ties that Bind: intelligence cooperation between the United Kingdom, United States of America, Canada, Australia and New Zealand. Jeffrey T. Richelson and Desmond Ball Allen, Unwin Hyman, (1990)

Titans: how the new Canadian establishment seized power. Peter C. Newman, Penguin (1998)

Too close for Comfort. Maude Barlow, McClelland & Stewart (2005)

Towards a Francophone Community. Robin S Gendron, McGill-Queen's University Press (2006)

Towers of Gold - Feet of Clay: The Canadian Banks. Walter Stewart, Collins (1982)

Transnational Corporations and Caribbean Inequalities. David Kowalewski, Praeger Publishers (1982)

Trouble with Africa: Why Foreign Aid Isn't Working. Robert Calderisi, MacMillan Press (2006)

The United Nations in the Congo: the quest for peace. King Gordon (1962)

Uncle Sam and Us: Globalization, Neoconservatism, and the Canadian State. Stephen Clarkson, University of Toronto Press (2002)

The Unexpected War: Canada in Kandahar. Janice Gross Stein and Eugene Lang, Viking Canada (2007)

Unlikely allies: Canada-Chile Relations in the 1990s. Janice Paskey and Roberto Duran Sepulveda, FOCAL Papers (1996)

Victorian Explorer: the African Diaries of Captain William G. Stairs (1887-1892). Janina M. Konczacki, Nimbus (1994)

War and Society: In Post-confederation Canada. Jeffery A. Keschen and Serge Marc Durflinger, Nelson Publisher (2007)

Weighing the Options: Case Studies in Naval Interoptability and Canadian Sovereignty. Richard Williams, Centre for Foreign Policy Studies (2004)

While Canada Slept: How We Lost Our Place in the World. Andrew Cohen, McClelland & Stewart (2004)

Who Killed the Canadian Military? J.L. Granatstein, Harper Flamingo, Canada (2004)

Words and Deeds: Canada, Portugal and Africa. Toronto Committee for the Liberation of South Africa, TCLSAC (1976)

The Worldly Years: The Life of Lester Pearson, volume 2: 1949-72. John English, Alfred A Knopf Canada (1992)

Worthwhile Initiatives? Canadian Mission-Oriented Diplomacy. Andrew F. Cooper and Geoffrey Hayes, Irwin Publishing Ltd. (2000)

Keeping track of Canadian foreign policy
Some of the best books

Northern Shadows Canadians in Central America by Peter McFarlane

Quiet Complicity: Canadian involvement in the Vietnam War by Victor Levant

Community Rights and Corporate Responsibility: Canadian mining and oil companies in Latin America Edited by Liisa North, Timothy David Clark and Viviana Patroni

Perpetuating Poverty: The Political Economy of Canadian Foreign Aid by Robert Carty, Virginia Smith and LAWG

Canadian International Development Assistance Policies edited by Cranford Pratt

The Ambiguous Champion: Canada and South Africa in the Trudeau and Mulroney Years by Linda Freeman

Words and Deeds: Canada, Portugal and Africa by the Toronto Committee for the Liberation of South Africa

Snowjob: Canada, the United States and Vietnam (1954-1973) by Charles Taylor

Complicity: Human Rights and Canadian Foreign Policy by Sharon Scharfe.

Holding the Bully's Coat by Linda McQuaig

Imperialism, Nationalism and Canada: Essays from the Marxist Institute of Toronto edited by Craig Heron

Ties that Bind: Canada and the Third World. Edited by Richard swift and Robert Clarke.

Renegades: Canadians in the Spanish civil war by Micheal Peprou

Between War and Peace in Central America. Edited By Liisa North and Capa

Canadian Gunboat Diplomacy: The Canadian Navy and Foreign Policy edited by Ann L Griffiths, Peter T Haydon, and Richard H Gimblett

Noir Canada: Pillage, corruption et criminalité en Afrique by Alain Denault, Delphine Abadie et William Sacher

Dark Threats and White Knights: The Somalia Affair, Peacekeeping and the New imperialism by Sherene H Razack

Exporting Danger by Ron Finch

Just Dummies: Cruise Missile Testing in Canada by John Clearwater

Making a Killing: Canada's Arms Industry by Ernie Regehr

Arms Canada: The Deadly Business of Military Exports by Ernie Regehr

Canadian Nuclear Weapons: The Untold Story of Canada's Cold War Arsenal by John Clearwater

Some of the best websites and magazines

www.dominionpaper.ca

www.zmag.org

www.rabble.ca

Canadian Dimension magazine

Briarpatch magazine

New Socialist magazine

Press for Conversion

The Dominion is a grassroots newspaper, published monthly online and in print. It seeks to provide a counterpoint to the corporate media and direct attention to independent critics and the work of social movements. *The Dominion* has published in-depth special reports on Canadian foreign policy, Alberta's tar sands, and the activities of Canadian mining companies abroad.

www.dominionpaper.ca

The Media Co-op is a network of community-based reader-funded cooperatives, established by the Dominion's editorial collective. Starting with Locals in Halifax and Vancouver, the Media Co-op aims to establish democratically run, cooperatively produced media that reflects the needs of its members. All are invited to take part in the Media Co-op's working groups, which cover topics such as Canadian foreign policy, labour, environment, Original Peoples, as well as local issues.

www.mediacoop.ca

For more information, visit our web sites or get in touch at *info@mediacoop*.ca